Praise for *Human-Centred Economics*

"John Maynard Keynes argued that the ideas of economists are more powerful than we realize; that they determine the framework in which we think about the economy and hence the specific policies that determine economic and social outcomes. This excellent volume argues that the framework of liberal economics is no longer fit for purpose. It proposes a revision of the standard framework to address issues such as rising inequality, climate change, and social polarization. It challenges us all to think afresh, building on the strengths of conventional economic analysis while at the same time recognizing its weaknesses."
—Ravi Kanbur, *T. H. Lee Professor of World Affairs, International Professor of Applied Economics and Professor of Economics at Cornell University and former Director of the World Development Report and Chief Economist for Africa at the World Bank*

"A new social contract and just climate transition are urgently needed, but they will require a fundamental reform of economics as it has been taught and practiced for the past half century. This book proposes the most serious and specific replacement of neoliberalism and the Washington Consensus I have seen. It should be required reading in academia, governments and international organizations—and for anyone interested in systemic rather than piecemeal action on social and environmental justice."
—Sharan Burrow, *Former General Secretary of the International Trade Union Confederation and President of the Australian Council of Trade Unions*

"Free market capitalism is sick and the soul searching of economists, who bear some responsibility for its weakened state, has yet to produce solutions. In "Human-Centred Economics," Samans focuses on non-market institutions to re-anchor the market economy. Institutions affecting distribution and average worker well-being—democratic political formations, collaborative international relations—should be as integral to economic thought as market forces. This friendly amendment to economic theorizing supports an important policy proposal that seeks to address persistent problems of underdevelopment, climate degradation, excessive financialization, and 21st century declines in human well-being. This provocative book deserves a wide readership."
—William Milberg, *Professor of Economics and Director, Heilbroner Center for Capitalism Studies, The New School for Social Research*

"This is such a timely and important book. It provides a crucially needed compass and roadmap for the growing number of governments who are setting national goals based on social and environmental wellbeing rather than a sole focus on GDP growth. And it brilliantly addresses the intellectual and moral flaws in current economic theory and practice by setting out a new human-centred operating system for the conduct of economic policy. I cannot recommend it too highly."
—Stewart Wallis, *Executive Chair of the Wellbeing Economy Alliance and former Executive Director of the New Economics Foundation*

"This book achieves a rare feat: anchored in a critique of the past, it sets a template for the future. Rather than go down the rabbit hole of academic shortcomings, Richard Samans goes straight to the key policy challenge of our times: particularly for middle-income and high-income economies 'more growth' is not the most important policy target; more inclusiveness, resilience and environmental sustainability is. He argues that the 'living standards of nations' needs to be internalized at the multilateral and national levels. In this respect, there is kinship between Samans and J. Bradford DeLong's *Slouching Towards Utopia*; Samans delves more decisively into the international development policy domain—and aims to show what liberal political economy could deliver in the 21st century."
—Achim Steiner, *Administrator of the United Nations Development Programme and former Executive Director of the United Nations Environment Programme and Director-General of the International Union for Conservation of Nature*

"In "Human-Centred Economics: The Living Standards of Nations," Richard Samans takes us back to the basics and lays out, in clear and compelling prose, where we have gone wrong. He identifies the gap between the concerns of classical political economy and much contemporary economic policy and explains what is at stake in this disjuncture. In deconstructing the social contact and framing it as indispensable to both national wealth and collective well-being, Samans provides an alternative vision for macroeconomics in a learned but accessible text that is as useful for advanced undergraduate and graduate students seeking a deeper understanding of the field as it is for policymakers interested in scaling action on inequality and climate change."
—Jennifer Lynn Bair, *Professor of Sociology and Associate Dean for the Social Sciences, University of Virginia*

"Richard Samans explores why modern economies have underperformed in terms of social inclusion, environmental sustainability and human wellbeing. In doing so, he provides a lucid critique of orthodox economics which seeks to focus on markets as means with growth and efficiency as ends. Invoking the intellectual tradition of classical political economy, the author argues that it will be possible to harmonize economic and social progress in the 21st century only if we can restore the balance between markets and institutions, production and distribution, and national income and living standards of people. This refreshingly different book is an engaging read."
—Deepak Nayyar, *Emeritus Professor of Economics, Jawaharlal Nehru University, New Delhi, Honorary Fellow, Balliol College, Oxford and former Vice Chancellor, University of Delhi*

Richard Samans

Human-Centred Economics

The Living Standards of Nations

Published in association with the International Labour Organization

Richard Samans
Chene-Bourg, Geneva, Switzerland

ISBN 978-3-031-37434-0   ISBN 978-3-031-37435-7 (Ebook)
https://doi.org/10.1007/978-3-031-37435-7

© ILO: International Labour Organization 2024, corrected publication 2024. This book is an open access publication.

Open Access This book is licensed under the terms of the Creative Commons Attribution 4.0 International License (http://creativecommons.org/licenses/by/4.0/), which permits use, sharing, adaptation, distribution and reproduction in any medium or format, as long as you give appropriate credit to the original author(s) and the source, provide a link to the Creative Commons licence and indicate if changes were made.

The images or other third party material in this book are included in the book's Creative Commons licence, unless indicated otherwise in a credit line to the material. If material is not included in the book's Creative Commons licence and your intended use is not permitted by statutory regulation or exceeds the permitted use, you will need to obtain permission directly from the copyright holder.

The use of general descriptive names, registered names, trademarks, service marks, etc. in this publication does not imply, even in the absence of a specific statement, that such names are exempt from the relevant protective laws and regulations and therefore free for general use.

The publisher, the authors, and the editors are safe to assume that the advice and information in this book are believed to be true and accurate at the date of publication. Neither the publisher nor the authors or the editors give a warranty, expressed or implied, with respect to the material contained herein or for any errors or omissions that may have been made. The publisher remains neutral with regard to jurisdictional claims in published maps and institutional affiliations.

This Palgrave Macmillan imprint is published by the registered company Springer Nature Switzerland AG.
The registered company address is: Gewerbestrasse 11, 6330 Cham, Switzerland

Paper in this product is recyclable.

Copyright © International Labour Organization 2024

This is an open access work distributed under the Creative Commons Attribution 4.0 International Licence (https://creativecommons.org/licenses/by/4.0/). Users can reuse, share, adapt and build upon the original work, as detailed in the Licence. The ILO must be clearly credited as the owner of the original work. The use of the emblem of the ILO is not permitted in connection with users' work.

Attribution – The work must be cited as follows: Samans, Richard. *Human-Centred Economics: The Living Standards of Nations*. Cham, Switzerland: Palgrave Macmillan, 2024.

Translations – In case of a translation of this work, the following disclaimer must be added along with the attribution: *This translation was not created by the International Labour Organization (ILO) and should not be considered an official ILO translation. The ILO is not responsible for the content or accuracy of this translation.*

Adaptations – In case of an adaptation of this work, the following disclaimer must be added along with the attribution: *This is an adaptation of an original work by the International Labour Organization (ILO). Responsibility for the views and opinions expressed in the adaptation rests solely with the author or authors of the adaptation and are not endorsed by the ILO.*

This Creative Commons licence does not apply to non-ILO copyright materials included in this publication. If the material is attributed to a third party, the user of such material is solely responsible for clearing the rights with the rights holder.

Any dispute arising under this license that cannot be settled amicably shall be referred to arbitration in accordance with the Arbitration Rules of the United Nations Commission on International Trade Law (UNCITRAL). The parties shall be bound by any arbitration award rendered as a result of such arbitration as the final adjudication of such a dispute.

All queries on rights and licensing should be addressed to the ILO Publishing Unit (Rights and Licensing), 1211 Geneva 22, Switzerland, or by email to rights@ilo.org.

The designations employed in ILO publications, which are in conformity with United Nations practice, and the presentation of material therein do not imply the expression of any opinion whatsoever on the part of the ILO concerning the legal status of any country, area or territory or of its authorities, or concerning the delimitation of its frontiers.

The responsibility for opinions expressed in this book rests solely with the author, and its publication does not constitute an endorsement by the ILO or its constituents of the opinions expressed herein.

Reference to names of firms and commercial products and processes does not imply their endorsement by the ILO, and any failure to mention a particular firm, commercial product or process is not a sign of disapproval.

Synopsis

This book engages in a fundamental reflection regarding the chronic underperformance of economies with respect to social inclusion, environmental sustainability, and systemic and human resilience. It asks and seeks to answer the question of how macroeconomic theory and policy should be reformed and even reformulated in a century facing the prospect of further inequality and disruption from artificial intelligence and machine learning, climate change and other shifts and shocks.

Some see AI as likely to usher in an era of abundance. But for whom? The digital transformation of economic activity thus far has tended to widen inequalities, both within and among countries. Generative and other advanced forms of AI could well magnify this effect, other things being equal. And policymakers have been promising for years to better internalize environmental and particularly climate externalities in the way our economies are managed. But nearly a decade since the Paris climate agreement's goals were set, humanity remains on a path to well over, rather than well below, two degrees Celsius of warming since pre-industrial times.

The commitment articulated by many political leaders and economists during the Great Financial Crisis to forge a rebalanced—that is to say, more inclusive, sustainable and resilient—growth and development model remains largely aspirational and incremental in practice. Fifteen years later, the question remains: how should the pedagogy and practice of macroeconomics be revised to better serve a world in which distributional and transitional considerations have become at least as important to many societies as the overall size of their economies as measured by GDP? In other words, how can liberal economics be refashioned to improve both the quantity and social quality of growth, and indeed to achieve the former through the latter? And what would a just digital or green transition mean in practical terms for the conduct of macroeconomic policy?

The book addresses these questions by first investigating the history of economic thought to determine whether the discipline's tendency to treat these considerations as afterthoughts, as "trickle-down" by-products of economic growth, can be traced to its original eighteenth- and nineteenth-century principles. Has this been a case of misconception or misapplication of the founding principles of liberal political economy—of original sin or wayward practice?

Concluding the latter, the author proposes a specific structural reform of the standard liberal growth and development model to remedy its nearly exclusive focus on markets and production and related underemphasis of the role of institutions—the norms, policy incentives and public administrative capacities which are the practical manifestation of a country's social contract—in enabling broad and sustainable progress in living standards. This more human-centred, living-standards-oriented model, focused as much on the policy and institutional enablers of household living standards as on the traditional factors of production, is then used as the point of departure for major proposed reforms of national and international economic policy, including the way international economic institutions are configured and cooperate. Many have called for a new Bretton Woods conference to renew the multilateral system and improve the coherence of its economic, social and environmental dimensions. But these appeals have never amounted to much, in part because they have lacked an organizing principle—a new or substantially revised policy model upon which to build a renovated institutional edifice.

The book concludes with a reflection on the relationship between the concepts and tools it proposes and the legacy of John Maynard Keynes, interpreting them as a way of reinforcing through structural and institutional policy his fiscal and monetary policy efforts to chart a Middle Way between laissez-faire capitalism and state-controlled socialism—to better reconcile liberal economics and social justice. By rebalancing economics so that it adopts a parallel and equal focus on the wealth, or production, of nations and the living standards, or lived experience, of their people, the human-centred approach outlined in these pages provides an actionable alternative to neoliberalism, a Roosevelt Consensus to replace the still reigning Washington Consensus. In so doing, it offers a potential lifeline to the liberal tradition and multilateral system at a time of rising economic disruption, social insecurity, and political polarization, phenomena which are profoundly corrosive of the liberal values underpinning democracy and the vision of global peace and stability framed by the ILO's 1919 Constitution and its 1944 Philadelphia Declaration annex and the United Nations' 1945 charter.

Preface

Capitalism and markets have made enormous contributions to human welfare, particularly by raising rates of economic growth above the negligible levels experienced by humanity in the millennia that preceded their introduction. But since the 2008–09 financial crisis, there has been a great deal of soul searching among even leading scholars and public advocates of liberal economics.

These reflections and self-criticisms tend to focus on the shortcomings of capitalism with respect to social inclusion, environmental sustainability and systemic and individual human resilience. Political leaders have raised the stakes by publicly committing to big improvements in performance in each of these respects, albeit usually in the form of long-term goals and targets.

The result has been a great deal of description and diagnosis of these problems, and some reform in response to them. But these changes have been incremental and inconsistent, generally of a piecemeal or workaround nature. Few if any achieve scale by intervening at what might be called the operating system level of capitalism, notwithstanding regular appeals for the replacement of "neoliberalism" and the Washington Consensus. The basic theory and practice of liberal economics—its conceptual model of growth and development—remain essentially undisturbed.

This essential stasis, despite the public's hue and cry for reform and the big international goals set by political leaders, raises uncomfortable questions, not only for the politicians who have gone out on a limb in making these public promises, but also for economists. Why are the solutions being proposed not scaling? Is there a deeper flaw—what might be called a systemic–theoretical problem—in capitalism which inherently prevents it from delivering satisfactory levels of inclusion, sustainability and resilience? If so, what is the nature of that flaw, and what can be done to correct it? These are the questions this book asks and seeks to answer.

Two fundamental theoretical critiques *have* emerged in recent years. Thomas Piketty has argued and presented evidence that capitalist economic systems are predisposed to a progressive concentration of wealth. But what accounts for capitalism's severe environmental, human rights and other social justice deficits? Some proponents of the de-growth movement question the very premise of capitalism. But what about low-income and lower-middle-income countries that haven't yet grown to the point of having sufficient means to provide jobs and basic necessities for their people?

The problem clearly runs deeper and wider than wealth concentration or wasteful and polluting consumption. Some new concepts helpfully capture this multidimensional nature of the challenge or appeal for a new modus vivendi of governance to address it, such as a new social contract, which the International Trade Union Confederation and its former general secretary, Sharan Burrow, have been advocating for years. But at the end of the day a veritable transformation of economic activity will be required for such inspiring visions to be realized—a systemic shift in incentives and behaviour. Achieving that scale of change will require altering the source code of capitalism: the intellectual discipline of economics. Absent this, it's hard to see how this transformation about which there is so much aspirational agreement—as evidenced by countless intergovernmental pronouncements committing to greater inclusion, sustainability and resilience—can be achieved.

Marx took broader aim at liberal economics' theoretical core, but some of the most fervent applications of his ideas proved disastrous. And those that survive have been substantially transformed through the administration of a big dose of capitalism and markets. China and Vietnam are prominent cases in point. It is as if Francis Fukuyama got his end-of-history thesis half right: the capitalism but not the democracy part.

Keynes's *General Theory* was arguably the last fundamental change in the operating system of capitalism. His insight about the role and practice of macroeconomic policy located a critical source of disequilibrium in the growth and development model of his day, and arguably ours too, and he proposed a theoretical—that is, systemic—solution. The profound implications of his insight live on; they changed how capitalism is conceptualized and applied everywhere and forever.

The ideas of Hayek, Von Mises, Friedman and other pioneers of neoliberalism certainly changed the course of capitalism. But they represented a purer application of it—of markets—rather than a basic change in the system itself. Indeed, they were in large part a reaction to one of the legacies of Keynes, namely a more active use of government in various policy domains.

Economics was originally known as "political economy", and therein lies an important part of the problem which this book explores in depth. In his book on the history of economic thought, *The Worldly Philosophers*—the title of which refers to economists and political economists of the past few centuries whose ideas he thought operated at a fundamental conceptual level—Robert Heilbroner asked whether end-of-history triumphalism and hubris, on one hand, and the increasingly abstract and quantitative nature of scholarship, on the other, were the last nails in the coffin of this liberal intellectual tradition. His concern has been justified thus far. Despite the considerable *Sturm und Drang* within the economics community during the past 15 years, including the considerable body of excellent analysis and diagnosis, no systemic–theoretical response has emerged yet from it. As a result, reform continues on its path-dependent, incremental course, glaringly out of proportion to social and political concerns about inclusion, sustainability and resilience. If anything, these challenges have grown.

The field seems to be stuck, not unlike in the 1930s when it was forced to dig deeper and re-examine its very mental model—the key design features of its operating system. The piecemeal and work-around nature of recent reforms seem increasingly out of sync with contemporary social concern about growing in-country inequality, environmental degradation, and poverty and precarity. One has the feeling that capitalism is again at a turning point—in need of a deeper, perhaps general, theory of what ails liberal economics.

This book engages in such a fundamental reflection. It examines whether circumstances have again exposed an underlying flaw or lacuna in capitalism at the systemic–theoretical level and, if they have, what that socially disequilibrating factor is. Was it a design error or oversight in the original principles laid down by Adam Smith and other founders of classical political economy? Or has a bug crept into the operating system somewhere along the way since? And, most importantly, how should the problem be corrected at scale, whatever it is?

I approach this inquiry with humility. For all of their social shortcomings, liberal economics and capitalism have been a major force for good. I go to considerable lengths to emphasize this and acknowledge the huge contributions that various pioneers and reformers of the field have made over the years.

The book is not intended to be an exhaustive or definitive survey of the intellectual history of liberal economics. Nor does it aim to present an all-encompassing reform agenda. But it does call out certain patterns of behaviour and limitations of analysis and practice which I believe are strategic hindrances. In my view, these render liberal economics less and less fit for the purpose of responding to the challenges of the mid twenty-first century, versus those of the late twentieth century, and more and more of a disequilibrating factor and source of political instability for the liberal project more generally—for democracy and the multilateral system.

These thoughts have been building up in my mind for some time. I've had the privilege of working for many years at the interface of economics and labour, environmental, trade, finance and development policy, on the one hand, and corporate and multilateral governance, on the other. The observations and ideas in the book reflect this interdisciplinary experience. Some draw from and build on prior working papers and other publications from as far back as 2006.

My institution, the International Labour Organization (ILO), has been at the forefront of this dilemma—indeed it was born in the crucible of the aftermath of conflict, pandemic and social unrest early in the last century. It was and remains a critical part of the solution; but only part. I believe the problem runs deeper and wider, deeper in the systemic–theoretical sense described above and wider in the bureaucratic–organizational sense of implicating a wide variety of ministry and international organization portfolios. For this reason, after presenting the *problématique* in greater detail in Chap. 2, I delve into relevant aspects of the history of economic thought in Chap. 3; propose, in Chap. 4, an alternative model of growth and development that internalizes the primary institutional dimensions of the social contract which have an important bearing on the rate and breadth of progress in living standards; and outline a corresponding domestic and international economic policy reform agenda in Chaps. 5 and 6, respectively, spanning multiple domains and institutions.

In sum, this book examines the chronic underperformance of economies with respect to inclusion, sustainability and resilience, investigating its origins in the history of economic thought and tracing its manifestation in policy practice and outcomes. It concludes that the growth and development model underpinning modern economics evolved over the past century in an unbalanced manner which departs from first principles of classical political economy in one fundamental respect. The field's most influential original theorists and codifiers, including Adam Smith, emphasized the crucial role of institutions—legal and other norms, policy incentives and related public administrative capacity—in translating market-oriented growth into broad and sustainable gains in social welfare. Correcting the modern imbalance in emphasis between markets and institutions, production and distribution, and national income and household living standards is the most important step required to replace twentieth-century trickle-down "neoliberalism" with a more human-centred model of economic progress in the twenty-first century.

The essential principle I posit is that the median living standards of households deserve at least as much direct policy attention and cultivation by economists and policymakers as the overall wealth, or national income, of nations. Broad progress in the lived experience of people, rather than GDP growth per se, is the bottom-line measure of national economic performance, and it depends on the strength of both markets of exchange and institutions in such areas as labour and social protection, financial and corporate governance, competition and rents, infrastructure and basic necessities, environmental protection, anti-corruption, education and skilling, etc.

To support implementation of this principle, I propose integrating these and other principal institutional dimensions of the social contract into the heart of macroeconomic theory on a co-equal basis with the traditional factors of production of the aggregate production function. Formally internalizing such "factors of distribution"—policy and institutional enablers of broadly diffused and sustainable gains in living standards—in the standard growth and development model through the introduction of a companion "aggregate distribution function" would help to refocus economists and politicians on the median living standards, rather than primarily aggregate wealth or GDP, of nations. This has the potential to transform the dismal science from its increasingly ineffective and unpopular capital-accumulation-centred, trickle-down construct to a more human-centred, lifting-all-boats dynamic in which governments are focused at least as much on the seaworthiness and ecosystem stewardship of vessels and their crews as they are on the level of the tide. It is the combination of the two that ultimately determines whether the entire marina rises with and profits fully and sustainably from the sea's incoming bounty.

Extensive comparative data are presented demonstrating that nearly every country has considerable policy space to narrow its social "welfare gap"—its underperformance on key dimensions of household living standards relative to the frontier of leading outcomes and enabling policy practices of peer countries—and that doing so can often also help to reduce its output gap, or underperformance on growth. I propose major corresponding reforms of international economic governance and cooperation to refocus them on supporting societies and the biosphere in this journey—a "Roosevelt Consensus" to replace the still reigning Washington Consensus. These include changes that would optimize deployment of the existing resources of international financial institutions to enable humanity to achieve the goals its leaders have set on sustainable development and climate change, mobilizing an additional $2 trillion to triple international development and climate financing from 2024 to 2030; double global renewable energy and sustainable agriculture R&D investment; and retire and replace the majority of the world's coal-fired power plants within the next fifteen years—a prerequisite for the fulfilment of the Paris climate agreement's objectives.

The aim is to fundamentally reform capitalism by hard-wiring in liberal economic theory and the analysis, advice and support provided by international economic organizations a systematic counterforce to its tendency towards inequality, environmental degradation and concentration of rents and power. I argue in the concluding chapter that such a macroeconomic reorientation of the sub-disciplines of welfare and institutional economics, which have been in an abstract, largely microeconomic state of semi-hibernation for nearly a century, would have the effect of adding a reinforcing structural-institutional dimension to John Maynard Keynes' "Middle Way" fiscal and monetary policy reforms of the 1930s. These were aimed at charting a more effective course between laissez-faire capitalism and state-centric socialism—at better reconciling capitalism with social justice—through the maintenance of full employment in decent work supported by sustained domestic demand and investor confidence in the real economy.

This imperative remains as critical as ever in a century experiencing the disruptive forces of algorithmic automation and climate change. Indeed, over the next generation, humanity will need to chart a new Middle Way in economics, this time between environmentally destructive growth and socially destructive economic stagnation or degrowth. The proposed systematic internalization of the key institutional drivers of inclusion, sustainability and resilience in macroeconomic theory and policy creates the basis for the construction of such a new neoclassical-Keynesian-ecological synthesis and realization of the socially-embedded, FDR-inspired vision of economic growth and development framed by the ILO's 1944 Declaration of Philadelphia.

This long overdue step towards the routine internalization of social and environmental externalities in the understanding and practice of macroeconomics also has the potential to brighten the political outlook for the liberal tradition in the twenty-first century, both within and among nations. With its sharp focus on median household living standards, human-centred economics is kitchen-table economics. It is a strategy to increase investment in the lived experience of people—their employment opportunity, disposable income, purchasing power and economic, environmental and social security. These are matters of tangible relevance to people of all demographics and political philosophies. As such, this approach would help political leaders to cut through the din of contemporary polemics over identity and immigration by responding more directly and effectively to the common aspirations of their people. By enabling a more direct angle of attack on popular concerns about inclusion, sustainability and resilience—on practical challenges people confront daily—human-centred economics creates the potential for a more effective response to illiberal forms of populism and political disaffection and polarization more generally. In doing so, it would strengthen the multilateral system, breathing new life into its underlying liberal values and norms while improving its effectiveness and thus credibility by greatly accelerating the translation of its Sustainable Development Goals into tangible improvements in the material well-being of people on the ground.

These are my thoughts and suggestions; they do not necessarily reflect the views of the ILO or its constituents, or any of the institutions with which I have been affiliated over the years; or, for that matter, any of the reviewers who have been kind enough to offer their comments and suggestions.

I sense that economics is approaching a turning point and am hopeful that this will be a turn towards society in the way the field's founders intended. This book can be read as a suggested navigational guide for that change of course by way of an inquiry into the nature and causes of the living standards of nations—the material lived experience, dignity and agency of their people.

Geneva, Switzerland R. Samans
June 2023

ACKNOWLEDGEMENTS

The tapestry of this book is woven of the threads of my experience in the worlds of economics, politics and policy at the domestic and international levels. In addition, I've had the great good fortune of working in several intellectual disciplines that should interact extensively but generally do not. In a professional culture that rewards specialization, this eclecticism—I prefer to call it "interdisciplinary depth"—has sometimes been a career disadvantage. But I've always believed that an expansive view of the economic policy landscape would ultimately be a strategic advantage as both an analyst and practitioner. The book is a product of that philosophy.

As a result, I've had the privilege of working with and listening to many remarkable people who've left a mark on the world view expressed in these pages. I'd like to acknowledge a number of them with gratitude and respect, while stipulating that they bear no responsibility for any errors, omissions or misplaced emphasis herein.

First are people who went out of their way to take a chance on or advocate for me over the years, in particular Bill Goold, Steve Bailey, Dawn Erlandson, Steve Clemons, Howard Rosen, Pete Rouse, Lael Brainard, Gene Sperling, Sharan Burrow, Philip Jennings, Rich Trumka, Guy Ryder, Achim Steiner and Liz Shuler. I am grateful to them all.

Next are a number of contemporary intellectual influences, including people with whom I've had the privilege of being acquainted, such as John Williamson, Fred Bergsten, Michael Spence, Joseph Stiglitz, Nicholas Stern and Jeff Sachs, and others with whom I have not had that privilege, such as Gerald Helleiner, Robert Kuttner, James Galbraith, Dani Rodrik and Amartya Sen.

Then there are my long-standing intellectual sparring partners and kindred spirits: Alan Rojer, Kurt von Mettenheim, Bill Drake, Simon Zadek, Jonathan Fried and Ricardo Melendez-Ortiz.

Special thanks are due to Robert Johnson for supporting publication of initial research related to this book at the Institute for New Economic Thinking (INET) as well as to Wyndham Hacket Pain of Palgrave Macmillan for his steadfast support of this project.

I'd also like to thank several people who read and provided comments on the manuscript, including Sangheon Lee, Janine Berg, Uma Rani, Kurt von Mettenheim, Jennifer Bair, Stewart Wallis, Lord Robert Skidelsky, Parag Khanna, Marva Corley-Coulibaly and Dorothea Hoehtker. Thanks are also due to Souleima El Achkar and Rossana Merola for work on some of the data; Chris Edgar on the publishing arrangement; Alessandro Ippolito and Judy Rafferty on production-related aspects; Carlos Mancini on infographics; and Anthony Nanson for copy-editing and other editorial advice.

Last but certainly not least, I thank my wife Catherine and children Elijah and Ava for their forbearance during the past several months, beginning with my abandonment of them in the middle of the summer to spend a week alone in the Swiss Alps to kick-start the writing process. I dedicate this book to my kids and their generation in the hope that some of these ideas and others they may inspire will serve to enlarge the economic, social and environmental possibilities of their time.

Jodhpur, India   R. Samans
February 2023

Contents

1 Introductory Overview: Institutionalizing Inclusion, Sustainability and Resilience in Market Economies   1

2 Liberal Economics' Track Record on Inclusion, Sustainability and Resilience   11

3 Original Sin or Wayward Practice? Living Standards as a Trickle-Down, Residual Consideration of Modern Economics   55

4 From the Wealth to the Living Standards of Nations: Internalizing the Social Contract in Macroeconomic Theory and Policy   107

5 Human-Centred National Economic Policy: Institutionalizing Inclusion, Sustainability and Resilience in Domestic Economic Governance   131

6 Human-Centred International Economic Policy: Institutionalizing Inclusion, Sustainability and Resilience in International Economic Governance and Cooperation   235

7 Conclusion: Building on Keynes's Middle Way to Renew the Liberal Tradition and Multilateral System in the 21st Century   319

Correction to: Human-Centred Economics   C1

Bibliography   343

Index   349

About the Author

Richard Samans is Director of the International Labour Organization's Research Department and has served as its Sherpa to the G20, G7 and BRICS processes. He previously founded and chaired the Climate Disclosure Standards Board and was a Managing Director of the World Economic Forum and Director-General of the Global Green Growth Institute. He served earlier as Special Assistant to the President for International Economic Policy and National Security Council Senior Director for International Economic Affairs in the US White House during the second Clinton-Gore administration as well as economic policy adviser to US Senate Democratic Leader Thomas A. Daschle. He has also served in the United Nations system as a member of the Secretary General's Task Force on Digital Financing of the Sustainable Development Goals, the ILO's Global Commission on the Future of Work and UNEP's Inquiry into the Design of a Sustainable Financial System. He is a member of the Transitional Advisory Group of the IFRS Foundation's International Sustainability Standards Board.

List of Figures

Fig. 2.1	Global income distribution in 1800, 1975 and 2015	14
Fig. 2.2	Global change in real income by income percentile, 1988–2008	15
Fig. 2.3	Since the Baby Boomer generation, each new generation has seen its chances of belonging to the middle-income class fall	18
Fig. 2.4	GDP relative to baseline in percentage points	35
Fig. 5.1	Relationship between GDP per capita and environmental performance	138
Fig. 5.2	Performance in three dimensions of SDG 8	140
Fig. 5.3	OECD—Product Market Regulation (PMR) indicators	145
Fig. 5.4	Social Market–Market Socialism Corporate Governance Continuum	153
Fig. 5.5	Financialization–Real Economy Investment Financial Regulation Continuum	158
Fig. 5.6	Net share buybacks and net capital formation as a share of net operating surplus for operating corporations	161
Fig. 5.7	Jobs multiplier effect of public infrastructure investment (per USD 1 million investment)	163
Fig. 5.8	Direct government funding and tax support for business enterprise R&D (BERD), 2019 (percent of GDP)	164
Fig. 5.9	Progress in reaching G20 Brisbane goal set back by COVID-19 pandemic (% point change in gender gap in labour force participation rate 2012–21)	172
Fig. 5.10	Evolution of real minimum wages, selected countries, 2015–22	174
Fig. 5.11	Dispersion of collective bargaining coverage rates	176
Fig. 5.12	Incidence of low pay, 2021 or latest available	177

Fig. 5.13	Redistribution decreased in a majority of countries after 2010 and before the COVID-19 pandemic. Percentage reduction of market income inequality owing to transfers and taxes, 2007–14 (or latest year), working-age population	178
Fig. 5.14	Differences in household income inequality pre- and post-tax and government transfers, 2018	178
Fig. 5.15	(a) Tax revenue, selected countries, as percentage of GDP and by country income group, 2018. (b) Tax revenue, selected countries, by type of tax and country income group, 2018	180
Fig. 5.16	Composition of tax revenue, selected countries, by country income group, 2018	182
Fig. 5.17	Level and composition of health spending in select high-income countries	183
Fig. 5.18	Net child care costs (% of average wage, 2021 or latest available)	184
Fig. 5.19	Development of social protection programmes anchored in national legislation by policy area, pre-1900 to 2020	196
Fig. 5.20	SDG indicator 1.3.1: effective social protection coverage, global and regional estimates, by population group, 2020 or latest available year	197
Fig. 5.21	Gross pension replacement rates, men, percentage of pre-retirement earnings, 2020 or latest available	198
Fig. 5.22	Spending on child benefit packages in 90 low- and middle-income countries, by country (percentage of GDP)	199
Fig. 5.23	Public unemployment spending (Percentage of GDP, 2021 or latest available)	200
Fig. 5.24	Coverage of unemployment benefits and average replacement rates	201
Fig. 5.25	Labour inspection	203
Fig. 5.26	High-homeownership countries tend to exhibit low wealth inequality	205
Fig. 5.27	Distribution pattern of country scores for the Green Growth Index by region, 2020	210
Fig. 5.28	Elements of a just transition	213
Fig. 6.1	Paris 1.5°C goal requires 80% drop in coal-fired power by 2030	260
Fig. 6.2	Tripling annual official development assistance (ODA) related external flows to low- and lower-middle-income countries from 2024 to 2030	277

LIST OF TABLES

Table 3.1	National legislation on social insurance before the German legislation of 1883	81
Table 5.1	Household access to water services in 15 cities and informal settlements in the global South	187
Table 5.2	European Union energy cost-of-living relief measures 2021–22	190
Table 5.3	Global Home ownership rates by country	205
Table 6.1	Fiscal expenditure and revenue reference ranges	247
Table 6.2	Decent work indicator reference ranges	249
Table 6.3	Financing gap for achieving universal social protection coverage in 2020 in billions US$ and as a percentage of GDP (low- and middle-income countries only)	263
Table 6.4	Resilience and Sustainability Trust (RST) allocation of rechannelled SDRs	278

LIST OF BOXES

Box 4.1 Aggregate Distribution Function: Policy and Institutional
         Ecosystem   116
Box 5.1 Aggregate Distribution Function: Policy and Institutional
         Ecosystem   132

CHAPTER 1

Introductory Overview: Institutionalizing Inclusion, Sustainability and Resilience in Market Economies

People evaluate their country's economic performance on the basis of the social quality of economic growth—its effect on the standard of living of their household and community. By contrast, economists and the politicians they advise have been trained to focus primarily on the quantity of growth—the volume of goods and services produced at a national level as measured by gross domestic product (GDP). These are related but distinct phenomena, and the relationship between them has weakened in many countries, in fact as well as social perception.

This widening disconnect is creating a growing social and political headache for the diverse range of governments that apply the teachings of liberal economics. For the past half-century, most have been advised to focus on boosting their overall national income or GDP through strategies that improve the efficiency of resource allocation: fiscal and monetary discipline; flexibility of labour and product markets; financial deregulation; trade liberalization; international capital mobility and exchange rate flexibility; and privatization. These are tools for improving market signals, efficiency of production and accumulation of tangible capital as a means of expanding the size of an economy.

An implicit assumption of this economic doctrine is that broad progress in living standards flows naturally from greater economic efficiency and the larger national and world economy it creates. The social benefits of expanded economic growth inevitably trickle down and out to the populace at large. This assumption is reinforced by the use of GDP as the standard basis for measuring a country's annual economic performance and its overall level of development, even though neither of these concepts is synonymous with what GDP actually measures: the aggregate production of goods and services measured at market prices.

In effect, generations of Western and other liberal economists and policymakers have been trained to behave as if Adam Smith's "invisible hand" of market-based resource allocation can be relied upon to optimize not only the wealth of nations (its core function as stated by Smith) but also the well-being of their populations at large. A rising tide of GDP, as it were, ultimately lifts all boats. But Smith and other important pioneers of the field assumed no such thing. They believed that market-oriented measures to increase the production and wealth of nations were a necessary but by no means sufficient condition for raising the broad standard of living of their people. A range of institutions—legal and other norms, policy incentives and administrative capacities mainly but not only in the public sector—were required to ensure broad social participation in the process and benefits of economic growth.

This excessive faith in markets and chronic underinvestment in institutions were embodied in the extreme in the most recent major course correction of liberal political economy—the wave of market liberalization that began in the late 1970s and 1980s and is often referred to as "neoliberalism". It has been a hallmark of international economic cooperation, as manifested in the proliferation of free trade agreements and international investment treaties focused almost exclusively on market access. Countries have integrated product, capital and labour markets nationally, regionally and globally through domestic regulatory reform and international trade and investment liberalization on the implicit assumption that the resulting boost in growth will have a positive downstream effect on the living standards of their populations.

However, in many countries this approach has collided with three socioeconomic realities. First, although economies have indeed responded to this policy mix and expanded significantly in size, inequality has often also grown and median living standards have stagnated as the distribution of national income has shifted appreciably from labour to capital. Second, this same policy mix has brewed a triple cocktail of human dislocation and insecurity in the form of accelerated industrial restructuring driven by technological disruption, increased trade and investment flows propelled in part by labour and tax arbitrage, and domestic deregulation and privatization. Third, the chickens have come home to roost regarding the long-standing failure of economies to internalize the large negative environmental externalities of industrial development. Environmental degradation has reached a tipping point in many ecosystems, with adverse consequences for social and political order in a growing number of countries that these ecosystems host.

These trends have combined to fuel a growing discrepancy between standard economic and financial measures of national economic performance (e.g., GDP and asset prices) and others more relevant to the everyday life of people (e.g., household income, access to decent work, level of social security). This disconnect between national income and household lived experience, between the wealth and broad living standards of nations, risks growing even wider over the next twenty years as artificial intelligence and algorithmic automation further disrupt manufacturing and service industries and governments implement tougher measures to decarbonize energy and industrial systems in line with their commitments under the Paris climate agreement.

Establishment politicians of the centre-right and centre-left have often appeared flat-footed in the face of these trends. Doubling down on more-of-the-same deregulatory and cost-of-capital-centred trickle-down economics increasingly resembles feet-of-clay economics to citizens, since it tends to widen rather than reduce this disconnect and exacerbate inequality. Large fiscal and monetary stimulus in the near term coupled with goals and targets for fundamental reform over the long term do not inspire great confidence either. These standard remedies of the conservative right and social democratic left are increasingly viewed by citizens as weak tea at best and cynical distraction at worst, relative to the scale of the challenge posed by the hollowing out of the middle class in advanced economies, increased marginalization of the poor in many developing countries, and growing disruption from automation and climate change. The longer that political leaders persist with these policies, the more they risk appearing complacent and ineffectual relative to the depth of change most people sense is required to deal with the disruption and dislocation that has already occurred, let alone what is fast approaching—and the more they risk feeding a vicious cycle of social disaffection and political cynicism and polarization.

Liberal economics' policy immobility and political tin ear in the face of these challenges is rooted in a certain indoctrinated incomprehension. The implicit assumption that GDP growth eventually diffuses or "trickles down" into broad socioeconomic progress and security has never been properly recognized and interrogated. As a result, it remains an almost subliminal article of faith that continues to be baked into the thinking of economists and political and business leaders, who are conditioned by their training to believe that measures to expand GDP are the best and indeed only intellectually credible way to advance broad living standards—safety net programmes for the poorest notwithstanding. This cognitive reflex is reinforced not only in the use of GDP per capita as the standard measure of a country's level of economic development but also by the relatively limited amount of theoretical and applied research on the relationship between economic growth and broad living standards as economics has developed as a social science over the past century and a half.

This blind spot of prevailing economic doctrine accounts for the widespread stasis of economic policy despite mounting social unease with the performance of economies in human terms—particularly with respect to social inclusion, environmental sustainability and human resilience and dignity. More than anything other factor, the trickle-down mental model of progress implicit in modern economics is responsible for the deer-caught-in-the-headlights political character of contemporary liberal governance, whether in its social democratic or conservative forms. It is increasingly out of step with the lived human experience and changing political attitudes of a growing cross-section of society as technological, environmental and demographic change (and geopolitical tumult) reorders the economic landscape.

The failure of modern economics to properly take account of the human implications of rapid and disruptive economic change has been roiling politics around the globe in recent years, creating an opening for demagogic populists to gain ground. It has done much to create the parched electoral landscape in which isolated wildfires of extremism have expanded into major infernos of social unrest and political instability, including in some countries that are traditional bulwarks of liberalism. Popular dissatisfaction with the way that socioeconomic opportunity and outcomes are being stewarded is providing the accumulated underbrush of kindling for these fires, making the job of political arsonists that much easier.

To be certain, the heated controversies over identity and immigration in many countries are not primarily a function of political economy. But, as Karl Polanyi famously observed when analysing the conditions that gave rise to fascism in Europe in the 1930s, such tensions are often fuelled by adverse economic conditions that reflect a failure of economic theory to reconcile high principle with the lived experience of people. While some actors appear to be working for various reasons to connect these blazes and whip them into a global political conflagration that would consume the liberal international order as we know it, the first step in extinguishing or at least controlling them is for friends of the liberal tradition and other users of its tools to recognize that the underlying hazard can be found closer to home—in the faulty wiring within our own mental model of economic growth and development.

Not since the Bolshevik Revolution and Great Depression has liberalism faced such an existential social and political threat. During that period in the early twentieth century, the academic and policy establishments struggled to understand and overcome the blind spots in the economic doctrine of the day that were preventing an adequate response to those two grave threats to capitalist democracies. The resulting course correction in political economy ultimately included a veritable revolution in monetary and fiscal policy; the creation of the so-called "welfare state"; and major new regulation of financial and labour markets, including the establishment of the International Labour Organization (ILO).

The ILO's 1919 Constitution and 1944 Philadelphia Declaration annex articulated a tripartite (business–labour–government) consensus behind a new way of combining market economics with broad social progress and justice. In effect, these remarkable multilateral accords, which pre-dated the birth of the United Nations system and Bretton Woods institutions, articulated a universal baseline social contract in which working people were to be protected from being treated as mere commodities by committing employers to respect certain legally enforceable worker rights, governments to provide certain minimum social protections, and all three stakeholders to engage in ongoing "social dialogue" aimed at surfacing and resolving differences in good faith (i.e., without resorting to violent political confrontation).

The combined effect of these domestic and international institutional reforms was to change many of the basic rules and relationships within economies, to reset their "growth model" and social contract. This course correction contributed to several decades of robust economic progress in which national income and household living standards progressed in tandem throughout much of the industrializing world. Liberal economic governance requires a similar restructuring of rules and relationships to reset the growth model and social contract of our own day. That is the stark message being sent by the electorate's vanishing confidence in the political and economic establishment in many countries.

A core thesis of this book is that the root of the increasingly serious crisis facing democratic capitalism can be located in a fundamental distortion in the way its canon of economic principles and tools have evolved since the eighteenth and nineteenth centuries, and especially in the way they have been applied over the past several decades. The key to reviving liberalism's fortunes in the twenty-first century—including its noble project of promoting mutually reinforcing gains in living standards within and among nations in an open international economic system anchored in the rule of law and universal human rights—is to reconstitute its political economy, the way it conceptualizes and pursues economic progress. Absent such fundamental reform, its domestic and international political prospects are likely to continue to deteriorate. Its leaders and elites are likely to continue to give the impression of rearranging the proverbial chairs on the deck of a governance model sinking under the weight of its inability to adapt to the profound economic, social and environmental transformations of a new era.

The book does not aim to add to the considerable literature describing or measuring this challenge. Rather, it seeks to locate more precisely the doctrinal cul-de-sac within liberal economics that has been preventing an adequate response. It then attempts to construct a revised theoretical model and corresponding policy framework that would enable countries to achieve a better balance between the quantity and social quality of growth, in particular with respect to the key dimensions of inclusion, sustainability and resilience.

The book is organized as follows. Chapter 2 summarizes the historical track record of liberal economics with respect to inclusion, sustainability and resilience. The seriousness and persistence of its shortcomings in these respects suggest a structural problem in the model—a possible constitutional flaw in liberal economic doctrine. Chapter 3 takes up this question, examining the extent to which current practice varies from the original framework and underlying assumptions of liberal political economy's eighteenth- and nineteenth-century intellectual pioneers. I find that the prevailing development model, by focusing so tightly on generating growth in national income—what Adam Smith called the "wealth of nations"—is out of sync with the mental model that Smith and other founders of liberal economics had of economic progress. Smith and two of the nineteenth century's most influential theorists and codifiers of what was then called "political economy", John Stuart Mill and Alfred Marshall, were moral philosophers before they were economists, literally and figuratively. They were quite explicit that markets alone could not deliver broad-based and lasting improvement in the material well-being of societies. Enabling policies and institutions were also needed in a wide variety of policy domains, which is to say that a robust social contract was every bit as essential as markets.

Their thinking in this regard was prescient. Increasing national income through a more efficient mechanism of resource allocation was precisely what was needed at the dawn of the industrial age, following a millennium of minimal productivity growth and wealth accumulation in poor, agrarian and feudal societies. But modern economic science, and particularly its late twentieth-century neoliberal variant, extrapolated these insights to near theocratic status, creating an intellectually consistent, mathematically rigorous construct with a growing real-world blind spot.

Particularly in high- and middle-income countries, the primary challenge today is not so much to boost the overall level of national wealth from abjectly low levels as it is to broaden the base of the growth process in order to expand its manifold benefits to the population as a whole and in so doing to make it more sustainable. If the planned-economy socialist experiment of the twentieth century failed because of its excessive focus on equity and control to the detriment of allocative efficiency and dynamism, the ongoing experiment in neoliberal capitalism is now staring its own political failure in the face for the opposite reason—an unbalanced focus on efficiency and aggregate wealth creation over the breadth of their payoff to society in the form of broad-based progress in living standards.

Chapter 3 probes the source of this blind spot and finds convincing evidence that it is not a congenital flaw; it cannot be attributed to the original principles of liberal policy economy. If there is an original sin, it is not in the thinking of the seminal political economists of the eighteenth and nineteenth centuries but rather in the highly context-specific interplay of circumstance, available tools and ideological overshoot as economics evolved into a more rigorous social science over the course of the twentieth century. The contemporary shortcomings of liberal economics are largely within our power to correct if we return to first principles and unlearn some of the reflexes and behavioural tics that have accumulated over the past century.

To this end, in Chap. 4, I present an alternative theoretical construct—or mental model—of growth and development which formally internalizes the role of enabling institutions related to inclusion, sustainability and resilience. It does so by defining the key channels by which gains in living standards propagate at the household level in an economy and modelling these as a system (a "function" in economics parlance). I argue that this "aggregate distribution function" is the de facto underlying income distribution system, or living standards diffusion mechanism, of modern economies, and that it deserves at least as much policy emphasis and investment as the factors of production in the aggregate production function. To support the operationalization of this reformulated growth model, I map the extensive ecosystem of policy domains and institutional features that correspond to the function's five "factors of distribution" and suggest policy principles and tools to assist in the development of a strategy to activate them more fully.

Chapter 5 considers the implications for domestic economic policy of this rebalanced growth and development model, with its explicit dual focus on strengthening the median living standards as much as the aggregate wealth, or GDP, of nations. For each of the areas of policy and institutional strength, identified in Chap. 4, that help to diffuse gains in household living standards, I provide examples of good policy practice and present comparative data demonstrating the wide range of performance among peer groups of countries. These data serve to illustrate the considerable unexploited policy space that countries have at every level of economic development to improve their performance on one or another aspect of median living standards—to narrow what I call their "welfare gap" through a process of systematic and sustained institutional deepening that can often also help to reduce their output gap, that is, to boost economic growth, given the importance of many of these institutional features for labour productivity and aggregate demand.

Chapter 6 applies this more human-centred, living-standards-oriented approach to economics to international economic cooperation and governance. Over the years, many have called for a new Bretton Woods conference to renew the multilateral system and improve the coherence of its economic, social and environmental dimensions. But these appeals have never amounted to much, in part because they have lacked an organizing principle—a new or substantially revised policy model upon which to build a renovated institutional edifice. I argue that the reformulated growth and development model and accompanying policy framework and principles articulated in these pages provide such a compass. I propose a corresponding set of priority reforms of international macroeconomic coordination, the international financial architecture and international trade and technology governance. These proposals are ambitious relative to the incrementalism of recent years, but I demonstrate that they are entirely feasible in both financial and political terms; they would simply activate much more fully the existing capital and capabilities, and in many cases stated intentions and current initiatives, of the corresponding international organizations.

Chapter 7 concludes with a reflection on the potential implications of this fundamental critique and reformulation of modern economics for the legacy of the most influential economist of the twentieth century, John Maynard Keynes, as well as the liberal tradition's political prospects in the twenty-first century. With its sharp focus on household living standards, human-centred economics is kitchen-table economics. It is fundamentally a strategy to invest in people—their employment opportunity, disposable income and purchasing power, and economic, environmental and social security. These matters are of tangible relevance to people of all demographics and political philosophies. Addressing them in a more direct and systematic manner would add a reinforcing structural dimension to Keynes's macroeconomic approach to charting a more viable "Middle Way" between laissez-faire capitalism and state-centric socialism. It would also provide the basis for a more socially just and thus politically durable transition to the major climate action required by Paris agreement.

It would constitute a growth and opportunity strategy as well, a means of increasing economic growth by broadening its base, investing in its fundamentals and thereby strengthening its resilience. Growth has been lagging or outright lacking in most advanced and an increasing number of developing economies, and this has contributed to a vast underutilization of resources and loss of human potential, as manifested in high rates of youth unemployment and widespread underemployment and informal and insecure work. Investing more in people through tangible improvements in their household purchasing power, financial security, social protection, skills and access to decent work would strengthen aggregate demand, worker productivity and investor and consumer confidence—Keynes's central preoccupation. These are the fundamental determinants of economic growth. By contrast, the standard trickle-down growth and development model has focused on improving conditions for capital investment through efficiency-enhancing supply-side reforms or boosting consumption through the periodic administration of fiscal and monetary stimulus—strategies that are well beyond the point of diminishing returns in many countries following decades of deregulation and privatization and years of extraordinary stimulus to combat the effects of the recent crises.

In sum, by establishing median progress in living standards as an explicit rather than residual consideration of economic theory, policy and measurement, the human-centred approach to economics suggested in these pages creates the prospect of capturing greater synergies—a stronger positive feedback loop—between production and distribution, markets and institutions, and efficiency and equity, that is to say, between growth and inclusion, sustainability and resilience. Chapter 2 begins with an examination of the historical track record of liberal economics in this regard.

Open Access This chapter is licensed under the terms of the Creative Commons Attribution 4.0 International License (http://creativecommons.org/licenses/by/4.0/), which permits use, sharing, adaptation, distribution and reproduction in any medium or format, as long as you give appropriate credit to the original author(s) and the source, provide a link to the Creative Commons licence and indicate if changes were made.

The images or other third party material in this chapter are included in the chapter's Creative Commons licence, unless indicated otherwise in a credit line to the material. If material is not included in the chapter's Creative Commons licence and your intended use is not permitted by statutory regulation or exceeds the permitted use, you will need to obtain permission directly from the copyright holder.

CHAPTER 2

Liberal Economics' Track Record on Inclusion, Sustainability and Resilience

Economics—that is, the nearly 250-year tradition of liberal political economy originating with Adam Smith and fellow eighteenth- and nineteenth-century pioneers—has been in something of an existential crisis for more than a decade. Despite its remarkable accomplishments over the years and outsized influence in the halls of government and academia, it is facing a chorus of fundamental criticism, including in its own professional ranks.

Difficult questions and unresolved tensions exposed by the Great Financial Crisis have combined with the extraordinary circumstances of the past few years—the COVID-19 pandemic, US–China trade rift, Russian invasion of Ukraine and accelerating algorithmic automation and climate change regulation—to trigger a period of searching reflection the likes of which have not been seen since economists and policymakers struggled to find solutions to the multiple crises they faced in the 1930s.

To be certain, modern economics, including its neoliberal variant of the past few decades, has made an enormous contribution to human progress by increasing economic growth. With the exception of a handful of countries bordering the North Sea, growth was nearly non-existent in all regions of the world until the nineteenth century,[1] when the market-oriented principles developed by Smith, David Ricardo, John Stuart Mill, W.S. Jevons, Leon Walras, Alfred Marshall and their twentieth-century successors began to be applied. While the technological advances of the First and Second Industrial Revolutions played a major role in this economic breakthrough—as, it must be said, did colonial and other forms of human and environmental exploitation—growth has often been strongest in countries that applied these market-oriented principles earliest and most consistently. Indeed, at different times over the past several decades, the growth rates of China, India and several Southeast Asian and Latin American countries shifted markedly upwards after their governments instituted policy changes that strengthened market signals, whether through domestic reforms or international trade and investment liberalization, or both.

The expansion of economic output that these principles helped to produce has improved the human condition unmistakably in at least one very important sense: poverty reduction. Roughly 90% of humanity lived on less than US$2 per day (in 2011 dollars) until about 1860.[2] Such absolute poverty declined fairly steadily to about two-thirds of the global population by 1950, mainly on the strength of progress in the West, where these principles were born and first consciously applied. Again, other factors such as technological advances, favourable geography and colonization figured prominently in the economic progress made by these countries; however, their liberal economic reforms contributed importantly, too.

This conclusion is corroborated by the more recent experience of many developing countries.[3] World Bank household survey consumption data show that the pace of extreme poverty reduction in the world increased after 1980. By then, absolute poverty had been virtually eradicated in Western Europe, North America, Japan, Australia and New Zealand. But the share of the global population living on less than US$1.90 per day in 2011 dollars declined dramatically from 44% in 1980 to less than 10% in 2015. Hundreds of millions of mainly Chinese, South and Southeast Asian, Latin American and other citizens were lifted beyond a subsistence level of existence or worse in little more than a generation. The timing of this remarkable—indeed, historically unprecedented—transformation coincided with the implementation of market-oriented reforms, which began in earnest in China in 1979, in India in 1991,[4] in Brazil in the mid-1990s[5] and in Indonesia[6] and Vietnam[7] in 1985 and 1986, respectively. Before these dates, the pace of economic growth and poverty reduction in these large developing countries had been modest by comparison.

China's progress has been nothing short of spectacular in this respect; extreme poverty has fallen from about 88% of its population of one billion in 1981 to below 1% today. Many other countries have also made strong progress. Nearly a third (29%) of the non-Chinese world population was living in extreme poverty in 1981, most of them in South Asia and sub-Saharan Africa. By 2013 this figure had fallen to 12%. From 1990 to 2013 alone, the number of people worldwide living on less than US$1.90 a day more than halved, from 1.8 billion to 766 million.[8]

Thus, the contribution of market-oriented economics to socioeconomic progress over the past 200 years is clear and impressive. It has a proud legacy of helping to raise economic output and incomes from the very low levels experienced by humanity for millennia. But modern liberal economics is manifestly struggling to respond effectively to three contemporary challenges on which societies everywhere are demanding much faster action: social inclusion; environmental sustainability; and resilience to major shifts and shocks. There is a growing body of evidence and criticism that it may be *constitutionally* incapable of responding effectively to these problems. Indeed, its theoretical models generally treat them as afterthoughts—as matters assumed to resolve naturally over time on the strength of a rising tide of national income generated by economic growth.

Incremental and halting progress on these three important questions is contributing to an erosion of popular confidence in the political dimension of the liberal tradition: the principles of democratic governance and the rule of law underpinning free, open and tolerant societies. Disillusionment with the track record of economies on inclusion, sustainability and resilience is playing into a growing cynicism and even nihilism in the political culture of many countries—a dangerous and potentially volatile belief that elites are either out for themselves or hopelessly out of their depth, or both, in the face of the disruptive changes sweeping our economies in the twenty-first century.

This dim view of the so-called dismal science's chances of effectively confronting these challenges is grounded in a considerable body of evidence.

INCLUSION

When viewed from a global historical perspective, much progress has been made on income inequality, particularly in the last half-century. As the people at *Our World in Data* have observed (see Fig. 2.1):

> In 1975, the world's income distribution was "bimodal", with the two-humped shape of a camel: one hump below the international poverty line and a second hump at considerably higher incomes. During the preceding

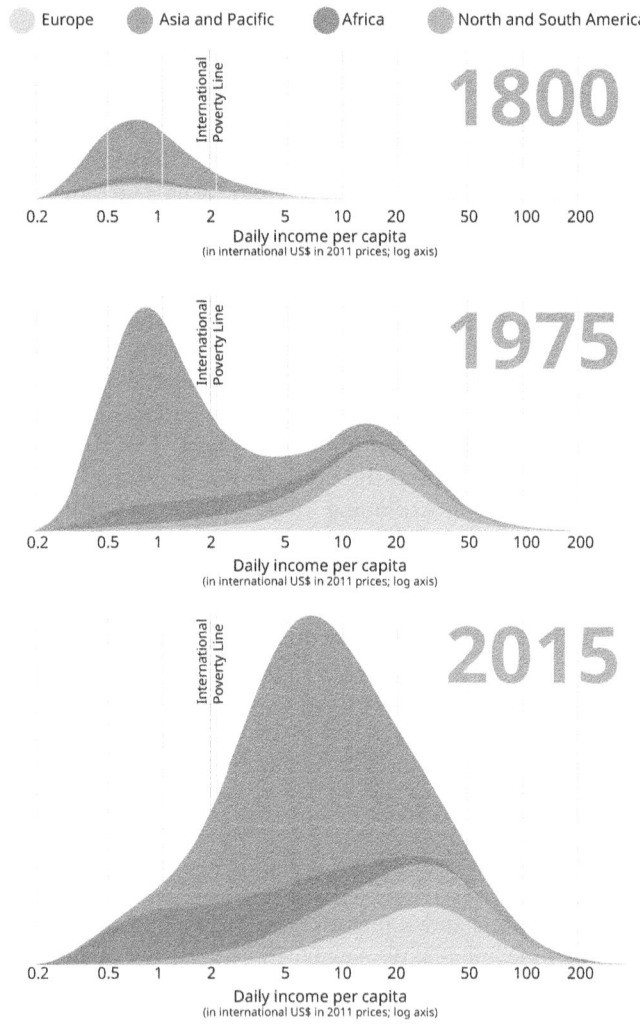

Fig. 2.1 Global income distribution in 1800, 1975 and 2015

century, the world had divided into a poor, developing world and a developed world that was more than 10-times richer. But over the following 4 decades, there has been a convergence in incomes: in many poorer countries, especially in South-East Asia, incomes have grown faster than they have in rich countries. Whilst enormous income differences remain, the world no longer neatly divides into the two groups of "developed" and "developing" countries. We have moved from a two-hump to a one-hump world. And at the same time, the distribution has also shifted to the right—the incomes of many of the world's poorest citizens have increased and extreme poverty has fallen faster than ever before in human history.[9]

Upon closer inspection, however, the record on inequality is less positive. There has been considerable variation in the pace of progress, and some large groups have barely progressed at all. This is the story told by the so-called "elephant curve" (Fig. 2.2),[10] which was widely interpreted to show that the poorest of the world and the middle and working classes in advanced economies were stagnating, while those of the emerging-market middle class and the richest 1% were enjoying disproportionate income gains. Subsequent refinements in both data and interpretation have qualified key parts of this story (in particular that post-Soviet countries and Japan account for most of the dip in the trunk and China accounts for most of the hump),[11] but much of it has been corroborated by other

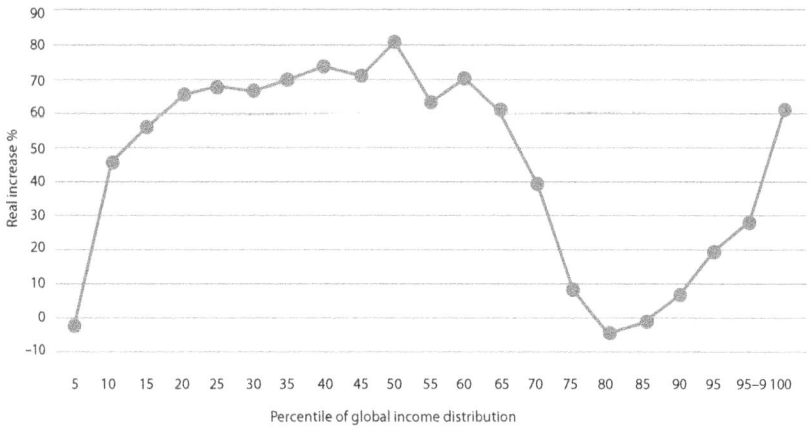

Branko Milanovic, "Global income inequality by the numbers: In history and now," World Bank, February 2013.

Fig. 2.2 Global change in real income by income percentile, 1988–2008

evidence and analysis showing a pronounced rise in within-country inequality across all levels of economic development.[12]

In fact, a more disaggregated look at the record of and prospects for social inclusion in the world reveals three serious and enduring problems.

First, in *advanced economies*, there has indeed been long-running stagnation in the income and living standards of the middle and working classes, especially relative to higher earners. The Organisation for Economic Co-operation and Development (OECD), an organization whose members are mainly advanced industrialized countries, reports that median household income in these countries has been stagnant since 2017, after growing 1% between the mid-1980s and mid-1990s and a more respectable 1.6% between the mid-1990s and mid-2000s. As the OECD's researchers observe, this tepid performance with respect to the middle and working classes contrasts with the fortunes of higher earners:

> Overall, over the past 30 years, median incomes increased a third less than the average income of the richest 10%. Moreover, in some countries the share of incomes at the very top has surged; in the United States, for example, the share of top 1% on total income has almost doubled from about 11% to 20% over the past three decades and almost half of all income growth over this period accrued to this group … Therefore, the economic influence of the middle class and its role as "centre of economic gravity" has weakened. Three decades ago, the aggregate income of all middle-income households was four times the aggregate income of upper income households, i.e. those with incomes above two times the national median; today, this ratio is less than three.[13]

At the same time …

> the prices of core consumption goods and services such as health, education and housing have risen well above inflation … while middle incomes have been lagging behind. In particular, ageing and new medical technologies have driven up the cost of health services; the race for diplomas is pressing parents to invest more and more in education while, at the same time, education services became more costly in a number of countries; the geographical polarisation of jobs is pushing up housing prices in large urban areas, precisely where most rewarding jobs are available … Housing, in particular, is key: at around one-third of disposable income, it constitutes the largest expenditure item for middle-income households—up from around a quarter in the 1990s. Despite large within-country variations, house prices have

been growing three times faster than household median income over the last two decades. Housing is more than just a standard consumption good: in many countries, being middle class is traditionally associated with owning a home, so soaring house prices have touched on the very meaning of being part of the middle class.[14]

This statistical analysis of widening inequality in advanced economies during the past generation—commonly referred to as the "hollowing out" of their middle classes—is based on a definition of the middle class as households earning between 75% and 200% of the national median. This group averaged 61% of the population across the OECD's member countries, ranging from roughly 50% in the United States to around 70% in a number of Nordic countries (with Czechia, France, Canada and Sweden not far behind).

The particular way these income thresholds are calculated makes them somewhat difficult to translate into terms with which people can readily identify, but the Pew Research Group runs its own more accessible calculation of the middle-class income thresholds of countries, and arrives at a similar definitional conclusion as the OECD (specifically, between 67% and 200% of current dollar median household income versus the OECD's range of between 75% and 200% of median household disposable income on a 2010 purchasing power parity [PPP] adjusted basis). On this very similar basis, Pew defines the US middle class as having household income for a family of three of between US$48,500 and US$145,500 in 2018, with those above this threshold regarded as higher-income households.[15] Other sources helpfully segment this higher income group further,[16] placing the line between upper-middle-income and wealthy households at around US$350,000 to US$400,000, near the point at which the next-to-highest US individual income tax bracket (35% rate) begins for married couples filing jointly.

In sum, these data paint a picture of middle and working classes in advanced economies being squeezed by a combination of stagnant real incomes, the rising cost of key necessities, and a job market undergoing polarization in skills and compensation. The OECD reports that

> one out of two middle-income households now report difficulties to make ends meet, though this ranges from one out of five or less in the Nordic countries and the Netherlands to two out of three or more in some Southern and Eastern European countries. Furthermore, almost 40% of middle-income

households are financially vulnerable: i.e. they are [i]n arrears or would not be able to absorb unexpected expenses or a sudden income fall.[17]

These trends have been building for over a generation and have become embedded in family perceptions of their intergenerational economic prospects. Fully "60% of parents list the risk that their children will not achieve the level of status and comfort that they have as one of the top-three greatest social and economic long-term risks".

Precarity and downward mobility is thus the current lived experience of much of the middle and working classes of these, the richest countries on the planet. The fear of downward intergenerational mobility is not an irrational one; in fact, this trend is increasingly evident in the data (see Fig. 2.3).

In sum, despite the significant increase in GDP, asset prices and affordable consumer conveniences in these countries during the past generation, a troubling expansion of inequality and insecurity has occurred within the largest segments of their populations. There is thus serious trouble in the

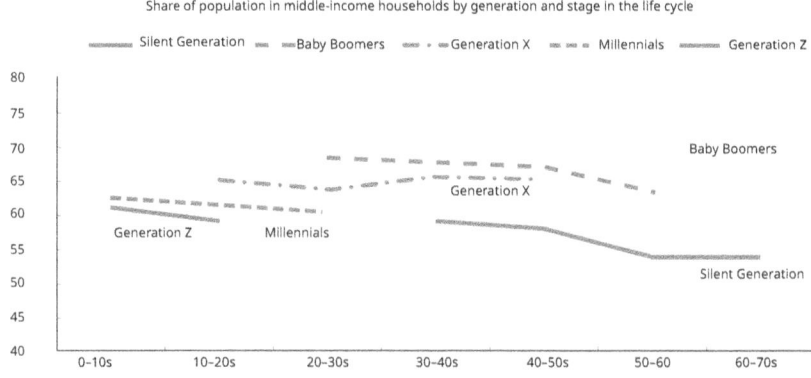

Note: Silent Generation: born before 1943, Baby Boomers: born 1943–64, Generation X: born 1965–82, Millennials: born 1983–2002; Generation Z: born since 2003. The middle-income class comprises individuals in households with income between 75% and 200% of the median. OECD average based on data from OECD average comprises available data from Canada, Denmark, Finland, France, United Kingdom, Ireland, Italy, Luxembourg, Mexico, Netherlands, Norway, Spain, Sweden and United States.

Source: OECD Secretariat calculations based on data from LIS Data Center, expect EU-SJLC for France (2014), Ireland (2014), Iceland (2014) and Sweden (2015).

Fig. 2.3 Since the Baby Boomer generation, each new generation has seen its chances of belonging to the middle-income class fall

supposed socioeconomic paradise of advanced economies, a status to which all developing countries aspire. Moreover, the problem appears to be getting worse, not better, and standard economic doctrine is seemingly impotent in the face of this.

Second, in many *middle-income countries*, progress in both economic growth and poverty reduction has been remarkable over the past few decades, thanks in large part to the waves of pro-growth reforms described above. However, it is not at all clear that their rapid convergence with the level of economic development of advanced industrialized economies—which has driven the two-humps-into-one-hump reduction in global inequality illustrated previously—can be sustained. Evidence of the existence of a so-called "middle-income trap", a seemingly systemic failure of even the most successful middle-income developing countries to join the ranks of wealthy advanced economies, is as compelling as it is vexing. South Korea is the only non-European-Union member of the United Nations with a population greater than 10 million to have unambiguously crossed this threshold over the past half-century.[18] This phenomenon, thus, increasingly appears to be structural, perhaps bred in the bone of the prevailing growth and development model.

Until now, progress in living standards and particularly poverty reduction in middle-income countries has been driven mainly by economic growth.[19] But, after more than forty years, it has become clear that the traditional growth-oriented prescription of reforms emphasizing improved economic efficiency and physical capital accumulation does not by itself provide a solution to the conundrum of the middle-income trap. Clues as to what might constitute a more effective strategy can be found in the experience of South Korea and its "Four Tigers" counterparts in East Asia.

The World Bank released the definitive analysis of this topic, *The East Asian Miracle*,[20] in 1993 under the leadership of Chief Economist Joseph Stiglitz. Colleagues and I have previously summarized this report and its policy implications for developing countries aspiring to high-income status as follows[21]:

> The World Bank's landmark 1993 study, *The East Asian Miracle*, examined how eight economies in the region succeeded in achieving a remarkable record of "high growth with equity" from 1960 to 1990. In a chapter entitled "An Institutional Basis for Shared Growth," its distinguished research team concluded: "Of course, few political leaders anywhere would reject, on principle, either the desirability of growth or that the benefits of growth

should be shared. What distinguished the High-Performing Asian Economies' leadership was the extent to which they adopted specific institutional mechanisms tailored to these goals, and that worked." The team then documented the institutional approaches that contributed importantly to this positive outcome in such areas as education, land reform, small- and medium-sized business support, housing, labor–management relations, insulation of policymaking from rent-seeking behavior, integrity in public administration, and business–government relations.

The blue-ribbon Commission on Growth and Development chaired by Nobel laureate Michael Spence drew a similar conclusion in its 2008 report, *The Growth Report: Strategies for Sustained Growth and Inclusive Development*:

> In recent decades governments were advised to "stabilize, privatize and liberalize." There is merit in what lies behind this injunction—governments should not try to do too much, replacing markets or closing the economy off from the rest of the world. But we believe this prescription defines the role of government too narrowly ... On the contrary, as the economy grows and develops, active, pragmatic governments have crucial roles to play ... [M]ature markets rely on deep institutional underpinnings, institutions that define property rights, enforce contracts, convey prices, and bridge informational gaps between buyers and sellers. Developing countries often lack these market and regulatory institutions. Indeed, an important part of development is precisely the creation of these institutionalized capabilities.[22]

My colleagues and I went on to conclude from these two studies that,

> In fact, economic institution-building has been a crucial part of the development path of essentially every country that has industrialized and achieved high living standards. Because development is a complex and multidisciplinary process—many conditions need to be fulfilled in order for widespread poverty to be replaced by ever-rising middle-class prosperity—this process of institutional deepening occurs across a wide spectrum of domains. But the process is not automatic. Although rising national income generates additional resources and policy space to establish and effectively implement such institutional mechanisms as public education systems, independent judiciaries, labor protections, social insurance systems, competition, investment climate, anti-corruption rules and enforcement agencies, and basic and digital infrastructure, they do not guarantee it. The pace and pattern of

economic institution-building is a choice, a function of policy decisions and public–private cooperation. Like other aspects of a country's growth model, it is shaped by the prevailing political economy and is largely endogenous to the development process. Because it is a policy choice, the size of the payoff from economic growth to broad socioeconomic progress is as well, to a considerable extent.

Indeed, the importance of economic institution-building for balanced and inclusive growth was a central lesson of the economic and financial crises of the early twentieth century. Beginning at the turn of the century and gathering force in the decades following the Great Depression, most of today's advanced industrialized countries underwent a sustained process of institutional deepening to broaden the base and strengthen the resilience of their economies. Labor, financial, social insurance, competition, and other reforms were deliberately aimed at engineering a more inclusive and sustainable growth model. They played a critical role in supporting the dramatic expansion of the middle class, eliminating poverty, and reducing economic insecurity in these societies during the latter half of the century.

If an economy can be thought of as a garden or arboretum, its macroeconomic and competitive environment sets the climate (basic conditions of moisture, sunlight, and temperature), while its institutions represent nutrients in the soil. Improvements in soil fertility can have a pronounced effect on the pace and consistency of plant growth, a process that takes years to get right and requires regular monitoring and modulation. Similarly, the essential fecundity of an economy—its yield of broad-based advancement of living standards—is shaped by the health of its macro-competitive environment as well as the strength of its institutions and policy-based incentives in areas particularly important for social inclusion. Like both weather conditions and soil quality, these factors require equal and ongoing attention. This fundamental lesson—and the rebalancing of emphasis in national policy that it implies—is where the journey toward a more socially-inclusive growth paradigm begins.[23]

Unfortunately, the lessons of these two landmark reports about the importance of institutions to achieving broad-based prosperity have never taken hold in the wider academic and policy communities. For all the hopeful talk after the 2008–09 financial crisis about the death of the Washington Consensus—the policy paradigm aptly described in the Commission on Growth and Development quote above—it continues to serve as the frame of reference for great majority of national policymakers as well as their international organization policy advisers and lenders. Such path dependency (i.e., it is hard to change old habits) perpetuates the middle-income trap, putting into question the durability of the impressive convergence of middle- and high-income countries and corresponding reduction in global cross-country inequality of recent decades.

Third, in *low-income countries* inequality and socioeconomic exclusion pose a particularly difficult challenge. These countries have been falling farther behind their middle-income counterparts in recent years while registering a very slow overall rate of convergence with advanced economies. Their performance has improved relative to before the mid-1990s,[24] but they continue to experience high levels of extreme poverty and deprivation of basic human needs. In richer economies, such material necessities are considered public goods and supported or provided by the state. But this tends not to be the case in the dire circumstances of the world's 28 low-income countries. As a result, traditional income-based measures of income poverty (e.g., the standard measure of extreme poverty of US1.90 per capita per day in 2011 prices or US$2.15 per day in 2017 prices) give an incomplete picture of the extent of material deprivation. Thus, the remarkable story of global poverty reduction of the past generation described earlier in this chapter, which is based on per capita GDP or income-based measures of poverty and disproportionately influenced by the progress of large middle-income countries like China and India, partially obscures the considerably less encouraging experience and lived reality of people in the world's poorest countries.

For this reason, new measures of poverty, so-called "multidimensional poverty indexes", have gained currency. By examining not only income but also key facets of people's lived experience with respect to the basic enabling necessities of life (e.g., access to health, education, employment, safe drinking water and sanitation, etc.), they track socioeconomic progress and poverty reduction more accurately. Studies comparing trends in income poverty and multidimensional poverty in low-income countries, as measured by the two leading such indexes—the Multidimensional Poverty Index (MPI) and Global Correlation Sensitive Poverty Index (G-CSPI)—have found a significant discrepancy, with the former providing a considerably rosier picture of progress in recent decades than the latter. One study concluded,

> A comparison between the trends in (extreme) income poverty and multidimensional poverty—based on a sample of 42 countries for which information was available for both indicators—reveals the former has declined significantly more than the latter (32% vs. 15%). Moreover, the prevalence

of multidimensional poverty (as measured by the headcount ratio of the G-CSPI) is substantially higher than the prevalence of extreme income poverty (as measured by the headcount ratio for USD 1.90 a day). These findings highlight that—once we take other, non-monetary dimensions into account—the progress in poverty eradication has not been as remarkable as believed and calls for stronger efforts in tackling the different forms of poverty.

Some additional analyses reveal further important policy information. While deprivations in all three dimensions of poverty have declined [the team of researchers focused on education; decent work; and access to potable water and adequate sanitation, which is a proxy for and strongly correlated with health status], the employment dimension has registered the smallest improvements. Moreover, [this] is the dimension that contributes the most to overall poverty; therefore, major attention should be given by policy makers to the functioning of labour markets. A preliminary analysis indicates that economic growth correlates with poverty reduction, but this elasticity is much lower for our G-CSPI than for income poverty. This finding is in line with that of Santos et al. who used the MPI as a measure of multidimensional poverty ... The direct policy implication is that, to address pockets of multidimensional poverty, a focus on the quantity aspect of growth is not enough. More attention must be given to the quality of the growth process and to the potential of social protection schemes and, more broadly, social policies to alleviate the multiple deprivations suffered by the poor.[25]

Thus, the crucial role of economic institutions in enabling social inclusion applies to low-income countries, too, albeit with a particular focus on the provision of basic needs. But such institutional deepening presents a particularly big challenge for these countries because of their more limited fiscal capacity and greater reliance on the often path-dependent policy advice and lending programmes of international organizations. This influential community, like the economics profession more broadly, continues to have as its primary frame of reference for economic development the traditional growth prescription of fiscal discipline, market competition and trade liberalization. It has traditionally placed much less emphasis on social protection, labour markets and public support of basic necessities.

In recent years and particularly since the onset of the pandemic, the leader-level messaging of these institutions has been changing in this regard; however, programmatic practice and resource allocation have yet to fully reflect this shift in narrative. For example, the United Nations

Children's Fund (UNICEF) reports that, before the COVID-19 crisis struck, 25 countries were already spending more on debt service than on social spending for education, health and social protection combined. By early 2021, the World Bank and the International Monetary Fund (IMF) were warning that 28 countries were at high risk of debt distress and 23 countries were at moderate risk. A quarter of all lower-middle-income countries were at high risk of debt distress. As of June 2021, the G20's Debt Service Suspension Initiative (DSSI) had offered an estimated US$13 billion in debt service relief to at least 43 participating countries, but just US$6 billion had been implemented. The programme was extended a final six months to December 2021, but it had become clear by then that permanent debt restructuring rather than the temporary deferrals of scheduled repayments was required. The G20 then launched a replacement programme, the Common Framework for Debt Treatment. However, it has been slow to take off despite a significant further deterioration of the finances of developing countries owing to rising fuel and food costs, increased US interest rates, a strengthened US dollar (in which many debts and imports are denominated) and the ongoing pandemic.

In fact, a formal consensus exists within the international community on the universal human right of social protection and its progressive realization through national social protection floors.[26] Social protection floors are nationally defined sets of four categories of basic social security guarantees that secure protection intended to prevent or alleviate poverty, vulnerability and social exclusion.[27] Despite this multilateral consensus, which should have a strong influence on the resource allocation decisions of bilateral and multilateral development finance institutions, less than half of humanity is covered by a single such category of basic social protection notwithstanding evidence that countries at all levels of development have the capacity to institute basic social protections, particularly if complemented with initial international support.[28] But while development donors in their own countries spend the same on social protection as they do on education and health combined, social protection receives one-seventh of the resources allocated to education and health in their foreign assistance budgets.[29]

In sum, there are serious and growing deficits in social inclusion within high-, middle- and low-income countries alike. According to the evidence of the past several decades, the stubborn persistence of these dimensions of inequality and insecurity appears to be a hallmark, not an aberration, of the prevailing liberal economic growth and development model, notwithstanding the dramatic reduction in income poverty and expansion of the global middle class, both driven in large part by the rapid, sustained economic growth of China, India and a number of other large middle-income countries.

SUSTAINABILITY

The problematic track record of liberal economic governance regarding environmental sustainability is less nuanced than its performance on social inclusion. There has been a systematic failure over the years and across all levels of development to internalize the adverse environmental impacts of economic growth in prices and policies. The evidence is unmistakable. Yes, environmental performance tends to improve with economic development, particularly once countries reach high-income status. But the overall environmental legacy of industrial development is abysmal verging on catastrophic, despite round after round of intergovernmental reform commitments beginning with the 1972 United Nations Conference on the Human Environment in Stockholm and the 1992 Earth Summit and Rio Declaration, which were inspired by the concept of sustainable development articulated by the landmark Brundtland Report, *Our Common Future*, published five years earlier.[30]

Prominent examples include:

- **Biodiversity:** According to the United Nations Environment Programme (UNEP), populations of species are declining and species extinction rates are increasing steadily. At present, 42% of terrestrial invertebrates, 34% of freshwater invertebrates and 25% of marine invertebrates are considered at risk of extinction. Between 1970 and 2014, global vertebrate species population abundances declined by on average 60%. Steep declines in pollinator abundance have also been documented. Ecosystem integrity and functions are declining. Ten out of every 14 terrestrial habitats have seen a decrease in vegetation productivity and just under half of all terrestrial ecoregions are classified as having an unfavourable status.[31]

    Moreover, loss of tropical forest is projected to increase from around 0.8% per year between 1981 and 1990[14] to an estimated 2% per year in the years ahead.[15] Projections show that a large fraction of species will be "committed to extinction" in the twenty-first century because of conflicting land use and climate change. The International

Union for Conservation of Nature (IUCN) Red List contains (as of September 2018) 26,000 threatened species or 27% of all assessed species, including: 41% of amphibians, 33% of reef-building corals, 25% of mammals, 13% of birds and 34% of conifers.[16] The average rate of vertebrate species loss over the last century is up to 100 times higher than the background rate.[17] Invasive species have contributed to more than half of the animal extinctions for which the cause is known.[18]

- **Climate change:** Global temperatures have risen by 1.2 °C so far, and already we are seeing an increase in natural disasters such as flooding and hurricanes. The UN Intergovernmental Panel on Climate Change (IPCC) 2022 report warned that the world is set to reach the 1.5 °C level within the next two decades and that only drastic cuts in carbon emissions from now would help prevent an environmental disaster. The report warned that the world is approaching certain tipping points, meaning that we will have gone beyond the point where the damage can be repaired. It highlighted, in particular, widespread forest die-off and global sea level rise from polar ice cap melting, the latter being likely to result in a one-metre rise, other things being equal.[32]

As important as comprehensive action is on all of the major drivers of greenhouse gas emissions,[33] nothing is more vital in the race to stabilize atmospheric concentrations of these gases by the mid-twenty-first century than rapidly reducing the burning of coal and preventing the installation of new coal-burning capacity.[34] Even if no new coal plants were built, the existing global fleet would consume most of world's remaining carbon budget of roughly 440 gigatons of carbon dioxide under a moderate-probability scenario of 1.5 °C in global warming, including a third of the budget in just the next 10 years.[35] For this reason, unabated coal-fired power generation must decline quickly—much faster than use of oil and natural gas[36]—if the world is to have a realistic chance of achieving either of the Paris climate agreement's 1.5 °C or "well-below-2 °C" goals: an 80% reduction by 2030 to achieve the 1.5 °C goal or the same reduction by 2038 to remain under the 2 °C limit, as well as virtual elimination (a 97% decline) within the following 10 years in both cases.[37] Although plans for many new plants have been cancelled in recent years, some 1000 coal boilers are still under construction or are being planned and permitted around the world, equivalent to around a quarter of existing capacity.[38] Coal is thus a central factor driving the current trajectory of 2.5% to 3 °C in global warming above pre-industrial levels,[39] which the bottom-up nationally determined contribution (NDC) process of the Paris climate agreement has yet to substantially alter on the ground. Some sort of extra-market intervention is clearly going to be required to achieve such a dramatic transition.

- **Oceans:** The United Nations Food and Agricultural Office (FAO) reports that nearly 85% of global fish stocks are currently overexploited, depleted or in recovery from exploitation.[40] According to Oceanos,[41] approximately 70% of world fish populations are now unsustainably exploited; the biomass of 25% of them has collapsed to less than 10% of historic levels; and 90% of worldwide stocks of large predatory fish are already gone. Species such as Orange Roughy, Chilean Sea Bass and Bluefin Tuna have collapsed. We are losing species as well as entire ecosystems. As a result, the overall ecology of our oceans is at risk of collapse and we, as a species, are at risk of losing a valuable food source that many depend on for social, economic or dietary reasons. Scientists now believe that, on current trends, nearly 90% of the world's fisheries will be overfished by 2050, meaning that they will be substantially depleted and on a path to collapse absent remedial action.[42] Moreover, they estimate that global coverage of living coral has declined by half since the 1950s[43] and many regions are expected to see their coral collapse entirely by late this century, according to current trends in global warming, ocean acidification and other pollution.
- **Freshwater and sanitation:** The World Meteorological Organization (WMO) concluded in a 2021 report that 3.6 billion people had inadequate access to water for at least one month per year in 2018, and that by 2050 this figure is expected to rise to more than five billion.[44] Water-related hazards have increased in frequency over the past 20 years; since 2000, flood-related disasters have risen by 134% compared with the two previous decades. The number and duration of droughts have also increased by 29% over this same period. In 2020, 3.6 billion people lacked safely managed sanitation services, 2.3 billion lacked basic hygiene services and more than two billion lived in water-stressed countries with a lack of access to safe drinking water. Seventy-five countries reported water efficiency levels below average, including 10 with extremely low levels. Current rates of

progress need to quadruple in order to reach the global Sustainable Development Goal (SDG) targets by 2030.

A group of scientists published a study in 2016 tracing the rise of water scarcity over the past century. Noting that the maximum global potential—the so-called "planetary boundary"[45]—for consumptive freshwater use is approaching rapidly,[46] they concluded from the data that, whereas water consumption increased fourfold, the population under water scarcity increased from 0.24 billion (14% of global population) in the 1900s to 3.8 billion (58%) in the 2000s. In other words, water scarcity has increased 16-fold since the 1900s despite the total population having roughly quadrupled.[47]

In sum, it should be abundantly clear from this partial summary[48] of global environmental degradation that a new and decidedly un-neoliberal approach is going to be required to stabilize let alone reverse this situation, notwithstanding all of the good intentions, initiatives and multilateral agreements of recent years. Any reasonable interpretation of the evidence leads to the conclusion that a revolution in economic policy—a fundamental reformulation of growth and development—is going to be required. The standard liberal economic model appears to be constitutionally incapable of internalizing negative environmental externalities in economic decision-making, both public and private, at the pace necessary to prevent catastrophic damage to the biosphere this century, despite growing recognition of the destabilizing effect this would have (and is already having) on economic and political stability.

Resilience

Liberal economic governance has also shown itself to be remarkably prone to major shocks having profound human consequences. It has a track record of systematically failing to learn from such difficulties in order to construct sufficient guard rails or buffers against the threat of future financial, food, energy, health and supply chain crises. It also has a chronic tendency to underinvest in a minimum level of human resilience and dignity through the construction of social security systems.

- **Finance:** The evidence with respect to financial crises is particularly damning. One comprehensive historical database covering the experience of 206 countries since the Second World War identified 151 systemic banking crises (1970–2019), 414 currency crises (1950–2019), 200 sovereign debt crises (1960–2019), 75 twin such crises (1970–2019) and 21 triple such crises (1970–2019).[49] If anything, the problem is getting worse and even more engrained despite growing evidence that financial crises are susceptible to prediction, since they are in large part an artifact of excess credit creation and therefore substantially preventable through anticipatory policy measures.[50]

The end of US dollar convertibility into gold in the early 1970s and the deregulation of financial services since have provided greater national policy autonomy. However,

> a combination of fiat currencies (those not linked to the price of gold or other physical commodity) and ever weakening financial market regulation has enabled exponential growth in credit and debt creation. This change has made boom and bust cycles more prevalent at a global level and ushered in an era of regular crises, but ones that have so far been tamed by even looser policy and debt/credit growth.[51]

There is every reason to believe that the papering over of vulnerabilities in the financial system and real economy over the past 15 years through the provision of extraordinary central bank liquidity and fiscal stimulus is likely to end in tears. Yes, there has been major progress in strengthening key aspects of bank regulation since the 2009 London G20 Summit and creation of the Financial Stability Board (FSB); however, major gaps in prudential regulation remain, notably with respect to shadow banking and fintech, including but not limited to crypto-assets. Moreover, banking interests have succeeded in rolling back some of the hard-fought safety measures agreed following the Great Financial Crisis. As former US Federal Reserve chairman Paul Volcker is reported to have quipped, "about every 10 years we have the greatest crisis in 50 years".

- **Food and energy:** The food and energy crisis of 2021–23 is also hardly unprecedented. As for food, history is replete with examples in which the international commodification and commercialization of agricultural production has degraded local food security, including the level of buffer stocks and cultivation of indigenous crops, to the social breaking point.[52] High food prices, often related to dependence on food imports, increase the "risk of conflict and political unrest in countries with weak social safety nets. Roughly four dozen countries experienced domestic political unrest or civil war during the 2008–12 global food price crisis. Governments in Haiti, Libya, Madagascar, and Tunisia fell, sometimes violently, and protracted civil wars erupted in Syria and Yemen."[53]

The world has experienced three major food crises in the past 50 years. Each time, it struggled to cobble together a tactical response to the immediate situation rather than channel the political urgency of the moment into a set of structural improvements in global food security institutions and frameworks. These need to include safety nets and buffer stocks, trade arrangements, international support for domestic productive capacity, and expanded public investment in areas with particular potential to strengthen the resilience of the system.

Global energy crises have typically originated in geopolitical tensions rather than structural weaknesses in global markets. Nevertheless, fuel-importing developing countries routinely pay a heavy price for related increases in oil and gas prices. They are usually not a party to the political tensions giving rise to these price spikes, but they bear the principal collateral damage in large part because the international community has never been able to agree on an effective mechanism to manage the resulting impact on their public finances and sovereign debt sustainability. The lack of such a systematic mechanism for external debt restructuring in such cases is a structural weakness in the resilience of the world economy from a human and social perspective. The consequence of this gap in the international financial architecture is austerity and increased poverty and deprivation that complicate an already difficult, and often dire, social situation. The world appears to be on the verge of repeating this vicious cycle—so evident in the Latin American debt crisis of the 1980s and heavily indebted poor country (HIPC) debt sustainability crisis of the 1990s and 2000s—albeit with different characteristics. In particular, a far larger proportion of the debt is privately held this time around, which is likely to complicate and delay the inevitable restructuring.[54]

- **Health:** The World Health Organization (WHO) and other bodies have warned of the threat of a disruptive pandemic for years. This risk has been rising along with the increased travel and migration that has accompanied the world economy's rapid integration over the past two generations. But the political will to strengthen the surveillance and early-warning and response capabilities of international health authorities has been lacking despite repeated appeals. This persistent lack of investment in a key aspect of the world economy's resilience was a contributing factor in WHO's uneven early response to the COVID-19 pandemic.[55] There are signs that this lesson is being learned. Governments agreed in May 2022 on a plan to strengthen the organization's finances[56] as well as create a new Pandemic Preparedness, Prevention and Response Fund.[57] Nevertheless, its ACT-A programme to support developing country COVID-19 vaccine access and related health system capacities was severely underfunded (to the tune of nearly two-thirds of its estimated needs for 2021–22 alone),[58] leaving the world that much more exposed to the potential further mutation and spread of the virus and ensuing economic dislocation.

- **Supply chains:** The global supply chain crisis of 2021–22 was produced by a "perfect storm" combination of US–China trade tensions, the snap-back in demand for goods during the pandemic and associated challenges in maintaining seafarer workforces during the lockdowns, and Russia's invasion of Ukraine. However unique, these circumstances exposed a systemic vulnerability in the prevailing model of industrial organization, with its heavy reliance on remote and highly distributed sourcing relationships and just-in-time delivery practices.

These severe supply chain disruptions have led to much reflection and debate about the resilience of supply chains across a range of risks—environmental, geopolitical, economic and technological.[59] Whether this rethink leads to companies assigning a higher priority to supply chain resilience in their strategic resource allocation and operational planning going forwards,[60] or they revert to least-cost but less secure and redundant options, remains an open question. This is ultimately a matter of corporate governance, i.e., whether boards and management teams see it as their duty to optimize near-term financial performance or the medium- to long-term value of the enterprise by also properly weighing material but often more intangible considerations, such as resilience to potential shocks. As such, structural weaknesses in the resilience of liberal economic governance are not just an issue for public policymakers; they also raise important questions for business leaders.

- **Social protection:** Arguably the biggest structural weakness in the resilience of the prevailing growth and development model is its pattern of underinvesting in human resilience and dignity. As noted earlier, half of humanity lacks access to even a single social security protection from among the five elements of a social protection floor: health; children; maternity; disability; and old age.

  The vast majority of the world's poor, including those without any social protection coverage, live in middle-income countries, which by definition should have the means to institute a social protection floor over time. The ILO reports that:

  > Today, many developing countries have levels of GDP per capita similar to those of high-income countries when the latter started to develop their social protection provision. For instance, Botswana and Indonesia today have a similar GDP per capita to that of the United Kingdom in 1911, when the Government enacted laws and established the first social insurance and social assistance programmes.[61]

  In fact, it has been estimated that all but six of the 51 countries classified by the World Bank as lower middle-income could afford to implement a social protection floor across the four areas of children, maternity, disability and old age, based on the updated extreme poverty threshold of US$2.15 per day, by raising over several years their tax revenues as a share of GDP to an average of 26% from the current level of 21% (which ranges from 15% to 42% depending on country circumstances) and allocating a "fair share" of 14% of such revenues to social protection (as compared with the OECD average of 33%).[62] Moreover, multilateral and bilateral donors clearly have the wherewithal to facilitate progress in this direction by increasing their funding for initial design and set-up costs; they currently allocate only 2.5% of their aid funds to social protection.[63] This is curiously at odds with their commitment to eradicate extreme poverty by 2030 as enshrined in SDG 1, since the people most susceptible to extreme poverty are precisely those who would benefit from the establishment of a social protection floor across these four domains.

A Self-Reinforcing Dynamic

In sum, notwithstanding its considerable success in helping to increase the rate of economic growth and poverty reduction over the years, liberal economic governance is demonstrably failing in its efforts to address the twenty-first-century imperatives of inclusion, sustainability and resilience. Its inadequacies in these respects appear to be deep-seated and structural. They have been largely impervious to the many expressions of commitment to fundamental reform by leaders dating back to the Rio Summit and Kyoto Protocol in the 1990s, the G20's pronouncements during the 2008–09 financial crisis,[64] the Paris climate agreement and SDGs agreed in 2015[65] and the ILO Centenary Declaration for the Future of Work[66] and Global call to action for a human-centred recovery from the COVID-19 crisis that is inclusive, sustainable and resilient[67] in 2019 and 2021, respectively.

This economic, social and environmental reform agenda has been memorialized in the 17 SDGs and their 169 corresponding policy targets.[68] Progress towards these 2030 targets is lagging badly, including with respect to such topics as inequality, universal social protection, climate change, poverty and hunger eradication. It was falling short even before the pandemic struck. Moreover, some aspects of the adverse trends summarized above are self-reinforcing. In a major study on the implications of inequality for macroeconomic policy, the Bank for International Settlements (BIS), the international organization of the world's central banks, recently concluded,

> We discover a two-way interaction between inequality and recessions. Higher levels of income inequality imply deeper recessions. And recessions tend to have a very persistent effect on income inequality. The income share of the wealthiest 10% of the population generally increases after recessions, usually remaining higher for years afterwards. In addition, we show that greater inequality makes monetary policy less effective when used either to stimulate or slacken aggregate demand. Finally, fiscal policy has tended to become less redistributive and less countercyclical, putting more onus on monetary policy as a tool for macroeconomic stabilisation. Taken together, these results suggest the importance of taking income inequality into account when designing and implementing both fiscal and monetary policy. First, both types of policy should seek to reduce the frequency and depth of recessions. Second, fiscal policy should seek to further limit the effects of recessions on the rise and persistence of income inequality. Third, policymakers should keep in mind how income inequality can erode the effectiveness of monetary policy.[69]

On the ground, governments are struggling to narrow the gap between social expectations and policy delivery on inclusion, sustainability and resilience. Civil impatience and frustration are on the rise and increasingly taking the form of street protests and social unrest affecting countries at all levels of development in all regions. In its 2021 report, the Global Peace Index found that anti-government demonstrations, general strikes and riots increased by 244% over the preceding decade, with an increase in the proportion relating to economic issues. More than 5000 pandemic-related violent events occurred between January 2020 and April 2021.

Recent examples of major social unrest (involving more than 10,000 people) triggered by socioeconomic conditions include: Chile (October 2019); Kazakhstan (January 2022); Tunisia (January 2021); France (November/December 2018); Iran (November 2019); Algeria (February 2019); Brazil (May 2019); Lebanon (October 2019); India (September 2020); Cameroon (October 2018); Ecuador (October 2019); Sri Lanka (March 2022); Greece (April 2022); Mauritius (August 2020); Mongolia (December 2018); the Netherlands (June 2022); Nicaragua (April 2018); Spain (March 2022); etc.[70]

Major social unrest is a threat to economies as well as governments. In 2018, the Gilets Jaunes (Yellow Vest) movement in France protesting fuel prices and economic inequality cost French retailers US$1.1 billion in revenue in just a few weeks.[71] A year later in Chile, large-scale demonstrations sparked by an increase in subway fares led to insured losses of US$3 billion. The 2020 protests in the United States over the death of George Floyd in police custody were estimated to have resulted in over US$2 billion insured losses.[72] And the South African riots of July 2021, which followed the arrest of former president Jacob Zuma and were fuelled by job lay-offs and economic inequality, caused damage worth US$1.7 billion.[73]

An IMF team examining this issue more comprehensively observed "a tight link between unrest and subsequent economic performance". It found that, on average, major unrest events are followed by a one percentage point reduction in GDP six quarters after the event (see Fig. 2.4). Unrest motivated by socioeconomic factors is associated with sharper GDP contractions than is unrest associated with political motives. Yet events triggered by a combination of both factors correspond to the sharpest GDP contractions.[74]

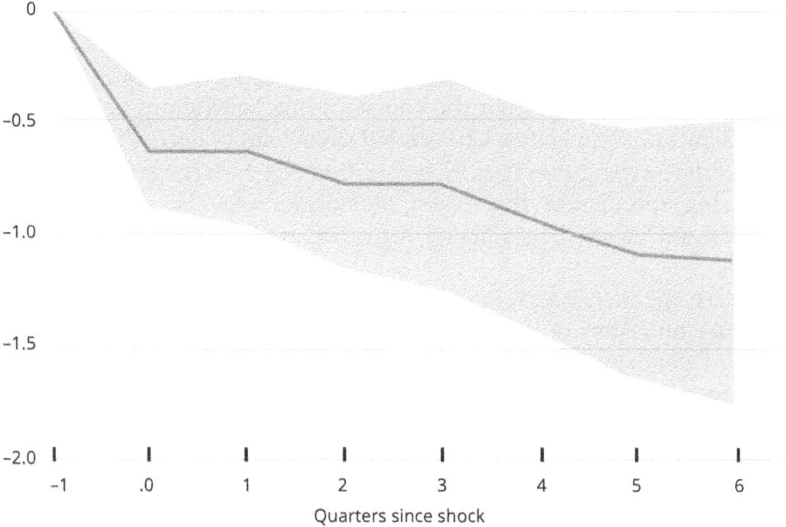

Note: A "new unrest event" is defined as an unrest event that follows eight quarters of no unrest events. The shaded area represents a 90% confidence interval.
Source: Hazdi-Vaskov, Pienknagura and Ricci, "The Macroeconomic Impact of Social Unrest", IMF Working Paper 21-135, 2021.

Fig. 2.4 GDP relative to baseline in percentage points

An Apparent Feature, Not a Bug

Thus, despite repeated appeals from both political leaders and people on the street for fundamental improvement in the performance of their economies with regard to social inclusion, environmental sustainability and resilience, standard liberal economic governance appears to be stuck, capable of mustering only incremental progress at best. Key institutions and the supporting policy and political establishment are blocked, unable to depart much from the path they have been on for decades.

This extended record of policy immobility relative to the scale of the challenge suggests a deeper problem than a lack of political will or the capture of policymaking by vested interests, as important as these problems are. It suggests a lack of imagination—a blind spot in the very model of economic progress framed by standard liberal economics, or at the very least a fundamental misunderstanding about how the principles of liberal political economy should be adapted to contemporary circumstances.

These shortcomings of a discipline that takes pride in its intellectual rigour and central relevance to real-world decision-making are clearly exacerbating the broader political travails of the liberal tradition in the twenty-first century.[75] Within the course of one generation, perspectives about democratic capitalism have shifted from "end of history" triumphalism to "the jungle grows back"[76] trepidation and even resignation. There is growing speculation that liberal democracy may be in irreversible decline[77] and eclipsed by illiberal forms of governance in the decades to come.

Indeed, the increasingly unabashed case against liberalism rests in no small part on claims of its ineffectiveness and fecklessness. The ongoing failure of democratic leaders to deliver the big improvements in social inclusion, environmental sustainability and human resilience and dignity demanded by their citizens strengthens this case. It certainly feeds the political cynicism and disaffection on which illiberal movements thrive.

Despite the high political stakes, the response by the economics community (both academic and policymaking) to these challenges has taken four indirect and mainly aspirational or incremental forms:

- **Description and analysis:** An avalanche of analysis has been produced in the past ten to twenty years, both descriptive and empirical, framing the shape and size of the problem economies face in strengthening their inclusion, sustainability and resilience.
- **Empathy, exhortation and goal-setting:** There have been repeated political efforts to give voice to these societal concerns and build an intergovernmental consensus on the broad changes in policy direction required to address them, including through the setting of long-term goals and targets for governments in UN agreements and companies in environmental, social and governance (ESG) and other sustainability initiatives and frameworks.
- **Measurement, advocacy and education:** Important work has been done to improve the measurement of these challenges (i.e., beyond-GDP indexes, SDG indicators; multidimensional poverty indexes; science-based targets, etc.) and apply these frameworks to raise public consciousness, enhance institutional accountability and expand frameworks of analysis, including in economics textbooks (e.g., the Curriculum Open-Access Resources in Economics, or "CORE Econ", curriculum[78]).

- **Individual initiative:** Countries and companies have not stood still; many have initiated actions—some significant, others less so—to address one or another of these challenges within the reach of their jurisdictions and operations.

In short, there has been a flurry of constructive movement in these four areas, particularly in the last five to ten years. Goal-setting, individual action and better measurement and analysis are all useful, but with few exceptions they do not rise to the scale of change required to reverse the serious adverse trends detailed earlier in this chapter. They are not producing the systemic shift in the performance of economies demanded by people and planet at the speed required by politics and physics, respectively.

One is left to conclude that such a shift will require an intervention at a deeper level—a change in the prevailing growth and development model itself. Inclusion, sustainability and resilience will need to be "designed into" market behaviour and economic policy and institutions more directly and systematically. Their positive and negative externalities will need to be routinely internalized in economic activity through corresponding incentives and disincentives in the policies, institutions and broader norms that make up the enabling environment within which market and policy decisions are made.

None of the four current modes of response operates at this level. Together, they may be helping to lay the groundwork for such a frontal response, but they are essentially working around the edges of the problem rather than confronting it directly in the form of a new theoretical construct and accompanying policy framework to guide the practical work of rebalancing priority-setting and resource allocation within governments and firms.

After 15-plus years of diagnosis, goal-setting and incremental action regarding globalization, neoliberalism and their discontents, where does this most fundamental dimension of the economic reform debate stand? What would be the nature of a more systemic fix?

A theory of the case is required to answer this question. A thesis regarding the nature and source of the essential disequilibrating factor or factors driving liberal political economy's chronic underperformance in these respects is needed in order to formulate a more sufficient response.

In some sense, this is an age-old debate; Marxists, socialists and social democrats have been rehearsing versions of it for the better part of two centuries. However, there are two prominent theses gaining momentum today:

- **Inherently unjust:** The first is the view that markets inherently produce socially unjust outcomes, including inequity and insecurity for broad sections of the population. They may be efficient mechanisms for allocating resources from the standpoint of maximizing production and returns on capital for owners of productive assets, but that is a different thing entirely from maximizing the economy's value for society. Advocates of this fundamental critique of liberal economics argue in particular that:

  i. Markets tend to commodify labour and people, even more so with digitalization, and this is in fundamental tension with the economic and social rights enshrined in the Universal Declaration of Human Rights and the ILO's corpus of multilaterally agreed labour and social security standards.
  ii. Capitalism was built on social and environmental exploitation through colonialism and natural resource extraction, the legacy of which endures in the global distribution of wealth and aspects of the business culture, skewing markets and market-oriented economies away from just socioeconomic and environmental outcomes.
  iii. There is an ongoing disconnect between the cross-border organization of economic activity and national organization of politics, leading the world economy's integration to reinforce commodification and exploitation and create a race-to-the-bottom dynamic that is already outpacing governance and poised to accelerate further as automation spreads throughout economies.

  Many adherents of this critique take a rights-based approach to fundamental reform. They advocate an agenda that not only recognizes the rights of all people to a basic level of material well-being and capacity but also advocates full implementation of these rights through the necessary collective action and policy intervention. This can take the form of mechanisms that supplant the role of markets either in whole (central planning) or in part (a mixed economy with a major role for state- or other collectively owned entities). Or it can take the form of large public investments and fiscal transfers that sit alongside markets and compensate for their inequitable and unsustainable processes and outcomes. In other words, rights-based approaches incline towards a reform agenda that would either replace markets to one degree or another, or tax the owners of capital more

heavily in order to generate sufficient public resources to ensure basic economic rights and capabilities, or both.
- **Inherently unstable:** The second ascendant school of fundamental criticism argues that markets and market economies (particularly highly financialized ones) are inherently unstable, and that this habitual instability imposes severe, unjustifiable costs on societies and particularly on the most vulnerable people within them. The tendency of market-oriented systems towards disequilibria, whether in financial, environmental or social terms, requires extra-market intervention. Absent this, liberal economies tend towards the dystopic in the form of volatility and instability that severely damage both the economy and social fabric.

The financial system aspect of this critique is supported by a long history of compelling theoretical and empirical work, including that of Hyman Minsky,[79] Charles Kindleberger,[80] Irving Fischer,[81] and Carmen Reinhardt and Kenneth Rogoff.[82] More expansive critiques of the inherent economic instability of capitalism include the work of Karl Marx,[83] John Maynard Keynes,[84] Thomas Piketty[85] and David Harvey.[86] Still broader critiques of capitalism's bias towards social and environmental disequilibria include the work of Karl Polanyi,[87] Pope Pius XI,[88] Herman Daly,[89] Robert Kuttner[90] and various proponents of zero growth or de-growth.[91] There has been important related work in recent years to take better account of social and environmental factors, such as through the construction of social accounting matrices and the efforts of ecological economics to introduce the concept of stocks and flows of resources, particularly with respect to natural capital and resources.[92] The Stiglitz–Sen–Fitoussi Commission[93] convened by the French government following the Great Financial Crisis served to galvanize additional thinking and initiatives in these respects; however, the practical manifestation of these innovations thus far has mainly been in the form of pilot projects.

There has been impressive growth in these two broad schools of thought in recent years, reflecting rising disillusionment with the failure of mainstream academic economists and policymakers to move beyond the four mainly aspirational and incremental modes of response described above. Citizen impatience with the slow pace of change is on the rise and may increase further as the combined after-shocks of the pandemic, war in Ukraine and monetary response to rising inflation are felt around the world, and as the disruptive effects of climate change become ever more visible and destabilizing in people's daily lives.

That said, the broad solutions associated with these two fundamental critiques have gained little traction, and they appear unlikely to do so for rather fundamental reasons. The first set of solutions tends to take the form of grand proposals for fiscal transfers that are in the nature of a workaround for the weaknesses in liberal economic governance (i.e., measures to compensate *ex post* for the unequal, unsustainable or fragility-inducing outcomes of market activity) rather than a structural fix of them. These typically take the form of big macroeconomic stimulus and public borrowing initiatives that would generate large sums to be spent on social and environmental objectives. Sometimes these proposals are linked to and find their ultimate expression in Modern Monetary Theory (MMT), with its potential to create the public resources necessary to finance a universal job guarantee or basic income as well as massive industrial restructuring. MMT advocates rightly observe that many countries have far more fiscal space than traditionally has been recognized, particularly if it is used to invest in areas that enhance labour productivity and the growth potential of economies, such as human capability, labour force participation, sustainable infrastructure, and technical progress. But the sheer scale of the deficit financing this approach implies can create its own uncomfortable risk of instability, namely unsustainable debt overhangs, particularly in countries that do not have the luxury of borrowing in their own currency or are already facing large structural deficits owing to their ageing populations and recent, crisis-related extraordinary stimulus packages.

The second focuses on measures to limit economic growth. However, zero growth or de-growth is not a particularly viable social or political proposition in developing countries seeking to eradicate poverty and boost modest living standards, as some of the proponents of this school of thought have acknowledged. Poor countries encompass the overwhelming majority of the world's population, and while they might be sanguine about a major reduction in consumption by their rich Northern counterparts, it is just as likely that they would regret the resulting drop in demand for their exports of goods, services and indeed people earning remittances to send to families back home. As long as there is significant poverty and inequality in the world, economic growth is going to continue to be a legitimate social priority. It is simply easier for everyone to obtain a larger piece of economic pie if the overall pie is growing. Thus, the critical challenge for policymakers is to improve the quality of growth, its sustainable contribution to broad-based progress in living standards. As Herman Daly argued, in environmental terms this means ensuring that renewable resources are exploited no faster than they can be regenerated, wastes are emitted no faster than they can be assimilated and non-renewable resources are depleted no faster than renewable substitutes can be developed to replace them.[94] In other words, the objective must be to sharply reduce the material and polluting content of growth rather than throttle its overall rate per se. Nevertheless, degrowth advocates do a service by challenging the wholly insufficient nature of progress in this respect and the underwhelming record of strategies that rely mainly on market mechanisms in particular.[95]

In Search of a Viable Theory of Fundamental Change

Such is the disappointing state of the global economic reform agenda with respect to social inclusion, environmental sustainability and resilience to major shifts and shocks. Economies give every appearance that they will continue to operate for the foreseeable future on the basis of the standard liberal economic growth and development model, making piecemeal or incremental progress on these three bottom-line social priorities. A viable theory of change of a more fundamental nature has yet to emerge. Massive ongoing fiscal deficits to finance a universal basic income or publicly bankrolled climate transition are not a feasible financial proposition for most if not all countries; and zero growth is not a feasible socioeconomic or political proposition in any except perhaps a small group of rich countries with shrinking populations.

In other words, the liberal economic reform project remains becalmed 15 years after the Great Financial Crisis, when neoliberal hubris was supposed to have been shattered and world leaders committed their governments to deep reform. The Washington Consensus has been declared passé, but nothing coherent or commensurate has taken its place. As a result, those in the forefront of reform are increasingly exposed to the criticism that their work is essentially hot air: a combination of unfulfilled political promises; piecemeal, incremental and often largely procedural measures; and grand but infeasible concepts.

To be certain, an impressive international consensus has been built on the direction of necessary reform. This process began at the 1972 UN Conference in Stockholm and it continued through the 1992 Rio Conference on Sustainable Development, 1994 Kyoto Protocol, 1995 Copenhagen Social Summit, 2009 G20 London and Pittsburgh Declarations, 2015 SDGs and Paris climate agreement, 2019 Centenary Declaration and 2021 Global Call to Action for a Human-Centred Recovery of the ILO and, most recently, the 2022 Kunming-Montreal Global Biodiversity Framework.

This combined economic, social and environmental agenda is actually a very important political achievement—a credit to the multilateral system in a world characterized by so much division. But it is not self-executing. As the product of *political processes*, it is a shared vision rather than a practical blueprint for the different model of economic growth and development and corresponding policy framework required for the achievement of much more inclusive and resilient societies and the stabilization, let alone reversal, of the planet's environmental degradation. That will require a deeper *thought process*—a more fundamental enquiry by scholars and practitioners in economics and adjacent social sciences.[96]

Specifically:

- What is the source of the conceptual or systemic flaw in liberal economic doctrine, that is to say, its disequilibrating feature with respect to inclusion, sustainability and resilience?
- How can these three factors be intentionally and systematically designed into the process of economic growth and development rather than assumed to obtain as an inevitable by-product of it?

In short, building a more viable theory of change is going to require a structural critique and deeper reformulation of liberal economic doctrine—a more forthright attempt to locate and confront its possible constitutional flaw instead of continuing to talk past, paper over or otherwise work around it.

This suggests that a re-examination of first principles is in order. Are the shortcomings of modern economics with regard to inclusion, sustainability and resilience—its treatment of living standards as a residual consideration—a matter of original sin or wayward and mistaken practice? In other words, are they due to an initial conceptual flaw or omission or to a misapplication of the field's foundational principles?

The next chapter undertakes this historical investigation; it traces the intellectual roots and evolution of liberal political economy with this question uppermost in mind.

NOTES

1. See Angus Maddison, *The World Economy: Historical Statistics*, Paris, OECD, 2003, p. 263, https://www.oecd-ilibrary.org/docserver/9789264104143-en.pdf?expires=1672760616&id=id&accname=ocid195767&checksum=FC44E6AF525F83E1156760B3D38D7E18; Jutta Bolt and Jan Luiten van Zanden, "The First Update of the Maddison Project Re-estimating Growth before 1820", Maddison Project Working Paper WP-4, January 2013, https://www.rug.nl/ggdc/historicaldevelopment/maddison/publications/wp4.pdf; and, for a closer look at Europe, Alexandra de Pleijt and Jan Luiten van Zanden, "A Tale of Two Transitions: The European Growth Experience, 1270–1900", Maddison Project Working Paper WP-14, February 2020, https://www.rug.nl/ggdc/historicaldevelopment/maddison/publications/wp14.pdf
2. See Francois Bourguignon and Christian Morrisson, "Inequality among World Citizens: 1820 to 1992", *American Economic Review*, September 2002, pp. 729–44, https://inequality.stanford.edu/sites/default/files/media/_media/pdf/Reference%20Media/Bourguignon%20and%20Morrisson_2002_History%20of%20Inequality.pdf
3. See, for example, Lant Pritchett with Addison Lewis, "Economic Growth *Is* Enough and Only Economic Growth Is Enough", 25 May 2022, https://lantpritchett.org/wp-content/uploads/2022/05/Basics-legatum-paper_short.pdf
4. See, for example, Montek Aluwahlia, "Economic Reforms in India since 1991: Has Gradualism Worked", *Journal of Economic Perspectives*, Vol. 16, No. 3 (2002), pp. 67–88.
5. See, for example, Teresa Ter-Minassian, "Structural Reforms in Brazil: Progress and Unfinished Agenda", Interamerican Development Bank, May 2012, https://publications.iadb.org/publications/english/viewer/Structural-Reforms-in-Brazil-Progress-and-Unfinished-Agenda.pdf
6. See, for example, Joseph J. Stern, "The Rise and Fall of the Indonesian Economy", Harvard Center for international Development Working Paper No. 100, June 2003, https://www.hks.harvard.edu/sites/default/files/centers/cid/files/publications/faculty-working-papers/100.pdf

7. See, for example, Jean-Raphael Chaponnière, Jean-Pierre Cling and Bin Zhou, "Vietnam Following in China's Footsteps: The Third Wave of Emerging Asian Economies", UNU-WIDER Research Paper No. 2008/84, September 2008, https://www.wider.unu.edu/sites/default/files/rp2008-84.pdf
8. World Bank, *World Development Indicators 2017*, Washington, 2017, p. 21, https://openknowledge.worldbank.org/handle/10986/26447
9. Max Roser and Esteban Ortiz-Ospina, "Income Inequality", *Our World in Data*, December 2013, https://ourworldindata.org/income-inequality
10. Christoph Lakner and Branko Milanovic, "Global Income Distribution: From the Fall of the Berlin Wall to the Great Recession", World Bank Policy Research Working Paper No. 6719, December 2013, https://openknowledge.worldbank.org/handle/10986/16935. For an adapted and updated version based on data from the World Inequality Database rather than household surveys, see Facundo Alvaredo, Lucas Chancel, Thomas Piketty, Emmanuel Saez and Gabriel Zucman, "The Elephant Curve of Global Inequality and Growth", World Inequality Lab Working Paper No. 2017/20, 2017, https://shs.hal.science/halshs-02797605/document
11. Caroline Freund, "Deconstructing Branko Milanovic's "Elephant Chart": Does It Show What Everyone Thinks?" Peterson Institute for International Economics, 30 November 2016. https://www.piie.com/blogs/realtime-economic-issues-watch/deconstructing-branko-milanovics-elephant-chart-does-it-show; Homi Kharas and Brina Seidel, "What's Happening to the World's Income Distribution: The Elephant Curve Revisited", Global Economy and Development Working Paper 114, April 2018. https://www.brookings.edu/wp-content/uploads/2018/04/workingpaper114-elephantchartrevisited.pdf
12. See, for example, World Inequality Lab, *World Inequality Report 2022*, 2022, https://wir2022.wid.world/; Anthony B. Atkinson, *Inequality: What Can Be Done?*, Cambridge, MA, Harvard University Press, 2015, pp. 237–9; Anthony B. Atkinson and François Bourguignon, *Handbook of Income Distribution*, Amsterdam, North-Holland, Vol. 2, 2015; Joseph Stiglitz, *The Price of Inequality: How Today's Divided Society Endangers Our Future*, New York, W.W. Norton, 2012; L. Chancel and T. Piketty, "Global Inequality 1820–2020: The Persistence and Mutation of Extreme Inequality", *Journal of the European Economic Association*, Vol. 19, No. 6 (2021), pp. 3025–62, https://academic.oup.com/jeea/article/19/6/3025/6408467?login=true; T. Piketty and G. Zucman, "Capital Is Back: Wealth-Income Ratios in Rich Countries 1700–2010", *Quarterly Journal of Economics*, Vol. 129, No. 3 (2014), pp 1255–310; O. Blanchard and D. Rodrik, *Combating Inequality: Rethinking Government's Role*, Cambridge, MA, MIT Press, 2021.

13. OECD, *Under Pressure: The Squeezed Middle Class*, Paris, 2019, p. 21, https://www.oecd-ilibrary.org/docserver/689afed1-en.pdf?expire s=1660309622&id=id&accname=ocid195767&checksum=506F4DD 0F0961FE5EA45598F7B6D13AD
14. Ibid., pp. 23–4.
15. Jesse Bennet, Richard Fry and Rakesh Kochhar, "Are You in the American Middle Class?" Pew Research Center, 23 July 2020, https://www.pewresearch.org/fact-tank/2020/07/23/are-you-in-the-american-middle-class/
16. See, for example, Stephen Rose, "The Upper Middle Class Continued to Grow from 2014 to 2019", Urban Institute, 24 February 2021, https://www.urban.org/research/publication/upper-middle-class-continued-grow-2014-2019
17. OECD, *Under Pressure*, pp. 25–6.
18. See, for example, Jim O'Neill, "Twenty Years On, the BRICS Have Disappointed", *Financial Times*, 29 November 2021, https://www.ft.com/content/034ba0e7-7518-437e-854c-7c0dd5d74e34
19. See, for example, D. Dollar and A. Kraay, "Growth Is Good for the Poor", *Journal of Economic Growth*, Vol. 7, No. 3 (2002), pp. 195–225; Augustin Kwasi Fosu, "Growth, Inequality, and Poverty Reduction in Developing Countries: Recent Global Evidence", WIDER Working Paper No. 2011/01, 2011, https://www.econstor.eu/bitstream/10419/54015/1/644542136.pdf
20. World Bank, *The East Asian Miracle: Economic Growth and Public Policy*, Washington, 1993, https://documents.worldbank.org/en/publication/documents-reports/documentdetail/975081468244550798/main-report
21. Richard Samans, Jennifer Blanke, Margareta Drzeniek Hanouz and Gemma Corrigan, *The Inclusive Growth and Development Report 2017*, Geneva, World Economic Forum, 2017, pp. 12–13, https://www3.weforum.org/docs/WEF_Forum_IncGrwth_2017.pdf
22. Commission on Growth and Development, *The Growth Report: Strategies for Sustained Growth and Inclusive Development*, Washington, World Bank, 2008, pp. 4–5, https://openknowledge.worldbank.org/handle/10986/6507
23. Richard Samans et al., *The Inclusive Growth and Development Report 2017*, p. 12. See also, for example, A. Hicks, *Social Democracy and Welfare Capitalism: A Century of Income Security Politics*, Ithaca, NY, Cornell University Press, 1999; and, with respect to the United States, Richard Samans and Jonathan Jacoby, "Virtuous Circle: Strengthening Broad-based Global Progress in Living Standards", Center for American

Progress, December 2007, p. 5, http://cdn.americanprogress.org/wp-content/uploads/issues/2007/12/pdf/virtuous_circle.pdf?_ga=2.89311579.156390069.1672825683-1607294752.1672825683
24. Dev Patel, Justin Sandefur and Arvind Subramanian, "The New Era of Unconditional Convergence", *Journal of Development Economics*, Vol. 152, September 2021, https://www.sciencedirect.com/science/article/pii/S030438782100064X?via%3Dihub
25. Francesco Burchi, Daniele Malerba, Nicole Rippin and Claudio E. Montenegro, "Comparing Global Trends in Multidimensional and Income Poverty and Assessing Horizontal Inequalities", German Development Institute/Deutsches Institut für Entwicklungspolitik Discussion Paper 2/2019, February 2019, pp. 36–7, https://www.idos-research.de/uploads/media/DP_2.2019.pdf
26. See Article 22, Universal Declaration of Human Rights (1948), https://www.un.org/en/about-us/universal-declaration-of-human-rights; ILO, "Social Protection Floor", https://www.ilo.org/secsoc/areas-of-work/policy-development-and-applied-research/social-protection-floor/lang%2D%2Den/index.htm#:~:text=Social%20protection%20floors%20are%20nationally%2Ddefined%20sets%20of%20basic%20social,poverty%2C%20vulnerability%20and%20social%20exclusion
27. Per relevant ILO standards and recommendations, national social protection floors should comprise at least the following four social security guarantees, as defined at the national level: (1) access to essential health care, including maternity care; (2) basic income security for children, providing access to nutrition, education, care and any other necessary goods and services; (3) basic income security for persons of active age who are unable to earn sufficient income, in particular in cases of sickness, unemployment, maternity and disability; (4) basic income security for older persons.
28. See, for example, Marcus Manuel, "Financing Social Protection: Domestic and External Options in Low-Income Countries", Friedrich Ebert Stiftung, June 2022, https://library.fes.de/pdf-files/iez/19401.pdf; Karuna Pal, Christina Behrendt, Florian Leger, Michael Cichon and Krzysztof Hagemejer, *Can Low-Income Countries Afford Basic Social Protection? First Results of a Modelling Exercise*, Geneva, ILO, 2005 https://papers.ssrn.com/sol3/papers.cfm?abstract_id=807366; European Report on Development, *Social Protection for Inclusive Development: A New Report in EU Co-operation with Africa*, Fiesole, 2010, p. 59, https://cadmus.eui.eu/bitstream/handle/1814/15496/ERD_Report_2010%5BEN%5D.pdf?sequence=2
29. Manuel, "Financing Social Protection", p. 2.

30. United Nations, *Stockholm Declaration and Action Plan for the Human Environment*, June 1972, https://www.un.org/en/conferences/environment/stockholm1972; United Nations, *Report of the Conference on Environment and Development*, August 12, 1992, https://www.un.org/en/development/desa/population/migration/generalassembly/docs/globalcompact/A_CONF.151_26_Vol.I_Declaration.pdf; and World Commission on Environment and Development, *Our Common Future*, 1987, https://sustainabledevelopment.un.org/content/documents/5987our-common-future.pdf
31. UNEP, *Sixth Global Environment Outlook: Summary for Policymakers*, Cambridge, UK, Cambridge University Press, 2019, p. 8. https://www.unep.org/resources/assessment/global-environment-outlook-6-summary-policymakers?_ga=2.149925366.1342757417.1660495706-726688390.1660495706. See also WWF, *Living Planet Report 2020*, Gland, 2020, https://livingplanet.panda.org/en-gb/
32. IPCC, *Climate Change 2022: Mitigation of Climate Change*, Cambridge, UK, Cambridge University Press, 2022, https://www.ipcc.ch/report/sixth-assessment-report-working-group-3/
33. This discussion is drawn from Richard Samans, "Financing Human-Centred COVID-19 Recovery and Decisive Climate Action: International Cooperation's Century Moment of Truth", ILO Working Paper 40, 7 October 2021, pp. 13–14, https://www.ilo.org/global/publications/working-papers/WCMS_821931/lang%2D%2Den/index.htm
34. See, for example, United Nations, "Secretary-General Urges Countries to End 'Deadly Addiction' to Coal", 2 March 2021 https://www.un.org/sg/en/content/sg/statement/2021-03-02/secretary-generals-video-message-powering-past-coal-alliance-summit
35. Kasia Tokarska and Damon Matthews, "Refining the Remaining 1.5C 'Carbon Budget'", *Carbon Brief*, 19 January 2021, https://www.carbonbrief.org/guest-post-refining-the-remaining-1-5c-carbon-budget/; International Energy Agency (IEA), "Global Energy Review 2021: CO2 Emissions", https://www.iea.org/reports/global-energy-review-2021/co2-emissions
36. IPCC, *Global Warming of 1.5 °C*, Geneva, 2018, pp. 132–4, https://www.ipcc.ch/sr15/
37. Paola A. Yanguas Parra, Gaurav Ganti, Robert Brecha, Bill Hare, Michiel Schaeffer and Ursula Fuentes, "Global and Regional Coal Phase-Out Requirements of the Paris Agreement: Insights from the IPCC Special Report on 1.5 °C", *Climate Analytics*, September 2019, pp. 10–11, https://climateanalytics.org/media/report_coal_phase_out_2019.pdf

38. Global Energy Monitor, "Global Coal Plant Tracker", https://globalenergymonitor.org/projects/global-coal-plant-tracker/. See also Global Energy Monitor, Sierra Club, CREA, Climate Risk Horizons, GreenID and Ekosfer, "Boom and Bust 2021: Tracking the Global Coal Plant Pipeline", April 2021, p. 15, https://globalenergymonitor.org/wp-content/uploads/2021/04/BoomAndBust_2021_final.pdf; Ted Nace, "A Coal Phase-Out Pathway for 1.5 °C", CoalSwarm and Greenpeace International, 2018, https://www.greenpeace.org/static/planet4-international-stateless/2018/10/7df76ee5-coalpathway-final.pdf; Jason Bordoff, "Yes, We Can Get Rid of the World's Dirtiest Fuel", *Foreign Policy*, 26 August 2020, https://foreignpolicy.com/2020/08/26/coal-mining-electricity-climate-change/
39. Climate Action Tracker, "Temperatures", https://climateactiontracker.org/global/temperatures/
40. FAO, "Fisheries and Aquaculture", https://www.fao.org/fishery/en/capture
41. Oceaneos, "State of the Oceans", 2021, https://www.oceaneos.org/state-of-our-oceans/
42. Boris Worm, "Avoiding a Global Fisheries Disaster", *Proceedings of the National Academy of Sciences*, Vol. 113, No. 18 (2016), pp. 4895–7, https://www.researchgate.net/publication/301539411_Averting_a_global_fisheries_disaster
43. Tyler D. Eddy et al., "Global Decline in Capacity of Coral Reefs to Provide Ecosystem Services", *One Earth*, Vol. 4 No. 9, 2021, https://www.cell.com/one-earth/fulltext/S2590-3322(21)00474-7
44. WMO, *2021 State of Climate Services: Water*, Geneva, 2021, https://library.wmo.int/doc_num.php?explnum_id=10826
45. See J. Rockström et al., "A Safe Operating Space for Humanity", *Nature*, Vol. 461 (2009), pp. 472–5, https://www.nature.com/articles/461472a; J.A. Dearing et al., "Safe and Just Operating Spaces for Regional Social-Ecological Systems", *Global Environmental Change*, Vol. 28, (2014), pp. 227–38, https://www.sciencedirect.com/science/article/pii/S0959378014001174?via%3Dihub
46. D. Gerten, H. Hoff, J. Rockström, J. Jägermeyr, M. Kummu and A.V. Pastor, "Towards a Revised Planetary Boundary for Consumptive Freshwater Use: Role of Environmental Flow Requirements", *Current Opinion in Environmental Sustainability*, Vol. 5 (2013), pp. 551–8, https://www.sciencedirect.com/science/article/abs/pii/S1877343513001498?via%3Dihub
47. M. Kummu et al., "The World's Road to Water Scarcity: Shortage and Stress in the 20th Century and Pathways towards Sustainability", *Scientific*

Reports, Vol. 6 (2016), 38495, https://www.nature.com/articles/srep38495

48. For further information about the nature and severity of the challenge posed by global environmental degradation, see Stockholm Resilience Center, "Planetary Boundaries", https://www.stockholmresilience.org/research/planetary-boundaries.html

49. Thanh Cong Nguyen, Vítor Castro and Justine Wood, "A New Comprehensive Database of Financial Crises: Identification, Frequency, and Duration", *Economic Modelling*, Vol. 108 (2022), 105770, https://www.sciencedirect.com/science/article/pii/S0264999322000165

50. See Robin Greenwood, Samuel G. Hanson, Andrei Shleifer and Jakob Ahm Sørensen, "Predictable Financial Crises", Harvard Business School Working Paper 20-130, March 2021, https://www.hbs.edu/ris/Publication%20Files/20-130_77e0879b-606a-4bbe-bd5a-1aa9dd77b6fe.pdf

51. Deutsche Bank Markets Research, "Long-Term Asset Return Study: The Next Financial Crisis", 18 September 2017, p. 22, http://www.tramuntalegria.com/wp-content/uploads/2017/09/Long-Term-Asset-Return-Study-The-Next-Financial-Crisis-db.pdf

52. See, for example, Philip McMichael, "The World Food Crisis in Historical Perspective", *Monthly Review*, 1 July 2009, https://monthlyreview.org/2009/07/01/the-world-food-crisis-in-historical-perspective/

53. Christopher B. Barrett, "The Global Food Crisis Shouldn't Have Come as a Surprise", *Foreign Affairs*, 25 July 2022, https://www.foreignaffairs.com/world/global-food-crisis-shouldnt-have-come-surprise?check_logged_in=1

54. See warnings issued by the World Bank in early 2022, for example Marcelo Estavao, "Are We Ready for the Coming Spate of Debt Crises?" World Bank, 28 March 2022, https://blogs.worldbank.org/voices/are-we-ready-coming-spate-debt-crises

55. See, for example, David Cutler, "The World Health Organization Is Not Powerful or Independent Enough to Deal with Pandemics", London School of Economics, 12 October 2021, https://blogs.lse.ac.uk/covid19/2021/10/12/the-world-health-organization-is-not-powerful-or-independent-enough-to-deal-with-pandemics/

56. Alexandra Finch, Kevin A. Klock, Eric A. Friedman and Lawrence O. Gostin, "At Long Last, Member States Agree to Fix the World Health Organization's Financing Problem", *Think Global Health*, 1 June 2022, https://www.thinkglobalhealth.org/article/long-last-member-states-agree-fix-world-health-organizations-financing-problem

57. WHO, "New Fund for Pandemic Prevention, Preparedness and Response Formally Established", 9 September 2022, https://www.who.int/news/item/09-09-2022-new-fund-for-pandemic-prevention%2D%2Dpreparedness-and-response-formally-established#:~:text=The%20fund%20will%20provide%20a,%2C%20regional%2C%20and%20global%20levels.
58. As of 25 July 2022, pledges towards the 2021–22 funding target totalled US$5.64 billion, counting towards the US$16.85 billion grant-financing ask, bringing the 2021–22 funding gap to US$11.20 billion. WHO, "Access to COVID-19 Tools Funding Commitment Tracker", 14 November 2022, https://www.who.int/publications/m/item/access-to-covid-19-tools-tracker
59. See, for example, Maria Grazia Attinasi, Mirco Balatti, Michele Mancini and Luca Metelli, "Supply Chain Disruptions and the Effects on the Global Economy", European Central Bank Economic Bulletin No. 8/2021, https://www.ecb.europa.eu/pub/economic-bulletin/focus/2022/html/ecb.ebbox202108_01~e8ceebe51f.en.html; Paul Wellener, Kate Hardin, Stephen Gold and Stephen Laaper, "Meeting the Challenge of Supply Chain Disruption", *Deloitte Insights*, No. 31, 2022, pp. 3–5, https://www2.deloitte.com/us/en/insights/industry/manufacturing/realigning-global-supply-chain-management-networks.html
60. See, for example, Knut Alicke, Edward Barriball, Tacy Foster, Julien Mauhourat and Vera Trautwein, "Taking the Pulse of Shifting Supply Chains", McKinsey, 26 August 2022, https://www.mckinsey.com/capabilities/operations/our-insights/taking-the-pulse-of-shifting-supply-chains
61. ILO, *Global Social Protection Report 2020–22*, Geneva, 2021, p. 49, https://www.ilo.org/wcmsp5/groups/public/%2D%2D-dgreports/%2D%2D-dcomm/%2D%2D-publ/documents/publication/wcms_817572.pdf
62. Manuel, "Financing Social Protection", p. 5.
63. Ibid., p. 11.
64. See, for example, Richard Samans, "Beyond Business as Usual: G-20 Leaders and Post-crisis Reconstitution of the International Economic Order", Center for American Progress Policy Brief, September 2009, http://cdn.americanprogress.org/wp-content/uploads/issues/2009/09/pdf/g20.pdf?_ga=2.122985483.1470839087.1660921370-175086094.1660921370
65. https://sdgs.un.org/goals
66. ILO, ILO Centenary Declaration for the Future of Work, 2019, https://www.ilo.org/global/about-the-ilo/mission-and-objectives/centenary-declaration/lang%2D%2Den/index.htm

67. ILO, Global call to action for a human-centred recovery from the COVID-19 crisis that is inclusive, sustainable and resilient, 2021, https://www.ilo.org/ilc/ILCSessions/109/reports/texts-adopted/WCMS_806092/lang%2D%2Den/index.htm
68. See SDG Tracker, "Measuring Progress toward the Sustainable Development Goals", https://sdg-tracker.org/
69. Luiz Awazu Pereira da Silva, Enisse Kharroubi, Emanuel Kohlscheen, Marco Lombardi and Benoît Mojon, "Inequality Hysteresis and the Effectiveness of Macroeconomic Stabilisation Policies", BIS, 19 May 2022, p. 1, https://www.bis.org/publ/othp50.htm
70. Carnegie Endowment for International Peace, "Global Protest Tracker", https://carnegieendowment.org/publications/interactive/protest-tracker
71. *New York Times*, "In Paris, 'Yellow Vest' Protests Cut Sharply into City's Luxury Trade", 17 December 2018.
72. Thomas Johansmeyer, "How 2020 Protests Changed Insurance Forever", World Economic Forum, 22 February 2021, https://www.weforum.org/agenda/2021/02/2020-protests-changed-insurance-forever/
73. Allianz, "Businesses Need to Prepare for a Rise in Social Unrest Incidents", press release, 14 June 2022, https://www.agcs.allianz.com/news-and-insights/news/civil-unrest.html
74. Philip Barret and Sophia Chen, "The Economics of Social Unrest", IMF, August 2021, https://www.imf.org/external/pubs/ft/fandd/2021/08/economics-of-social-unrest-imf-barrett-chen.htm
75. See, for example, V-Dem Institute, *Democracy Report 2022: Autocratization Changing Nature?*, Gothenburg, University of Gothenburg, 2022, https://v-dem.net/media/publications/dr_2022.pdf
76. Robert Kagan, *The Jungle Grows Back: America and Our Imperiled World*, New York, Vintage, 2019
77. See, for example, Patrick Deneen, *Why Liberalism Failed*, New Haven, Yale University Press, 2018.
78. https://www.core-econ.org/about/
79. See, for example, Hyman P. Minsky, "Capitalist Financial Processes and the Instability of Capitalism", *Journal of Economic Issues*, Vol. 14, No. 2 (1980), pp. 505–23.
80. Charles P. Kindleberger, *Manias, Panics, and Crashes: A History of Financial Crises*, 4th ed., London, Palgrave Macmillan, 2001.
81. Irving Fischer, "The Debt-Deflation Theory of Great Depressions", *Econometria*, Vol. 1, No. 3 (1933), pp. 337–57; Irving Fisher, *The Purchasing Power of Money*, New York: Macmillan, 1931.
82. Carmen M. Reinhardt and Kenneth S. Rogoff, *This Time Is Different: Eight Centuries of Financial Folly*, Princeton, NJ, Princeton University Press, 2011.

83. Karl Marx, *Das Kapital*, Otto Meisner, 1867.
84. John Maynard Keynes, *The General Theory of Employment, Interest and Money*, London, Palgrave Macmillan, 1936.
85. Thomas Piketty, *Capital in the Twenty-First Century*, trans. Arthur Goldhammer, Cambridge, MA, Belknap Press of Harvard University Press, 2014, p. 14.
86. David Harvey, *The Limits to Capital*, London, Verso Books, 1982.
87. Karl Polanyi, *The Great Transformation*, New York, Farrar & Reinhart, 1944.
88. Pope Pius XI, *Quadragesimo anno*, 1931.
89. See for example Herman E. Daly, *Steady-State Economics: The Economics of Biophysical Equilibrium and Moral Growth*, W.H. Freeman, 1977 and Peter Victor, "Herman Daly and the Steady-State Economy," 2009, http://gesd.free.fr/pvictor.pdf
90. Robert Kuttner, *Can Democracy Survive Global Capitalism?*, New York, W.W. Norton, 2018.
91. See, for example, Jason Hickel, *Less Is More: How Degrowth Will Save the World*, London, Penguin Books, 2022; Serge Latouche, Farewell to Growth, *Cambridge, UK, Polity Press, 2009: and* Christian Kerschner, "Economic de-growth vs. steady-state economy," Volume 18, Issue 6, April 2010, Pages 544–551, https://www.sciencedirect.com/science/article/abs/pii/S0959652609003473
92. Yannis Dafermos, Maria Nikolaidi and Giorgos Galanis, "A stock-flow-fund ecological macroeconomic model," Ecological Economics, 131 (2017), 191–207, https://www.sciencedirect.com/science/article/pii/S0921800916301343
93. Government of France, "Report by the Commission on the Measurement of Economic Performance and Social Progress," 2009, https://ec.europa.eu/eurostat/documents/8131721/8131772/Stiglitz-Sen-Fitoussi-Commission-report.pdf
94. See Herman E. Daly, "Towards Some Operational Principles of Sustainable Development," *Ecological Economics*, 2 (1990) 1-6, Elsevier Science Publishers B.V.. Amsterdam, https://www.sciencedirect.com/science/article/abs/pii/092180099090010R and Thomas O. Wiedmann, Heinz Schandl, Manfred Lenzen and Keiichiro Kanemoto, "The Material Footprint of Nations", *Proceedings of the National Academy of Sciences*, Vol. 112, No. 20 (2013), pp. 6271–6, https://www.pnas.org/doi/10.1073/pnas.1220362110
95. Wiedmann, T., Lenzen, M., Keyßer, L.T. *et al.* "Scientists' warning on affluence," *Nat Commun* **11**, 3107 (2020), https://www.nature.com/articles/s41467-020-16941-y

96. For promising examples of such a thought process, see Fleurbaey, Marc and Kanbur, Ravi and Snower, Dennis, "Efficiency and Equity in a Socially Embedded Economy," (August 7, 2021). Available at SSRN: https://ssrn.com/abstract=3900962 and the agenda framed by the Transitional Economics Commission in its 2022 report to the Club of Rome: Sandrine Dixson-Decleve, Owen Gaffney, Jayati Ghosh, Jorgen Randers, Johan Rockstrom and Per Espen Stokne, *Earth for All: A Survival Guide for Humanity*, Gabriola Island, BC, New Society, 2022, https://newsociety.com/books/e/earth-for-all?_ga=2.15415094.1659597184.1656940929-1752902652.1656940929&sitedomain=row

Open Access This chapter is licensed under the terms of the Creative Commons Attribution 4.0 International License (http://creativecommons.org/licenses/by/4.0/), which permits use, sharing, adaptation, distribution and reproduction in any medium or format, as long as you give appropriate credit to the original author(s) and the source, provide a link to the Creative Commons licence and indicate if changes were made.

The images or other third party material in this chapter are included in the chapter's Creative Commons licence, unless indicated otherwise in a credit line to the material. If material is not included in the chapter's Creative Commons licence and your intended use is not permitted by statutory regulation or exceeds the permitted use, you will need to obtain permission directly from the copyright holder.

CHAPTER 3

Original Sin or Wayward Practice? Living Standards as a Trickle-Down, Residual Consideration of Modern Economics

The first two chapters of this volume have examined shortfalls in the track record of modern economics with respect to three important dimensions of socioeconomic progress—inclusion, sustainability and resilience. I have argued that the evidence suggests a certain structural weakness or blind spot in liberal economic doctrine—a tendency to treat these considerations in both theory and practice as a residual, a natural outcome of increased economic efficiency and growth.

This chapter investigates where this imbalance in emphasis between efficient resource allocation and growth, on the one hand, and material well-being and broad progress in living standards, on the other hand, originated. Was it hard-wired into the principles of liberal political economy at conception? Did the liberal economic tradition always have such a tight focus on the technical functioning of markets—on prices, exchange, production, consumption and national income or "wealth" creation—and place much less emphasis on broader notions of material improvement in the human condition and the lived experience of the bulk of the population? Or did the residual treatment of the latter develop sometime later, in the refinement of the original doctrine and its translation into practice?

The natural first place to look for clues in this regard is the writing of Adam Smith, who is widely regarded as the founder of economics as an intellectual discipline and the father of capitalism. Smith is famous for

---

The original version of the chapter has been revised. A correction to this chapter can be found at https://doi.org/10.1007/978-3-031-37435-7_8

© The Author(s) 2024, corrected publication 2024
R. Samans, *Human-Centred Economics*,
https://doi.org/10.1007/978-3-031-37435-7_3

having made the original comprehensive case for market-based economic systems in his opus *An Inquiry into the Nature and Causes of the Wealth of Nations* (*TWN*).[1] Familiar to many are his metaphor of the "invisible hand" to illustrate the superior economic efficiency of markets of individual actors pursuing their rational self-interest in self-organized, distributed fashion; his theory that the division and specialization of labour serve as the engine of productivity growth and wealth creation; and his critique of mercantilism and political restraints on domestic commerce and foreign trade.

The following passages elaborate on each of these foundational concepts. First, with respect to the "invisible hand":

> It is not from the benevolence of the butcher, the brewer, or the baker, that we expect our dinner, but from their regard to their own interest. We address ourselves, not to their humanity but to their self-love, and never talk to them of our own necessities but of their advantages.[2]
>
> Every individual is continually exerting himself to find out the most advantageous employment for whatever capital he can command. It is his own advantage, indeed, and not that of the society, which he has in view. But the study of his own advantage naturally, or rather necessarily leads him to prefer that employment which is most advantageous to the society.[3]
>
> As every individual, therefore, endeavours as much as he can both to employ his capital in the support of domestic industry, and so to direct that industry that its produce may be of the greatest value; every individual necessarily labours to render the annual revenue of the society as great as he can. He generally, indeed, neither intends to promote the public interest, nor knows how much he is promoting it. By preferring the support of domestic to that of foreign industry he intends only his own security; and by directing that industry in such a manner as its produce may be of the greatest value, he intends only his own gain, and he is in this, as in many other cases, led by an invisible hand to promote an end which was no part of his intention.[4]

On the division and specialization of labour:

> In general, if any branch of trade, or any division of labour, be advantageous to the public, the freer and more general the competition, it will always be the more so.[5]
>
> It is the great multiplication of the productions of all the different arts, in consequence of the division of labour, which occasions, in a well-governed society, that universal opulence which extends itself to the lowest ranks of the people.[6]

On governmental intervention in commerce:

[Without trade restrictions] the obvious and simple system of natural liberty establishes itself of its own accord. Every man ... is left perfectly free to pursue his own interest in his own way ... The sovereign is completely discharged from a duty [for which] no human wisdom or knowledge could ever be sufficient; the duty of superintending the industry of private people, and of directing it towards the employments most suitable to the interest of the society.[7]

According to the system of natural liberty, the sovereign has only three duties to attend to ... first, the duty of protecting the society from the violence and invasion of other independent societies; secondly ... the duty of establishing an exact administration of justice; and, thirdly, the duty of erecting and maintaining certain public institutions and certain public works.[8]

These and other well-known quotations from *TWN* have established Smith in the popular imagination as a pure free-marketeer, the original exponent of a free enterprise system unfettered by distortionary government intervention. During the wave of enthusiasm for market reform that crested in the 1980s, 1990s and early 2000s, his public image underwent a revival of sorts. Adam Smith institutes, centres and student societies proliferated with the aim of spreading the gospel of capitalism, free markets and limited government. He was often cast as a kind of patron saint of neoliberalism, particularly by those with libertarian leanings.

In fact, this is a distorted or, at best, partial interpretation of *TWN*. A closer reading of the voluminous work reveals a rather eclectic and pragmatic approach to the role of markets and government regulation as well as the relationship between efficiency, productivity and wealth creation, on the one hand, and labour, social welfare and socioeconomic progress, on the other.

The Adam Smith of *TWN* is a heterodox analyst by modern standards. He did not assume that market actors left to their own devices could be counted on to ensure perfect competition and high rates of productivity growth, advance the broader interests of society, workers and the poor in particular, or self-regulate against market excesses and imperfections such as self-dealing and collusion. Indeed, he outlined an extensive critique and remedial agenda to the contrary. Taken in its entirety, *TWN* paints a balanced picture of what Smith considered to be the inherent strengths and shortcomings of "commercial society" (his precursor term for "capitalism") as well as appropriate responses to these, including by governments.

His eclectic or "catholic" approach to such a complex subject spanning multiple social science disciplines was generally emulated by his successors and in particular the next two most important theorists of liberal economics' first 150 years: John Stuart Mill and Alfred Marshall. This is no coincidence, since Smith, Mill and Marshall all considered themselves fundamentally to be moral philosophers who worked in the field of political economy in order to deepen understanding of the *material* aspects of what could be done to improve the human condition. They regarded themselves as engaging in the study of political economy as part of a broader enquiry into the drivers and determinants of social progress and the betterment of people as human beings. Even Marshall, the widely acknowledged father of neoclassical economics and most important bridge between the qualitative analysis of his classical predecessors and the quantitative approach of modern economists, deliberately placed his groundbreaking technical notation in annexes so as not to distract from understanding of the relevance of his work to the real world—to people.

Smith enumerated multiple imperfections in the markets he theorized and witnessed. In his view, these market imperfections or failures required countervailing intervention because they undermined growth in labour productivity and/or the equitable social distribution of its benefits. Some of these he viewed as inherent in human nature and thus markets themselves. Others he attributed to either the absence or poor design of government regulation in his country.

These extensive caveats about the natural attributes of markets and the shortcomings of those he witnessed in action in eighteenth-century Great Britain and Europe betray the popular caricature of Smith as a doctrinaire laissez-faire advocate. For example:

On the tendency of market actors towards collusion:

> People of the same trade seldom meet together, even for merriment and diversion, but the conversation ends in a conspiracy against the public, or in some contrivance to raise prices.[9]

The interest of those who "live by profit" is "directly opposite to that of the great body of the people," the workers and landlords. "Any profit-seeker will exploit their deeper knowledge of economic realities, as did stockjobbers and bankers." "The mean rapacity, the monopolizing spirit of merchants and manufacturers" are constant characteristics of any capital-holder [according to Smith]. This structural fact meant that profit-seekers should always be mistrusted and counterbalanced. The interests of merchants are aligned with those of the public only under specific and rare conditions: only when traders are isolated and merchant collusion is structurally constrained.[10]

On the tendency towards exploitative labour practices, including forced labour:

Masters [employers] are always and every where in a sort of tacit, but constant and uniform combination, not to raise the wages of labour above their actual rate ... We seldom hear of this combination, because it is the usual, and one may say, the natural state of things which nobody ever hears of.[11]

Smith viewed the lengthy apprenticeships of the day as a form of servitude: "the epitome of the restrictions of the principles of competition and liberty." It is unjust, he argued, that "during the continuance of the apprenticeship, the whole labour of the apprentice belongs to his master". By prohibiting the apprentice from bringing his skills to market ... the master took away the student's ability to negotiate for better wages, conditions, or other terms of employment.[12]

Rent and profit eat up wages, and the two superior orders of people oppress the inferior one.[13]

Folly and injustice seem to have been the principles which presided over and directed the first project of establishing those [overseas] colonies; the folly of hunting after gold and silver mines, and the injustice of coveting the possession of a country whose harmless natives, far from having ever injured the people of Europe, had received the first adventurers with every mark of kindness and hospitality.[14]

On the tendency towards regulatory capture by rent-seeking employers and merchants:

The proposal of any new law or regulation of commerce which comes from this order ought always to be listened to with great precaution, and ought never to be adopted till after having been long and carefully examined, not only with the most scrupulous, but with the most suspicious attention. It comes from an order of men, whose interest is never exactly the same with that of the publick, who have generally an interest to deceive and even to oppress the publick, and who accordingly have, upon many occasions, both deceived and oppressed it.[15]

We have no acts of parliament against combining to lower the price of work; but many against combining to raise it.[16]

Whenever the legislature attempts to regulate the differences between masters and their workmen, its counsellors are always the masters.[17]

On the tendency towards speculation and instability in financial markets:

Men commonly overestimate their chances of success in risky ventures, with the consequence that too great a share of the nation's stock of capital goes into such ventures.[18]

On the tendency towards usury and exploitative lending practices in financial services:

> the greater part of the money which was to be lent [in the absence of regulation of rates charged by banks] would be lent to prodigals and projectors, who alone would be willing to give this high interest ... A great part of the capital of the country would thus be kept out of the hands which were most likely to make a profitable and advantageous use of it, and thrown into those which were most likely to waste and destroy it.[19]

On the concentration of rents stemming from Great Britain's system of land inheritance, including primogeniture and entail:

> The former allocated all land to the first-born, even though "nothing can be more contrary to the real interest of a numerous family, than a right which, in order to enrich one, beggars all the rest of the children." It also undermined productivity, because large plots could not be efficiently cultivated. Concentration was increased by entails, which constrained the sale of land over successive generations. Entails were "founded upon the most absurd of all suppositions ... that every successive generation of men have not an equal right to the earth ... but that the property of the present generation should be restrained and regulated according to the fancy of those who died perhaps five hundred years ago."[20]
>
> If landed estates ... were divided equally among all the children, upon the death of any proprietor who left a numerous family, the estate would generally be sold. So much land would come to market, that it could no longer sell at a monopoly price ... The property rights crucial for development are those of the yeoman or small farm owner.[21]

On the risks of private management of public goods:

> Private initiative cannot be trusted to take proper care of the roads.[22]
>
> Where there is an exclusive corporation, it may perhaps be proper to regulate the price of the first necessary of life.[23]

These are not the observations and admonitions of a free market ideologue. They are the measured reflections of a keen and disinterested observer of human behaviour in the context of the commercial activity of his day. Smith clearly did not assume that government's appropriate role was simply to get out of the way of private enterprise through deregulation and low or flat taxes. To the contrary, he outlined in *TWN* an extensive programme of what today we might call smart, pre-distributive regulation aiming to ensure broad labour force participation under conditions of decent work, including a living wage, since he viewed these as the essential prerequisites of rising productivity and broadly based socioeconomic progress.

For example, he saw the broad scope of government's role in "establishing an exact administration of justice" as "that of protecting, as far as possible, every member of the society from the injustice or oppression of every other member of it".[24] Furthermore:

On the regulation of monopolies and anti-competitive business practices:

> To widen the market and to narrow the competition, is always the interest of the dealers. To widen the market may frequently be agreeable enough to the interest of the public; but to narrow the competition must always be against it, and can serve only to enable the dealers, by raising their profits above what they naturally would be, to levy, for their own benefit, an absurd tax upon the rest of their fellow-citizens.[25]
>
> Our woollen manufacturers have been more successful than any other class of workmen in persuading the legislature that the prosperity of the nation depended upon the success and extension of their particular business. They have not only obtained a monopoly against the consumers by an absolute prohibition of importing woollen cloths from any foreign country, but they have likewise obtained another monopoly against the sheep farmers and growers of wool by a similar prohibition of the exportation of live sheep and wool. The severity of many of the laws which have been enacted for the security of the revenue is very justly complained of, as imposing heavy penalties upon actions which, antecedent to the statutes that declared them to be crimes, had always been understood to be innocent. But the cruellest of our revenue laws, I will venture to affirm, are mild and gentle in comparison of some of those which the clamour of our merchants and manufacturers has extorted from the legislature for the support of their own absurd and oppressive monopolies. Like the laws of Draco, these laws may be said to be all written in blood.[26]

On labour regulation in general:

> [when] regulation ... is in favour of the workmen, it is always just and equitable.[27]

On prevention of wage fraud:

[requiring wages to be paid in money rather than in kind] imposes no real hardship upon the masters. It only obliges them to pay that value in money, which they pretended to pay but did not always really pay, in goods.[28]

On a minimum, living wage:

No society can surely be flourishing and happy, of which the far greater part of the members are poor and miserable. It is but equity, besides, that they who feed, cloath and lodge the whole body of the people, should have such a share of the produce of their own labour as to be themselves tolerably well fed, cloathed and lodged.[29]

By necessaries I understand, not only the commodities which are indispensably necessary for the support of life, but whatever the custom of the country renders it indecent for creditable people, even of the lowest order, to be without."[30]

On prudential financial regulation (of banks issuing fiat money):

[This] may, no doubt, be considered as in some respect a violation of natural liberty. But those exertions of the natural liberty of a few individuals, which might endanger the security of the whole society, are, and ought to be, restrained by the laws of all governments; of the most free, as well as of the most despotical. The obligation of building party walls, in order to prevent the communication of fire, is a violation of natural liberty, exactly of the same kind with the regulations of the banking trade which are here proposed.[31]

On public goods provision:

[Governments have a duty of] erecting and maintaining certain public institutions and certain publick works, which it can never be for the interest of any individual, or small number of individuals, to erect and maintain; because the profit could never repay the expence to any individual or small number of individuals, though it may frequently do much more than repay it to a great society.[32]

This class of government duties "are chiefly those for facilitating the commerce of the society, and those for promoting the instruction of the people." Smith supports the participation of the government in the general education of the people because it will help prepare them for industry, will make them better citizens and better soldiers, and happier and healthier men in mind and body. Public education is made necessary to check as far as may be the evil effects on the standards, mentality, and character of the working classes of the division of labor and the inequality in the distribution of wealth.³³

[Similarly, regarding public health,] it would deserve its [government's] most serious attention to prevent a leprosy or any other loathsome and offensive disease, though neither mortal nor dangerous, from spreading itself among them.³⁴

On progressive taxation:

It is not very unreasonable that the rich should contribute to the public expence, not only in proportion to their revenue, but something more than in that proportion.³⁵

More specifically, he proposed special taxes on:

- luxury vehicles (carriages): so that "the indolence and vanity of the rich [be] made to contribute in a very easy manner to the relief of the poor".³⁶
- monopoly profits: "the gains of monopolists, whenever they can be come at [are] certainly of all subjects the most proper" for taxation.³⁷
- land values: "Ground-rents, so far as they exceed the ordinary rent of land, are altogether owing to the good government of the sovereign ... Nothing can be more reasonable than that a fund which owes its existence to the good government of the state, should be taxed peculiarly, or should contribute something more than the greater part of other funds, towards the support of the government."³⁸

Smith's fundamental concern is the incidence of taxation: whom does the tax really affect and how does that impact productivity? Smith repeatedly emphasizes the negative effects of shifting the burden to the poor ... He also opposes the taxation of labor for the same reasons: advocates fail to understand that the tax is passed onto the consumer through higher prices, without increasing productivity ... Smith thus clearly opposes regressive taxes both on labor and on necessary consumption. The other systematic goal of taxation in Smith was to counterbalance asymmetries in wealth. Burdening the rich "more than in proportion" to their wealth and lightening the burden on the poor were criteria he applied repeatedly—not because morality demanded it, but because sound economics did.³⁹

Thus, Smith envisioned an important role for the state in enabling fair market competition and promoting social inclusion. Why did he go to great lengths to identify what he considered to be inherent market imperfections requiring countervailing government action?

Smith had a clear theory of change based on his belief that economic value fundamentally flows from the services applied by labour—by working people. His view in *TWN* is that, with few exceptions, restraint of competition—whether from monopolies, collusive business practices, concentration of rents, or legal barriers to trade—undermines the natural tendency of markets to promote the division and specialization of labour and hence growth in productivity, that is, economic output per unit of labour.

In his analysis, regulation of restrictive business practices and monopolies raises productivity growth by lowering barriers to entry, increasing competition and promoting more efficient allocation of resources. Regulation of other rents (e.g., land, financial system) ensures broader access to the factors of production within the economy, expanding the incentives for individual initiative and innovation, boosting labour productivity further. Labour regulation to ensure that wages reflect productivity ensures that a growing economy translates into a more educated, healthy and thus productive workforce, and this in turn increases the production and consumption of goods and services, that is, the "wealth", of the nation. Finally, government support for the supply of affordable public goods—the "necessaries of life"—including but not limited to quality public education and a safe and healthy environment (Smith had the urban slums of his day in mind), enhances the well-being and capabilities of the workforce as a whole, increasing the productivity of the nation's factories, trades and farms still further.

Thus, for Smith, unleashing the "animal spirits" of private enterprise by freeing up the "invisible hand" of markets was a necessary but not sufficient condition for optimizing both the productive output of nations and broad socioeconomic progress within them. As a moral philosopher and political economist, he considered the latter to be the ultimate objective of his enquiry. Recall that political economy or economics did not exist in his day as a separate intellectual discipline. He approached the topic as a subdiscipline within the larger intellectual canvas of moral philosophy, having as its fundamental purpose the improvement of the human condition across its moral and spiritual as well as material dimensions.

Accordingly, increasing the "wealth of nations" meant more to him than boosting production or what we today call GDP. It also meant enabling and justly compensating the entire workforce and clearing away discriminatory and outright exclusionary practices through the targeted application of anti-trust, labour, financial, education and social protection law and regulation. In *TWN*, Smith sketched the outlines of the institutional infrastructure that he thought should underpin market economies in order to optimize production and distribution simultaneously in recognition of their latent positive synergy. In this way, he anticipated the early- to mid-twentieth-century anti-trust, labour, financial system and social protection reforms of industrial economies and even Amartya Sen's more recent emphasis on human capability and agency in economic development.

Thus, a fair reading of *TWN* suggests that the residual treatment of living standards and distributional considerations of modern economics does not have its source in the original "scripture" of liberal political economy. Next, we turn to the landmark work of two of the most influential theorists of liberal political economy's pantheon in the century after Smith's, John Stuart Mill and Alfred Marshall. In his 1848 *Principles of Political Economy: With Some of Their Applications to Social Philosophy*, Mill integrated and extended the work of the classical theorists of the late eighteenth and early nineteenth century, notably Smith, David Ricardo and Mill's father James. In so doing, he set the stage for the advent of the neoclassical school in the late nineteenth century, which found its most comprehensive and authoritative expression in the work of Marshall, whose 1890 *Principles of Economics* synthesized and built upon the work of the early marginalists and W.S. Jevons in particular.

Mill's *Principles of Political Economy* was the most widely used economics textbook for nearly a half a century until the appearance of Marshall's *Principles of Economics*, which enjoyed this distinction for a similarly lengthy period. Both treatises combined specific theoretical innovations and refinements with a comprehensive overview of the field. As such, they are the best available nineteenth-century reference points for our continuing investigation into the origins of modern liberal economics' structural underemphasis of inclusion, sustainability and resilience.

John Stuart Mill is considered one of the most important figures in all of liberalism. However, emulating his mentor and the pioneer of utilitarianism, Jeremy Bentham, he was sceptical of a general application of the notion of natural rights, stating in his earlier seminal work "On Liberty",

> It is proper to state that I forgo any advantage which could be derived to my argument [for liberty] from the idea of abstract right as a thing independent of utility. I regard utility as the ultimate appeal on all ethical questions; but

it must be utility in the largest sense, grounded on the permanent interests of man as a progressive being.[40]

Mill drew a distinction between individual actions that are by their very nature "personal" or "self-regarding", that is, actions that pertain exclusively to the actor themself, and other conduct that is "social", meaning behaviour that has consequences—whether immediate or distant—for other people.[41]

> Whether conduct is purely self-regarding or generates externalities that potentially affect others is decisive for determining if and when society may intervene ... Commerce is chief among the kinds of social conduct that Mill deems amenable to social regulation. He stipulates that "trade is a social act," and as such, it belongs in a different class than the self-regarding freedoms defended in On Liberty [e.g., freedom of expression and religion].He states: "Whoever undertakes to sell any description of goods to the public, does what affects the interests of other persons, and society in general; and thus his conduct, in principle, comes within the jurisdiction of society."[42]

Mill's *Principles of Political Economy* hews to the market-oriented tradition of Adam Smith in emphasizing that "laissez-faire should be the general practice: every departure from it, unless required by some great good, is a certain evil".[43] He elaborated:

> [E]very restriction of [competition] is an evil, and every extension of it, even if for the time injuriously affecting some class of labourers, is always an ultimate good. To be protected against competition is to be protected in idleness, in mental dullness; to be saved the necessity of being as active and as intelligent as other people; and if it is also to be protected against being underbid for employment by a less highly paid class of labourers, this is only where old custom, or local and partial monopoly, has placed some particular class of artisans in a privileged position as compared with the rest; and the time has come when the interest of universal improvement is no longer promoted by prolonging the privileges of a few.[44]

Thus, as a moral philosopher, Mill like Smith saw the ultimate purpose of political economy as contributing to social progress and the moral and spiritual development of individuals. This larger perspective opened the door to a similarly clear-eyed, pragmatic assessment of the imperfections present and possibly inherent in markets as well as the legitimacy and indeed necessity at times of remedial societal and governmental action, notwithstanding his general view that "the great majority of things are worse done by the intervention of government, than the individuals most interested in the matter would do them, or cause them to be done, if left to themselves".[45]

Like Smith, Mill never formalized the many exceptions he enumerated to the general principle of laissez-faire in a specific theoretical construct, but his extensive discussion of such challenges and appropriate responses to them accounts for a substantial proportion of both his *Principles of Political Economy* and later works.

For example, Mill objected to Great Britain's inheritance laws, describing them as

> the feudal family, the last historical form of patriarchal life[46] ... I see nothing objectionable in fixing a limit to what any one may acquire by the mere favour of others, without any exercise of his faculties, and in requiring that if he desires any further accession of fortune, he shall work for it.[47]

Regarding private property more generally, in his autobiography Mill refers to the influence on his thinking of the St Simonian school of French philosophy:

> Their criticisms on the common doctrines of Liberalism seemed to me full of important truth; it was partly by their writings that my eyes were opened to the very limited and temporary value of the old political economy, which assumes private property and inheritance as indefeasible facts, and freedom of production and exchange as the *dernier mot* [last word] of social improvement.[48]

A pioneer of gender equality, he advocated changes in legal restrictions and customs (guild practices and social attitudes) that severely discriminated against women in regard to wages and employment opportunity:

> This most desirable result would be much accelerated by another change, which lies in the direct line of the best tendencies of the time; the opening of industrial occupations freely to both sexes. The same reasons which make it no longer necessary that the poor should depend on the rich, make it equally unnecessary that women should depend on men; and the least which justice requires is that law and custom should not enforce dependence (when the correlative protection has become superfluous) by ordaining that a woman, who does not happen to have a provision by inheritance, shall have scarcely any means open to her of gaining a livelihood, except as a wife

and mother. Let women who prefer that occupation, adopt it; but that there should be no option, no other carrière possible for the great majority of women, except in the humbler departments of life, is a flagrant social injustice.[49]

He advocated government provision of public goods, invoking the existence of certain

> "things of the worth of which the demand of the market is by no means a test." These are sublime goods "whose utility does not consist in ministering to inclinations, nor in serving the daily uses of life, and the want of which is least felt where the need is greatest." ... These goods include matters of personal cultivation such as education. They also include non-immediate goods such as retirement or saving for the future that are so far off on the horizon that one cannot reasonably expect people to place any weight on them given the natural tendency to discount the future. They also include many instances that require overcoming a collective action problem such as agitating for higher pay or fewer hours for labor. In all these instances, Mill allows that there is some role for government intervention.[50]

More generally, he viewed distribution as ultimately a social construct, a matter for societies to decide through their political processes:

> The distribution of wealth ... is a matter of human institution solely. The things once there, mankind, individually or collectively, can do with them as they like. They can place them at the disposal of whomsoever they please, and on whatever terms ... Even what a person has produced by his individual toil, unaided by any one, he cannot keep, unless by the permission of society. Not only can society take it from him, but individuals could and would take it from him, if society only remained passive ... The distribution of wealth, therefore, depends on the laws and customs of society. The rules by which it is determined, are what the opinions and feelings of the ruling portion of the community make them, and are very different in different ages and countries; and might be still more different if mankind so chose.[51]

These views are fundamentally at odds with the laissez-faire notion that government should intervene minimally in the economy. Like Smith, Mill clearly conceived of this principle as applying specifically to the exchange of goods and services in commercial activity. It was not to be extrapolated to the whole of political economy, but should, rather, be complemented by "human institution" to address related socioeconomic questions of fairness, human dignity and equitable participation in the benefits that market competition brings. He went so far as to suggest,

> Whether "individual agency in its best form" or some variant of socialism will prove superior in satisfying these needs is a "mere question of comparative advantages, which futurity must determine." The question of "which of the two will be the ultimate form of human society" remains open. Again we are thrown back—as in the question of liberty itself—on amorphous notions of "progress," "development," and "improvement" as the benchmarks of social policy.[52]

Moreover, anticipating the arguments of contemporary ecological economics, Mill envisioned natural limits to the process of economic growth. He thought that national economies would at some point reach a "stationary state" in which productive output and population would stabilize at a high level of wealth and material comfort. He argued that "in those most advanced, what is economically needed is a better distribution" and added:

> It is scarcely necessary to remark that a stationary condition of capital and population implies no stationary state of human improvement. There would be as much scope as ever for all kinds of mental culture, and moral and social progress; as much room for improving the Art of Living, and much more likelihood of its being improved, when minds ceased to be engrossed by the art of getting on. Even the industrial arts [technology] might be as earnestly and as successfully cultivated, with this sole difference, that instead of serving no purpose but the increase of wealth, industrial improvements would produce their legitimate effect, that of abridging labour. Hitherto it is questionable if all the mechanical inventions yet made have lightened the day's toil of any human being. They have enabled a greater population to live the same life of drudgery and imprisonment, and an increased number of manufacturers and others to make fortunes. They have increased the comforts of the middle classes. But they have not yet begun to effect those great changes in human destiny, which it is in their nature and in their futurity to accomplish. Only when, in addition to just institutions, the increase of mankind shall be under the deliberate guidance of judicious foresight, can the conquests made from the powers of nature by the intellect and energy of scientific discoverers become the common property of the species, and the means of improving and elevating the universal lot.[53]

To be certain, Mill like Smith was deeply sceptical of the ability of government to perform the functions of distribution well. He was wary of what he considered to be its natural tendency towards bureaucratic centralization and political capture by moneyed interests, and this led him to express a distinct (but not necessary fully confident) preference for voluntary associations to perform many of them. In this, he was presumably influenced by the analysis of Tocqueville, with whom he corresponded actively for a number of years.[54] However, he did not allow these practical considerations, informed as they were by the relatively underdeveloped state of public administration in mid-nineteenth-century Great Britain, to prevent him from highlighting the essential role he thought should be played by human institutions shaped by political rather than market processes, even if he did not package and advertise these arguments very coherently.

This dual approach—emphasizing simultaneously the importance of market signals in commercial exchange in order to raise an economy's productive output, on the one hand, and the need for markets to be underpinned by an institutional infrastructure of rules and incentives to translate such increased output into broad-based improvement in material living standards and hence the human condition—was embraced and deepened by Alfred Marshall in both dimensions. Marshall was one of the conceptual pioneers and the original codifier of neoclassical economics. His models and reasoning remain at the foundation of much of economics scholarship and policy practice today.

In particular, Marshall integrated the perspectives of classical economists who emphasized production-related and particularly labour costs as a principal determinant of value and the later marginalist school that emphasized marginal utility, that is, the degree of additional satisfaction or value gained from consuming a given product or service relative to other choices. He expanded the application of mathematics to political economy, developing tools and models such as supply and demand curves to help one understand determinants of price and, on an aggregate level, market equilibria. In this way, he took the study of markets begun by Smith to an altogether new level, refining and codifying the work of the original marginalists W.S. Jevons, Leon Walras and Carl Menger.

This more rigorous approach to understanding the nature of markets and the decision-making behaviour of actors within them consolidated political economy's evolution into a social science in its own right. The field's name eventually changed to "economics", and it came to be understood as the science of modelling rational decision-making under conditions of scarce or otherwise constrained choices.

Given Marshall's pioneering emphasis on the technical workings of markets and the mathematical modelling of them, one might have expected him not to pay as much attention to the broader socioeconomic issues that weighed so heavily upon Smith and Mill. In fact, Marshall doubled down on their twin emphasis of the role of markets in raising productive efficiency and output, on the one hand, and the role of "human institutions" in improving distribution and social welfare, on the other. He, too, had come to the study of political economy from a wider vantage point, having earlier studied metaphysics, ethics and social philosophy in addition to maths and physics. This was reflected in his definition of economics, which remains one of the most cited:

> Political Economy or Economics is a study of mankind in the ordinary business of life; it examines that part of individual and social action which is most closely connected with the attainment and with the use of the material requisites of well-being. Thus it is on the one side a study of wealth; and on the other, and more important side, a part of the study of man.[55]

In this definition, the production–distribution, markets–institutions duality of approach is quite explicit. It flows coherently from Mill's definition that political economy "investigate[s] the nature of Wealth, and the laws of its production and distribution".[56]

Marshall focused increasingly on the second part of this duality—the promotion of broad human welfare through stronger social institutions—as his work progressed across the eight editions of *Principles of Economics* and various other writings between 1879 and 1923. He underscored the importance of market limitations and imperfections and the role of government in most of the same areas emphasized by Smith and Mill cited above. He did so out of a similar larger philosophical conviction that "the growth of mankind in numbers, in health and strength, in knowledge, ability, and in richness of character is the end of all our studies"[57] as well as a pragmatic sense that "the health and strength of the population" are the basis of industrial efficiency and that man's "vigour" is the source of all progress.[58] He saw the abject living conditions of much of the population in his day as both a moral stain and an economic opportunity cost:

> There are vast numbers of people both in town and country who are brought up with insufficient food, clothing, and house-room; whose education is broken off early in order that they may go to work for wages; who thenceforth are engaged during long hours in exhausting toil with imperfectly

nourished bodies, and have therefore no chance of developing their higher mental faculties.[59]

Accordingly, he turned increasingly to distributional considerations and related enabling environment conditions. In the fifth edition of *Principles*, he added a long chapter entitled "Progress in Relation to Standards of Life"—an early reference to the modern term "standard of living".[60] In Appendix K, he argued that "a certain minimum of means is necessary for material wellbeing" and suggested both there and in his earlier (1879) volume, *The Economics of Industry*—which was written with his wife and frequent collaborator Mary Paley—a decidedly multidimensional definition of well-being and economic progress not unlike the contemporary ones cited in Chap. 2:

> True well-being or welfare requires, besides a necessary level of material wealth, a number of elements that are of fundamental importance for human nature. Quality of life is one, but a good quality of life can be achieved only by means of a good level of education, the true and most important engine of progress and welfare. Through education people can improve their condition both in the work place and in society. Through education people can improve in character and evaluate aspects of life that are not strictly "material". And through education a nation can upgrade in the competitive international arena. Education therefore is a fundamental aspect of true welfare, its premise. But various other elements are also essential: a good quality of life requires a good place to live in (clean and spacious houses, green open spaces, good quality of air and so forth); a good place to work in and good labour conditions; good social relations; open opportunities for personal advancement. We cannot simply sum up all these components in the concepts of surpluses, nor of national dividend which, at most, can only be approximations.[61]
>
> These necessaries, comforts, and luxuries are for a man's children as well as for himself; indeed the chief of them is a good physical, mental and moral education for his children. Economic progress depends much on change in the Standard of Comfort of the people, and therefore on the strength of their family affections … Just as a man who has borrowed money is bound to pay it back with interest, so a man is bound to give his children an education better and more thorough than he has himself received.[62]

To this end, he sketched a public policy reform agenda that mirrored those of Smith and Mill while reaching beyond them in important respects. For example, on a minimum, living wage:

When … the home of children is such that there is no considerable chance of their growing up to be good citizens, healthy in mind and body, the State is bound as a duty and for self-preservation to intervene. It may improve the home; or close it, and take charge of the family. In the rare cases in which when the wages of any kind of adult male labour are so low that, even when supplemented by the utmost earnings that wife and children are likely to bring in, they would not suffice to maintain a wholesome family life, then it may conceivably be advisable to prohibit such low wages.[63]

An increase of wages … almost always increases the strength, physical, mental and even moral of the coming generation … an increase in the earnings that are to be got by labour increases its rate of growth; or, in other words, a rise in its demand-price increases the supply of it.[64]

On investment in human capital:

Many of the children of the working classes are imperfectly fed and clothed; they are housed in a way that promotes neither physical nor moral health … At least they go to the grave carrying with them undeveloped abilities and faculties; which, if they could have borne full fruit, would have added to the material wealth of the country … many times as much as would have covered the expense of providing adequate opportunities for their development.[65]

"There is no extravagance more prejudicial to the growth of national wealth than that wasteful negligence which allows genius that happens to be born of lowly parentage to expend itself in lowly work." No change would be more conducive to a rapid increase of material wealth as an improvement in the schools, provided it be combined with an extensive system of scholarships. His observation was that "progress is most rapid in those parts of the country in which the greatest proportion of the leaders of industry are the sons of working men."[66]

The older economists took too little account of the fact that the human faculties are as important a means of production as any other kind of capital; and we may conclude, in opposition to them, that any change in the distribution of wealth which gives more to the wage receivers and less to the capitalists is likely, other things being equal, to hasten the increase of material production … if … it provided better opportunities for the great mass of the people, increased their efficiency, and developed in them such habits of self-respect as to result in the growth of a much more efficient race of producers in the next generation. For then it might do more in the long-run to promote the growth of even material wealth than great additions our stock of factories and steam-engines.[67]

On public goods provision in areas "which must be regulated more or less by Government":

> Streets ... Canals, Light houses (some); Surveys and information of all kinds which are beyond the reach of private effort: ... Free parks and Recreative grounds etc ... Markets ... slaughter houses; fairs; cemeteries; action in the case of infectious diseases. The supply of meat, fruit, and other things which the consumer cannot test for himself at all or until too late to escape ... Telegraphs, Telephones, Water, Gas, Electricity supply, Tramways Building on public streets, Railways Pipe lines, Agricultural drainage and Irrigation works, Educational and medical provisions on too large a scale for private enterprise, in which public and private foundations may well be mingled under public control. Universities[,] Museums[,] Art Galleries[,] Hospitals (with paying cards).[68]

On environmental regulation and subsidies:

> The most important capital of a nation is that which is invested in the physical, mental and oral nurture of its people. That is being recklessly wasted by the exclusion of, say, some ten millions of the population from reasonable access to green spaces, where the young may play and the old may rest. To remedy this evil is ... even more urgent than the provision of old-age pension; and I wished the first charge upon the rapidly-growing value of urban land to be a "Fresh Air" rate (or general tax), to be spend [sic] on breaking out small green spots in the midst of dense industrial districts, and on the preservation of large green areas between different towns and between different suburbs which are tending to coalesce. I thought that the gross amount of the Fresh Air rate or tax should be about ten millions a year, till we have cleared off the worst evils caused by many generations of cruel apathy and neglect.[69]

These theoretical principles regarding the critical importance of institutional reforms to advance public welfare and well-being were expressed by Marshall in qualitative rather than quantitative terms. They were not translated into supporting mathematical notation and graphs such as those he famously pioneered for modelling price determination and related consumer and producer behaviour in markets of exchange. However, he forcefully and repeatedly argued that higher investment by society in the skills and lived experience of the poor would ultimately have a major quantitative impact in the form of higher productivity and national economic output. It would influence the supply of and demand for a critical factor of production, labour, and thereby shape the positioning of these curves in key industries and across the economy over the medium to long term. In other words, these aspects of his *Principles of Economics* regarding social welfare promotion were part and parcel of his theory and not separate or subordinate observations.

In this way, Marshall deepened the holistic and, by modern standards, heterodox tradition of Smith and Mill. He took their two-track argument about strengthening market signals and economic growth, on the one hand, and institutions and broad social welfare, on the other, to a new level of sophistication, including by underscoring the latent synergy between the two.

However, he also unintentionally set the stage for the imbalance in emphasis between these two dimensions that was to emerge in succeeding decades. His very act of applying mathematical methods more rigorously to the modelling of behaviour in markets of exchange inspired successive waves of impressive scholarship aiming to refine and more broadly apply these neoclassical tools of analysis to this more quantifiable of the two domains. Such concentration of scholarly attention evolved to such an extent that the young field of "economics" rapidly became synonymous with, in essence, the study of the mechanics of price determination and equilibrium in markets composed of rational actors. This shift was reflected in the most commonly used definition of economics that emerged in the years following Marshall's death, Lionel Robbins's 1932 formulation: "Economics is the science which studies human behavior as a relationship between ends and scarce means which have alternative uses."[70]

The dual emphasis of Smith, Mill and Marshall is nowhere to be found in Robbins's characterization of the field, and these men scarcely would have approved of it. But this is not to say that welfare considerations were not an ongoing focus of the profession. In fact, Marshall's hand-chosen successor as professor of political economy at Cambridge University, Arthur Cecil Pigou, became the father of a new subdiscipline known as "welfare economics". But whereas Marshall's and his two predecessors' focus on welfare and well-being was at the broad societal—that is, macro- and institutional—level, Pigou's was mainly at the micro- or individual consumer or producer level. Pigou made this choice for very practical reasons; he was able to apply the rapidly evolving quantitative methods of his day far more readily to markets, prices and incomes than to the comparatively intangible and subjective domains of human institutions and notions such as equity and sufficiency. He explained,

Welfare is a thing of very wide range. It is necessary to limit our subject-matter. In doing this we are naturally attracted towards that portion of the field in which the methods of science seem likely to work at best advantage. This they can clearly do when there is present something measurable … The one obvious instrument of measurement available in social life is money. Hence, the range of our inquiry becomes restricted to that part of social welfare that can be brought directly and indirectly into relation with the measuring-rod of money.[71]

There is no guarantee that the effects produced on the part of welfare that can be brought into relation with the measuring-rod of money may not be cancelled by effects of a contrary kind brought about in other parts, or aspects, of welfare; and, if this happens, the practical usefulness of our conclusions is wholly destroyed. The difficulty, it must be carefully observed, is not that, since economic welfare is only a part of welfare as a whole, welfare will often change while economic welfare remains the same, so that a given change in economic welfare will seldom synchronise with an equal change in welfare as a whole. All that this means is that economic welfare will not serve for a barometer or index of total welfare. But that, for our purpose, is of no importance.[72]

By contrast, for Marshall, welfare is not simply reduced to a measurable quantity but is something extremely complex; and the idea of measurability "should be always present" but "it should not … be prominent".[73] As his protégé, Pigou was fully cognizant of the limitations of his own partial approach, which focused solely on what he called "economic welfare":

[W]hat we wish to learn is, not how large welfare is, or has been, but how its magnitude would be affected by the introduction of causes which it is in the power of statesmen or private persons to call into being. The failure of economic welfare to serve as an index of total welfare is no evidence that the study of it will fail to afford this latter information: for, though a whole may consist of many varying parts, so that a change in one part never measures the change in the whole, yet the change in the part may always affect the change in the whole by its full amount. If this condition is satisfied, the practical importance of economic study is fully established. It will not, indeed, tell us how total welfare, after the introduction of an economic cause, will differ from what it was before; but it will tell us how total welfare will differ from what it would have been if that cause had not been introduced: and this, and not the other, is the information of which we are in search.[74]

Despite the limitations of his approach, which he freely acknowledged, Pigou was working unambiguously in the two-lens production-and-distribution, growth-and-social-welfare political economy tradition of Marshall,

Mill and Smith. He viewed economic welfare as being advanced by "any cause which, without the exercise of compulsion or pressure upon people to make them work more than their wishes and interests dictate, increases productive efficiency, and, therewith, the average volume of the national dividend, provided that it neither injures the distribution nor augments the variability of the country's consumable income (emphasis supplied)." He also considered it being enhanced by "any cause which increases the proportion of the national dividend received by poor persons" (emphasis supplied), "provided that it does not lead to a contraction of the national dividend and does not injuriously affect its variability"[75] (emphasis supplied). He posited further that economic welfare will not be maximized if there is a divergence between what he called the marginal social net product and marginal private net product of economic activities.

Thus, Pigou was keenly interested in the determinants of distribution at the macroeconomic level, and he did not necessarily intend his partial pecuniary approach to define or dominate how economics would deal with larger distributional and ethical dimensions of social welfare, including those relating to inclusion, sustainability and resilience. But this turned out to be what happened, and while there has been plenty of scholarly debate among welfare and development economists over the years about these limitations[76] and possible alternative or additional avenues of enquiry,

> The richness and complexity of the reflections developed by Marshall went lost in Pigou's systematization [which focused on] ... the sum of producers' and consumers' surplus that are measured in terms of money and maximized according to the doctrine of maximum satisfaction. The maximization of welfare (that is of consumers' and producers' surpluses and National Dividend) becomes simply the solution of an analytical maximization problem. The condition of welfare maximization is that marginal social costs (benefits) are equal to marginal private costs (benefits). If they are not equal (market failure), then there is scope for state intervention.[77]

This gave the role of government a far narrower scope on matters of social welfare than that envisioned by Smith, Mill and Marshall and many of their contemporaries. Thus, remarkably, even the branch of modern economics called "welfare economics" ended up largely sidestepping broader considerations of social welfare, never developing a strong macro- and institutional component of the kind implied by the two-track framework of analysis of liberal economics' most influential original theorists.

This is not to say that economic policy did not pursue the kinds of investments in people and related institutional and legal reforms advocated by Smith, Mill and Marshall. Major such reforms were introduced in Western countries in the latter part of the nineteenth and first half of the twentieth centuries. However, these were driven by rising social and political pressure, not the teachings and techniques of welfare economics. The neoclassical school had an important influence on the competition (e.g., anti-trust) and certain other reforms of this period, but it followed rather than led society when it came to the distributional agenda. To this day, it has not found a formula for integrating Smith's, Mill's and Marshall's dual approach in its increasingly elaborate theoretical framework. If anything, this imbalance in emphasis in the way their founding principles were applied became more entrenched as the twentieth century wore on.

By contrast, classical liberal political economists and Smith in particular had a major influence on both market and social policy reforms in the early nineteenth century. Smith's views and prescriptions on mercantilism and the Corn Laws (restricting the importation of cheaper grains), on the guild, apprenticeship, labour mobility and inheritance rules of his day, and on government's role in taxation and public goods provision contributed to a policy shift in Great Britain and elsewhere, as illustrated by this account of Parliament's early consideration of minimum wage legislation and reform of the Settlement Laws (restrictions on the movement and other rights of workers, women, illegitimate children, orphans and other poor or vulnerable people)[78]:

> In 1795–6, and again in 1799–1800, sudden increases in food prices set off an intense discussion of wage rates and poor relief. One episode—Samuel Whitbread's proposed minimum wage legislation of 1795—provides a particularly clear illustration of the changing interpretation of Smith's ideas. Whitbread was a reform M.P., and his bill would have given magistrates powers "to regulate the wages of Labourers in Husbandry" by fixing minimum wages. He was strongly influenced by Smith, and introduced the Commons debate on the bill by explaining that "he felt as much as any man … that the price of labour, like any other commodity, should be left to find its own level". But he was prepared to countenance some "legislative interference" to protect the "rights" of the poor. Whitbread followed the *Wealth of nations* closely in his parliamentary presentation. Smith himself was tolerant, after all, of some wage regulation …
>
> Whitbread's Smith-inspired rhetoric was greeted, however, with a quite different interpretation of political economy. [Prime Minister William] Pitt answered Whitbread with a resounding defence of the "unassisted operation

of principles". He invoked "the most celebrated writers upon political economy" as testimony that the House should "consider the operation of general principles, and rely upon the effects of their unconfined exercise". His solution was to remove restrictions on the "free circulation of labour", and to begin reform of the laws of settlement. Whitbread and his friends pointed out that such reforms "would take a considerable time"; a barley loaf, meanwhile, cost rather more than "the whole of the labourer's daily wages". But "the present case", for Pitt, was not "strong enough for the exception".

There is something of Smith on both sides of the parliamentary debate … Smith was considered, like Whitbread, as a friend of the poor. In the *Wealth of nations* he describes "the liberal reward of labour" as the "necessary effect and cause of the greatest public prosperity"; in the "Early draft" he had written that a "high price of labour" was the "essence of public opulence." Smith's language, more generally, is quite different from Pitt's. Pitt followed Smith in criticizing the law of settlements. But where Smith described an "evident violation of natural liberty and justice", by which the "poor man" is "most cruelly oppressed", Pitt saw no more than a "grievance": "instances where interference had shackled industry". Whitbread and his friends, like Smith, wished "to rescue the labouring poor from a state of slavish dependence". The labourer should not "receive his due as an eleemosynary gift"; the dependence of the poor was especially evil because people who had received relief were excluded from the franchise, and thus from their constitutional rights. But for Pitt, the poor were concerned with prices and not with rights; the workman was prevented, at worst, "from going to that market where he could dispose of his industry to the greatest advantage".[79]

This story attests to *TWN*'s influence in not merely informing public policy debate but shifting its very frame of reference—with respect to both the role of markets and that of governments in advancing social welfare. Such was Smith's paradigmatic influence that Pitt eulogized him and his treatise in a speech before the House of Commons soon after his death.[80]

Looking back in 1881, Lord Acton, the eminent editor, historian and political adviser of Prime Minister William Gladstone, remarked, "government with the working class" was the irresistible consequence of Smith's ideas of freedom of contract, and of labour as the source of wealth: "That is the foreign effect of Adam Smith—French Revolution and Socialism."[81] Similarly, Carl Menger, founder of the Austrian School of economics, characterized Smith as a friend of the poor and noted that he was quoted frequently by Louis Blanc, Ferdinand Lassalle and Karl Marx[82]:

> A. Smith placed himself in all cases of conflict of interest between the poor and the rich, between the strong and the weak, without exception on the

side of the latter. I use the expression "without exception" after careful reflection, since there is not a single instance in A. Smith's work in which he represents the interest of the rich and powerful as opposed to the poor and weak.[83]

Of course, Smith was by no means solely or even principally responsible for the wave of social reform legislation that swept his own country and others during the early nineteenth century. But *TWN* had a powerful legitimating and political-base-broadening effect. As it came to dominate political economy discourse and pedagogy, it helped to accelerate the pace of reform in Great Britain and abroad.

Great Britain's Parliament passed its first factory legislation in 1802 which

> prevented apprentices under the age of 21 from working at night and for longer than 12 hours a day, and made provision for them to receive some basic education. Much of the labour in the nation's burgeoning cotton mills was provided by "pauper apprentices", who were often children below the age of ten. Many of them were orphans sent into factory employment by the Poor Law authorities, often very far from their home parishes. In the first decades of the 1800s, as many as a fifth of workers in the cotton industry were children under the age of 13.[84]

Between 1819 and the 1880s, Parliament adopted a succession of increasingly expansive legislation regulating factories, mines, chimney sweeps and the provision of poverty relief, addressing many of the gaps criticized by Smith and Mill.[85] Indeed, by the mid nineteenth century, most European countries were legislating social and labour protections for specific vulnerable groups as summarized in Table 3.1.[86]

This was a period plagued by rolling waves of industrial unrest across Europe,[87] leading governments of many countries to pursue labour and social protection reforms in order to limit the risks to political stability. With an eye to its restive working class, the German government of Chancellor Otto von Bismarck became the first to adopt a comprehensive social insurance programme, beginning with his proposal in 1881 for old-age insurance:

> The German system provided contributory retirement benefits and disability benefits as well. Participation was mandatory and contributions were taken from the employee, the employer and the government. Coupled with

Table 3.1 National legislation on social insurance before the German legislation of 1883

Accident insurance	Sickness insurance	Old-age and/or invalidity pensions
1838: Prussia: employers' liability law for railway workers. (b)	1844: Belgium: compulsory insurance for seamen. (d)	1791: France: establishment of the right of seamen to pensions in cases of invalidity. (d)
1842: Norway: compensation for miners recognized in Mining Law. (e)	1851: Belgium: state subsidies for workers voluntarily insured in mutual benefit societies. (c)	1844: Belgium: compulsory invalidity and old-age insurance for seamen. (d)
1854: Austria: compulsory insurance for miners. (c)	1852: France: state subsidies to voluntary insurance societies. (c)	1854: Austria: compulsory invalidity insurance for miners (but not insurance against old-age). (c)
1860: Norway: compensation for seamen recognized in Marine Law. (a)	1854: Prussia: compulsory insurance for miners. (c)	1856: France: state subsidies to approved funds. (c)
1868: Belgium: compulsory insurance for miners. (c)	1854: Austria: compulsory insurance for miners. (c)	1861: Italy: establishment of seamen's invalidity funds covering the risks of invalidity, old age, death. (d)
1871: Germany: employers' liability for workers in specific industries. (b)	1868: Saxony: compulsory insurance for all workers. (c)	
1877: Switzerland: employers' liability for factory workers. (c)	1869: Bavaria: communal aid to factory workers, servants, apprentices. (a)	
1880: United Kingdom: employers' liability for workers in specific industries. (c)	1873: Finland: seamen to receive medical aid/treatment in cases of sickness/accidents according to Marine Law. (g)	
1882: New Zealand: workmen's compensation act. (t)		

Source: Stein Kuhnle, "The Beginnings of the Nordic Welfare States: Similarities and Differences"

the workers' compensation program established in 1884 and the "sickness" insurance enacted the year before, this gave the Germans a comprehensive system of income security based on social insurance principles. (They would add unemployment insurance in 1927, making their system complete.)[88]

Following the passage of Bismarck's reforms, the Nordic countries and others began to examine and adopt aspects of the new and more comprehensive German social security system. By the First World War, 32 countries had introduced some sort of legislation providing insurance or compensation for industrial accidents or occupational hazards, 18 countries had introduced sickness insurance or benefit schemes—Germany (1883), Norway (1909), the United Kingdom (1911) and the Netherlands being pioneers of compulsory schemes. Some sort of old-age, survivors' or disability insurance or scheme was in place in 13 countries, whereas only seven countries had introduced unemployment benefit schemes.[89]

These efforts by Western governments to widen the social benefits of industrialization were influenced by a growing political radicalization of the working class in many countries. Industrial strikes and trade unions proliferated from the 1860s to 1890s, since many of the limited reforms governments enacted suffered from weak implementation and enforcement. Marx's *Das Kapital* appeared in 1867, inspiring much debate about the plight of workers and the possibility of a more equitable approach to organizing economies: socialism. The global economic depression of 1873–77 and ensuing stagnation up to and including much of the 1890s (e.g., the Panic of 1893 in the United States) exacerbated social pressures.

By the twentieth century's second decade—which witnessed the economic and political convulsions of the First World War, Bolshevik Revolution, Spanish influenza and major industrial strikes such as those in the United Kingdom during the 1911–14 "Great Unrest" and those in the United States affecting the textile, coal and steel industries and even Boston's entire police force—governments were seized by fears of civil unrest, political instability and the prospect of Bolshevik-style communist revolution. This was the febrile environment in which discussions began soon after the war on a new global "social contract" through the formation of the ILO. As the ILO's second director, Edward Phelan, who in 1919 helped to draft its constitution, recounted:

> The three Great Powers, the United States of America, Great Britain and France were … preoccupied with a critical post-war situation, more immediately dangerous than that which followed the Second World War. A revolutionary temper was widespread: the Bolshevik Revolution in Russia had been followed by the régime of Bela Kun in Hungary; the shop steward movement in Great Britain had honeycombed many of the larger trade unions and undermined the authority of their constitutional executives; the trade union movements in France and Italy showed signs of becoming more and more

extremist; millions of men, trained in the use of arms, to whom extravagant promises had been freely made were about to be demobilised; the wave of unrest had spread even to such stable and peaceful democracies as the Netherlands and Switzerland. How gravely the situation was viewed may be indicated by the fact that during the [Versailles] Peace Conference itself, Clemenceau moved many thousands of troops into Paris as a precaution against rioting in the streets. The decision to give labour matters a prominent place in the Peace Treaty was essentially a reflection of this preoccupation. The Peace Conference accepted the proposals of its Labour Commission without much concern either for the generalisations of the Preamble or for the details of the proposed organisation. In other circumstances, it is indeed highly probable that some of the more daring innovations in the latter, such as the provision that non-Government delegates should enjoy equal voting power and equal status with Government delegates in the International Labour Conference, would have been considered unacceptable.[90]

Following the First World War, the ILO Constitution was adopted as part of the Treaty of Versailles, alongside but separate from the part that established the League of Nations. Its brief preamble contained distinct echoes of the admonitions and principles of Smith, Mill and Marshall:

Whereas universal and lasting peace can be established only if it is based upon social justice;
  And whereas conditions of labour exist involving such injustice, hardship and privation to large numbers of people as to produce unrest so great that the peace and harmony of the world are imperilled; and an improvement of those conditions is urgently required; as, for example, by the regulation of the hours of work, including the establishment of a maximum working day and week, the regulation of the labour supply, the prevention of unemployment, the provision of an adequate living wage, the protection of the worker against sickness, disease and injury arising out of his employment, the protection of children, young persons and women, provision for old age and injury, protection of the interests of workers when employed in countries other than their own, recognition of the principle of equal remuneration for work of equal value, recognition of the principle of freedom of association, the organization of vocational and technical education and other measures;
  Whereas also the failure of any nation to adopt humane conditions of labour is an obstacle in the way of other nations which desire to improve the conditions in their own countries[91];

In essence, the unfinished institutional development agenda advocated by the founding theorists of capitalism had become an international political priority of the highest order. Its underdevelopment and lack of international coordination had come to be perceived as a direct threat to peace and stability within and among countries.

Years later, US President Franklin D. Roosevelt reflected on his unanticipated role in helping to organize the ILO's first International Labour Conference in 1919 in Washington:

> I well remember that in those days the ILO was still a dream. To many it was a wild dream. Who had ever heard of Governments getting together to raise the standards of labor on an international plane? Wilder still was the idea that the people themselves who were directly affected—the workers and the employers of the various countries—should have a hand with Government in determining these labor standards.[92]

Roosevelt was referring to the special governance arrangements of the ILO, which to this day allot governments and social partners equal voting rights (a 2:1:1 ratio for governments, worker organizations and employer organizations, respectively). The purpose was

> to promote social progress and overcome social and economic conflicts of interest through dialogue and cooperation. In contrast to the revolutionary movements of the time, it brought together workers, employers and governments at the international level—not in confrontation, but in a search for common rules, policies and behaviours from which all could benefit. It included a number of unique features. Above all, it gave these economic actors equal power of decision with states, and it introduced new forms of international treaty concerned with social aims, along with new ways to apply them. Politically it drew on the main European democratic political currents of the time, in particular social democracy, Christian democracy and social liberalism, and actors from each of these perspectives participated in its work and contributed to its development.[93]

In essence, the ILO was given the task of forging a new "social contract" to accompany and soften the rough edges of industrial capitalism along the lines envisioned by Smith, Mill and Marshall—to fill the institutional lacuna in liberal economic theory and practice through the creation of formal international labour and social protection norms ratified by governments and translated by them into national law and regulation. In the organization's first 20 years, 67 conventions were adopted pursuant to tripartite agreement on such topics as hours of work, maternity protection, forced labour, minimum age, lead paint, night work, sickness insurance, accident protection, old-age insurance, and invalidity insurance.[94]

In 1944, as part of its landmark Philadelphia Declaration, the organization's tripartite constituents elaborated upon the nature and significance of the emerging universal social contract—this corpus of multilaterally agreed socioeconomic norms—constructed during the interwar period, and they began to look ahead. Of particular note, they affirmed a bedrock principle (contained in the first substantive clause) that "labour is not a commodity"[95] and framed a related series of individual *economic* rights and corresponding governmental responsibilities:

> the Conference affirms that:
> (a) all human beings, irrespective of race, creed or sex, have the right to pursue both their material well-being and their spiritual development in conditions of freedom and dignity, of economic security and equal opportunity;
> (b) the attainment of the conditions in which this shall be possible must constitute the central aim of national and international policy;
> (c) all national and international policies and measures, in particular those of an economic and financial character, should be judged in this light and accepted only in so far as they may be held to promote and not to hinder the achievement of this fundamental objective;
> (d) it is a responsibility of the International Labour Organization to examine and consider all international economic and financial policies and measures in the light of this fundamental objective;
> (e) in discharging the tasks entrusted to it the International Labour Organization, having considered all relevant economic and financial factors, may include in its decisions and recommendations any provisions which it considers appropriate.[96]

The statement "labour is not a commodity" was an implicit criticism of not only the often parlous state of industrial working conditions but also the clinical way that labour was generally treated in liberal economics—particularly in the abstract mathematical models of neoclassical theory including the peculiarly circumscribed realm of "welfare economics". Similarly, the assertion of individual economic rights and the notion that the "central" responsibility of economic policy is to create conditions conducive to the attainment of these for everyone can be read as an implicit rebuff of the imbalanced, "markets-first" way the field has taken forward the two-track framework of principles it inherited from Smith, Mill and Marshall.

An institutionalist school of economics did emerge during the interwar period as important social reforms were being adopted in industrialized countries. These scholars defined "institutions" broadly as "durable systems of established and embedded social rules that structure social interactions",[97] encompassing governmental institutions as well as voluntary associations and informal customs and practices having an important bearing upon economic activity. The group argued that such "human institutions", in the words of J.S. Mill, were important endogenous factors in economic progress and therefore should be more fully internalized in economic theory and practice.

The widely acknowledged founder of the field, Thorstein Veblen, argued that "an evolutionary theory of value must be constructed out of the habits and customs of social life". He criticized the rationality assumption of the neoclassicists, maintaining that people were not "lightning calculators of pleasures or pains, who [oscillate] like a homogeneous globule of desire of happiness under the impulse of stimuli that shift [them] about the area, but leave [them] intact".[98] Rather, they were driven by habits and custom and by whatever constituted achievement in the currently reigning system of status emulation (echoing Smith's earlier opus, *The Theory of Moral Sentiments*). This led him to conclude that

> marginal utility analysis, indeed the entire apparatus of neoclassical marginalism, was static. It therefore could not capture the important evolutionary, processual elements of the economy, including the changing institutional and power structures of society. Because mainstream economics was not an evolutionary science, Veblen argued in a famous essay, it had become little more than a sophisticated and subtle defense, albeit selectively, of existing institutions, the existing power structure, and the systemic and ideological status quo.[99]

Another principal member of the school, John R. Commons, elaborated:

> It is not only principles of mechanism and scarcity conceived as working themselves out automatically and beneficently, through commodities, feelings and individual selfishness, but also principles of the collective control of transactions through associations and governments, placing limits on selfishness, that [must be] ... included in economic theory... [F]our verbs [describe such] guidance and restraint of individuals in their transactions. [Such institutions] tell what the individuals *must* or *must not* do (compulsion or duty), what they *may* do without interference from other individuals

(permission or liberty), what they *can* do with the aid of the collective power (capacity or right), and what they *cannot* expect the collective power to do in their behalf (incapacity or exposure). In short, the working rules of associations and governments, when looked at from the private standpoint of the individual, are the source of his rights, duties and liberties, as well as his exposures to the protected liberties of other individuals.[100]

For a time, it appeared that these pragmatic, empirically based perspectives desiring to better integrate market and institutional considerations might lead to a more explicit internalization of social welfare considerations in mainstream economics. However, this heterodox approach ultimately met with strong resistance:

> It is widely known that the old institutionalists were hostile to the narrow vision of economics as the "science of choice" and the utility-maximizing version of "economic man", which have prevailed for the second half of the twentieth century. [But] so keen to dismiss these criticisms, many mainstream economists have resorted to the dismissive tactic of describing any broader version of their discipline, or any approach that is not based on individual utility maximization, as "not economics".[101]

In any event, by the 1930s this debate had been overshadowed by and largely absorbed into the intense focus of economists and policymakers on the dire macroeconomic crisis gripping the world. In the context of deflation, widespread unemployment and depressed levels of domestic demand and international trade, necessity became the mother of invention for macroeconomists, ultimately producing a revolutionary new theory and tool: respectively, John Maynard Keynes's *The General Theory of Unemployment, Interest and Money* and Simon Kuznets's and the US Department of Commerce's national income (gross national product) accounts.

Keynesian demand management dominated the field during the generation following the Second World War, focusing on fiscal and monetary policy intervention to lessen the amplitude of the business cycle. This period also saw important innovations in the theory and empirical measurement and decomposition of economic growth. Both of these avenues of enquiry were concerned principally with the production side of the economy and made extensive use of national income accounting as a measurement tool and the aggregate production function as a conceptual model. At its simplest level, the latter posited that output was a function of key factor inputs (e.g., labour, capital, land and natural resources, technical progress). Both of these topics—Keynesian macro-management of the business cycle and the neoclassical aggregate production function (particularly its use in estimating the relative weight of factor inputs)—came under vigorous criticism that persists to this day. Nonetheless, both remain at the heart of the way that economies are generally conceived of today.

These and other elements of the dominant post-war framework of analysis—the so-called "neoclassical synthesis" combining these and other neoclassical and Keynesian elements—were primarily concerned with the growth and stabilization of productive output. They paid comparatively little attention to distribution and the role of institutions therein. To be certain, public policy and politics continued to make strong advances on this front, many industrialized countries adding considerably in the 1960s and 1970s to their health care, education, labour market, social security, environmental and other social programmes. However, the economics profession was primarily focused elsewhere, both before and after the stagflation of the 1970s brought to the fore in the 1980s the monetarist and deregulatory neoliberal agenda—which had even less interest in distribution and the social contract and indeed often sought to roll aspects of them back.

Institutional economics did experience a revival of sorts from the 1970s to 1990s, but with a microeconomic focus on such topics as transaction costs, information asymmetries and principal–agent incentive challenges in the decision-making behaviour of firms and consumers. Scholars such as Ronald Coase, Oliver Williamson, Albert O. Hirschman and Douglass North made important and celebrated contributions, but these remained some distance from the original macro-institutional, social welfare focus of Smith, Mill and Marshall.

This deepening of mainstream economics' focus on production and GDP growth during the second half of the twentieth century, whether from a Keynesian or neoliberal perspective, had the effect of leaving unanswered the question raised by the ILO Philadelphia Declaration and the Universal Declaration of Human Rights regarding economic and social rights. How are governments to make these the "central aim" of economic policy? How are they to ensure that "all national and international policies and measures, in particular those of an economic and financial character" will be "judged in this light and accepted only in so far as they may be held to promote and not to hinder the achievement of this fundamental objective".[102]

The Universal Declaration of Human Rights was adopted in 1948, four years after the Philadelphia Declaration. It specified a set of economic rights that in 1966 were included in an international treaty, the International Covenant on Economic, Social and Cultural Rights (ICESCR), that has been ratified by over 170 countries:

- equal rights for men and women (Article 3);
- the right to work (Article 6);
- the right to just and favourable conditions of work (Article 7);
- the rights of workers to organize and bargain collectively (Article 8);
- the right to social security and social insurance (Article 9) and protection and assistance for the family (Article 10);
- the right to an adequate standard of living (Article 11), which includes: (i) adequate food, (ii) adequate clothing and (iii) adequate housing;
- the right to freedom from hunger (Article 11);
- the right to the highest attainable standard of physical and mental health, including the right to health care (Article 12);
- the right to education (Article 13).

The *ICESCR* is a legally binding instrument in which state parties assume responsibility to implement and maintain the rights guaranteed therein. Article 28 provides that the Covenant's provisions "shall extend to all parts of federal States without any limitations or exceptions".

The Universal Declaration, ICESCR and Philadelphia Declaration articulate a social contract, a commitment by governments to their citizens and the international community to place attainment of these economic rights at the heart of their economic and social policies. They are a modern manifestation of Smith's, Mill's and Marshall's shared principle that markets are but a means to the fulfilment of the more fundamental objective of improving the general welfare of society, and that this requires a complementary project by governments to construct enabling institutions—legal and other norms, policy incentives, administrative capacities—that facilitate access for all to the opportunities and benefits of the increased economic growth that market-based resource allocation helps to generate.

Smith:
> what improves the circumstances of the greater part can never be regarded as an inconveniency to the whole. No society can surely be flourishing and happy, of which the far greater part of the members are poor and miserable.[103]

Mill:

> many, indeed, fail with greater efforts than those with which others succeed, not from difference of merits, but difference of opportunities; but if all were done which it would be in the power of a good government to do, by instruction and by legislation, to diminish this inequality of opportunities, the difference of fortune arising from people's own earnings could not justly give umbrage.[104]

Marshall:

> It is reasonable to suppose that the chief aim of the Government of a Western country is to promote the well-being of the people.[105]

Unfortunately, these first principles and modern rights remain largely outside the field of vision of today's economists, chief economic advisers, and ministers of finance and trade, who tend to engage with them only peripherally. This begs the uncomfortable question of whether a social contract is something apart from economics. Is it merely an aspirational moral and political statement? That would be a rather cynical reading of the intentions of the governments that signed up to these rights. It also would suggest a certain intellectual laziness on the part of economists and economic policymakers. Is it really not possible for the field to walk and chew gum at the same time as it was challenged to do by its founding fathers—to explicitly integrate market-based resource allocation and institutionally based promotion of inclusion, sustainability and resilience in the same growth and development model?

The world has been warned of the cost of this disconnect before—most memorably by Marx in the nineteenth century and Karl Polanyi in the twentieth century. In his 1944 treatise *The Great Transformation: The Political and Economic Origins of Our Time,* Polanyi argued that the capitalist economies which emerged in the late nineteenth and early twentieth centuries became "disembedded" or decoupled from the priorities of society—of people. Their self-regulatory, laissez-faire ethos disregulated society. "The origins of the cataclysm [of the 1920s and 1930s] lay in the utopian endeavor of economic liberalism to set up a self-regulating market system," spawning a vicious circle of financial and economic instability and social and political tensions.[106]

Echoing Smith, Mill and Marshall, Polanyi argued that markets needed to be re-embedded in society through "human institution", e.g., labour, social protection, competition, financial and other regulation. He observed that these institutional innovations began to emerge organically in the nineteenth century in an effort to re-embed markets in social values:

> Human society would have been annihilated but for protective counter-moves which blunted the action of this self-destructive mechanism. Social history in the nineteenth century was thus the result of a double movement ... While on the one hand markets spread all over the face of the globe ... on the other hand a network of measures and policies [arose] to check the action of the market relative to labor, land, and money ... Society protected itself against the perils inherent in a self-regulating market system.[107]

He diagnosed the underlying problem of liberal economics as a

> distorted and obsolete conception of freedom. The liberal conception has yet to transcend its origins. Born into a cultural milieu in which the state represented the most serious obstacle to liberty, the liberal view of freedom has always been freedom from government. Liberal economic theory has been preoccupied with free (from government) enterprise and private property and neglectful of the vital changes in the social situation.[108]
>
> With the liberal, the idea of freedom thus degenerates into a mere advocacy of free enterprise—which is today reduced to a fiction by the hard reality of giant trusts and princely monopolies. This means the fullness of freedom for those whose income, leisure and security need no enhancing.[109]

Looking ahead, Polanyi envisioned the possibility of realizing a set of *positive* rights and freedoms

> made possible by the wealth created by industrialism as a way of life ... Freedom can be made wider and more general than ever before; regulation and control can achieve freedom not only for the few, but for all. Freedom not as an appurtenance of privilege ... but as a prescriptive right extending far beyond the narrow confines of the political sphere into the intimate organization of society itself.[110]

In this way, he anticipated the global social contract of economic and social rights established by multilateral agreement following the Second World War. However, if he were alive today, he no doubt would be disappointed with the continuing lack of traction of this agenda in economic theory and practice. Indeed, he might well view the persistence of this disconnect between society and economics, particularly in the context of our concurrent economic, environmental and geopolitical crises, as evidence of a new and equally disorderly Great Transformation in the making.

Simon Kuznets, the father of national income accounting and GDP, extended Polanyi's basic point and applied it to the burgeoning field of development economics in the 1950s and 1960s. He is best known in this respect for his postulation of an inverted U-shaped relationship between growth and development, on the one hand, and inequality, on the other.[111] Many observers interpreted this "Kuznets curve" as suggesting the existence of a quasi-natural law of economic development in which inequality rises as a country begins to industrialize and then subsides upon reaching an advanced, or high-income, stage of development. However, neither the subsequent empirical evidence[112] nor Kuznet's original writing on the subject[113] supports this notion. Instead, both suggest that sociopolitical factors are the more decisive factor in changing the direction of the curve; at some point, a political backlash to rising inequality occurs that results in countervailing institutional reforms. My ILO colleague Sangheon Lee has referred to this as a "Kuznets moment"[114]—in effect a catch-up step change in the development of a country's social contract.

The essential question raised by Polanyi's and Kuznets's analyses (and those of Smith, Mill and Marshall) still hangs over modern economics: how can the prevailing growth and development model be reformulated so that it is proactive rather than reactive when it comes to diffusing gains in living standards from growth and industrialization? How can it break the cycle of relying on "Kuznets moments" of disruptive political backlash by becoming more human and institutionally centred and less capital and market centred—that is, more bottom-up and less trickle-down? In other words, how can the social contract be more fully internalized in economic theory and instrumentalized in policy practice?

Keynes vigorously engaged with this question in his *General Theory* but primarily through the prism of macroeconomic policy rather than that of the many structural–institutional dimensions of the social contract emphasized by Smith, Mill and Marshall. He wrote that the social justice deficits or "outstanding faults of the economic society in which we live are its failure to provide for full employment and its arbitrary and inequitable distribution of wealth and incomes".[115] And he argued that this pathology required governments to be prepared to make active use of fiscal policy to countervail deficits in aggregate demand directly through their own spending as well as indirectly through redistribution of income and wealth via the tax code from richer to poorer households, which have a higher propensity to consume and thereby support demand and employment. It also required governments to keep interest rates low in order to encourage investment in productive capacity and discourage financing of rent-seeking activities primarily benefiting owners of existing assets—that is to say, the same wealthier households that have a lower propensity to consume and support aggregate demand than those of more modest means.

Keynes characterized this macroeconomic policy mix as spelling

> the euthanasia of the rentier, and, consequently, the euthanasia of the cumulative oppressive power of the capitalist to exploit the scarcity-value of capital. Interest to-day rewards no genuine sacrifice, any more than does the rent of land. The owner of capital can obtain interest because capital is scarce, just as the owner of land can obtain rent because land is scarce. But whilst there may be intrinsic reasons for the scarcity of land, there are no intrinsic reasons for the scarcity of capital.[116]

For this reason, he argued,

> The State will have to exercise a guiding influence on the propensity to consume partly through its scheme of taxation, partly by fixing the rate of interest, and partly, perhaps, in other ways. Furthermore, it seems unlikely that the influence of banking policy on the rate of interest will be sufficient by itself to determine an optimum rate of investment. I conceive, therefore, that a somewhat comprehensive socialisation of investment will prove the only means of securing an approximation to full employment; though this need not exclude all manner of compromises and of devices by which public authority will co-operate with private initiative. But beyond this no obvious case is made out for a system of State Socialism which would embrace most of the economic life of the community. It is not the ownership of the instruments of production which it is important for the State to assume. If the State is able to determine the aggregate amount of resources devoted to augmenting the instruments and the basic rate of reward to those who own them, it will have accomplished all that is necessary.

Thus, Keynes was no "socialist" in the strict sense of the term. Rather, he was grappling with the larger economy-wide or macroeconomic imperfections of the liberal economic model, analogous to the way Smith, Mill and Marshall deconstructed the largely microeconomic market failures and imperfections they witnessed in the "commercial society" of their day. Like them, he framed his critique in both moral and practical terms, in the interest of advancing social justice and economic growth and efficiency simultaneously: "For if effective demand is deficient, not only is the public scandal of wasted resources intolerable, but the individual enterpriser who seeks to bring these resources into action is operating with the odds loaded against him."[117]

Indeed, Keynes regarded his theory as revitalizing classical liberal political economy by addressing one of its most fundamental blind spots—its excessive focus on market mechanics and corresponding inability to address the secular uncertainty chilling investment in productive capacity and accompanying underutilization of human resources—that is to say, the severe deficits of inclusion and resilience he witnessed in the macroeconomy around him during the 1920s and 1930s:

> Our criticism of the accepted classical theory of economics has consisted not so much in finding logical flaws in its analysis as in pointing out that its tacit assumptions are seldom or never satisfied, with the result that it cannot solve the economic problems of the actual world. But if our central controls succeed in establishing an aggregate volume of output corresponding to full employment as nearly as is practicable, the classical theory comes into its own again from this point onwards. If we suppose the volume of output to be given, *i.e.* to be determined by forces outside the classical scheme of thought, then there is no objection to be raised against the classical analysis of the manner in which private self-interest will determine what in particular is produced, in what proportions the factors of production will be combined to produce it, and how the value of the final product will be distributed between them. Again, if we have dealt otherwise with the problem of thrift, there is no objection to be raised against the modern classical theory as to the degree of consilience between private and public advantage in conditions of perfect and imperfect competition respectively. Thus, apart from the necessity of central controls to bring about an adjustment between the propensity to consume and the inducement to invest, there is no more reason to socialise economic life than there was before.[118]

A more contemporary and arguably still the most direct and influential attempt to reconcile the liberal growth and development model with a human-centred perspective on social welfare is Amartya Sen's work in the 1980s and 1990s on human capability and agency. Sen challenged the utility basis of welfare economics frontally:

> What is missing from these traditional models, Sen argues, is a notion of what activities we are able to undertake ("doings") and the kinds of persons we are able to be ("beings"). Sen calls this notion *capabilities*. Capabilities are the *real freedoms* that people have to achieve their potential doings and beings. Real freedom in this sense means that one has all the required means

necessary to achieve that doing or being if one wishes to. That is, it is not merely the formal freedom to do or be something, but the substantial opportunity to achieve it.

In this way, the capability approach changes the focus from means (the resources people have and the public goods they can access) to ends (what they are able to do and be with those resources and goods). This shift in focus is justified because resources and goods alone do not ensure that people are able to convert them into actual doings and beings. Two persons with similar sets of goods and resources may nevertheless be able to achieve very different ends depending on their circumstances.[119]

Sen's capabilities approach encompasses non-monetary (capabilities, functioning and agency) as well as monetary aspects of well-being. It considers the overriding objective of development to be the expansion of human capabilities rather than economic growth. In this way, he addressed an important blind spot in income- and GDP-based metrics of poverty and economic development: the lived experience of people. While growth may be necessary for development, it is not always sufficient.[120] Policy should therefore distinguish between growth-mediated (top- or trickle-down) and support-led (bottom- or level-up) development.[121]

Sen was not doctrinaire; he did not insist on only one defined set of important capabilities and did not exclude or minimize the importance of economic growth and the provision of basic needs and commodities. However, his critique of welfare economics and development strategy struck a lasting chord among economists and philosophers and has been translated into practical tools, most notably the UN Human Development Report (HDR). The HDR's Human Development Index (HDI) measures life expectancy, mean and expected years of school, and per capita gross national income across 191 countries.[122] It defines human development as being about "expanding the richness of human life rather than simply the richness of the economy in which human beings live. It is an approach that is focused on people and their opportunities and choices."[123]

Before he introduced his capabilities approach, Sen published extensively on related aspects of welfare economics, social choice theory and development economics. He participated in the ILO's World Employment Programme (WEP), for which he conducted a landmark study on famines.[124] In it, he found that a drop in food production was often not the proximate cause of catastrophe; rather, it was inequality and vulnerability in other aspects of the economy which prevented equitable access to food supplies. In the 1970s, the WEP advanced the view that the central objective of development is improvement in the well-being of the people. Thus development policies should focus on poverty eradication, meeting of the basic needs of the people and creation of remunerative employment and work opportunities ... Perhaps the high point of the WEP was the World Employment Conference of 1976, which proposed the satisfaction of basic human needs as the overriding objective of national and international development policy. The basic needs approach to development was endorsed by governments and workers' and employers' organizations from all over the world. It influenced the programmes and policies of major multilateral and bilateral development agencies, and was the precursor to the human development approach.[125]

The United Nations Development Programme's (UNDP's) original director of the HDR, Mahbub ul Haq, would later remark,

> It is fair to say that the human development paradigm is the most holistic development model that exists today. It embraces every development issue, including economic growth, social investment, people's empowerment, provision of basic needs and social safety nets, political and cultural freedoms and all other aspects of people's lives. It is neither narrowly technocratic nor overly philosophical. It is a practical reflection of life itself.[126]

Sen's influence can be seen to this day in the growing interest in multidimensional poverty and "beyond-GDP" indices. But, as important as these and other more human-centred, lived-experience metrics are, they measure *ex post* outcomes. They do not define or prioritize the universe of relevant policy inputs that can be deployed to achieve such outcomes. Performance metrics like these can help show the way, but they are not a substitute for the internalization and instrumentalization of these considerations in policy itself.

In addition, Sen's capabilities approach has been critiqued as being incomplete in the sense of missing or at least underemphasizing the important role of collective (not just individual) capabilities in advancing social welfare.[127] An economy's productive transformation depends heavily on institutionally enabled norms, incentives and capacities that influence the organization of knowledge and work and inculcate behaviours and patterns of industrial relations and investment. These collective capabilities of societies can have a profound impact on both the pace and pattern of development, particularly with respect to access and inclusion and the concentration of rents and power. Yet they remain largely outside the focus of policy and practice.[128]

The fact remains that the social contract remains largely disembodied from modern macroeconomics. The Washington Consensus neoliberal model of growth and development is widely criticized, but it remains the de facto frame of reference in government councils and university classrooms. The responsibility for this cannot be placed at the doorstep of the founders of liberal political economy; they clearly advised and expected the field of political economy to develop differently, placing parallel emphasis on markets and economic growth, on the one hand, and institutions that support broad improvement in social welfare, on the other. The abiding tendency of modern economics to assume the latter to be a residual outcome of former is clearly a case of wayward and mistaken practice rather than original sin.

Social concerns about such broader welfare considerations as inclusion, sustainability and resilience arguably loom larger today than ever before in the politics of countries. The world's economies appear to be entering a period of particularly disruptive transformation driven by the concurrent forces of automation, climate change, population ageing and geopolitical conflict. These *structural* transformations exacerbate all three of these challenges. The standard policy toolbox of the past two generations, whether the macroeconomic stimulus agenda preferred by the left or the deregulatory cost-of-capital-reduction agenda preferred by the right, are an indirect response to them. Such strategies have been applied on and off for decades and proven to be blunt and largely ineffective instruments in addressing *these* challenges, even if they have been effective at times in addressing others (e.g., combating recessions and sluggish productivity growth).

The reason is that they operate through only one of the two channels, or tracks, envisioned by Smith, Mill and Marshall (and, in their own ways, Polanyi, Sen and—particularly with respect to financial system regulation, taxation and public investment—Keynes). Despite their important philosophical differences, the centre-left and centre-right traditions come at the problem from the same point of departure. Their remedies respond to concerns about the social quality of economic growth mainly via a strategy to expand its quantity through a strengthening of demand or supply or both, in the belief that the resulting increased output will eventually translate, or trickle down, into commensurate gains in broad living standards.

The complementary systematic institutional strategy advocated by Smith, Mill and Marshall remains the road not taken by modern economics, even if it has been forced on to the political agenda from time to time by restive polities, usually in times of crisis. The social, economic and environmental costs of failing to activate this second channel of liberal political economy more directly and fully are rising. Having established that the field's original theoretical framing poses no inherent obstacle to doing so, I take up the question in the next chapter of how economic theory and policy practice should be reformulated to achieve such a rebalanced, more human-centred, growth and development model—one that accommodates living standards as an explicit rather than essentially residual feature.

NOTES

1. Adam Smith, *An Inquiry into the Nature and Causes of the Wealth of Nations* (*TWN*), London, W. Strahan & T. Cadell, 1776.
2. Ibid., Book I, Chapter II.
3. Ibid., Book IV, Chapter II.
4. Ibid., Book IV, Chapter II.
5. Ibid., Book II, Chapter II.
6. Ibid., Book I, Chapter I.
7. Ibid., Book IV, Chapter IX.
8. Ibid.
9. Ibid., Book I, Chapter X.
10. Deborah Boucoyannis, "The Equalizing Hand: Why Adam Smith Thought the Market Should Produce Wealth without Steep Inequality", *Perspectives on Politics*, Vol. 11, No. 4 (2013), p. 1055, quoting Smith, *TWN*, https://www.cambridge.org/core/journals/perspectives-on-politics/article/abs/equalizing-hand-why-adam-smith-thought-the-market-should-produce-wealth-without-steep-inequality/5F88C6D86DD80C3420E85982D72FAF50
11. Smith, *TWN*, Book I, Chapter VIII.
12. Jack Russell Weinstein, "Adam Smith on Slavery", *Adam Smith Works*, 15 May 2019, https://www.adamsmithworks.org/documents/adam-smith-on-slavery
13. Smith, *TWN*, Book IV, Chapter VII.
14. Ibid., Book IV, Chapter VII.
15. Ibid., Book I, Chapter XI.
16. Ibid., Book I, Chapter VIII.
17. Ibid., Book I, Chapter X.
18. Adam Smith, *TWN*, ed. Edwin Cannan, London, Methuen, 1904, pp. 64–5.
19. Smith, *TWN*, Book II, Chapter IV.
20. Boucoyannis, "The Equalizing Hand", p. 1061, quoting Smith, *TWN*.

21. Smith, *TWN*, Book III, Chapter IV.
22. Smith, *TWN* (1904), p. 217.
23. Ibid., p. 144.
24. Smith, *TWN*, Book V, Chapter I.
25. Ibid., Book I, Chapter XI.
26. Ibid., Book IV, Chapter VIII.
27. Ibid., Book I, Chapter X.
28. Ibid.
29. Ibid., Book I, Chapter 8.
30. Ibid., Book V, Chapter II.
31. Ibid., Book II, Chapter II.
32. Smith, *TWN* (1904), p. 185.
33. Jacob Viner, "Adam Smith and Laissez-Faire", *Journal of Political Economy*, Vol. 35, No. 2 (1927), p. 209, quoting Smith, *TWN*, https://www.jstor.org/stable/1823421#metadata_info_tab_contents
34. Smith, *TWN* (1904), p. 272.
35. Ibid., p. 327.
36. Ibid., p. 216.
37. Ibid., p. 377.
38. Ibid., p. 329.
39. Boucoyannis, "The Equalizing Hand", p. 1059, quoting Smith, *TWN*.
40. John Stuart Mill, "On Liberty", in John Gray, ed., *On Liberty and Other Essays*, Oxford, Oxford University Press, 1991, p. 15.
41. Ibid., pp. 16, 83–4, 86–8.
42. Richard Boyd, "John Stuart Mill on Economic Liberty and Human Flourishing", in Michael R. Strain and Stan A. Veuger, eds, *Economic Freedom and Human Flourishing: Perspectives from Political Philosophy*, Washington, DC, American Enterprise Institute, 2016, pp. 113–14.
43. John Stuart Mill, *Principles of Political Economy*, Vol. 2, Book V, Chapter 11.
44. Ibid.
45. Ibid.
46. Ibid., Vol. 1, Book II, Chapter 1.
47. Ibid.
48. John Stuart Mill, *Autobiography*, Boston, Houghton Mifflin, 1969, p. 100.
49. John Stuart Mill, *Principles of Political Economy*, Toronto, University of Toronto Press, 1965, p. 765. See also Virginie Gouverneur, "John Stuart Mill on Wage Inequalities between Men and Women", Working Paper, Bureau d'économie théorique et appliquée, October 2018.
50. Boyd, "John Stuart Mill on Economic Liberty and Human Flourishing", p. 121, quoting Mill, *Principles of Political Economy*.
51. Mill, *Principles of Political Economy*, Vol. 1, Book II, Chapter 1.

52. Boyd, "John Stuart Mill on Economic Liberty and Human Flourishing", p. 118, quoting Mill, *Principles of Political Economy*.
53. Mill, Principles of Political Economy, Book IV, Chapter 6.
54. H.O. Pappe, "Mill and Tocqueville", *Journal of the History of Ideas*, Vol. 25, No. 2 (1964), pp. 217–34.
55. Alfred Marshall, *Principles of Economics*, London, Macmillan, 1961, Chapter 1.
56. Mill, *Principles of Political Economy*, Vol. 1, Introductory.
57. Marshall, *Principles of Economics*, p. 139.
58. Ibid., pp. 161–2.
59. Ibid., pp. 2–3.
60. Katia Caldari and Tamotsu Nishizawa, "Marshall's Welfare Economics and 'Welfare': A Reappraisal Based on His Unpublished Manuscript on Progress", *History of Economic Ideas*, Vol. 22, No. 1 (2014); Tamotsu Nishizawa, Katia Caldari and Marco Dardi, *Aspects of the History of Welfare Economics*, Pisa, Fabrizio Serra, 2014, p. 57.
61. Ibid., p. 56.
62. Alfred Marshall and Mary Paley, *The Economics of Industry*, Bristol, Thoemmes Press, 1994, pp. 28, 32.
63. John K. Whitaker, ed., *The Correspondence of Alfred Marshall, Economist*, Cambridge, UK, Cambridge University Press, 1996, Vol. 5.
64. Marshall, *Principles of Economics*, p. 532.
65. Ibid., p. 562.
66. Tamotsu Nishizawa, "Alfred Marshall on Human Capital and Future Generations", *Economic Review*, Vol, 53, No. 4 (2002), p. 311, quoting Marshall, *Principles of Economics*.
67. Marshall, *Principles of Economics*, pp. 227–8.
68. Whitaker, *The Correspondence of Alfred Marshall*, Vol. 5.
69. Ibid., Vol. 3, pp. 235–6.
70. Lionel Robbins, *An Essay on the Nature and Significance of Economic Science*, London, Macmillan, 1932, https://cdn.mises.org/Essay%20on%20the%20Nature%20and%20Significance%20of%20Economic%20Science_2.pdf
71. A.C. Pigou, *The Economics of Welfare*, London, Macmillan, 1920, p. 11.
72. Ibid., p. 12.
73. Alfred Marshall, *The Present Position of Economics*, London, Macmillan, 1885, https://books.google.ch/books?id=4f4OAAAAQAAJ&printsec=frontcover&source=gbs_ge_summary_r&cad=0#v=onepage&q&f=false
74. Pigou, *The Economics of Welfare*, p. 12.
75. A.C. Pigou, *The Economics of Welfare*, Palgrave Macmillan, 1920, pp. 47 and 53.
76. For a recent example, see Meghnad Desai, The Poverty of Political Economy: How Economics Abandoned the Poor, Harper Collins India, 2022.

77. Tamotsu Nishizawa, "An Alternative History of Welfare Economics and Alfred Marshall: History of Welfare Economic Studies Reconsidered", presentation at Teiko University, pp. 20–21, 43.
78. See, for example, Marjorie Bloy, "The 1662 Settlement Act", *Victorian Web*, 12 November 2002, https://victorianweb.org/history/poorlaw/settle.html
79. Emma Rothschild, "Adam Smith and Conservative Economics", *Economic History Review*, New Series, Vol. 45, No. 1 (1992), pp. 84–5, https://www.jstor.org/stable/pdf/2598329.pdf?refreqid=fastly-default%3A9802e811cdccdf15e4d19b03232a00b4&ab_segments=0%2Fbasic_search_gsv2%2Fcontrol&origin=search-results
80. Salim Rashid, "Adam Smith's Rise to Fame: A Reexamination of the Evidence", *Eighteenth Century*, Vol. 23, No. 1 (1982), p. 82, https://www.jstor.org/stable/41467257?read-now=1&refreqid=excelsior%3A1216a984a28a9e9c6b8ba205ed5ef599&seq=19#page_scan_tab_contents
81. Lord Acton, *Letters of Lord Acton to Mary, Daughter of the Right Hon. W. E. Gladstone*, London, George Allen, 1904, p. 92.
82. Rothschild, "Adam Smith and Conservative Economics", p. 88.
83. C. Menger, "Die Social-Theorien der classischen National-Oekonomie und die moderne Wirtschaftspolitik", p. 223, as quoted in Rothschild, "Adam Smith and Conservative Economics", pp. 88–9.
84. UK Parliament, "Reforming Society in the 19th Century", https://www.parliament.uk/about/living-heritage/transformingsociety/livinglearning/19thcentury/
85. Ibid.; see also, for example, Anderzej Dniejko, "A Chronology of Social Reform and Social Change in Great Britain in the Nineteenth and Early Twentieth Centuries", *Victorian Web*, 15 February 2014. https://victorianweb.org/history/socialism/chronology.html
86. Stein Kuhnle, "The Beginnings of the Nordic Welfare States: Similarities and Differences", *Acta Sociologica*, Vol. 21, No. 1 supplement (1978), p. 13, https://journals.sagepub.com/doi/pdf/10.1177/000169937802101s02
87. See, for example, George Rudé, "Protest and Punishment in Nineteenth-Century Britain", *Albion*, Vol. 5, No. 1 (1973), pp. 1–23, https://www.jstor.org/stable/pdf/4048354.pdf?refreqid=excelsior%3A8cc5b71cdab54e4977fce3cf359e36e4&ab_segments=&origin=
88. *Social Security*, "Otto von Bismarck", https://www.ssa.gov/history/ottob.html
89. Stein Kuhnle and Anne Sander, "The Emergence of the Western Welfare State", in Francis G. Castles, Stephan Leibfried, Jane Lewis, Herbert Obinger and Christopher Pierson, eds, *The Oxford Handbook of the Welfare State*, Oxford, Oxford University Press, 2010, p. 69. https://books.google.ch/books?id=lLawRZJhlqAC&pg=PA67&redir_esc=y#v=onepage&q&f=false

90. E. Phelan, "The Contribution of the ILO to Peace", *International Labour Review*, Vol. 59, No. 6 (1949), pp. 607–32.
91. Constitution of the International Labour Organization, Treaty of Versailles, Part XIII, 1919, https://www.ilo.org/dyn/normlex/en/f?p=NORMLEXPUB:55:0::NO::P55_TYPE,P55_LANG,P55_DOCUMENT,P55_NODE:KEY,en,ILOC,/Document
92. Franklin D. Roosevelt, Address to the International Labor Organization, 6 November 1941, *American Presidency Project*, http://www.presidency.ucsb.edu/ws/index.php?pid=16037
93. Gerry Rodgers, Eddy Lee, Lee Swepston and Jasmien Van Daele, *The International Labour Organization and the Quest for Social Justice, 1919–2009*, Geneva, ILO, 2009, p. 3, https://www.ilo.org/wcmsp5/groups/public/@dgreports/@dcomm/@publ/documents/publication/wcms_104643.pdf
94. https://www.ilo.org/dyn/normlex/en/f?p=1000:12000:::NO
95. This principle was one of nine adopted in the recommendations of the Commission *on International Labour Legislation appointed by the 1919 Paris Peace Conference. The Commission, which was tasked by the Conference with developing recommendations on the design of what became the ILO,* was chaired by Samuel Gompers, head of the American Federation of Labour (AFL), and included representatives of eight other countries. See ILO, *Paris Peace Conference (1919–1920): Commission on International Labour Legislation*, Geneva, 1923, pp. 305–8, https://labordoc.ilo.org/discovery/delivery/41ILO_INST:41ILO_V1/1257239620002676
96. ILO Declaration of Philadelphia, 10 May 1944, p. 1. https://www.ilo.org/legacy/english/inwork/cb-policy-guide/declarationofPhiladelphia1944.pdf
97. Geoffrey M. Hodgson, *The Evolution of Institutional Economics: Agency, Structure, and Darwinism in American Institutionalism*, London, Routledge, 2004, p. 14.
98. Thorsten Veblen, "Why Is Economics Not an Evolutionary Science?" *Cambridge Journal of Economics*, Vol. 22 (1998), pp. 403–14.
99. Warren J. Samuels, "Foreword", in Rick Tilman, ed., *Thorstein Veblen and His Critics, 1891–1963: Conservative, Liberal, and Radical Perspectives*, Princeton, NJ, Princeton University Press, 1992, pp. ix–x.
100. John R. Commons, *Legal Foundations of Capitalism*, New York, Macmillan, 1924, p. 6, https://socialsciences.mcmaster.ca/econ/ugcm/3ll3/commons/LegalFoundationsCapitalism.pdf
101. Hodgson, *The Evolution of Institutional Economics*, p. 4.
102. ILO, Declaration of Philadelphia.
103. Smith, *TWN*, Book I, Chapter VIII.
104. Mill, *Principles of Political Economy* (1965), p. 811.
105. Whitaker, *The Correspondence of Alfred Marshall*, Vol. 5.

106. Karl Polanyi, *The Great Transformation: The Political and Economic Origins of Our Time*, New York, Farrar & Rinehart, 1944, p. 29.
107. Karl Polanyi, *The Great Transformation: The Political and Economic Origins of Our Time*, Boston, Beacon Press, 1957, p. 76.
108. C.E. Ayres, *The Theory of Economic Progress*, quoted in J. Ron Stanfield, "The Institutional Economics of Karl Polanyi", *Journal of Economic Issues*, Vol. 14, No. 3 (1980), p. 605, https://www.jstor.org/stable/pdf/4224945.pdf
109. Polanyi, *The Great Transformation*, p. 257.
110. Ibid., p. 256.
111. Simon Kuznets, "Economic Growth and Income Inequality", *American Economic Review*, Volume 45, No. 1 (1955), pp. 1–28, https://www.jstor.org/stable/1811581#metadata_info_tab_contents. See also Simon Kuznets, "Inequalities in the size distribution of income', *Economic Growth and Structure: Selected Essays*, London, Heinemann, 1965, pp. 288–303.
112. Seem for example, Daron Acemoglu and James Robinson, "The Political Economy of the Kuznets Curve", *Review of Development Economics*, Vol. 6 No. 2 (2002), pp. 183–203.
113. Sangheon Lee and Megan Gerecke, "Economic Development and Inequality: Revisiting the Kuznets Curve", in Janine Berg, ed., *Labour Markets, Institutions and Inequality: Building Just Societies in the 21st Century*, Cheltenham and Geneva, Edward Elgar and ILO, 2014.
114. Ibid., pp. 48–50.
115. J.M. Keynes, *The General Theory of Employment, Interest and Money*, London, Macmillan, 1936, p. 372.
116. Ibid., p. 376.
117. Ibid., p. 380–1.
118. Ibid., p. 378–9.
119. *Stanford Encyclopedia of Philosophy*, "The Capability Approach", 10 December 2020, https://plato.stanford.edu/entries/capability-approach/. See also Amartya Sen, *Commodities and Capabilities*, Amsterdam, North-Holland, 1985.
120. David A. Clark, "The Capability Approach: Its Development, Critiques and Recent Advances", Economic and Social Research Council Global Poverty Research Group, p. 10, https://base.socioeco.org/docs/developments_critiques_advances.pdf
121. See Jean Dreze and Amartya K. Sen, *Hunger and Public Action*, Oxford, Clarendon Press, 1989; Amartya K. Sen, *Development as Freedom*, Oxford, Oxford University Press, 1999.
122. https://hdr.undp.org/data-center/human-development-index#/indicies/HDI
123. https://hdr.undp.org/

124. Amartya Sen, *Poverty and Famines: An Essay on Entitlement and Deprivation*, Geneva and Oxford, ILO and Clarendon Press, 1981, https://www.prismaweb.org/nl/wp-content/uploads/2017/06/Poverty-and-famines%E2%94%82Amartya-Sen%E2%94%821981.pdf
125. Dharam Ghai, "Building Knowledge Organizations: Achieving Excellence," unpublished paper, 1999), pp. 3–4, https://www.ilo.org/wcmsp5/groups/public/%2D%2D-dgreports/%2D%2D-inst/documents/genericdocument/wcms_193047.pdf. Ghai held a number of ILO posts between 1973 and 1987, including chief, Research Branch, WEP; head of the secretariat for the World Employment Conference of 1976; and chief, Rural Employment Policies Branch.
126. Mahbub ul Haq, *Reflections on Human Development*, Oxford, Oxford University Press, 1995, p. 23.
127. For an excellent overview and crystallization of this critique, see Antonio Andreoni, Ha-Joon Chang and Isabel Estevez, "The Missing Dimensions of the Human Capabilities Approach: Collective and Productive," *The European Journal of Development Research*, vol. 33(2), 179–205, March 2021, https://link.springer.com/article/10.1057/s41287-020-00356-y.
128. See for example Ha-Joon Chang and Antonio Andreoni, "Institutions and the process of industrialisation: Towards a theory of social capability development," in: Nissanke, M., Ocampo, J.A. (eds) *The Palgrave Handbook of Development Economics*, Palgrave Macmillan, Cham. 2019, https://link.springer.com/chapter/10.1007/978-3-030-14000-7_12.

Open Access This chapter is licensed under the terms of the Creative Commons Attribution 4.0 International License (http://creativecommons.org/licenses/by/4.0/), which permits use, sharing, adaptation, distribution and reproduction in any medium or format, as long as you give appropriate credit to the original author(s) and the source, provide a link to the Creative Commons licence and indicate if changes were made.

The images or other third party material in this chapter are included in the chapter's Creative Commons licence, unless indicated otherwise in a credit line to the material. If material is not included in the chapter's Creative Commons licence and your intended use is not permitted by statutory regulation or exceeds the permitted use, you will need to obtain permission directly from the copyright holder.

Pioneers of Human-Centred Economic Thought

Adam Smith

John Stuart Mill

Alfred Marshall

Thorstein Veblen

John R. Commons

Arthur Cecil Pigou

John Maynard Keynes

Amartya Sen

Herman Daly

Gro Harlem Brundtland

ILO Director-General Edward J. Phelan signing the Declaration of Philadelphia at the White House in the presence of (left to right) President Franklin D. Roosevelt, Cordell Hull (US Secretary of State), Walter Nash (President of the 26th Session of the ILC), Frances Perkins (US Secretary of Labor) and Lindsay Rogers (ILO Assistant Director), Washington DC, May 17, 1944. Photo credit: ILO Archives

Indira Gandhi, Prime Minister of India, addressing the UN Conference on the Human Environment in Stockholm, Sweden, June 14, 1972. Photo credit: United Nations

Sadako Ogata (right), former UN High Commissioner for Refugees, and Professor Amartya Sen (left), economist and Nobel Prize laureate, present the "Report of the Commission on Human Security" to UN Secretary-General Kofi Annan, May 1, 2003. Photo credit: United Nations/Eskinder Debebe

CHAPTER 4

From the Wealth to the Living Standards of Nations: Internalizing the Social Contract in Macroeconomic Theory and Policy

Since the publication by Adam Smith of *The Wealth of Nations* nearly 250 years ago, humanity has made tremendous economic and social progress. Most of the world's population have become more affluent and are living healthier, longer and more productive lives in no small part owing to the insights and tools of liberal economics. Nevertheless, Chap. 2 presented evidence of significant shortcomings in its track record on inclusion, sustainability and resilience. Deficits in these three areas are serious and persistent, and they have been fuelling a decline in social cohesion and a rise in political polarization in many countries and regions.

Chapter 3 investigated whether these deficits can be traced to the discipline's original conceptualization. It concluded that, to the contrary, the field's most influential founding theorists and codifiers explicitly contextualized their insights about the power of market-based resource allocation in a larger perspective and complementary set of prescriptions. These emphasized the important role of institutions—legal and other norms, policy incentives and public administrative capacity in multiple domains—in helping to translate the increased economic growth enabled by market-based resource allocation into broad improvement in social welfare. Smith, John Stuart Mill and Alfred Marshall considered increased production and national income, the wealth of a nation, as a means and not an end in itself. The ultimate purpose of an economy, they each emphasized, was to advance the material well-being, or standard of living, of society as a whole.

© The Author(s) 2024
R. Samans, *Human-Centred Economics*,
https://doi.org/10.1007/978-3-031-37435-7_4

Nevertheless, during the twentieth century the discipline grew far more focused on production than on distribution, drawn by the pressing need to boost output during the Great Depression and Second World War and the related advent of Keynesian demand management techniques and national income accounting. These achievements made and are continuing to make an enormous contribution to human welfare. However, the parts of the economics profession ostensibly dedicated to the study of social welfare—e.g., welfare and social choice economics—came to be narrowly focused on modelling utility-maximizing behaviour by individuals and organizations within markets and extrapolating these micro-level insights into highly abstract "social utility functions" based on simplified normative assumptions, e.g., equal distribution of utility gains, weighted distribution or Rawlsian distribution (initial fulfilment of minimum thresholds). These models have little to say about well-being or societal welfare in the macroeconomic sense emphasized by Smith, Mill and Marshall. They mirror the ongoing emphasis of most of the rest of the profession on the drivers of allocative efficiency within markets and the role that these play in optimizing the overall size of the economic pie, as opposed to the drivers of socio-economic inclusion, sustainability and resilience and the role that these play in optimizing the pie's distribution and contribution to the material well-being of society as a whole.

From time to time, scholars and polities have pushed back against this imbalance in the theory and practice of capitalism, notably in the form of rights- and capabilities-based critiques and labour and social protection legislation, as summarized in Chap. 3. More often than not, the latter has been triggered not by theory and pedagogy but by social and political pressures arising from economic crises. The actions taken by many countries during the COVID-19 crisis to expand their social protection programmes and occupational safety and health (OSH) requirements are a recent case in point. Nevertheless, this imbalance in the standard liberal growth model—its disproportionate emphasis on increasing allocative efficiency through markets relative to improving distributional equity and sustainability through institutions—persists.

In effect, inclusion, sustainability and resilience were lost in translation during the evolution of eighteenth- and nineteenth-century political economy into twentieth-century economic science. These important priorities and the range of institutions that facilitate their implementation have yet to meaningfully penetrate the dominant *production cum capital accumulation* mental model of growth and development. This is despite the increasingly insistent pleadings of political leaders, who have repeatedly committed to pursue fundamental reform of their economies in these three respects, beginning at the 1972 United Nations Conference on the Human Environment in Stockholm and continuing with the 1992 Rio Summit on Environment and Development, 2008 and 2009 G20 Summits, 2015 UN Paris climate agreement and 2030 Agenda, 2019 ILO Centenary Declaration and, most recently, the 2022 Kunming-Montreal Global Biodiversity Framework. Taken literally, each of the outcome documents of these historic summits is an unfulfilled promise of deep economic reform.

Smith, Mill and Marshall established the theoretical foundations of a more balanced growth and development model long ago through their explicit distinction between social welfare and economic efficiency and their corresponding explicit emphasis on institutions as well as markets. The principles they articulated in this respect have been refined and extended by the likes of Veblen, Commons, Sen, North, Acemoglu, Rodrik and others. However, the standard model remains largely unreformed by these insights; in economic theory and policy practice, growth and production remain largely disconnected from living standards and distribution.

Institutions are the underexploited link. They play a vitally important role both in production and distribution and in capturing synergies between the two. Rebalancing liberal economics by elevating and formalizing the role of institutions in core economic theory and practice is an increasingly urgent priority. The prospect of a twenty-first-century version of Polanyi's Great Transformation cannot be discounted, as algorithmic automation, net-zero regulation, population ageing and geopolitical and geoeconomic fragmentation gather force.

The place to begin is a recognition that production of goods and services (GDP) is just a top-line measure of national economic performance, analogous to the way that revenues (sales) are commonly considered the top-line measure of business performance and profits are considered the desired bottom-line result.[1] The bottom-line way that societies—people—judge their economy's success is progress in the living standard of their household and community, i.e., in the lived experience of ordinary families. And yet, like in a business, it is very difficult to grow the bottom line over time without increasing the top line. GDP growth remains vitally important to progress in living standards for the simple reason that it is easier for everyone to receive a larger piece of pie if the entire pie, in this case the national economy, is expanding.

To be certain, the correlation between economic growth, or change in real GDP per capita, and broad progress in living standards is strongly positive, particularly with respect to poverty alleviation.[2] However, it is far from lockstep. The evidence suggests that this relationship can be closer in poorer countries than more affluent ones, which is intuitive given that economies dominated by subsistence agriculture and having little industrial production and service sector activity are starting from a low base. The superior labour productivity associated with more specialized and industrial uses of labour is the *sine qua non* of economic growth, as Smith famously argued. A very poor economy cannot become significantly richer, at least not durably so, without such a structural transformation of its economy and the more productive and remunerative deployment of its workforce that this enables. Over the medium to long term, labour productivity growth is also the main driver of living standards in wealthier countries. But the incremental payoff from additional economic growth for poverty reduction and living standards tends to decline as countries become rich.[3] In these countries, the challenge is more about inclusion and distribution—involving more of the population in their already substantial industrial and other productive economic activity.

In fact, production and distribution both matter greatly—in poor and rich countries alike. And institutions matter greatly for both production and distribution, as emphasized by the original principles of liberal political economy. Many of the world's least developed countries remain mired in extreme poverty, despite large infusions of foreign aid over decades, in no small part because they have struggled to assimilate the lessons of the East Asian miracle; for a variety of reasons they have failed to develop an enabling environment of rules and institutional systems and administrative capacities conducive to productive investment, job creation and human development—the cornerstones of economic growth. At the same time, many of the world's middle- and high-income countries have failed during the course of their development to sufficiently upgrade aspects of their institutional enabling environment which promote inclusion, sustainability and resilience. Regulations, policy incentives and public investments and administrative capacity in certain areas of economic policy help to diffuse the benefits of national income across society as a country develops, often in ways that further increase labour productivity and economic growth.

Thus, achieving strong *bottom-line* national economic performance—broad progress in household living standards—requires policymakers to adopt an explicit twin focus, as Smith, Mill and Marshall taught. Their work—as well as that of a number of leading twentieth-century figures in the field of institutional economics, such as Veblen, Commons, Polanyi and Sen—strongly suggests that governments at all levels of economic development should formally adopt a dual economic policy anchor or strategic focus—GDP and median household living standards—in order to capture the material well-being or lived experience of people much more directly in their conceptualization, pursuit and measurement of economic progress. This is particularly true when markets are undergoing substantial liberalization, integration or technological or environmental disruption, since these impose increased human costs in the form of dislocation, insecurity and income dispersion. Each of these two policy anchors requires deliberate policy effort and performance measurement in its own right. Moreover, there is an important feedback loop between them, a circle that can be either vicious or virtuous depending upon circumstance and policy.

Like a person who can only see through one eye, standard liberal economics suffers from limited depth perception and peripheral vision in managing the performance of economies because it neither conceptualizes nor sets policy priorities, nor measures national economic performance explicitly and simultaneously through these two lenses. Rebalancing capitalism in the twenty-first century—reclaiming it from its late-twentieth-century neoliberal diversion—begins with reconstituting economics, both scholarship and policy practice, so that it is focused on cultivating the *median living standards* at least as much as the *aggregate wealth* of nations. This in turn requires a better understanding of the mix of policies and public and private sector institutional features that can best activate the latent synergy between the two.

This new principle—that GDP growth and broad progress in living standards deserve equally explicit and direct policy effort—is also an old one, to judge from the writings of the eighteenth- and nineteenth-century founders of market economics. But instrumentalizing it in the twenty-first century will require countries, and especially capitalist democracies, to revise the mental model, policy toolbox and progress metric they have relied upon to develop their economies.

An elaborate canon of theory and policy tools for conceptualizing and influencing GDP growth has accumulated over many decades of scholarship and practice. But comparatively little has developed in this respect regarding living standards and their relationship with economic growth. As a result, the tree of accumulated economics knowledge is lopsided and at risk of toppling over and taking the rest of the Enlightenment's precious legacy of individual liberty and empowerment with it. What should have been one of its major branches of enquiry is severely stunted, whether owing to lack of imagination, path dependency or the natural tendency of analysts to go where the data are, which happened to be GDP after the establishment of national income accounting in the 1930s and 1940s.

At the centre of the prevailing mental model of economic progress, familiar to everyone who has studied university macroeconomics, is the aggregate production function. This is an analytical framework that deconstructs the growth process into its main building blocks or "factors of production". It typically takes the form of an equation in which an economy's output or overall production of goods and services (Y) is represented as a function of available production technology (A) and the quantity of capital (K), labour (L) and sometimes other factors such as natural resources (R), human capital, etc. Thus:

$$Y = A \times f(K, L, R...)$$

The aggregate production function provides a cognitive roadmap for addressing the challenge of raising the level of production in an economy (GDP). It has been the focus of extensive theoretical and empirical enquiry. Great effort has gone into developing policies to optimize this equation by strengthening these individual factor inputs through better policy and understanding of how they relate to each other.

Policymakers need an analogous mental map for enabling the broad diffusion of material well-being—an aggregate distribution function—in order to fully operationalize the principle that an economy's production (GDP) and median living standards deserve equal and parallel emphasis. On the inspiration of its production function counterpart, such an aggregate distribution function should deconstruct the main drivers or channels by which gains in a country's standard of living manifest in distributed fashion across society. By modelling such *factors of distribution*, we can better understand the full range of policy levers available to promote this process of diffusion—that is to say, to render the economic development process more socially inclusive, environmentally sustainable, and resilient.

There is no single, generally accepted definition of "standard of living" or "material well-being" within any social science let alone across all of the relevant ones. However, *employment and entrepreneurial opportunity*—the availability of decent work and livelihoods—certainly lies at that heart of the concept inasmuch as the great majority of the income of median households in rich and poor countries alike is derived from labour compensation of some form. In addition, work confers skills that can help to improve the resilience of workers and their households to economic and social change. Finally, decent work also confers a certain purpose and dignity upon one's everyday existence. This may be more of an intangible than material aspect of well-being, but for many people it is just as important as the money they earn.

Disposable income—financial resources available to spend after taxes and debt service—is obviously fundamental to one's standard of living. It is the principal enabler of consumption, that is, purchases ranging from life's immediate necessities to its more ephemeral pleasures. Whether one is well or poorly paid for productive services rendered and whether equal work is equally remunerated are key determinants in the material well-being of workers and their households. A household's disposable income also determines its ability to invest in future well-being, for example in the acquisition of skills and competencies that lead to greater employment opportunity or in self-insurance against risks or unforeseen developments.

The *availability and affordability of material necessities*, such as housing, food, shelter and energy, also have a major influence on a household's standard of living. Indeed, in all but the wealthiest households, such expenses account for a large proportion of the use of disposable income. They therefore tend to represent a major variable in the typical household's perception of its standard of living.

Basic *economic security*—a reasonable degree of protection against major risks to a household's ability to provide for itself—is another vital element of its standard of living. Such risks include loss of employment, serious illness, disability and old age. In the absence of basic social protection in these areas, households remain in constant, if underlying, anxiety about the prospect of downward mobility, i.e., a sudden, sharp drop in their standard of living.

Meanwhile, basic *environmental security*—a reasonable degree of protection against risks of disruption to the household's natural environment—is a rising preoccupation and important element of material well-being for many families. This applies not only to disruptions related to the climate and global warming, such as droughts, floods and heat stress, all of which can seriously and rapidly impair livelihoods, property and labour productivity, but also to threats to the same from air, water and soil pollution and collapsing natural habitats and species populations. The viability and quality of the natural environment is an integral part of material well-being for a wide spectrum of households, from those depending on it directly for their livelihoods, to those whose health is threatened directly or indirectly by its degradation, to those relying on it for a significant share of their leisure and recreation.

Thus, an economy's aggregate distribution function can be represented as follows:

$$Z = f(O, I, N, EcS, EnS)$$

where Z represents the median household's standard of living, O is its employment and entrepreneurial opportunity, I is its disposable income, N is the affordability and availability of its material necessities, EcS is its economic security or capacity to withstand adverse shocks, and EnS is its environmental security.

These five "factors of distribution" represent the core components of family or household material well-being. They are the main channels through which a country's standard of living is expressed in the lived experience of ordinary people, defined for these purposes as households earning the median level of income.

Combining the two functions enables us to represent the drivers of a nation's material well-being more completely:

$$W = A \times f(K, L, R) + f(O, I, N, EcS, EnS)$$

This is an economy's aggregate social welfare function. It comprises both an aggregate production function and an aggregate distribution function, reflecting the crucial importance for a nation's socioeconomic progress of *both* its overall level of national income (the size of the pie) and the everyday lived experience or material well-being and security of its people (the breadth of social participation in its benefits).

A few important caveats are in order. This is not a mathematical function; it is a representation of a social science system—a mental model or heuristic. Not only do its two component functions represent different things (output of goods and services at the national level versus material well-being at the household level), but some of the latter's factor inputs are also less quantifiably measurable than those of the former. That said, the aggregate production function itself has been demonstrated to have limited, if any, meaningful mathematical validity, despite its ambitions in this regard when it was originally developed and empirically tested in the mid twentieth century.[4] The aggregate social welfare function described here has no such pretension. It is simply a cognitive roadmap—an expanded and thus more balanced and complete way of thinking about how to mobilize economic progress in the modern world, in which inequality or *relative* poverty and insecurity is at least as big a problem as absolute poverty for many countries and their citizens.

This rebalanced mental model of national economic progress resurrects the lapsed first principle of Smith, Mill and Marshall that growth through greater allocative efficiency is a necessary but not sufficient condition for the ultimate measure of a nation's economic performance: improvement in its general standard of living. It does so by formally integrating the critical role of institutions—particularly those that promote inclusion, sustainability and resilience—into the standard "neoclassical synthesis" growth and development model, restructuring it to explicitly cover both the productive quantity and social quality of growth—that is, both the wealth *and* the living standards of nations.

Such a reformulation of the standard growth and development model has a key policy implication for both developed and developing countries: the production and distribution functions of their economies require equal and ongoing cultivation. Like the supply of capital and labour and the pace of technical change reflected in the aggregate production function, the strength of each of the aggregate distribution function's factor inputs is heavily influenced by policy rules and incentives as well as public and private institutional capacities.

Box 4.1 is a representation of this institutional ecosystem, a summary of the primary domains of policy and institutional strength corresponding to each of the aggregate distribution function's five factor inputs.

Box 4.1 Aggregate Distribution Function: Policy and Institutional Ecosystem

Employment and entrepreneurial opportunity (O)

Competition and rents

- Anti-trust
- Anti-corruption
- Property rights and land tenure rules and enforcement capacity
- Technology governance, e.g., intellectual property rights, data ownership and access

Investment in real-economy productive capacity

- Corporate governance rules and protections
- Financial system governance rules and protections
- Public investment in infrastructure, R&D, key industries, public works

Labour force skills, transitions and participation

- Skills, e.g., basic K-12 education,[5] school-to-work, tertiary education, lifelong education
- Active labour market policies, e.g., employment services, training, skills matching, income maintenance, credentialing
- Rights: elimination of forced and child labour; non-discrimination, e.g., gender, race and ethnicity, disabilities, age, etc.
- Formalization of work arrangements

Disposable income (I)

Wage compensation

- Minimum/living wage regulations
- Rights, e.g., freedom of association and collective bargaining
- Social dialogue rules, institutions, practices
- Taxation of wage income and relative treatment of earned and unearned income

Non-wage compensation

- Health insurance rules, policy incentives
- Pension rules, policy incentives

(*continued*)

Box 4.1 (continued)
- Dependent care rights, benefits, incentives
- Working hours, annual leave, work–life balance regulations
- Profit-sharing and employee, community ownership regulations, incentives

Availability and affordability of material necessities (N)

Regulation, policy incentives, and subsidies

- Water and sanitation
- Food
- Housing
- Energy
- Transport
- Telecommunications
- Recreation

Economic security (EcS)

Social protection—coverage and adequacy of benefits

- Health care
- Pension
- Unemployment insurance
- Disability
- Anti-poverty

Worker protection regulation and enforcement capacity

- Occupational safety and health
- Arbitrary dismissal
- Consumer protection

Asset-building/wealth accumulation policies and incentives

- Homeownership
- Private pensions
- Business ownership
- Small saver protection

(*continued*)

> **Box 4.1 (continued)**
> **Environmental security (EnS)**
> *Climate change policies*
> - Mitigation
> - Adaptation
>
> *Other natural capital regulation*
> - Water
> - Air
> - Soil
> - Natural habitat and biodiversity

These are the primary areas of policy and institutional design that influence the nature and extent to which a country's rising prosperity (traditionally understood as GDP growth) takes expression in a general improvement in its standard of living. As discussed in greater depth in Chap. 5, this process is far from automatic within countries or uniform across them. Policy choices within and across these policy domains make a big difference, resulting in considerable variation in median household living standards among countries with similar levels of GDP per capita.

In short, this policy and institutional ecosystem is the de facto income distribution system—or, more precisely, living standards diffusion mechanism—of modern market economies. It is the practical manifestation of their social contracts—how they apply their society's values with respect to inclusion, sustainability and resilience to the rules of the game within their economies.

This institutional infrastructure tends to be constructed over time in an ad hoc and piecemeal manner. In many countries, it remains poorly or unevenly developed or has been left to wither on the vine because policymakers have not been trained to think of it *as a system* (a "function" in economics parlance) that has an important bearing on *bottom-line* national economic performance and therefore requires deliberate, ongoing construction. Most top policymakers as well as the economists who advise them tend to be macroeconomists or financial market specialists who have been conditioned by modern economic science to treat living standards mainly as a residual—a trickle-down outcome of more efficient and better capitalized production. They therefore concentrate on policies (macroeconomic, financial stability, trade) that boost the economy's top-line performance as measured by GDP, asset prices and trade flows, rather than on domains like these which are particularly important in shaping its bottom-line intended outcome: broad-based progress in household living standards.

This policy framework and the aggregate distribution function to which it corresponds are tools to help modify these reflexes, to rebalance liberal economics away from patterns of thought and behaviour which have developed over the past century and especially the last four decades. They are vehicles to help restore the explicit dual focus of classical political economy on markets, production and national income, on the one hand, and institutions, distribution and broad social welfare, on the other. Ours is a century that badly needs economies—and economists—to establish a better balance and stronger synergy between the two.

Towards Human-Centred Economics

Economics and capitalism are ripe for fundamental reform. And while it is important not to throw the baby out with the bathwater (markets, production and economic growth remain important challenges about which modern economics has much to contribute), it is also important not to underestimate the current degree of stasis within the field relative to the transformation underway in economies, business and politics.

Frustration regarding inclusion, sustainability and resilience has been building within many societies and appears to be close to the boiling point in some. The gap between the promises of political leaders and the facts on the ground in these respects has reached uncomfortably stark levels. Social patience appears to be running thin at precisely the moment when a major cyclical challenge (the unwinding of over a decade of unsustainable macroeconomic stimulus) is coinciding with three extraordinary shocks (the break in US–China economic relations, COVID-19 pandemic and Russia–Ukraine war) and increased disruption from climate change and automation.

We appear to have arrived at another hinge point of history when the liberal tradition is being challenged to evolve, to summon the imagination and will necessary to pre-empt a gathering storm of economic, social and political disruption that has the potential to rip it asunder. It nearly missed the boat in this regard a century ago, as it descended into financial panic, depression, industrial unrest and political extremism in the 1920s and 1930s. Can it respond more proactively this time around? Can economists find a better way to help the world's political leaders deliver what they have promised in multiple international declarations—a growth and development model that is stronger for being more inclusive, sustainable and resilient?

That is the spirit in which this conceptual model and policy framework are presented. The aggregate social welfare and distribution functions formally integrate important institutionally enabled dimensions of social welfare into the standard mental model of economic growth and development. They define the social contract in practical terms and insert it into the core of macroeconomic theory. In so doing, they provide a formula for better reconciling the rights-based and economic-utility-based conceptions of economic progress, which have been like two ships passing in the night for a very long time.

In other words, these are concepts and tools for re-embedding economics in society, to use Polanyi's terminology. Placing institutions that matter for distribution and social welfare at the heart of liberal economics in this manner would go a long way towards overcoming its long-standing blind spot with respect to inclusion, sustainability and resilience—that is to say, the weakness of its implied assumption that these matters are ultimately sorted out through the indirect, trickle-down effects of growth. It would help to make market economies—and the intellectual discipline of economics—more *human-centred*, that is, more focused on living standards and the lived experience of people and less on GDP and financial markets.

The aggregate distribution function looks at national economic strategy and performance through the other end of the telescope—from the bottom-up perspective of the material well-being and security of households as opposed to the top-down, abstract statistical construct of national income. Its vantage point is the kitchen rather than boardroom table or financial trading desk. It adds a missing practical *macroeconomic* dimension to welfare economics, which has been a highly abstract, microeconomically oriented subdiscipline for too long.

In effect, the aggregate distribution function describes the larger social welfare policy "switch" at which many economic policymakers have fallen asleep over the past few decades as inequality and insecurity mounted while digital disruption, economic integration and environmental degradation accelerated. The aggregate distribution function of an economy extends well beyond transfer payments and education and skilling, the two most commonly proposed responses to the centrifugal forces of technological disruption and globalization upon societies. It provides a wider view of the playing field for policymakers—the full range of pre- and post-transfer policy responses available to shift an economy from a socially polarizing trickle-down mode to a levelling-up, lifting-all-boats dynamic.

Countries wishing to make faster progress on social inclusion, environmental sustainability, and resilience should be investing in strengthening the distribution function at least as much as the production function of their economies. Some have managed to forge a more perfect union than others between individual economic liberty and shared socioeconomic progress by taking a more direct and systematic approach to managing this side of their economies—the social *quality* of economic growth. They have maintained competitiveness while achieving greater inclusion through a mixture of sharper policy incentives and stronger public and private institutions designed for this purpose.[6] Governments should not be too proud to learn from their peers in this regard, no matter how particular they perceive their own history, culture and political institutions to be.

Fuller activation of an economy's aggregate distribution function is fundamentally a strategy to increase investment in *people*—their capabilities, purchasing power, fair employment and entrepreneurial opportunity, and material well-being and security. The standard of living of working people and their households overwhelmingly depends on employment-related compensation and publicly enabled (but not necessarily publicly delivered) services and protections in such areas as education, consumer safety, asset-building, social insurance, and infrastructure. Investing in these translates much more directly into people's lived experience than do the blunter instruments of general fiscal and monetary stimulus and cuts in business regulation.

Business and political leaders commonly describe people as an economy's most important resource, but they have perennially failed to walk this talk by investing adequately in them and their standard of living and economic security. The trickle-down frame of reference of liberal economics with its emphasis on boosting investment in physical and financial capital, often through huge, untargeted expenditure of public resources (e.g., across-the-board personal and corporate tax cuts), has at best an indirect and blunt effect on jobs and living standards. Optimizing an economy's aggregate distribution function, by contrast, focuses on increasing public and private investment in multiple aspects of the lived experience of households. It aims more directly and structurally (as part and parcel of the growth process itself) to improve the capacity of market economies to democratize participation and diffuse the benefits of growth in economic activity, thereby bringing more of society along on a nation's upward development journey.

This more comprehensive and direct *human* investment and security agenda also happens to be what is most needed at this juncture to strengthen the growth prospects of many economies. There are three big prevailing and vexing challenges here. First, economists were debating for several years before the COVID-19 pandemic whether the United States and other advanced economies are characterized by a chronic underlying deficit of demand—so-called "secular stagnation"—owing to technology, globalization, population ageing and other structural factors. The recent sharp rise in inflation related to the COVID-19 pandemic and war in Ukraine has transformed this concern into open fear of a prolonged period of stagflation. Second, despite the technological innovation in our midst, productivity growth has been very slow for the past decade—about 1% per year—and this phenomenon has spread to major emerging economies.[7] And third, with interest rates rising to combat inflation and balance sheets still bloated from two rounds of extraordinary monetary stimulus in the past 15 years, many central banks have limited policy space to fight the next downturn, even before it has begun. They may need to work more closely with fiscal authorities to devise more direct and effective methods of transmitting stimulus into the economy in the event monetary policy is severely constrained during a future major downturn.

The aggregate distribution function offers policymakers an additional way of addressing each of these growth conundrums. First, its fuller activation would have the effect of adding a bottom-up, *structural* dimension to Keynesian demand management, in contrast to the top-down, indirect and transitory nature of traditional macroeconomic stimulus packages. A full-court press of structural policy and institutional reforms that reinforce household disposable income, purchasing power, economic security and labour market participation and transitions would support aggregate demand and consumer and investor confidence on an ongoing basis. Other things being equal, this would raise the labour share of national income and level of consumption within an economy—Keynes's key preoccupation as discussed in Chap. 3—and so help it to escape the grip of *secular* forces weighing it down, whether the after-shocks of recent crises or the income- and opportunity-dispersing effects of automation and the climate transition.

Second, fuller activation of an economy's aggregate distribution function would also address slow productivity growth more directly and effectively by prioritizing investment in skills development, research and development, sustainable infrastructure and anti-trust and anti-corruption protection, placing these at the centre of national economic policy rather than at the periphery where they too often have languished. Finally, the function represents a menu of potential channels to transmit stimulus more directly into the economy, particularly in the event that central bankers find themselves in the monetary black hole of a liquidity-trap or stagflationary recession. During such a crisis, an extraordinary increase in financing corresponding to one or more of these factors of distribution (such as disposable income or material necessities), through either conventional government borrowing or direct central bank financing, would help to stabilize the economy in the near term while advancing its structural rebalancing and reform over the longer term.

Thus, strengthening an economy's aggregate distribution function represents a *growth as well as social justice strategy*—a way to render its growth model more dynamic, resilient and sustainable by making it more inclusive. Finding such a way to add a sustained bottom-up impetus to growth could scarcely come at a better time for many economies around the world that are struggling to wean themselves from a decade and a half of unsustainable and decreasingly effective monetary and fiscal stimulus. While such stimulus was crucial to stabilizing their economies in the aftermath of the 2007–08 financial crisis, this strategy has run its course. So has the other approach many economies have relied upon over the past generation—trade surpluses. Trade volumes are growing again after the pandemic, but they are not likely to return soon to the rates experienced earlier in the century given the geopolitical and other forces of global economic fragmentation at work.

The world economy also requires a new growth paradigm because of the very real prospect that artificial intelligence and machine learning will hollow out employment, purchasing power and aggregate demand over the next ten to twenty years as much as or more than digitalization and globalization did over the previous two decades. If projections about the speed of this disruption are anywhere near accurate, then shifting the economic strategy from pushing-on-a-string, trickle-down mode to a lifting-all-boats, level-up dynamic becomes a long-term macroeconomic imperative as much as a sociopolitical one. Direct, systematic action to strengthen the living-standards diffusion mechanism of economies may prove to be an indispensable tool in countervailing a technology-driven erosion of demand within them as automation spreads.

Enabling Country Practice

Thus, a country can improve not only the inclusiveness and sustainability of its economy but also the dynamism and resilience of its growth by systematically strengthening its aggregate distribution function. That is the larger significance of this theoretical construct and policy framework. They point towards a new type of structural economic reform that is pro-growth as well as pro-equity, sustainability and resilience. Indeed, it is pro-growth *because* it is pro-equity, pro-sustainability and pro-resilience.

The principles and framework presented here can help to fundamentally reform and rebalance capitalism while correcting its neoliberal blind spot regarding the human costs of technological change, policy liberalization and environmental externalities. By more directly and systematically activating the broad spectrum of rules, policy incentives and institutional frameworks that support the equitable diffusion of employment and entrepreneurial opportunity, disposable income, affordable material necessities and economic and environmental security, they provide a comprehensive roadmap for practising and not just preaching the mantra of inclusive, sustainable and resilient growth at the country level.

However, developing a specific strategy to strengthen an economy's aggregate distribution function is necessarily a bespoke, rather than cookie-cutter, exercise. Each country has its own institutional strengths and weaknesses, fiscal constraints and political mandates conferred through elections and other channels. But each also has an interest in understanding how this institutional ecosystem functions *as a system* and in basing decisions regarding priorities for its improvement on better data and evidence. This is no small challenge given the complex, interdisciplinary scope of this important dimension of economic policy and its underemphasis for so long by mainstream economics.

In fact, this challenge presents an enormous opportunity for economics as an applied social science—a chance to renew its relevance to society and government on some of the biggest challenges humanity confronts this century. The fact that the aggregate social welfare and distribution functions presented here are not mathematical functions does not mean they are impervious to sophisticated quantitative analysis. Better data and analysis on both policy effort and efficacy in each of these five domains can support better, evidence-based decision-making by political leaders and technocrats.

In other words, a big empirical research agenda beckons. Comparable and comprehensive data are needed to help countries benchmark policy effort and institutional strength and assess their remaining policy space for improved design and increased investment in each of the five domains of the aggregate distribution function. These data could ultimately be used to construct cross-country indices of policy inputs and outcomes within these domains and perhaps across them as well.

Some important cross-country data sets and analytics of this nature exist, but most benchmarking of policy effort and investment in these domains has limited country coverage (mainly OECD countries). The most recognized indices comparing performance across multiple policy domains measure *outcomes* rather than these kinds of *inputs*. Examples include the UNDP's HDI,[8] the OECD's Better Life Index,[9] the Genuine Progress Indicator/Index of Sustainable Economic Welfare[10] and the Oxford Global Multidimensional Poverty Index.[11] These hint at but do not directly measure the nature and extent of policy effort and institutional strength contributing to such outcomes. The first priority of this new macro-welfare economics research agenda therefore should be to develop data and tools to help countries gauge the strength of their policy design and institutional capacity across the aggregate distribution function in relation to the experience of other countries. Comparable global databases of such information would help governments to better understand where the development of their economy's distribution function stands relative to that of peer countries, and why, and thus to take better decisions about the priorities for further investment in it.

A handful of major data sets exist on these topics, and these could be the building blocks of such an effort. For example, the OECD tracks fiscal expenditures by major category of social spending; the ILO compiles decent work indicators, which measure various dimensions of labour protection; and the ILO also has an extensive database on social protection systems, including with respect to their coverage, benefit levels, and financing. These and other databases corresponding to the aggregate distribution function's five factor inputs are explored in greater depth in Chap. 5 as part of a more extensive examination of what these concepts and tools imply for national policymaking.

A second research priority should be to establish a generally accepted *outcome* index, or composite panel of indicators, corresponding to the aggregate social welfare function. Such a multidimensional measure of a country's progress in advancing its standard of living would include GDP, insofar as this is part of the production function component of the aggregate social welfare function; however, as a more complete measure of bottom-line national performance, the entire composite should replace GDP per capita as the main international metric of annual performance and overall level of economic development. Considerable effort would be required to select an appropriate handful of indicators corresponding to outcomes related to the aggregate distribution function as well as to assign a combined weight to these relative to GDP.

An existing example of such a composite index is the Inclusive Development Index, which I helped to create and publish at the World Economic Forum in 2017–18.[12] It placed equal weights on its three pillars of Growth, Inclusion, and Intergenerational Equity and Sustainability and their 12 constituent indicators but invited users to vary these according to their preference via an online tool. Other examples of multidimensional indices and databases related to living standards include the HDI, including its inequality-adjusted income component[13]; the Social Progress Index (SPI)[14]; and the Environmental Performance Index published by the Yale Center for Environmental Law and Policy and the Center for International Earth Science Information Network at Columbia University's Earth Institute.[15] These are somewhat less representative measures of median progress in living standards and material well-being, because they either cover only a subset of the function's five factors of distribution or, in the case of the SPI, additional topics. The ILO has published a composite set of indicators for gauging country progress on Sustainable Development Goal 8: "promoting sustained, inclusive and sustainable economic growth, full and productive employment and decent work for all".[16] These 12 indicators are displayed in "rosebud" charts to provide a more holistic perspective on national economic progress than do traditional GDP-based measures.

A third important area of research would be to examine the historical evidence regarding the correlation between the aggregate production and distribution functions—between GDP growth and median living standards and their constituent factors. As Chap. 5 will illustrate, some evidence suggests there is a weak and inconsistent correlation between growth and key dimensions of living standards.

An integrated research agenda of this nature could add substantially to our understanding of the institutional infrastructure that underpins modern market economies and how it can be upgraded to deliver the better user experience that leaders have been promising for decades in terms of inclusion, sustainability and resilience. Economists could make a major contribution to both scholarship and society by greatly expanding quantitative work on the *qualitative* dimension of economic growth and development— applying empirical analysis in ways that give policymakers the tools they need to fulfil the distinctly heterodox principles and vision of liberal political economy's founders. Such work would have the effect of revitalizing two important subdisciplines of economics which have been in semi-hibernation for the past generation: welfare and institutional economics. It could also help economics to transcend its long-standing reputation as the "dismal science", focused on scarcity and narrow, economic-utility maximization, by rendering it more relevant to and enabling of the economic, social and environmental possibilities of *our* time.

In particular, this reformulated growth and development model would go a long way towards reconnecting liberal economics with the foundational principles articulated in the 1944 Philadelphia Declaration of the ILO. The Declaration stated that "all national and international policies and measures, in particular those of an economic and financial character", should have as their "central aim" and "be judged . . . and accepted only in so far as they may be held to promote and not hinder" the attainment of the conditions in which "all human beings, irrespective of race, creed or sex, have the right to pursue both their material well-being and their spiritual development in conditions of freedom and dignity, of economic security and equal opportunity."

This multilateral statement of the bottom-line social purpose of economic policy strongly evokes the explicit two-lens, growth-and-living-standards, markets-and-institutions framework of analysis of Smith, Mill and Marshall as reflected in the aggregate social welfare function presented above. The Philadelphia Declaration was agreed only a few months before the Bretton Woods conference creating the IMF and World Bank, providing important context for their design as well as that of the General Agreement on Tariffs and Trade and Havana Charter of 1947-1948 and the Universal Declaration of Human Rights of 1948. The initial articles of the charters of the IMF, World Bank, GATT and WTO all reflect the logical policy hierarchy set out in the Declaration, stating that the ultimate purpose of each institution is to advance employment, standards of living and sustainable development. All of these texts embody Roosevelt's conviction, expressed in his State of the Union message to Congress and the American people a few months before ILO delegates arrived in the "City of Brotherly Love," that a Second Bill of Rights of an economic and social character was needed because "true individual freedom cannot exist without economic security and independence" and "people who are hungry and out of a job are the stuff of which dictatorships are made."[17] The aggregate distribution function is a device for systematizing this sense of solidarity—this appreciation of the ultimate social purpose of economies—within a country's economic policy through the ongoing institutional development of its social contract, that is to say, through acts of political economy mediated optimally through representative democratic processes including social dialogue.

Chapters 5 and 6 apply this rebalanced and re-embedded model of economic growth and development to contemporary domestic and international economic governance, respectively. Chapter 5 derives several important lessons for its application in national economic policy from existing cross-country data. These demonstrate that nearly every country has ample scope to make substantial progress on inclusion, sustainability and/or resilience by working to strengthen correspondingly weak areas of its aggregate distribution function, its social contract, relative to the experience and practices of peer countries. One size cannot fit all in this regard, since social contracts are highly context-specific in a cultural, historical and political sense. Because they are so polity-specific, the discussion refrains from prescribing a single policy mix. Rather, it provides a methodology—a set of tools, frameworks and comparative data—that can be applied by governments in a wide range of political and economic contexts to integrate priorities regarding inclusion, sustainability and resilience systematically into the design and implementation of their economic policy.

Notes

1. Important elements of this chapter are drawn from and build upon an earlier working paper: Richard Samans, "Level-Up Economics: Beyond the Wealth of Nations", INET Working Paper, January 2020, https://www.ineteconomics.org/research/research-papers/level-up-economics-beyond-the-wealth-of-nations
2. See, for example, David Dollar and Art Kray, "Growth Is Good for the Poor", *Journal of Economic Growth*, Vol. 7, No. 3 (2002), pp. 195–225, https://papers.ssrn.com/sol3/papers.cfm?abstract_id=632656
3. Lant Pritchett with Addison Lewis, "Economic Growth *Is* Enough and Only Economic Growth Is Enough", 25 May 2022, https://lantpritchett.org/wp-content/uploads/2022/05/Basics-legatum-paper_short.pdf
4. For an overview of this long-running debate, see, for example, Jonathan Temple, "Aggregate Production Functions and Growth Economics", *International Review of Applied Economics*, Vol. 20, No. 3 (2006), pp. 301–17, http://www2.econ.iastate.edu/tesfatsi/AggregProdFunctionsDontExist.Temple.pdf; and A.J. Cohen and G.C. Harcourt, "Whatever Happened to the Cambridge Capital Theory Controversies?" *Journal of Economic Perspectives*, Vol. 17, No. 1 (2003), pp. 199–214; F.M. Fisher, *Aggregation: Aggregate Production Functions and Related Topics*, Cambridge, MA, MIT Press, 1993; R.M. Solow, "Review of Capital and Growth", *American Economic Review*, Vol. 56, No. 5 (1966), pp. 1257–60.

4 FROM THE WEALTH TO THE LIVING STANDARDS OF NATIONS… 129

5. K-12 = kindergarten to 12th grade.
6. See, for example, Richard Samans, Jennifer Blanke, Gemma Corrigan and Margareta Drzeniek Hanouz, *Inclusive Growth and Development Report 2017*, Geneva, World Economic Forum, 2017, pp. 1–46, https://www3.weforum.org/docs/WEF_Forum_IncGrwth_2017.pdf
7. See ILO, *World Employment and Social Outlook: Trends 2023*, Geneva, pp. 87–126, https://www.ilo.org/global/research/global-reports/weso/WCMS_865332/lang%2D%2Den/index.htm
8. UNDP, "Human Development Index (HDI)", https://hdr.undp.org/data-center/human-development-index#/indicies/HDI
9. OECD, "Better Life Index", https://www.oecdbetterlifeindex.org/#/11111111111
10. See for example Ida Kubiszewski et al., "Beyond GDP: Measuring and achieving global genuine progress," Ecological Economics, Volume 93, September 2013, Pages 57-68, https://www.sciencedirect.com/science/article/abs/pii/S0921800913001584
11. Oxford University Poverty and Human Development Initiative, "Global Multidimensional Poverty Index", https://ophi.org.uk/multidimensional-poverty-index/
12. World Economic Forum, *The Inclusive Development Index 2018*, Geneva, 2018, https://reports.weforum.org/the-inclusive-development-index-2018/ and https://www3.weforum.org/docs/WEF_Forum_IncGrwth_2018.pdf
13. See UNDP, "Inequality-Adjusted Human Development Index (IHDI)", https://hdr.undp.org/inequality-adjusted-human-development-index#/indicies/IHDI
14. "2022 Social Progress Index", https://www.socialprogress.org/static/8a62f3f612c8d40b09b3103a70bdacab/2022%20Social%20Progress%20Index%20Executive%20Summary_4.pdf
15. M.J. Wolf et al., *2022 Environmental Performance Index*, New Haven, Yale Center for Environmental Law & Policy, 2022, https://epi.yale.edu/
16. ILO, *Time to Act for SDG 8: Integrating Decent Work, Sustained Growth and Environmental Integrity*, Geneva, 2019, https://www.ilo.org/global/publications/books/WCMS_712685/lang%2D%2Den/index.htm
17. Franklin D. Roosevelt, "State of the Union Message to Congress," January 11, 1944, https://millercenter.org/the-presidency/presidential-speeches/january-11-1944-fireside-chat-28-state-union; see also Cass R. Sunstein, The Second Bill of Rights, Basic Books, 2006.

Open Access This chapter is licensed under the terms of the Creative Commons Attribution 4.0 International License (http://creativecommons.org/licenses/by/4.0/), which permits use, sharing, adaptation, distribution and reproduction in any medium or format, as long as you give appropriate credit to the original author(s) and the source, provide a link to the Creative Commons licence and indicate if changes were made.

The images or other third party material in this chapter are included in the chapter's Creative Commons licence, unless indicated otherwise in a credit line to the material. If material is not included in the chapter's Creative Commons licence and your intended use is not permitted by statutory regulation or exceeds the permitted use, you will need to obtain permission directly from the copyright holder.

CHAPTER 5

Human-Centred National Economic Policy: Institutionalizing Inclusion, Sustainability and Resilience in Domestic Economic Governance

In Chap. 4, I posited that countries should devote at least as much attention to strengthening the aggregate distribution function as the aggregate production function of their economies, irrespective of their level of economic development. This is the golden rule of human-centred economics. It is the key to rebalancing modern market economies so that they deliver the more inclusive, sustainable and resilient pattern of growth and development which their populations have been demanding and leaders have been promising.

In practical terms, this means governments should place as big a priority on strengthening and investing in the policies and institutions corresponding to the five factors of distribution represented in the aggregate distribution function as on those related to the factors of production in the aggregate production function. This is the key to increasing not only the wealth (national income or GDP) of their nation but also its median standard of living, which is the bottom-line measure of national economic performance for individual households and society at large. The former is but a means to achieve the latter, and median living standards are influenced by more than the rate, or quantity, of economic growth. The pattern, or quality, of growth matters as well, and this is shaped to a considerable extent by institutional design and capacity in the five domains outlined in Chap. 4 and summarized again in Box 5.1 below.

The original version of the chapter has been revised. A correction to this chapter can be found at https://doi.org/10.1007/978-3-031-37435-7_8

© The Author(s) 2024, corrected publication 2024
R. Samans, *Human-Centred Economics*,
https://doi.org/10.1007/978-3-031-37435-7_5

Box 5.1 Aggregate Distribution Function: Policy and Institutional Ecosystem

Employment and entrepreneurial opportunity (O)

Competition and rents

- Anti-trust
- Anti-corruption
- Property rights and land tenure rules and enforcement capacity
- Technology governance, e.g., intellectual property rights, data ownership and access

Investment in real economy productive capacity

- Corporate governance rules and protections
- Financial system governance rules and protections
- Public investment in infrastructure, R&D, key industries, public works

Labour force skills, transitions and participation

- Skills, e.g., basic K-12 education, school-to-work, tertiary education, lifelong education
- Active labour market policies, e.g., employment services, training, skills matching, income maintenance, credentialing
- Rights: elimination of forced and child labour; non-discrimination, e.g., gender, race and ethnicity, disabilities, age, etc.
- Formalization of work arrangements

Disposable income (I)

Wage compensation

- Minimum/living wage regulations
- Rights—e.g., freedom of association and collective bargaining
- Social dialogue rules, institutions, practices
- Taxation of wage income and relative treatment of earned and unearned income

Non-wage compensation

- Health insurance rules, policy incentives
- Pension rules, policy incentives

(*continued*)

Box 5.1 (continued)

- Dependent care rights, benefits, incentives
- Working hour, annual leave, work–life balance regulations
- Profit-sharing and employee, community ownership regulations, incentives

Availability and affordability of material necessities (N)

Regulation, policy incentives, and subsidies

- Water and sanitation
- Food
- Housing
- Energy
- Transport
- Telecommunications
- Recreation

Economic security (EcS)

Social protection—coverage and adequacy of benefits

- Health care
- Pension
- Unemployment insurance
- Disability
- Anti-poverty

Worker protection regulation and enforcement capacity

- Occupational safety and health
- Arbitrary dismissal
- Consumer protection

Asset-building/wealth accumulation policies and incentives

- Homeownership
- Private pensions
- Business ownership
- Small saver protection

(*continued*)

> **Box 5.1 (continued)**
> **Environmental security (EnS)**
> *Climate change policies*
> - Mitigation
> - Adaptation
>
> *Other natural capital regulation*
> - Water
> - Air
> - Soil
> - Natural habitat and biodiversity

The practice of human-centred economics begins with a recognition that the construction and ongoing refinement of this policy and institutional ecosystem are an integral part of the development process, equal in importance to the traditional strategy of seeking to boost GDP through measures that increase allocative efficiency and capital accumulation. This is a different approach to structural economic reform. Since the 1980s, structural economic reform has been synonymous with short-term packages of austerity and efficiency measures intended to stabilize public finances and currencies in the context of a crisis. These administer a concentrated dose of the general neoliberal prescription of fiscal and monetary belt-tightening combined with supply-side measures that liberalize labour, product and capital markets. By contrast, a sustained strategy to progressively invest in the policy incentives and institutions that more directly support household employment opportunity, disposable income, availability and affordability of material necessities, and economic and environmental security is a formula for improving both demand and supply—for increasing *both* the living standards *and* the growth potential of an economy.

In simple terms, an economy's growth potential is its maximum sustainable rate of economic growth. Its output gap is the difference between its actual GDP and the level implied by this potential rate. Macroeconomists often think in terms of how to narrow this gap through policy, particularly during recessions or periods of stagnation. They generally consider a country's long-run growth potential to be primarily a function of the size and productivity of its active labour force, whereas its near-term output gap is more related to business cycle conditions and the restrictive or stimulative posture of macroeconomic policy with respect to aggregate demand.

Economies with roughly the same level of national income per capita can have a higher or lower growth potential than each other depending upon the characteristics of their policy and institutional ecosystem that influence the size and productivity of the workforce (e.g., those affecting capital investment, technological development and diffusion, skills, immigration, gender discrimination). In other words, a country's output gap can vary depending on the policy choices it makes in these and other policy areas (and, in the near term, the phase in which its economy is situated in the business cycle).

The practice of human-centred economics requires governments and economists to think in analogous terms about median living standards. Countries at roughly the same level of national income per capita can have quite different levels of median household living standards. This difference is influenced significantly by the relative robustness of their policy and institutional ecosystem in the five dimensions of household living standards represented in the aggregate distribution function.

In this sense, an economy can be conceived of as having not only an output gap but also a living standards gap or social welfare gap. In conceptual terms, this is the difference between its current median household living standard relative to the level that would obtain if its government more fully activated the policy and institutional ecosystem underpinning its aggregate distribution function. In practical terms, this *welfare gap* can be represented by comparing the current state of the country's median household standard of living (or major component thereof) with that of the best-performing countries at a similar level of development, be they high, upper-middle, lower-middle or low income.

In other words, just as national economies can have a higher or lower growth potential and corresponding gap in output (GDP) relative to this potential, so they can have a higher or lower potential median standard of living and corresponding social welfare gap depending on the extent to which they have exploited the possibilities for activating the aggregate social welfare function of their economy and, in particular, its aggregate distribution function component (its social contract).

ESTIMATING WELFARE GAPS

Four cross-country indices of multidimensional living standards help to illustrate in quantitative terms the social welfare gaps of countries, that is, differences between actual and potential median household living standards, as well as the considerable potential for variation in such gaps among countries with similar GDP per capita. First, the Inclusive Development Index (IDI) is a composite measure of 12 indicators, four each in the areas of Growth and Employment; Inclusion; and Intergenerational Equity and Sustainability.[1] IDI data for 103 economies published in 2018 suggest that that GDP per capita correlates somewhat weakly with performance on indicators other than labour productivity and healthy life expectancy (and poverty rates in advanced economies). For example, all but three of 29 advanced economies experienced GDP growth over the preceding five years, but only 10 registered clear progress in the IDI's Inclusion pillar (median household income; poverty rate; income Gini and wealth Gini). A majority, 16 of 29, saw their Inclusion score deteriorate, and the remaining three were stable. A majority of countries with the best GDP growth performance failed to improve on Inclusion.

This pattern was repeated in the relationship between GDP growth and performance on Intergenerational Equity and Sustainability, with 11 of 29 showing clear progress and 18 of 29 deteriorating. This pillar includes indicators on public indebtedness relative to GDP; the dependency ratio (active workforce relative to retiree population); carbon intensity of GDP; and adjusted net savings, which measures the rate of savings in an economy more holistically, that is, after taking into account investment in human capital, depletion of natural resources, and damage caused by pollution.

Developing country data showed a similar weakness in the relationship between GDP growth and Inclusion. Of the 30 such economies with the highest GDP per capita growth over the preceding five years, only six scored similarly well on a majority of the Inclusion indicators, while 13 registered mediocre performance and 11 outright poor performance. With respect to Intergenerational Equity and Sustainability, only eight scored similarly well on a majority of indicators, while 12 were no better than mediocre and 10 registered outright poor performance. Most developing economies recorded a deteriorating performance on this pillar. Notable exceptions included Brazil, China and India, which reported strong levels of human capital investment that offset high levels of natural resource depletion.

In sum, over 40% of developing countries had IDI scores that were more than nine places different from their GDP per capita scores, suggesting that policy and institutional factors can make a considerable difference in a country's broader socioeconomic performance. Among the 30 advanced economies for which comparable data was available, the United States had an IDI score that was 14 places lower than its GDP per capita ranking, suggesting that it has substantial room for improvement in many of the policy domains corresponding to its aggregate distribution function.

Second, on the narrower question of the relationship between poverty reduction and economic growth in poor countries, there is considerable evidence that growth is strongly correlated with reduction in *income* poverty (e.g., number of people living on less than US$1.90 per day in 2011 prices on a PPP basis). However, its relationship with country performance in *multidimensional* poverty reduction (on broader measures of living standards such as employment, education and health) is more nuanced and significantly weaker, albeit still positive, particularly for poorer developing countries. The authors of one of the few existing studies on this question concluded,

> The elasticity of income-based poverty to growth is between five to eight times higher than that of multidimensional poverty, depending on the specific measure of poverty used ... our results indicate that economic growth is an important instrument to alleviate multidimensional poverty, but its effect is substantially lower than that on monetary poverty. Therefore, countries aiming for progress in SDG 1, Target 1.2—or specifically, to "reduce at least by half the proportion of men, women, and children of all ages living in poverty in all its dimensions"—must identify other policies or interventions to reduce poverty in these other dimensions. This is particularly urgent in the present day given the already emerging and forecasted impacts of the COVID-19 pandemic on both income and multidimensional poverty. For these reasons, future researchers should focus on an investigation of other factors and policies, starting from social policies that could have a substantial impact on multidimensional poverty.[2]

Third, GDP per capita and environmental performance are positively related in a general sense. For example, the Environmental Performance Index (EPI)[3] has a strong overall correlation between its overall scores and GDP per capita globally. However, there is wide variation in scores among countries at the same level of GDP per capita, driven by weak correlations in two of the EPI's three pillars, those of Climate Change and Ecosystem Vitality. These variations are explained in substantial part by governance factors, both substantive and procedural. In other words, policies and

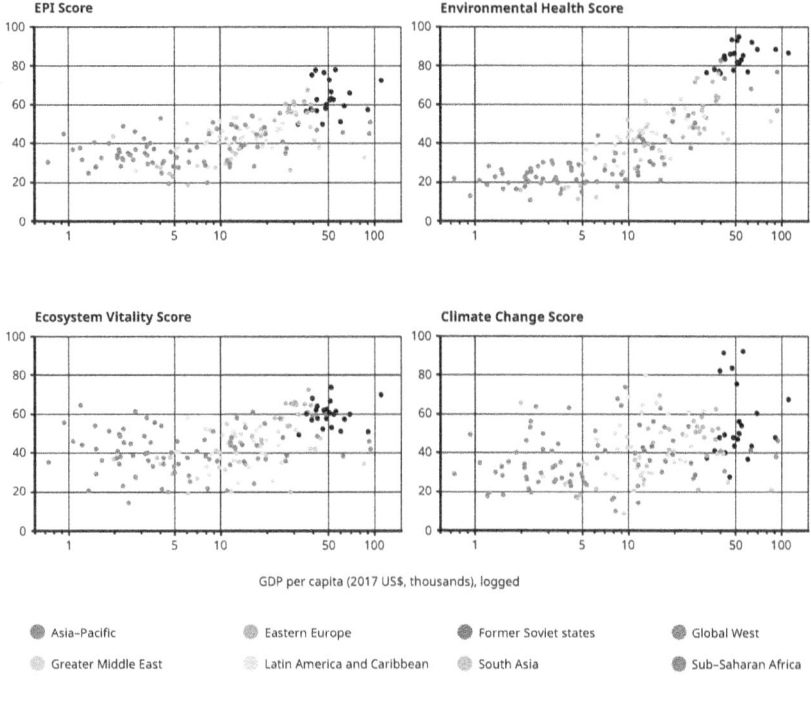

Fig. 5.1 Relationship between GDP per capita and environmental performance

institutions matter. Figure 5.1 illustrates such variability in performance on the EPI's individual pillar scores among countries with similar levels of GDP per capita in the same region.

Finally, SDG 8 sets a goal of promoting "sustained, inclusive and sustainable economic growth, full and productive employment and decent work for all". As such, it covers growth, social inclusion and environmental integrity, similarly to the IDI. The ILO is the custodian of SDG 8 within the UN system. It has developed a measurement framework of 22 indicators across these three dimensions and calculated the scores of each for 11 subregions of the world. These are presented in "rosebud" graphics in which stronger scores are represented by longer petals shaded green whereas moderate and low scores have shorter petals shaded yellow and red, respectively. Certain subregions with comparable levels of GDP exhibit significant differences in scores within and across the three sets of indicators. For example, there is considerable variation in the environmental scores of the three relatively advanced regions of Northern, Western and Southern Europe; Eastern Europe; and North America. Similarly, scores varied considerably in all three pillars among three subregions predominantly composed of lower-middle-income countries: Western and Central Asia; South Asia; and North Africa (Fig. 5.2). While geography and culture inevitably contribute to these variations, policies and institutions appear to play a more important role given that there is also significant variation in performance on many of these indicators among countries in the same subregion. This recalls the findings of the 1993 World Bank study on the East Asian miracle, which found that key institutional features were decisive in distinguishing the performance of eight high-performing Asian economies from that of many other developing countries both within and outside Asia.

NARROWING WELFARE GAPS BY STRENGTHENING
THE AGGREGATE DISTRIBUTION FUNCTION OF ECONOMIES

What strategies can a country use to narrow its welfare gap—to increase its median standard of living, or important dimensions thereof, relative to that of well-performing countries at a comparable level of economic development? What policy and institutional levers can it feasibly activate more fully to improve one or more of household employment and entrepreneurial opportunity, disposable income, availability and affordability of material necessities, and economic and environmental security relative to the frontier of country practice and performance in its cohort?

There follows a discussion of *some* of the most salient opportunities in this respect for each of the aggregate distribution function's five factors of distribution. This presentation is not intended to be exhaustive of the policy opportunities with respect to each such factor. Nor is it meant to suggest that the effect on living standards of any one, let alone all, of these policy interventions occurs only through the factor of distribution under which it is listed. In fact, many have an influence on more than one of the five factors (employment, income, affordability of necessities, and economic and environment security). They are listed in their area of primary or most direct influence.

In each of the five sections below, I first summarize the relevance of the policy area in question for the lived experience of median households;

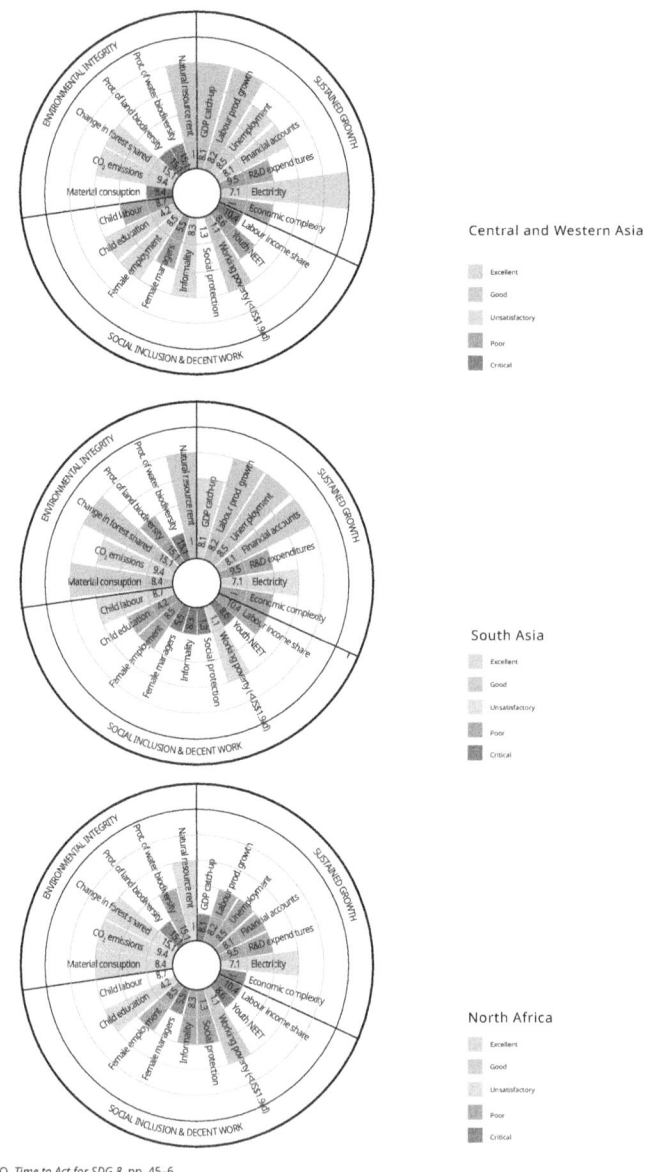

Source: ILO, *Time to Act for SDG 8*, pp. 45–6

Fig. 5.2 Performance in three dimensions of SDG 8

second, I describe some of the primary policy and institutional strategies countries use to strengthen their performance in that aspect of household living standards; and, third, I illustrate the extent of unutilized policy space most countries have to narrow their welfare gap in each policy domain—to more fully activate the relevant policies and institutions—by presenting data on the wide range of experience and performance among peer countries, that is, those with a comparable level of national income per capita.

The primary point of this lengthy presentation is to illustrate the considerable agency virtually every country at every level of economic development has to make its economy perform more equitably and sustainably for the benefit of its entire population by taking a comprehensive view of its relative strengths and weaknesses across the entirety of the policy and institutional ecosystem described by the aggregate distribution function. Readers looking for a single recommended policy prescription—a one-size-fits-all solution—in this regard will be disappointed, as the contours of countries' welfare gaps across the five dimensions of household living standards represented by the function vary widely. The book's more prescriptive policy recommendations are reserved for international governance and cooperation in Chap. 6. These describe in considerable detail how the international institutional architecture should be recast to provide much more effective support of countries wishing to render their economies more inclusive, sustainable and resilient, i.e., to strengthen the rate and breadth of progress in living standards by addressing weaknesses or areas of underdevelopment in their social contracts.

As emphasized in Chap. 4, the policy and institutional ecosystem presented in Box 5.1 is the practical manifestation of a country's social contract. The policy choices and investments the country makes in these five domains largely determine how well it translates its society's values with respect to inclusion, sustainability and resilience into the way its economy functions.

EMPLOYMENT AND ENTREPRENEURIAL OPPORTUNITY (O)

The relative quantity and quality of jobs within economies at similar levels of GDP are influenced by many structural and institutional factors. Prominent among them are those which influence competition and innovation, investment in productive capacity, workforce skills, labour market discrimination and exclusion, and support for the transition of dislocated workers.

Competition and Rents

Restrictive business practices and public policies that suppress competition and concentrate rents within an economy were arguably Adam Smith's top preoccupation in writing *The Wealth of Nations*. These practices and policies constrain the spread of enterprise and innovation on which broad-based employment opportunity and improved productivity depend. There are considerable differences in how countries set and enforce anti-trust, anti-corruption, property rights and land tenure, and intellectual property and data stewardship rules, and these have an important influence on industry and employment—on the fairness and equality of access to opportunity and concentration and potential for abuse of power within an economy.

Anti-trust Policy
Over the past generation anti-trust interpretation and enforcement have shifted in a number of advanced economies. In some cases, this has contributed to a notable rise in industrial concentration, expanding the power of large firms to set the terms of their relationship with distributors and suppliers, extract rents and arbitrage labour costs, including by changing (or suggesting they could change) the location and job intensity of production. About two-thirds of employment and a substantial share of innovation take place in small and medium-sized enterprises, a level that is fairly consistent across rich and poor economies.

In 2019, the OECD reported

> a clear increase in industry concentration in Europe as well as in North America between 2000 and 2014 on the order of 4 to 8 percentage points for the average industry. Over the period, about 3 out of 4 (2-digit) industries in each region saw their concentration increase. The increase is observed for both manufacturing and non-financial services and is not driven by digital-intensive sectors.[4]

The following year, the organization issued a study of business dynamism across 18 countries and 22 industries over the past two decades and found that

> declines in business dynamism have been pervasive in many countries and are driven by dynamics occurring at a disaggregated sectoral level, rather than reallocation across sectors … In particular, entry rates and job reallocation rates declined on average by about three and five percentage points, respec-

tively. Although declines have been pervasive—all countries display some signs of declining business dynamism—there is significant heterogeneity in their magnitude and speed across countries and sectors.[5]

Business dynamism is important for employment and entrepreneurial opportunity because

> Young firms, and more specifically a few high-growth firms, are the engine of job creation and are crucial for the introduction of new business models and the introduction and diffusion of innovation. Furthermore, young businesses can be a springboard for younger workers ... and represent employment opportunities for women, immigrants and labour market outsiders, e.g. unemployed and entrants in the labour markets ... Business dynamism is also significantly related to aggregate productivity. Job reallocation and dynamism are key for an efficient allocation of resources, allowing successful firms to grow and the less productive ones to shrink. This allocation of resources importantly relies on both reallocation between incumbents, but also the extensive margins on firm dynamics, i.e. the continuous process of firm entry and exit. In addition, business dynamism may favour the introduction of radical innovation and the diffusion of technology and knowledge, the key drivers of within-firm productivity growth.[6]

The OECD's researchers identified market structure and firm heterogeneity to be factors correlated with the decline in business dynamism, and concluded that

> institutions and framework conditions are found to play an important role in explaining cross-country differences in the observed trends ... Thus, policy reforms can significantly help limit declines in business dynamism. Indeed, reforms reducing administrative requirements and barriers to entrepreneurship, improving the enforcement of contracts, and enhancing innovation potential and skills may boost business dynamism with positive longer-term effects. Focusing on these policy areas together may reduce barriers to entry and to knowledge diffusion, allow experimentation and favour creative destruction, while increasing absorptive capacity and the potential to benefit from technological change.[7]

As for market structure, economist Thomas Philippon has observed that the US and Europe have reversed roles over the past twenty years with respect to competition policy: "Until the 1990s, US markets were more competitive than European markets. Today, however, many European markets have lower excess profits and lower regulatory barriers to entry."[8]

The deterioration of competitive conditions in the United States is further illustrated by the extent to which increases in the ratio of market to book value within industries (known as Tobin's q) results in new firms entering the market. This relationship has deteriorated markedly over the past generation.[9]

More specifically, Philippon and colleagues observed that,

> Twenty years ago, access to the internet was cheaper in the US than in Europe. In 2018, however, the average monthly cost of fixed broadband in the US was twice as high as in France or Germany. Air transportation is another industry in which the US has fallen behind. The rise in concentration and profits aligns closely with a controversial merger wave that included the merging of Delta and Northwest in 2008, United and Continental in 2010, Southwest and AirTran in 2011, and American and US Airways in 2014. In Europe, over the same period, the growth of low-cost carriers has driven competition up and prices down.
>
> European industries did not become cheaper and more competitive by chance. In all the cases that I have studied, there was a significant policy action, such as the removal of a barrier to entry or an antitrust action. The French telecom industry, for instance, was an oligopoly with three legacy carriers that lobbied hard to prevent entry. The oligopoly lost in 2011, a fourth operator obtained a license, and prices decreased by 50 percent within two years.[10]

By contrast, in the United States, Philippon found evidence of a decrease in the independence and vigour of anti-trust regulation accompanied by an increase in industry lobbying and campaign contributions. He explained that

> Incumbents may, for example, influence antitrust and merger enforcement as well as regulations, ranging from the length and scope of patents and copyright protection to financial regulation, non-compete agreements, occupational licensing, and tax loopholes. Consistent with these ideas, we find that the elasticity of firm entry to Tobin's q has decreased more in industries that have experienced larger increases in lobbying and regulations.[11]

Similarly, the OECD's Product Market Regulation database documents a decrease in restrictive market entry regulation during a recent fifteen year period in all countries except the United States and Hungary. Figure 5.3 illustrates the significant variation in the level and trend of this and other aspects of policy relating to the competitiveness of product markets, underscoring the point that policy design and implementation

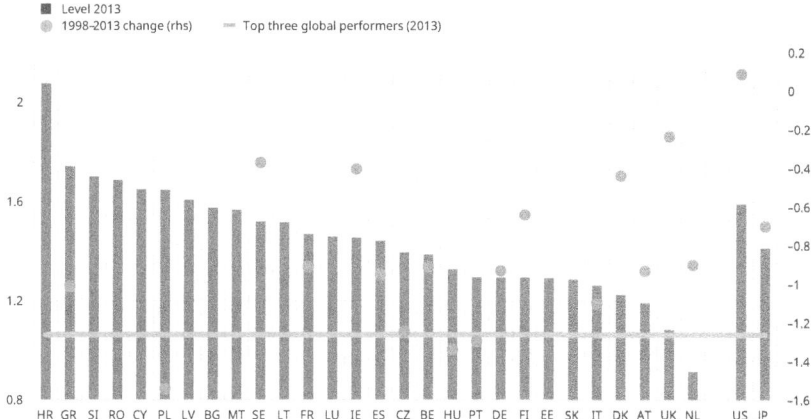

Fig. 5.3 OECD—Product Market Regulation (PMR) indicators

matter, and many countries have considerable room for improvement relative to their peers.[12]

Governments and citizens wishing to benchmark their countries' policies and institutional capacities relating to competition policy and the entrepreneurial climate have a relatively new source of data at their disposal. The Columbia University and University of Chicago Law Schools recently established a Comparative Competition Law Dataset, which covers competition laws in 130 jurisdictions between 1889 and 2010 and includes a second Comparative Competition Enforcement Dataset providing data on competition agencies' resources and activities in 100 jurisdictions between 1990 and 2010. These global data sets, which cover far more countries than those of the OECD, offer "the most comprehensive picture of competition law yet assembled and provide a new foundation for empirical research on the legal regimes used to regulate markets".[13] Some additional relevant global data on relevant aspects of the policy and institutional enabling environment for business dynamism can be found in the World Governance Indicators, and in particular their Regulatory Quality and Rule of Law pillars.[14]

Anti-corruption Policy
The strength of anti-corruption policies and institutions also has a big influence on the concentration of rents and restriction of competition and entrepreneurial dynamism in an economy. While this is a particular challenge in many developing countries, it also remains a significant issue in some advanced economies in both hard (outright bribery) and soft (electoral financing and lobbying) forms.

Systemic corruption exacts a major toll on employment and entrepreneurial opportunity. It siphons rents, restricts competition, suppresses investment, exacerbates inequality and reduces government tax revenue.[15] In a 2017 Transparency International survey of more than 160,000 adults in 119 countries, 25% of people reported that they had to pay a bribe to access public services in the preceding 12 months. A majority, 57%, judged their government to be performing "badly" in the fight against corruption, with police and elected officials ranked as the most corrupt public sector actors on average.[16]

Global estimates vary and suffer from methodological challenges,[17] but there is broad agreement that corruption is a pervasive problem and acts as a significant drag on economic growth and employment, including in the formal sector.[18] It has many causes and dimensions, but historical experience demonstrates that it can be markedly reduced through concerted action, in particular stronger public policy and institutional capacity in key areas. These include corporate liability and asset forfeiture laws; measures to ensure the independence of anti-corruption investigators and prosecutors; rules regarding plea bargains and whistleblowers; open procurement processes; increased citizen access to information regarding public budgets and services; digitalization of tax systems; participation in international cooperative initiatives; and special initiatives applying several of these tools at once to accelerate progress in problematic industries. Countries and jurisdictions as diverse as Hong Kong, India, Rwanda, Indonesia, Prague, Mauritius, Costa Rica, Uruguay and Bratislava have had important successes through applying these and other strategies.[19]

A number of cross-country benchmarking databases of the policy and institutional strength of anti-corruption frameworks in these and other dimensions have become available relatively recently. These complement and are an important evolution beyond the well known Corruption Perceptions Index, which has been issued since 1995.[20] They can be used by countries wishing to gain a better understanding of how they can strengthen this important aspect of their aggregate distribution function by moving their policies and institutional frameworks closer to good or leading country practice.

To be specific, the Capacity to Combat Corruption Index benchmarks policy and institutional strength in 15 Latin American countries across 14 key variables, including the independence and efficiency of judicial, prosecutorial and anti-corruption agency institutions, quality and enforceability of campaign finance legislation, access to public information, strength of investigative journalism, level of resources available for combating white-collar crime, and the extent of civil society mobilization with respect to corruption. The Index relies on extensive data and a proprietary survey conducted among leading anti-corruption experts from academia, civil society, media and the private sector.[21]

The British Commonwealth Secretariat has created its own set of anti-corruption policy enabling environment benchmarks as part of a voluntary initiative by member countries. The Commonwealth Anti-Corruption Benchmarks are intended primarily to help governments and public sector organizations assess their anti-corruption laws, regulations, policies and procedures against international good practice and consider implementing appropriate improvements. There are 25 benchmarks, each of which comprises a principle supported by a corresponding benchmark. The benchmarks address corruption across key areas of the public and private sectors which are either important for combating corruption or vulnerable to significant corruption. In relation to each key area, the benchmarks promote the concepts of honesty, impartiality, accountability and transparency and provide for specific anti-corruption measures.[22]

Finally, the OECD is constructing a new Public Integrity Indicators database, which is intended to measure "the preparedness and resilience of the public integrity system at the national level to prevent corruption, mismanagement and waste of public funds, and to assess the likelihood of detecting and mitigating various corruption risks by different actors in the system". The effort will seek to frame

> minimum legal, procedural and institutional safeguards for the independence, mandate and operational capability of essential actors in the integrity system with more outcome-oriented sub-indicators drawing on administrative data and surveys ... [The aim is to] help enhance the capacity of countries to measure corruption, corruption risks, effects of anti-corruption interventions and the resilience of the public integrity system and will provide an evidence-based approach to developing and implementing better integrity policies for better lives.[23]

Land Governance

Restrictive and discriminatory land tenure systems have historically played an important role in hindering socially inclusive development, particularly in rural settings. As discussed in Chap. 3, Adam Smith was particularly critical of the land tenure system of his day in Great Britain, which he argued was not only unfair and exclusionary but also economically counterproductive. It inhibited improvement in agricultural productivity by severely limiting ownership of land by individuals who would be motivated by such ownership to invest, innovate and steward the land more effectively.

Unfortunately, distorted and exclusionary land use systems are still common in much of the world (indeed vestiges remain in the United Kingdom itself). Seventy per cent of land is unregistered in developing countries, a situation that makes residents vulnerable to displacement and less likely to invest in productivity-enhancing improvements. In many countries, land governance regulation and compliance systems are weak. Rights and claims are often undocumented and overlapping,[24] which leads to uncertainty, conflict and increased inequality. Outdated and insecure land tenures and institutions undermine both the rule of law and government revenues.[25]

There is a long, cross-cultural track record of the crucial role that broadly distributed and secure land rights for smallholder farmers have played in advancing sustainable and inclusive development.[26] A study of 33 countries found that stronger property rights were associated with a 5% increase in GDP growth.[27] A study of 108 countries found that stronger property rights were associated with an increase of 6 to 14 percentage points in the average annual growth of per capita income.[28] And another global study of 101 countries found that more secure property rights were associated with higher private investment.[29] In sum, when land rights for smallholder farmers, both women and men, are strong and broadly distributed, they can increase agricultural investment, reduce hunger, feed the rural poor and growing urban population and promote equitable and inclusive growth.[30]

The World Bank advises that

> Secure land titles provide incentives for farmers to invest in land, borrow money for agricultural inputs and improvements to their land, and enable land sale and rental markets to ensure full utilization of land. They are also crucial for sustainable urbanization. By 2050, about two-thirds of the global population, six billion people, will be living in urban settlements and one-third in rural areas, a complete reversal from the pattern in 1950. Most of this increase will be in Africa and Asia. Failure to clarify land rights and fix distorted land policies contributes to increased property values, making them potentially unaffordable to the urban poor. These gaps have already led to

the formation of large informal settlements in many cities around the world. According to the World Bank report *Africa's Cities: Opening Doors to the World*, the top priority for African cities to create more affordable and livable urban environments is to formalize land markets, clarify property rights, and institute effective urban planning.[31]

Thus, institutional improvements in land governance, including taxation, can make a big difference for growth, employment and inclusion. It is important for sustainability as well, since half the forests in developing countries have insecure tenure, and this is often a driver of deforestation. Countries and stakeholders wishing to compare the strength of their policy and institutional ecosystem against good and best practice in this domain can consult the Global Land Governance Index, a project of the International Land Coalition (ILC). The ILC is a network of over 200 civil society and intergovernmental organizations committed to advancing people-centred land governance that "responds to the needs, and protects the rights, of the women, men and communities who live on and from the land, respecting that they should be the ultimate decision-makers on how their land and natural resources are used". The Index includes data on 33 cross-country indicators in three broad areas: legal and institutional framework; implementation; and outcomes.[32]

Technology Governance
Technology policy and governance are playing an increasingly important role in ensuring fair competition and preventing concentration of rents. There has been a resurgence of interest in intellectual property rights regimes in recent years, with critics arguing that advanced economies have failed to strike an appropriate balance between maintaining adequate incentives for innovators and their investors, on the one hand, and protecting the public's interest in having affordable access to technological advances with important implications for social welfare (especially when these advances have benefited from public R&D expenditure), on the other.[33] Similarly, as industries digitally transform and algorithmic automation gathers force, data have become a crucial factor of production. Much of this information concerns the personal behaviour and preferences of individual citizens, whether or not they provided it in the act of consuming a product or service. Proprietary monetization of such data is an increasingly important business model for many companies and industries, but it raises questions about whether, as a matter of fairness, citizens should have a measure of control over and even ownership of such data. These include whether citizens should have the right to port their data to competitors and

whether firms should have to obtain consent before using data for commercial purposes beyond the services individuals have purchased.

Fair competition and distribution of rents in the digital economy are increasingly contested concepts. Good and leading policy practice remain under development, including in advanced economies. For this reason, the benchmarking of country practice is difficult and in need of further international research and cooperation. Given the cross-border nature of such policy questions, they are taken up again in Chap. 6, which examines the implications of human-centred economics and its emphasis on institutions for *international* economic policy.

Real Economy Investment

Macroeconomic conditions are principally responsible for the overall level of investment within an economy. However, corporate governance and financial system rules have an important influence on the pattern of investment—the extent to which the private sector finances the productive capacity, innovation and skills upon which the quantity and particularly the quality of job creation depend. Policies in these areas shape the balance between short- and long-term investment, corporate profits and labour's share of national income, greenfield investment and the levering, exchange or combination of existing assets, and tangible and intangible investment.

In poor economies characterized by financial repression, weak rule of law and a large unbanked population, the first priority is to establish basic investor protections, promote financial inclusion for households and small businesses and ensure the prudential regulation of banks. These policies help to create a system that progressively expands the flow of domestic savings and foreign investment to productive uses. In more developed economies with financial systems supported by sound legal and regulatory frameworks, the challenge is to continue the process of financial deepening—more efficient intermediation—but in a way that remains true to a key "first principle" of human-centred corporate governance and financial regulation: corporations and financial institutions are social constructs. They are vehicles to intermediate savings to productive economic uses and the satisfaction of society's material welfare. They must not be permitted to become the tail that wags the dog of these real economy imperatives by erecting barriers to entry, concentrating rents or creating excessive leverage and other risks to financial stability.

A sophisticated financial and corporate sector in the form of deep and liquid financial markets and well-managed and accountable corporations is a boon to economic development. But there is a crucial balance to be struck through law and regulatory oversight in ensuring that capital serves the real economy rather than the other way around.

As discussed in Chap. 2, history has repeatedly demonstrated that this balance cannot be taken for granted by societies and their governments—or assumed by economists in their models of economic growth and development. Businesses are constantly in search of higher margins and, as Adam Smith emphasized, not infrequently succumb to the temptation to suppress competition in order to achieve them. At the same time, financial markets are prone to herd behaviour that leads to periodic panics and crashes that destroy jobs and household income through recessions and even depressions. Thus, an additional "first principle" of sound regulation of corporate and financial governance is that market actors are not self-regulating. Fair competition and financial stability are not equilibrium conditions of capitalism; they do not obtain and sustain naturally. They rely on sound institutional frameworks and diligent regulatory oversight.

What are the practical implications of these first principles of human-centred corporate governance and financial system regulation? Where specifically is this policy balance to be struck in order to ensure that excessive rents are not created for the owners of capital and their agents to the detriment of progress in the real economy?

During the twentieth century, this debate revolved around the question of state ownership of enterprises and banks, that is, socialism. How extensively should governments intervene directly in capital allocation by owning firms and financial institutions? But state ownership is a very crude instrument for improving an economy's intermediation of private savings to productive real economy investment. Moreover, it generates negative externalities of its own, including the concentration of information and reduction in individual initiative which tend to accompany centralized systems of control. Moreover, the politics of state enterprise and credit allocation were highly charged during the Cold War. The capitalism–socialism ideological polemic of the time had a polarizing effect on this debate, partially obscuring the wider spectrum of corporate governance and financial system policy options available to ensure that finance serve the purpose of mobilizing investment in real economy productive capacity.

Corporate Governance

In a modern market economy, the essential question for policymakers with respect to corporate governance is not whether to promote laissez-faire or state ownership. It is how to balance shareholder and broader enterprise value creation, and in particular how to incentivize firms to pursue the former within the broader and more fundamental pursuit of the latter.

If corporations are a social construct—vehicles for channelling capital to purposes that increase employment, labour productivity and living standards—then by definition they cannot be run solely in the interests of generating short-term financial returns to investors. Near-term profitability does not necessarily equal medium- to long-term firm strength in terms of market share and employment or indeed profitability and market valuation. The value of an enterprise over time is shaped by a more complex mixture of tangible and intangible as well as short- and long-run factors than those which influence its current returns to shareholders.

How should a country's corporate governance legal framework reflect this larger social purpose of companies without diminishing their ability to raise capital from investors? Rather than a binary choice between private shareholder primacy and state ownership, this policy challenge is better represented today as a continuum reflecting the considerable diversity of corporate structures and market economy systems in operation around the world. There are multiple corporate governance constructs in use that place varying degrees of emphasis on shareholder versus broader enterprise value creation—on near-term financial versus medium- to long-term economic and social returns—as represented in the Social Market–Market Socialism Corporate Governance Continuum shown in Fig. 5.4.

At one extreme of this continuum is the laissez-faire, self-regulatory approach best captured by the dictum attributed to economist Milton Friedman: "the business of business is business".[34] At the other is comprehensive state ownership of the means of production—direct alignment of resource allocation with social priorities through direct or indirect government control. Few if any economies today are characterized by these two extremes; all are mixed economies in the sense of not only combining private and state ownership to one degree or another but also employing different corporate legal structures that balance shareholder and wider company stakeholder interests in differing ways and degrees.

This spectrum of mixed approaches has developed across the world economy in part because the Friedman, or neoliberal, approach relies on assumptions that do not hold in the real world—particularly that corporate boards and financial markets weigh all relevant factors in allocating capital,

5 HUMAN-CENTRED NATIONAL ECONOMIC POLICY: INSTITUTIONALIZING... 153

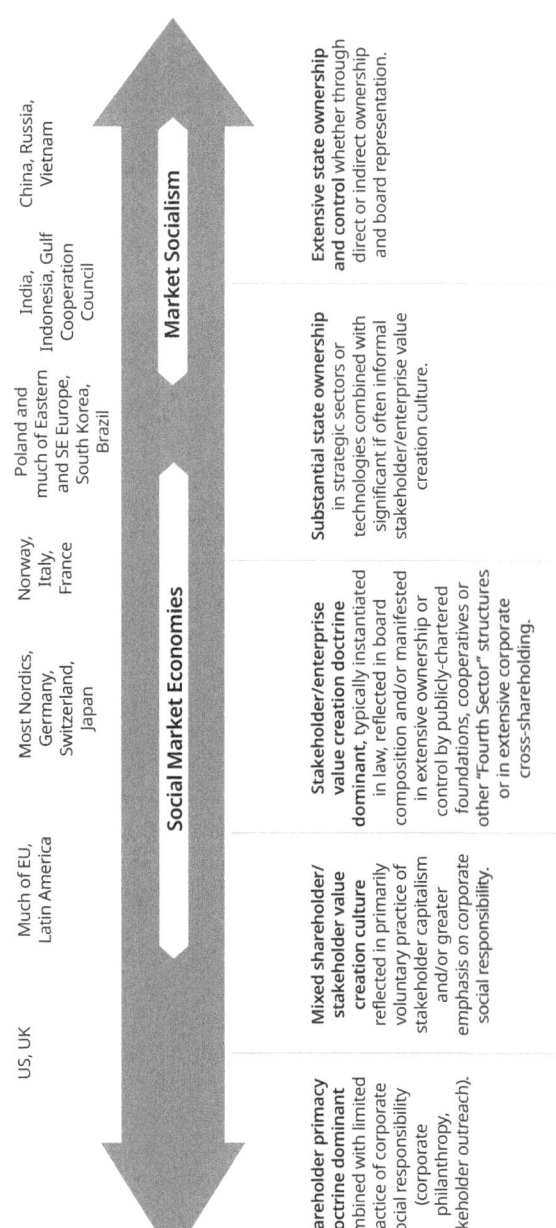

Fig. 5.4 Social Market–Market Socialism Corporate Governance Continuum

making rational decisions on the basis of complete information. We know from long experience that financial markets and corporate boards do not always have access to or properly weigh information about all material tangible and intangible factors—that is, those which can reasonably be expected to influence a firm's value over the medium term.[35] Moreover, they sometimes exhibit significant biases in their decision-making, whether because of principal–agent issues, moral hazard, groupthink, herd behaviour, or misaligned incentives related to executive compensation practices or rent-seeking opportunities in the form of regulatory capture or collusion.

The other reason these mixed approaches have proliferated is that, in contrast to the United States, most societies fundamentally accept the notion of the corporation as a social construct and seek to reflect this in their corporate governance statutes and practices. Whether formally or informally, the enterprise value (as opposed to shareholder value) concept is pre-eminent in most countries,[36] albeit in different ways as reflected in the Social Market—Market Socialism Corporate Governance Continuum. For example, Germany legally mandates employee board seats in large firms and either requires or encourages the formation of works councils that serve as an employee–employer consultative interface in virtually all firms.[37] In Scandinavia, Germany and Switzerland, there are over 3000 family-controlled shareholder foundations and holding companies, which have as their legal purpose the continuation of the firm, that is, sustainable *enterprise* value creation, as opposed to shareholder value creation alone. These account for over a third of the GDP of Sweden and over half of the market capitalization of the Copenhagen Stock Exchange as well as a significant share of the German and Swiss corporate communities.[38] The European Union has been moving more formally in this direction by establishing new rules regarding sustainability-related corporate disclosure and due diligence in supply chains.[39]

In Latin America and Asia, family-owned or -controlled businesses dominate the corporate landscape. Many retain a strong sense of responsibility to the communities hosting their major operations. India has codified such behaviour as a legal requirement of larger firms, mandating the expenditure of 2% of their average net profit on corporate social responsibility projects in communities.[40] In Northeast Asia, corporate governance is characterized by cooperation and consensus-building, with a sense of the company's shared responsibility for maintaining social cohesion. In addition, there is a tradition of extensive corporate cross-shareholding, which tends to reinforce the creation of durable enterprise value as opposed to near-term shareholder value.

Even the United States has experienced considerable experimentation with alternative structures and practices to those emphasizing shareholder primacy, whether in the form of chartered "B corporations"[41] or the expanding practice of stakeholder capitalism, which seeks to overcome the information asymmetries and incentive misalignments described above by explicitly recognizing the purpose of the corporation as creating enterprise rather than solely shareholder value and instituting processes to ensure that the key material interests of all of the firm's key stakeholders—employees, customers, suppliers, distributors, communities hosting operations, etc.— are properly considered.[42] Nevertheless, the shareholder primacy ethos remains dominant in US boardrooms and capital markets for reasons of both law and tradition, which is to say, the path dependency of accumulated, customary practice.

Countries are positioned on the Social Market–Market Socialism Corporate Governance Continuum according to the extent to which the legal mission of corporations is socialized beyond a narrow duty to shareholders and how this is most commonly manifested in ownership structure. The role of the private sector is extensive all along the continuum, but countries appearing on the left side are those in which there is a strong *de jure* or de facto primary corporate governance duty to shareholders, while broader economic and social considerations are integrated on a more informal—that is, less systematic—basis, for example through the growing voluntary practice of stakeholder capitalism. Those appearing towards the right side of the spectrum instantiate the duty of a corporation to multiple stakeholders and society at large more formally and systematically, for example through substantial use of state-owned enterprises[43] and sometimes an emphasis on the primacy of enterprise value creation in statutory law. At the far right of the continuum are countries in which state-owned enterprises play an extensive role in the economy, a defining feature of "socialism". Finally, countries positioned in the centre make extensive use of alternative corporate governance legal frameworks, e.g., non-profit foundations, cooperatives and public-purpose B corporation or "fourth sector"[44] firms, all of which are privately held but governed by a formal legal obligation to maximize wider enterprise and stakeholder or societal value rather than solely or principally shareholder value. Governments in this category take steps through various aspects of law and regulation to incentivize the use of these ownership structures within their economies, expanding the "social and solidarity economy".[45]

Corporate governance codes and cultures are in flux in much of the world, moving along this continuum in one direction or other in response to social, environmental and economic pressures. Countries wishing to achieve a more inclusive, sustainable and resilient pattern of economic growth and development should give serious thought to where on this continuum they wish to position their own corporate governance legal and institutional regime. Unfortunately, existing sources of comparative benchmarking information on country corporate governance legal environments do not yet adequately capture the policy trade-offs represented in the continuum. They tend to focus only on more traditional dimensions of corporate governance practice.[46] Thus, this aspect of the aggregate distribution function is particularly ripe for further policy research and benchmarking analysis by scholars and international organizations.

Financial System Governance
If financial markets and institutions like corporations are fundamentally a social construct—vehicles for channelling capital to purposes that increase employment, labour productivity and living standards—then by definition they also cannot be run in the primary let alone sole interest of generating returns for their investors. While such returns are an entirely necessary and legitimate objective, they cannot be the driving logic of financial system governance. This is especially so when the government serves as a lender of last resort and more generally underwrites the financial sector's stability, as is the case to one degree or another in all countries.

Financial sector development is critically important to economic development, but policymakers have a duty to set it in this larger context. They should certainly seek to build the public and private institutional foundations of more efficient and sound financial intermediation, as summarized by such important policy guidelines and benchmarking resources as the IMF Financial Development Index.[47] But they must also work to ensure that the process of financial deepening does not overshoot, creating negative social externalities and collateral financial stability risks. These may include increased inequality and the diversion of capital to uses that contribute relatively little to employment, productivity and living standards, such as financial engineering that is essentially speculative in nature and results in the churning of existing assets rather than investment in new ones.

Striking the right balance in financial sector regulation in these respects will require policymakers to think seriously and expansively about the policy tools available to manage the degree of leverage and risk-taking throughout the financial system, on the one hand, and to promote the system's net performance in intermediating funds for primary investment in real economy productive capacity and innovation, on the other. These are crucial parameters of human-centred financial sector regulation—of ensuring that finance serves the purpose of enhancing both the growth and living standards potential of economies, which includes but is not limited to strengthening their capacity to avoid and withstand crises.

The full panoply of tools relevant to these two policy challenges are not yet fully covered by cross-country policy analysis and guidance, since some of them extend beyond the traditional focus of banking and securities regulators. But, as in the case of corporate governance, the challenge confronting policymakers is not a binary one—such as between the polar extremes of a laissez-faire, self-regulatory approach and state-directed credit allocation. A spectrum of approaches to controlling credit creation and leverage and promoting real economy investment exists in theory and increasingly in practice as well. This typology of policy options and practices is represented in the Financialization–Real Economy Investment Financial Regulation Continuum in Fig. 5.5.

With respect to credit creation and leverage, the international capital and liquidity requirements for large banks were raised following the Great Financial Crisis (Basel III reforms).[48] This has reduced the degree of leverage in the banking system appreciably[49] but is only a partial response to the inherent pro-cyclicality of financial sector behaviour which makes financial markets prone to instability and outright crisis, as observed by Hyman Minsky, Charles Kindleberger and others. While financial regulators are to be commended for increasing the discipline of regulatory oversight, including by stress-testing their banks against these post-crisis capital and liquidity requirements, such efforts are insufficient for two reasons. First, these requirements and tests do not yet adequately cover non-bank financial institutions, which represent a large and growing proportion of financial intermediation, particularly in advanced, systemically important countries.[50] Non-bank institutions like hedge funds, private equity firms, asset managers and other institutional investors, cryptocurrency exchanges and the trading operations of investment banks often operate at very high rates of leverage that create risk for the financial system as a whole. Second, the adequacy of the existing requirements for banks remains questionable given their central role in credit creation. It is now widely accepted that credit creation is endogenous to the banking system; bank loans actually create deposits rather than the other way around, and banks borrow reserves from central banks on demand at the prevailing rate for such funds.[51]

Thus, the status quo, in the form of the post-crisis Basel III requirements, is represented towards the left side of the continuum, just to the right of the very light regulatory approach that characterized international macroprudential supervision before the crisis. The new supervisory regime

Fig. 5.5 Financialization–Real Economy Investment Financial Regulation Continuum

is a significant improvement over its pre-crisis predecessor, even if it is still in the process of implementation[52] and falls well short of what many experts consider prudent, particularly with respect to bank capital adequacy.[53] Most countries fall within this category, but some of them impose or are considering imposing somewhat tighter capital and leverage requirements on banks as well as non-bank institutions in order to limit further the risk within their financial systems. They also encourage socially inclusive and environmentally sustainable credit *allocation* by creating a significant role for social, postal and microfinance banking institutions focused on serving communities and small businesses[54] as well as requiring related portfolio management and disclosure requirements for banks, such as those promoted by the Network for Greening the Financial System (NGFS), a group of 121 central banks and other financial regulatory authorities,[55] and the supporting corporate disclosure standards being developed by the new International Sustainability Standards Board (ISSB) of the International Financial Reporting Standards Foundation.[56] These strategies, combined with accelerated implementation of the modest agenda of regulatory oversight of non-bank financial institutions agreed by the FSB in 2014,[57] constitute an approach to advancing financial sector reform moderately beyond the status quo. This is therefore represented towards the centre of the continuum.

A more ambitious strategy to de-risk the financial system and prioritize the capital investment requirements of real economy firms would involve government intervening at a more structural level while maintaining credit creation and allocation within the private sector. This approach appears further to the right on the continuum. First, all financial activities characteristic of the role of depository institutions would be statutorily ring-fenced from riskier financial service provision such as investment banking and proprietary trading, irrespective of what kinds of institutions sponsored them, and subjected to some combination of significantly higher capital requirements, restrictions on the classes of assets in which they could invest, and public deposit insurance. Second, these measures would be accompanied by others that provided preferred regulatory and possibly tax treatment for lending for economically viable purposes that also have positive real economy, social or environmental externalities, including certain small business, community and household loans such as those supporting disadvantaged communities or climate mitigation and resilience as well as the activities of alternative or social banking institutions. Third, non-bank activities would be subjected to a thorough financial supervisory regime going well beyond current FSB and BIS mandates in order to mitigate substantially the stability risks their large flows and complex structures create, potentially including stricter capital and margin requirements, liquidity buffers, clearing system requirements, transparency, stress-testing, etc.

This approach would treat the payment-processing and retail and business financing functions of banks like a regulated public utility owing to their vital importance to the robustness and resilience of real economy activity. It would segment and more fully de-risk the part of the financial system which government is prepared to stand behind in the event of a crisis as well as focus it on the financing of business capital formation and working capital as well as the practical needs of households. Other parts of the financial system that do not merit government backstopping (non-bank institutions, the trading and securities structuring and underwriting activities of universal banks, crypto, etc.) would nevertheless be subjected to a substantial tightening of regulation given their still considerable potential to generate systemic risk.[58] This more proactive regulatory posture would further reduce the risk of financial instability in riskier markets spilling over into and becoming the tail that wags the dog of the real economy, as such instability has done so many times before. It would privilege and therefore likely reduce the cost of financing of employment- and wage-supporting real economy investment, a crucial priority of Keynes's *General Theory*, as discussed in Chap. 3. Given the pressures building within the financial system that relate to fintech trends, debt levels and societal demands for greater inclusion, sustainability and resilience, this could well be where consensus thinking about financial regulation will lead in the coming years, particularly in the event of another severe global financial crisis.

This regulatory posture would return the core of the financial system to its roots and fundamental purpose. Up until about a century ago, banks primarily financed industry and to a lesser extent households on a relatively short-term, collateralized basis. They engaged in very little maturity transformation, let alone financial engineering designed to multiply leverage and effectively enable speculation. In the absence of deposit insurance, they tended to operate conservatively, matching the tenure of assets and liabilities while serving real economy purposes—financing tangible investment in trade, inventory and plant and equipment that could be collateralized.[59] This stands in contrast to today's highly financialized economies in which financial market activity is largely decoupled from the core task of mobilizing primary investment in productive capacity. The former chairman of the United Kingdom's Financial Services Authority, Adair Turner, estimated that "no more than 15% of lending by the UK banking system is funding the 'new investment projects' on which theoretical descriptions of banking

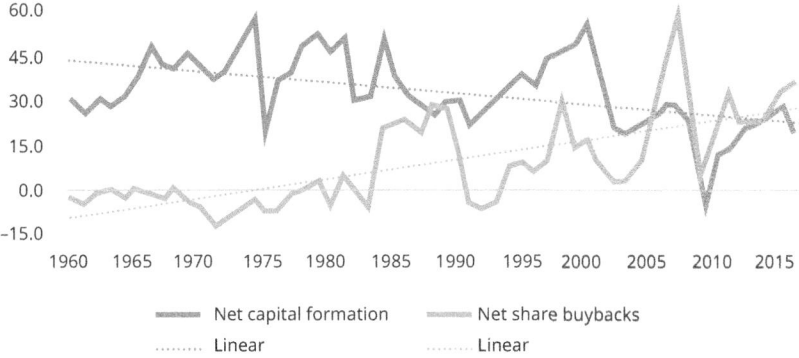

Fig. 5.6 Net share buybacks and net capital formation as a share of net operating surplus for operating corporations

systems still tend to concentrate".[60] This phenomenon is also evident in the US economy, as illustrated in Fig. 5.6, where

> the separation of asset valuations from underlying economic performance is perhaps the most conspicuous feature … with firms being managed to maximize asset valuations separately from, or even at the expense of, growth, productivity, and other socially beneficial objectives.[61]

Finally, further to the right along the continuum are even more fundamental and interventionist approaches to ensuring that credit creation and capital allocation are aligned with broader economic and social priorities. At the far end of the spectrum is state ownership or effective control of major financial institutions, such as one sees to a considerable extent in China, Russia, India and Gulf Cooperation Council countries and, to a lesser but still substantial extent, Brazil, Mexico and Indonesia. Another, less statist approach would not go so far as to place credit *allocation* under the control of government, but it would place credit *creation* more strictly within its purview. Following the 1929 crash and the Great Depression of the 1930s, there was considerable debate about this option, known as the "Chicago Plan", that calls for the

> separation of the monetary and credit functions of the banking system, first by requiring 100% backing of deposits by government-issued money, and second

by ensuring that the financing of new bank credit can only take place through earnings that have been retained in the form of government-issued money, or through the borrowing of existing government-issued money from non-banks, but not through the creation of new deposits, ex nihilo, by banks.[62]

Theoretically, this approach would have several advantages:

First, preventing banks from creating their own funds during credit booms, and then destroying these funds during subsequent contractions, would allow for a much better control of credit cycles, which were perceived to be the major source of business cycle fluctuations. Second, 100% reserve backing would completely eliminate bank runs. Third, allowing the government to issue money directly at zero interest, rather than borrowing that same money from banks at interest, would lead to a reduction in the interest burden on government finances and to a dramatic reduction of (net) government debt, given that irredeemable government-issued money represents equity in the commonwealth rather than debt. Fourth, given that money creation would no longer require the simultaneous creation of mostly private debts on bank balance sheets, the economy could see a dramatic reduction not only of government debt but also of private debt levels.[63]

The Chicago Plan was never implemented. It raises a number of practical questions and remains in the realm of theoretical debate.[64] However, it did attract renewed interest in the immediate aftermath of the Great Financial Crisis.

Public Investment
In addition to incentivizing private investment in productive capacity through appropriate corporate and financial system governance, governments have an important investment role of their own to play in supporting employment and entrepreneurial opportunity. The public sector typically accounts for a large share of investment in infrastructure, technology, public works and, in many countries, strategically important industries. These kinds of public investments can be crucial enablers of productivity and economic growth if structured well, and they often create a further multiplier effect by "crowding in" additional private investment in industry and innovation.

The public sector finances the vast majority of infrastructure globally—an average of 83% in emerging market and developing countries, where private financing is limited mainly to renewable energy.[65] There is solid evidence that such investment contributes importantly to productivity growth, particularly in developing countries[66] and especially in the absence

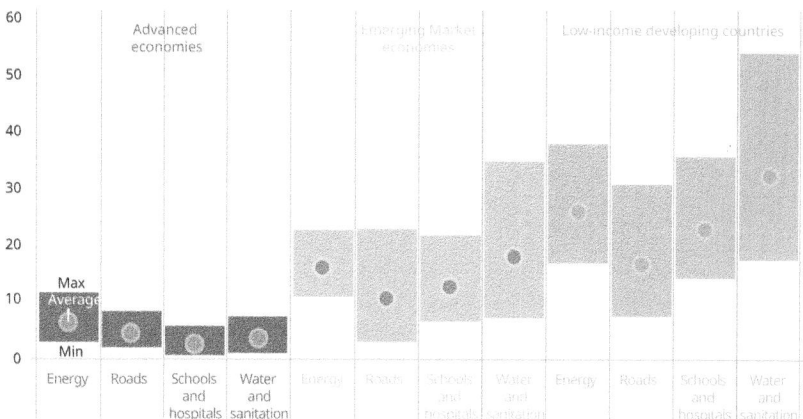

Sources: Compustat, Orbis and IMF staff calculations.

Fig. 5.7 Jobs multiplier effect of public infrastructure investment (per USD 1 million investment)

of major cost overruns, project delays or political manipulation of site selection. As illustrated in Fig. 5.7, it is also relatively employment intensive. An IMF study of 41 countries over 19 years determined that US$1 million of public spending in infrastructure creates an estimated 3–7 jobs in advanced economies, 10–17 jobs in emerging market economies and 16–30 jobs in low-income developing countries.[67] Countries wishing to maximize the job creation potential of infrastructure can access policy guidance and databases permitting cross-country comparison and benchmarking, such as the World Bank's Benchmarking Infrastructure Development tool[68] and the G20 Global Infrastructure Hub.[69]

Similarly, public investment in technological research, development and diffusion also plays a critical role in economic progress. Indeed, most economists believe that so-called "total factor productivity", a residual measure of the contribution of technical progress after accounting for changes in labour and capital, accounts for a majority of economic growth. Detailed estimates of the US economy in the twentieth century found that total factor productivity accounted for about 60% to 65% of growth, with about 26% attributable to improvements in labour quality and 14% to growth in capital inputs.[70] While these proportions likely vary across countries and time, economists who have studied the topic do broadly agree that how well an economy integrates better technologies and techniques largely determines (in addition to

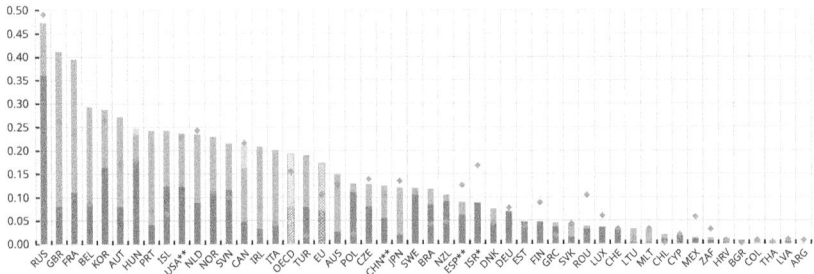

Fig. 5.8 Direct government funding and tax support for business enterprise R&D (BERD), 2019 (percent of GDP)

population growth) how fast it will grow and hence generate employment and entrepreneurial opportunity for its people.

This implies that the policy and institutional enabling environment for research, development and the application of knowledge and innovation deserves priority attention from policymakers seeking to advance median living standards. In high- and upper-middle-income countries, where most of the world's R&D investment occurs, roughly 60% of R&D expenditure is in the private sector. For this reason, many governments provide considerable support for such activities through preferential tax treatment in addition to directly funding basic research in universities and government laboratories. In other words, it is quite common for technical progress to be subsidized by governments, whether directly or indirectly. Figure 5.8 shows the diversity of policy practice in public subsidization of private R&D investment, mainly through the tax code.[71]

For example, 20 OECD countries have special deduction rules for R&D costs, 18 have a tax credit for R&D, and 19 countries have a patent box (preferential tax treatment for patents and certain other intellectual property). These policies vary in their definitions of R&D costs, deduction amounts, credit rates, and eligibility rules. Three countries (Belgium, Ireland and the United Kingdom) have versions of all three policies in their tax systems. Only Estonia and Sweden have none of the three policies, although Sweden directly finances business R&D at twice the level of the OECD average. Five countries, including the United States, only apply their R&D tax benefits to incremental R&D expenses. The country with the most generous tax credit is Australia (43.5% on a refundable basis for smaller firms and 38.5% for larger ones), whereas the United Kingdom has the least generous credit rate, at 13% on qualifying expenses.[72]

In sum, empirical research suggests that public R&D financing has a sizable payoff for the economy and job creation, with US$1 million in such spending yielding an average range of 5–11 jobs in R&D in OECD countries, a higher ratio than for infrastructure spending in those countries.[73] However, as the work of Ricardo Hausmann, a leading international development economist, and colleagues have emphasized,[74] policy support for technological progress is not just an issue for wealthy countries, where most advanced research takes place. In fact,

> the two main ingredients for the development of new technology are codified knowledge in the form of theories, frameworks, scientific papers, patents, recipes, protocols, routines and instruction manuals and tacit knowledge or knowhow, which is acquired through learning by doing in a long process of imitation and repetition and which exists only in brains.[75]

The key policy objective is therefore to cultivate economic *innovation*, whether through development of new or the application of existing technology and processes within industry and agriculture. This implies a wider range of policy and institutional tools than direct financing or tax subsidies. It argues for a broader effort to diversify and upgrade an economy's industrial base, using a blend of industrial, foreign investment, human capital, technology and immigration policy to activate both formal and tacit channels of innovation more fully.[76]

This wider conceptualization of *innovation cum industrial* policy has been gaining momentum in theory and practice in recent years.[77] It combines elements of traditional state subsidization of industries deemed strategically important for an economy's next stage of economic development, for example the much-publicized initiatives of China, Europe and the United States in frontier technologies, with cross-cutting strategies to promote economic diversification and value-added industrial production by improving the institutional enabling environment in multiple domains. Active industrial policy is particularly in vogue in middle-income countries worried about the so-called "middle-income trap". Of the 101 countries that were middle income or below in 1960, the only non-EU countries and jurisdictions with a population greater than five million to have since graduated to high-income status are Japan, South Korea, Taiwan Province of China, Israel and Singapore.[78] In fact, South Korea is the only country to have ascended from low-income to high-income status during this period, a feat China may also achieve in the next few years according to recent trends. Whether China will be able to maintain this status—a few countries, such as Russia, Argentina and Venezuela, attained and later lost it—will likely depend on the effectiveness of its approach to innovation cum industrial policy, a consideration not lost on its leadership given the ambitious policy targets and state-driven investment strategies it has set.[79]

Two comparative databases are useful tools for identifying country strengths and weaknesses and planning strategies with respect to innovation cum industrial policy; one is focused on the innovation ecosystem and the other on economic complexity and diversification. They are, respectively, the World Intellectual Property Organization's Global Innovation Index[80] and Harvard Growth Lab's Country and Product Complexity Rankings[81] based on the Economic Complexity Index,[82] which measures the diversity and sophistication of the productive capabilities embedded in the exports of countries.

Labour Force Skills, Transitions and Participation

A person's job prospects depend crucially on his or her skills and capabilities. The general skill level of a community or nation is determined mainly by public policy. Through their policy and funding decisions, governments at the national and subnational levels heavily influence the extent of access to quality primary and secondary schools, school-to-work training programmes; universities, and worker and lifelong training. They also influence the job market through the extent of their implementation and enforcement of key norms—in particular, international labour standards that prohibit forced and child labour and discrimination on the basis of gender, ethnicity or other personal characteristics. Beyond upholding universal human rights, the abolition of forced and child labour ensures that workers do not compete against people whom society has determined should not be in the workforce. Regulation against discrimination ensures that employers draw from the widest possible pool of eligible talent and must consider applicants fairly, on the basis of their capabilities.

As the empirical work discussed above has found, the quantity and quality of labour are second only to technical progress in their importance for an economy's growth potential. Since skilling and labour rights profoundly influence both the quantity and quality of a country's workforce, they deserve to be a central focus of economic policy. However, this is far from uniformly the case—a situation contributing to substantial inequality in employment and entrepreneurial opportunity among and within countries.

Skills and Transitions

In most low- and lower-middle-income developing countries, the primary skilling imperative is to expand basic literacy and numeracy by increasing access to and the quality of primary and secondary education. The advent of mass schooling in Europe and North America in the latter decades of the nineteenth century was instrumental to rapid productivity gains and economic development in these regions. But while enrolment in primary school has risen significantly in developing countries over the past two decades, serious problems remain.

First, primary and secondary school completion rates are lagging in many of these countries. Even when children do reach the last grade of primary or lower secondary school, they often fail to attain basic levels of literacy and numeracy. For example, in Central, South and Western Asia as well as North Africa, only about half of students complete primary school education and acquire a basic level of reading proficiency; roughly 40% complete but do not attain such proficiency and 10% do not complete their primary education. These figures are much worse for sub-Saharan Africa (10%, 53% and 37%, respectively) and better for Latin America (75%, 18% and 7%, respectively).[83] Moreover, they vary considerably within regions, even among countries with similar GDP per capita.

The corresponding figures for basic numeracy are markedly worse. And while reading and numeracy proficiency improves for children of lower secondary school age, scores remain far behind levels in high-income countries, in part because in developing countries fewer students complete lower secondary than complete primary school—more than a third fewer in low-income countries and about one-sixth fewer in their lower-middle-income counterparts.[84] On current rates of progress, it will take an estimated 70 to 100 years for these developing countries to attain the 12 twelve years of schooling of today's developed countries.[85]

These large inequalities in educational access and attainment within and among developing countries—in the basic skill set of their populations—reflect differences in policy priorities and resourcing. For example, public education expenditures in about a third of developing countries are below both of the SDG targets of 4% of GDP and 15% of total government expenditure.[86] In a cross-regional sample of 30 lower-middle-income countries, per capita public education spending ranged between about US$50 and US$700—a factor of 14![87] This wide disparity owes partly to similarly wide differences in the level of domestic resource mobilization. Tax revenues vary between about 20% to 60% of GDP in lower-middle-income countries and roughly 12% to 40% in low-income countries.[88] This striking divergence in available fiscal resources contributes to similarly wide variation in the proportion of education expenses that households incur out of pocket, anywhere from 25% to 80% in low-income, lower-middle-income and upper-middle-income countries, with the highest average burden falling on households in lower-middle-income nations.[89]

By contrast, the main policy challenge in advanced economies is strengthening training and tertiary education in terms of both access and job market relevance. A major exception in a number of countries is the need to improve the regional consistency of basic education quality and attainment. In particular, the United States relies to an unusual extent on local property taxes to finance its public primary and secondary schools, a practice that results in public expenditure per pupil being about three times higher in the wealthiest communities than in the poorest.[90] Most countries' school-financing systems do the opposite; to a greater or lesser extent they cross-subsidize schools in disadvantaged communities in order to promote more equitable educational attainment and consistent basic skills within their economies, leading to much smaller geographic variation in public education spending per pupil. Moreover, on average, US teachers earn about 60% of the average wage of all tertiary-educated workers and 50% of that of similarly educated workers. Out of 26 OECD countries for which data were available, only Hungary has a lower performance; the overwhelming majority of these countries have teacher pay rates between 80% and 100% of those of all tertiary-educated and of similarly educated workers.[91]

Public investment in school-to-work and workforce training also varies widely among high-income countries. For example, the proportion of youth between the ages of 18 and 24 not in employment, education or training (NEET) ranges from 7% or 8% in the Netherlands and Germany to about 15% in the United Kingdom and United States and 24% in Italy (2019 figures).[92] And public expenditure on active labour market policies—e.g., worker training, employment services and income maintenance during retraining—varied before the pandemic in these countries between about 0.2% and 1% of GDP—a factor of five.[93]

Enrolment rates in tertiary education are similarly disparate, ranging from near universal (95% and above) in Japan, Belgium, the Netherlands and the United States to about two-thirds in Sweden, Switzerland and Israel (with female enrolment rates substantially above those for males in the latter two). This partly reflects considerable differences in the use of public versus private institutions to deliver tertiary education and in the total amount of expenditures devoted to tertiary versus basic education. Tertiary spending varies widely, from about 1% of GDP for several OECD countries at the bottom of the distribution to about 2.5 times this proportion in the United States, Canada and Chile at the top of the distribution.[94]

Finally, advanced economies are increasingly recognizing the importance of investing in early childhood education, given the significant cognitive and social benefits that have been demonstrated by research.[95] Participation in early childhood education is increasingly compulsory and publicly supported in these countries, with an average of 87% of 3–5-year-olds enrolled in such programmes. Even where it is not compulsory, countries often offer universal legal entitlements for at least one or two years before the start of compulsory schooling. As a result, in more than half of 42 OECD member and partner countries with available data, enrolment of children between the ages of three and five is nearly universal, that is, at least 90%. The highest enrolment rates of 3–5-year-olds are in Belgium, Denmark, France, Iceland, Ireland, Israel, Norway, Spain and the United Kingdom, where they equal or exceed 97%. In contrast, less than 50% of 3–5-year-olds are enrolled in education in Saudi Arabia, Switzerland and Turkey. Public support of such education also varies considerably, ranging from 98% in Belgium and Luxembourg to two-thirds in the United Kingdom and about half in Japan, the rest of the funding coming from households and other private sources.[96]

Rights and Participation
Households and communities are composed of people with diverse workforce and demographic profiles with respect to age, experience, gender, ethnicity and time availability, etc. Given the central role of labour income in living standards, progress at the median depends on fair access to employment and entrepreneurial opportunity for all who seek it, irrespective of gender, race, ethnicity, age, disability, etc. This in turn relies upon the implementation and enforcement of laws regarding non-discrimination and the elimination of forms of work so odious that society has deemed them illegal, particularly forced and child labour.

Since the early 1920s, the world's governments and employers' and workers' organizations have negotiated through the ILO a large number of international legal standards covering these and other dimensions of the world of work. In 1998, a subset of these conventions were designated as Fundamental Principles and Rights at Work,[97] meaning that the ILO's 187 member governments agreed to "promote, respect and realize" these instruments irrespective of whether they had ratified them domestically. These so-called "core labour standards" are universal; governments and employers of all kinds are obliged to create the policy and institutional environment necessary to ensure their faithful implementation.

In addition to providing technical assistance to help governments and social partners translate international labour standards into domestic regulation and practice, the ILO tracks implementation on the ground. Its most recent estimates find that progress has been mixed on forced and child labour; there is a long way to go to full realization of international norms. For example:

- **Forced labour and human trafficking:**[98]

    i. In 2021, 49.6 million people were living in modern slavery, of which 27.6 million were in forced labour and 22 million in forced marriage. There was an increase of 2.7 million in the number people in forced labour between 2016 and 2021, which translates into a rise in the prevalence of forced labour from 3.4 to 3.5 per thousand people in the world.
    ii. Of the 27.6 million people in forced labour, 17.3 million are exploited in the private sector, 6.3 million in forced commercial sexual exploitation and 3.9 million in forced labour imposed by the state. Women and girls account for 4.9 million of those in forced commercial sexual exploitation and for six million of those in forced labour in other economic sectors. Twelve per cent of all those in forced labour are children. More than half of these children are in commercial sexual exploitation.
    iii. Forced labour is a concern regardless of a country's wealth. It is highest in the Arab States (5.3 per thousand people), followed by Europe and Central Asia (4.4 per thousand), the Americas and Asia and the Pacific (both at 3.5 per thousand) and Africa (2.9 per thousand). More than half of all forced labour occurs in either upper-middle income or high-income countries.

- **Child labour:**[99]

    i. At the beginning of 2020, 160 million children worldwide—63 million girls and 97 million boys—were in child labour, accounting for almost one in 10 of all children worldwide. Seventy-nine million children—nearly half of all those in child labour—were in hazardous work that directly endangered their health, safety and moral development.
    ii. The percentage of children in child labour remained unchanged from 2016 to 2020. The global picture masks continued progress

against child labour in Asia and the Pacific as well as Latin America and the Caribbean. In both regions, child labour trended downwards over the preceding four years, whereas sub-Saharan Africa has seen an increase in both the number and percentage of children in child labour since 2012. There are now more children in child labour in sub-Saharan Africa than in the rest of the world combined.

iii. Child labour continued to decline over the preceding four years among children aged 12 to 14 and 15 to 17; however, it rose by 16.8 million among young children aged five to 11.

- **Gender discrimination:**

  i. The gender pay gap is substantial and remains high in nearly all G20 countries, between 5% and 40%. When adjusted for education, the gap is even larger. Women are twice as likely as men to be in low-paid jobs, and they continue to be under-represented in leadership positions across the G20, accounting for 15% to 45% of managerial jobs, depending on the country.

  ii. The share of women in informal employment is greater than that of men in eight of the 12 G20 countries where such data are available. Women work disproportionately in the home, in domestic work or in own-account work—the lowest echelons of the informal economy. The rate of self-employment for women is on average 7.5 percentage points below that of men.

  iii. At their 2014 Summit in Brisbane, G20 leaders committed to reduce the gender gap in labour force participation by 25% relative to 2012 by the year 2025. G20 ministers of labour further agreed on a set of key principles to improve the quality of women's employment. Most countries have been making progress towards the goal despite the recent pandemic, as illustrated in Fig. 5.9.

As with other drivers of employment and entrepreneurial opportunity, labour rights and protections can be improved on the ground through increased policy and institutional effort. The ILO helps strengthen their legal frameworks and administrative oversight and enforcement capacity. Upon request, it can prepare a Decent Work Country Profile,[100] a data-based analysis of the strengths, weaknesses and opportunities for progress of a country's laws and institutional strength in employment, labour rights, social protection systems, active labour market policies, etc. Given the centrality of these policy domains to median progress in living standards—they

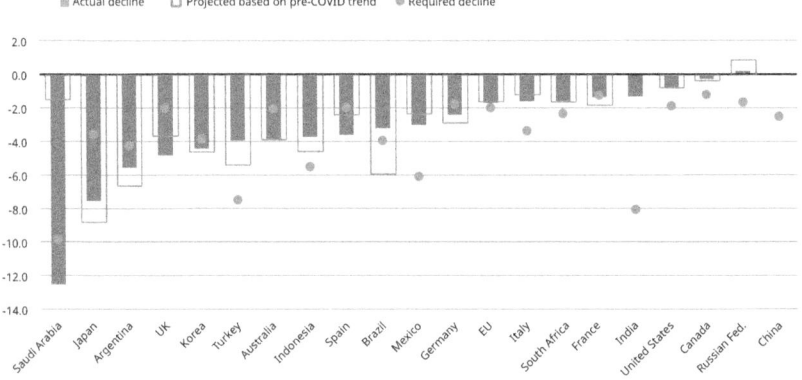

Fig. 5.9 Progress in reaching G20 Brisbane goal set back by COVID-19 pandemic (% point change in gender gap in labour force participation rate 2012–21)

correspond to three of the aggregate distribution function's five factors of distribution—countries should consider undergoing such an evidence-based review and tripartite consultation on a regular basis, perhaps every three or five years, analogous to the IMF's Article 4 policy consultations on macroeconomic and financial system conditions and policies.[101] For developing countries, such strategic, evidence-based reviews on a periodic basis could also help to mobilize additional tangible support from the development cooperation community for their related institutional development priorities.

Disposable Income (I)

While the composition of household income varies somewhat according to wealth, the typical household relies overwhelmingly on wages from employment. Labour income, including from self-employment, accounts on average for roughly 70% of gross household income; pension, social insurance and other benefits account for about 20%; and investment income, including rental income, for about 1% to 4%. Payment of taxes and social insurance contributions typically reduces the gross amount by about 25%. The remainder is the household's disposable income—the money it has available to spend on material necessities and discretionary purchases and to save and invest.[102]

Public policy has a significant influence on the three largest of these variables: wages, benefits and taxes. Policy choices on each help to shape the extent to which disposable income is widely distributed among households. For example, with respect to wages, the statutory minimum wage has an important bearing on *median* living standards because it not only influences the pay of workers in entry-level and low-skill jobs but also has a knock-on effect on the earnings of workers several tiers above. Along with policies relating to benefits and taxes, the minimum wage has an important effect on the absolute level of household income at the bottom of the distribution (on working poverty) as well as on the degree of dispersion along the entire distribution (on income inequality).

Statutory minimum wage levels vary considerably among market economies, including among those at a similar level of development. Figure 5.10 illustrates this variation among a number of OECD economies; it presents the evolution of both nominal and real (inflation-adjusted) wages.

A critical consideration for policymakers is the relationship between the legal minimum wage and a "living wage", defined as the gross wage income necessary for a typical household to meet its necessary living costs. In many countries plagued by high levels of working poverty and inequality, there is a large gap between the two. Moreover, this gap varies considerably among countries with a similar GDP per capita, suggesting that policymakers in many countries have plenty of scope to increase their legal minimum wage to levels consistent with human dignity and social justice without hindering business activity and employment. Among upper-middle-income countries, for example, the minimum wage is about 60% to 70% of a living wage in Malaysia and Guatemala, but only about half of this level, 30% to 40%, in Kazakhstan, Iraq and Azerbaijan. As for lower-middle-income countries, the ratio is 62% in Pakistan but only 34% in Egypt and 9% in Bangladesh.[103]

Among high-income countries, in Spain and New Zealand the statutory minimum wage is above the living wage (108% and 167%, respectively), whereas in the United States it is well below: 30% for people earning the federal minimum wage, and rising to about 50% to 60% in states with a higher mandated minimum wage than the federal rate of US$7.25 per hour, which was last adjusted in 2009.[104] As the US example demonstrates, policymakers need to pay attention to not only the current level of the minimum wage in relation to the cost of living but also its adjustment mechanism given the tendency of prices to rise over time, sometimes dramatically so as with the recent round of inflation.

An additional policy variable that influences wages is the enabling environment created by government with respect to another Fundamental

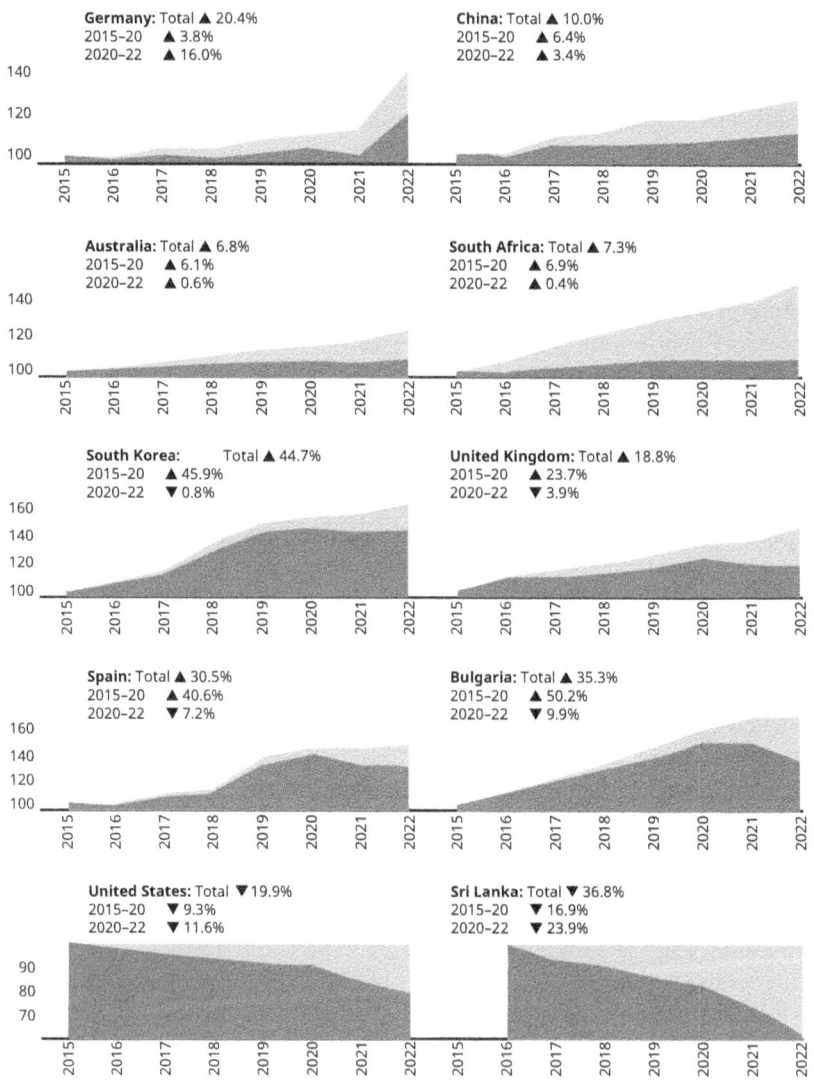

Fig. 5.10 Evolution of real minimum wages, selected countries, 2015–22

Principle and Right at Work: freedom of association and the effective recognition of the right to collective bargaining. Collective bargaining agreements play an important role in many countries in securing decent work, guaranteeing equality of opportunity and treatment, reducing wage inequality and stabilizing labour relations. They can promote trust, cooperation and stability and thus reduce labour turnover, including by enhancing the retention of experienced workers during periods of inactivity such as was experienced during the COVID-19 pandemic. Collective agreements can also reinforce compliance with statutory or negotiated standards, relieving labour administration systems of some of the costs of monitoring and enforcing labour standards. There is evidence, for example, of a positive relationship between collective agreements and compliance with OSH standards at the enterprise level. In short, collective bargaining can help to forge resilience in the short term while transforming and improving the productivity of work practices in the long run.[105]

From the perspective of workers, collective bargaining is an important vehicle for securing a fair share of the fruits of their labour in the form of compensation that rises in proportion to their firm's financial success and their increased productivity. But, as with minimum wage regulation, policies with respect to freedom of association and collective bargaining vary widely among countries. Developed economies tend to have higher proportions of their workers covered by collective bargaining agreements than do developing countries; however, there is considerable variation within all income groups and regions, as illustrated in Fig. 5.11.

Among the features of the policy and institutional environment that influence collective bargaining coverage rates are the nature and enforcement of rules regarding union campaigns and elections; the extent to which bargaining is carried out in a single- or multi-employer setting; and the extent of coverage of such agreements, such as whether their terms apply to both members and non-members of the trade union that negotiated the agreement. For example, a recent ILO survey of 93 countries with available data found that multi-employer or a mixture of multi- and single-employer bargaining was the norm in about half of them, and single-employer bargaining was the common practice in the other half. Collective bargaining coverage rates were significantly higher in the former category of countries than in the latter. In sum, with respect to

> shaping the regulatory coverage of collective bargaining, the effective recognition of the right to collective bargaining for all workers and the promotion of the full development of collective bargaining are foundational. It is when the

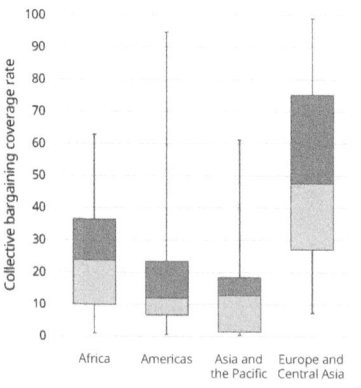 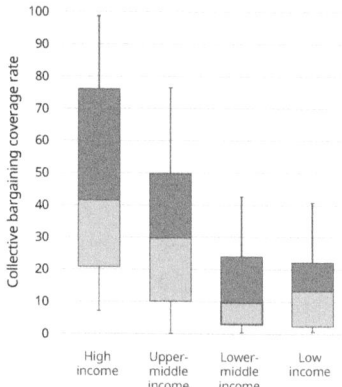

Fig. 5.11   Dispersion of collective bargaining coverage rates

process involves trade unions representing a significant proportion of workers and takes place in multi-employer settings at the territorial, sectoral and/or interprofessional levels that collective bargaining achieves the broadest and most inclusive regulatory coverage. In some countries, the manner in which collective agreements are applied, whether through their extension or through *erga omnes* applicability [automatic application to non-union members of the bargaining unit], can contribute to the inclusive governance of work.[106]

Citizens and policymakers interested in understanding the relative conduciveness of their country's regulatory ecosystem to freedom of association and trade union density,[107] on the one hand, and the effective realization of the right to collective bargaining, on the other, can consult a range of ILO resources. These include the country-specific reports of its labour standards supervisory mechanism[108] and the overall quantitative indicators it presents on a cross-country basis as part of its role in monitoring progress on SDG Target 8.8.2.[109]

Thus, minimum wage and labour rights regulation, among other regulatory and non-regulatory factors, play an important role in shaping the level and distribution of wages within an economy. One useful barometer of whether these and other dimensions of labour market governance deserve increased attention within a given country is the country's "low pay rate", defined as the proportion of the workforce earning less than two-thirds of

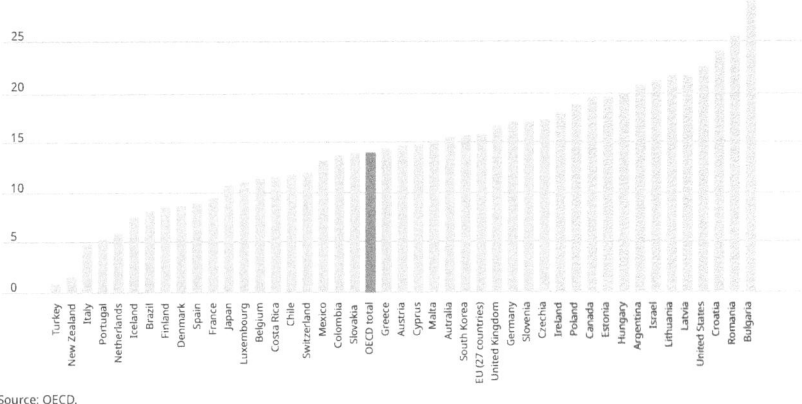

Source: OECD.

Fig. 5.12 Incidence of low pay, 2021 or latest available

the median wage. Figure 5.12 presents this statistic for OECD countries. It demonstrates that this rate can vary by a factor of five or more among such high-income countries. For example, whereas the low pay rate in Italy, the Netherlands, Portugal and New Zealand is in the low single digits, the US rate is 23%!

Taxes, fiscal transfers and non-wage employee compensation are also important factors in the distribution of disposable income among households, especially in countries plagued by a high incidence of low pay, working poverty and income inequality. The progressivity of a country's tax system and the generosity and scope of coverage of its social insurance and employer-provided benefits are shaped by public policy. In a supportive policy environment, these additional sources of income and compensation can offset much of the precarity and deprivation resulting from highly unequal labour market outcomes. Figure 5.13 illustrates the extent to which taxes and transfers reduce market inequality in a selection of advanced economies, reflecting the wide variation in the overall level of such policy support and the trend in OECD countries before the COVID-19 pandemic.

Figure 5.14 completes this picture by also showing the level of household income inequality *before* taxes and transfers. Most OECD countries' policies reduce their Gini coefficients (a standard measure of income inequality) by 10 to 15 coefficient points, typically from around 0.40 before taxes and transfers to about 0.30 or just below. The United States and, to a lesser extent, the United Kingdom are outliers, since they start and end at significantly higher levels of inequality: 0.47 pre-redistribution

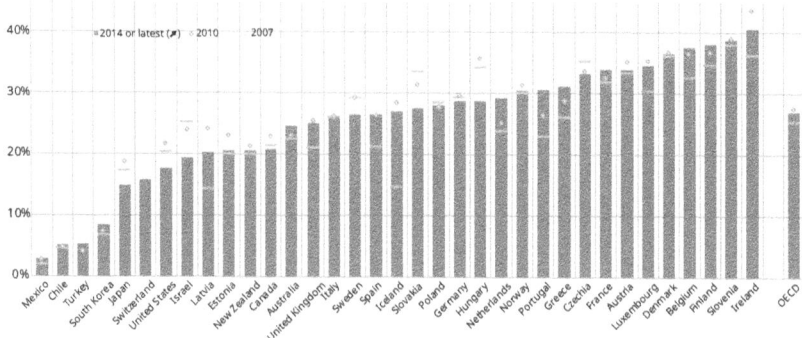

Notes: Redistribution is defined as the difference between market income and disposable income inequality, expressed as a percentage of market income inequality. Market incomes are net of taxes in Hungary, Mexico and Turkey.
Source: OECD Income Inequality Update November2016.

Fig. 5.13 Redistribution decreased in a majority of countries after 2010 and before the COVID-19 pandemic. Percentage reduction of market income inequality owing to transfers and taxes, 2007–14 (or latest year), working-age population

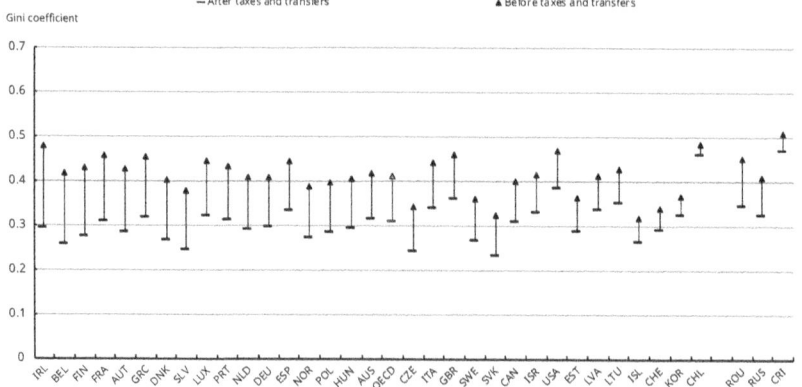

Note: All Gini coefficients are based on the 2012 new income definition and are for the working-age population, disregarding the effect of public pension schemes.
Data for Chile, Denmark, Germany, Hungary, Ireland, Iceland, Switzerland and the United States are for 2017 rather than 2018. Data for the Netherlands and Russia are for 2016 rather than 2018. Data for Costa Rica are for 2019 rather than 2018.
Source: OECD Income Distribution Database.

Fig. 5.14 Differences in household income inequality pre- and post-tax and government transfers, 2018

versus 0.39 post-redistribution for the United States and 0.46 pre-redistribution versus 0.36 post-redistribution for the United Kingdom.

Higher pre-transfer income inequality and lighter use of tax system progressivity and social insurance transfer payments translate into higher levels of poverty, other things being equal. OECD estimates of relative poverty rates, that is, the proportion of households whose disposable income is less than 50% of their country's median, reveal that the United States and Israel had the highest relative poverty rates—nearly 18% of households, three times the 5% to 6% rates of Nordic countries such as Denmark and Finland. More than 20% of American and Israeli children (as well as those of Turkey, Spain and Chile) live in relative poverty.[110]

Child, old-age, disability and other social insurance benefit programmes that augment household disposable income will be addressed in the "Economic Security (EcS)" section below. With respect to tax system progressivity, it is necessary to consider the way a government both raises revenue and redistributes it through the tax code. Each has an important impact on median household disposable income and inequality. There is considerable variation in both the amount and composition of tax revenue among countries at a similar level of economic development, as illustrated in Fig. 5.15a, b.

In particular, countries differ significantly in the degree to which they rely on the taxation of capital and income versus the taxation of labour and consumption. Greater emphasis on the former (e.g., corporate, inheritance and individual income taxes) than on the latter (e.g., payroll and goods and services or value-added taxes) tends to enhance a tax system's contribution to the partial correction of market inequality discussed above. As Fig. 5.15b suggests, there is plenty of scope for most countries at all levels of economic development to improve the progressivity of their tax systems by increasing the emphasis on the former relative to the latter. Unfortunately, just the opposite has been occurring, by and large, over the past two generations.

A recent World Bank study found that over the past 50 years average effective labour and capital tax rates have converged as a result of a 10-percentage-point increase in labour taxation and a five-point decline in capital taxation. The global rise in labour taxation is driven by the expansion of payroll-based social security contributions in the 1970s and 1980s. Yet, as reflected in Fig. 5.16, the most striking pattern is the marked decline of capital taxation: in high-income countries, effective capital tax rates were close to 40% in high-income countries in 1965 and fell to about 32% in 2018, driven by the sharp decline in the taxation of corporate profits. In developing countries, both capital and labour taxation have risen, but capital taxation has been rising at a faster pace.[111]

Finally, policies that support *non-wage* compensation—employee benefits—have an important bearing on the disposable income of households as well. For example, the cost of health and child care diverge significantly among countries as a function of their policy and institutional set-up. With

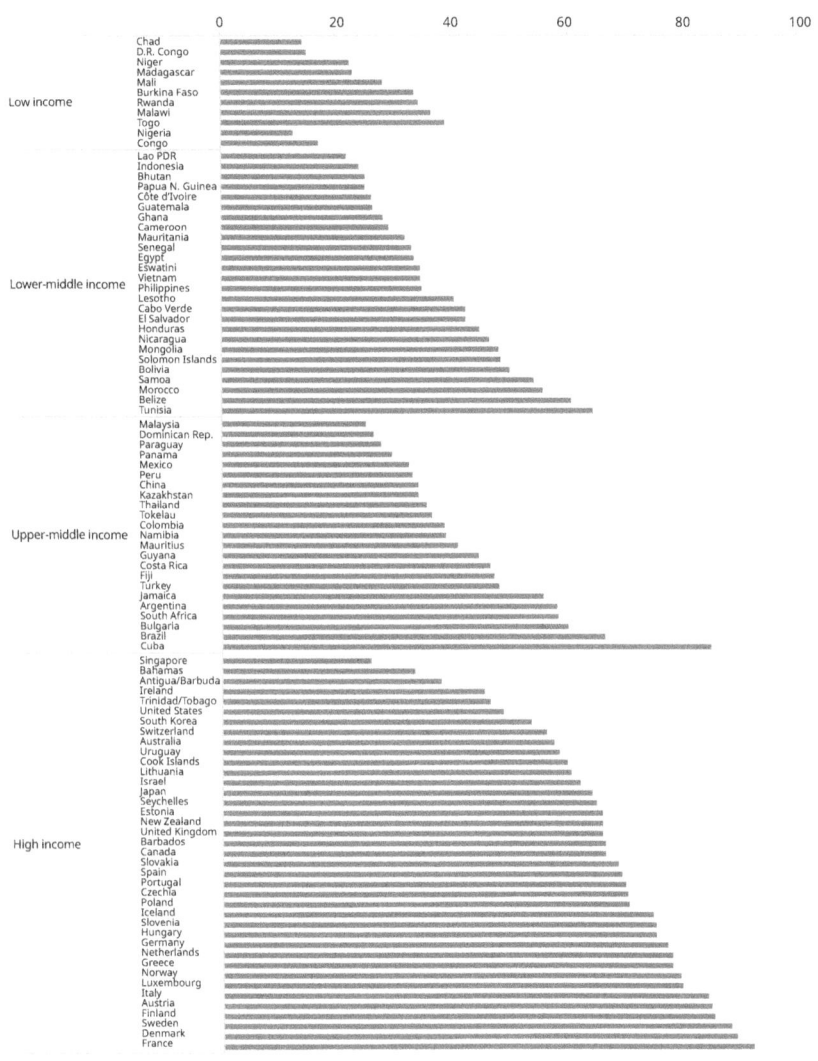

GEM Statlink: https:// bit.ly/GEM2021_fig21_6
Source: UNESCO GEM Report team analysis based on OECD data.

Fig. 5.15 (a) Tax revenue, selected countries, as percentage of GDP and by country income group, 2018. (b) Tax revenue, selected countries, by type of tax and country income group, 2018

5 HUMAN-CENTRED NATIONAL ECONOMIC POLICY: INSTITUTIONALIZING... 181

GEM StatLink: https://bit.ly/GEM2021_fig21_6
Source: UNESCO GEM Report team analysis based on OECD data.

Fig. 5.15 (continued)

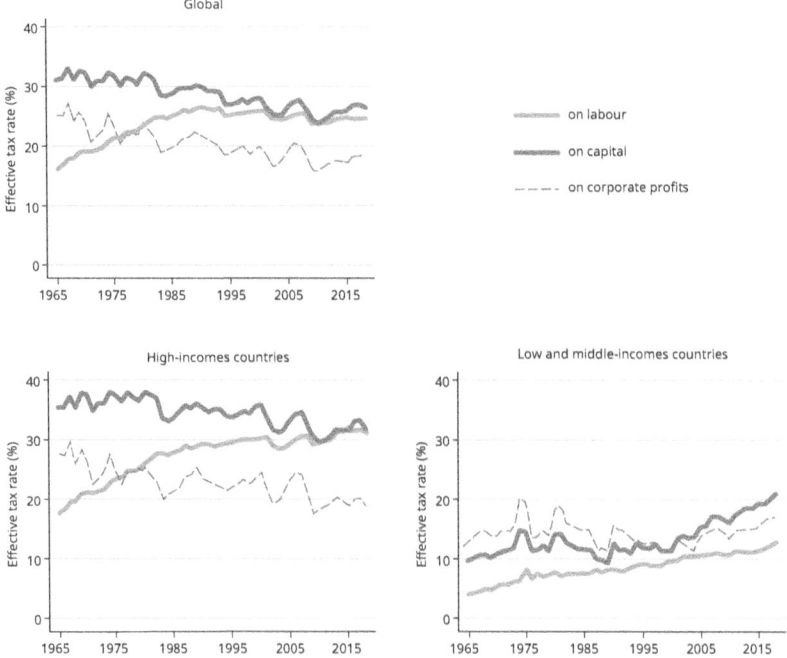

Notes: This figure plots the time series of average effective tax rates on capital (blue) and labour (red), as well as the effective tax rate on corporate profits (red dashed line).
The top-left panel corresponds to the global average, weighting country-year observations by their share in that year's total net domestic product (NDP), in constant 2019 US$ (= 156).
The bottom-left panel shows the results for high-income OECD countries (= 37), and the bottom-right panel for low- and middle-income countries (= 119).
Source: Bachas et al., "Globalization and Factor Income Taxation", World Bank, 2022.

Fig. 5.16 Composition of tax revenue, selected countries, by country income group, 2018

respect to health care, not only does total spending per capita vary significantly among countries, but the structure of their systems, particularly the extent of their reliance on private health insurance and out-of-pocket expenses, diverges as well. The latter costs are borne by households directly (through the payment of insurance premiums and doctors' and pharmaceutical bills) or indirectly (through a reduction in wages that offsets at least in part the premiums paid by employers). Figure 5.17 summarizes cross-country differences within these two dimensions for an illustrative group of advanced economies.[112]

Similarly, public support of the cost of child care, a major expense of young families, differs across countries. Figure 5.18 illustrates these

5 HUMAN-CENTRED NATIONAL ECONOMIC POLICY: INSTITUTIONALIZING... 183

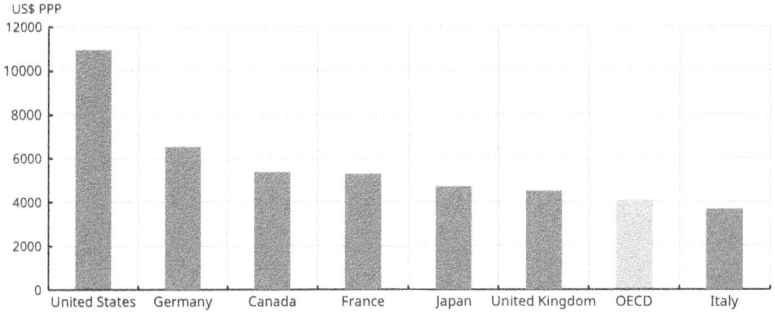

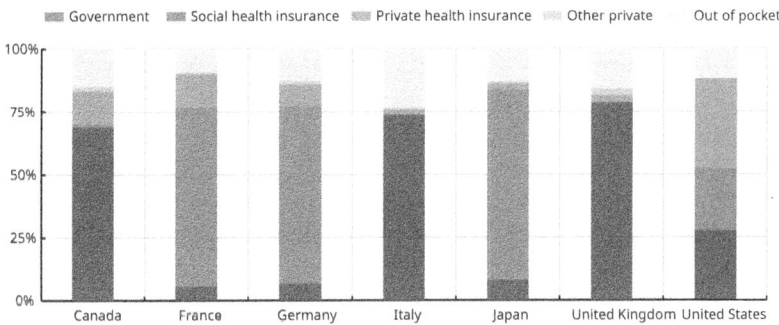

Fig. 5.17 Level and composition of health spending in select high-income countries

differences, which translate into very different impacts on the monthly budgets of these households, particularly in countries with limited child allowances or "family benefits".[113]

Availability and Affordability of Material Necessities (N)

The recent rise in inflation related to the COVID-19 pandemic and the war in Ukraine has revived appreciation of the state's enabling and stabilizing role in ensuring access to material necessities. The moral and economic case

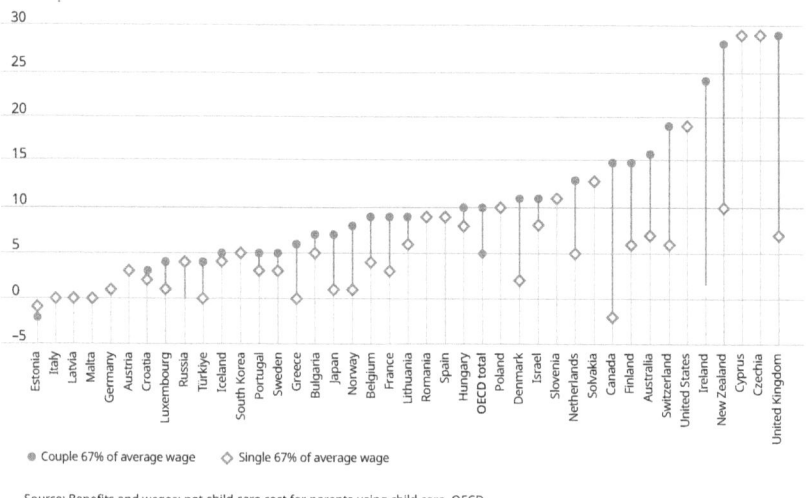

Fig. 5.18 Net child care costs (% of average wage, 2021 or latest available)

for such policies and institutions was made long ago by Adam Smith in *The Wealth of Nations*, as discussed in Chap. 3. During the twentieth century, a strong legal basis for this important function of government also emerged, becoming embedded in international human rights treaties and the constitutions and domestic statutes of many countries.

The 1948 Universal Declaration of Human Rights states in Article 25(1) that "everyone has the right to a standard of living adequate for the health and well-being of himself and his family". It refers in particular to the right to adequate food, clothing, housing, medical care and necessary social services. The 1966 ICECSR codified these rights and defined them further in the General Comments issued by its Committee on Economic, Social and Cultural Rights with respect to adequate housing (General Comments 4 and 7), food (General Comment 12), water (General Comment 15) and social security (General Comment 19).[114] The criteria elaborated by these General Comments provide the single most comprehensive international legal interpretation of the right to the material necessities of life, the "progressive realization" of which states are committed to achieve "using available resources".[115]

Governments seek to ensure the availability and affordability of material necessities in three main ways: investment in related infrastructure; regulation of public utilities; and subsidies targeted to needy populations or special policy objectives.

Public Infrastructure Investment

Adequate drinking water, food, shelter, energy and telecommunications are all dependent on infrastructure systems for both production and delivery. Thus, the level and effectiveness of a country's infrastructure investment largely determine how well it fulfils its duty to ensure broad access to the basic necessities of life, including in relation to the targets set by the SDGs on clean water and sanitation (SDG 6),[116] zero hunger (SDG 2),[117] affordable and clean energy (SDG 7)[118] and sustainable cities and communities (SDG 11).[119]

Unmet needs in these areas are enormous in many countries, and not just the poorest. For example, approximately two billion people worldwide lack access to safely managed drinking water at home, and about 3.6 billion, or half the world's population, lack access to safely managed sanitation. About one in 10 people suffers from hunger; and a third lack regular access to adequate food, including 149 million children under the age of five who suffer from stunting. Roughly 700 million people lack electricity, and 2.4 billion still use inefficient and polluting cooking systems. One billion or so live more than two kilometres from an all-weather road. In addition, an estimated one billion people live in urban slums and 1.6 billion live in inadequate housing. The best available data suggest that over 100 million people are homeless, including half a million in the United States.[120]

The Global Infrastructure Hub, an initiative of the G20 launched during Australia's 2014 presidency, has estimated global energy, water, transport and telecommunications infrastructure investment trends and needs to 2030 and beyond. It estimates there is a gap of roughly US$800 billion, or 25%, per year, totalling about US$15 trillion over the next two decades.[121] A World Bank study estimates that low- and middle-income countries invest an average of about 4% of GDP, or US$1 trillion globally, per year on infrastructure, with the public sector accounting for nearly 90% of this amount, albeit with considerable variation from a low of 53% to 64% in South Asia to a high of 98% in East Asia and the Pacific.[122]

Given the pressure on public finances in the aftermath of the COVID-19 crisis, closing this investment gap is going to require greater innovation and efficiency. When it comes to innovation, there is growing interest in blended finance, the combination or "stacking" of public and private forms of risk mitigation and finance in order to enlarge the flow of infrastructure investment in developing countries from global and domestic capital markets. These currently allocate only a tiny proportion of the US$120 trillion or so of funds under institutional management to such purposes. Since this portfolio shift would require considerable improvement in *international* economic policy and cooperation, this topic will be addressed in greater depth in Chap. 6. As for improved efficiency, it has been estimated that up to 38% of global infrastructure investment is not spent effectively because of bottlenecks, lack of innovation, and market failures. Improving the efficiency of infrastructure investment (fact-based project selection, streamlined delivery, and the optimization of operations and maintenance of existing infrastructure) could reduce spending by more than US$1 trillion a year for the same amount of infrastructure delivered.[123]

These abstract statistical estimates have a very tangible manifestation in impaired living conditions and well-being on the ground. Taking the freshwater infrastructure gap as an example, Table 5.1 shows the impact on daily lives of inadequate infrastructure in each of 15 cities and nearby informal settlements across a range of middle- and low-income countries. Even in those locations with regular piped water, researchers found that the quality is poor and unhealthy, requiring remedial treatment. As a result, a substantial share of the income and time of people is spent on life's most basic necessity, even in countries without high levels of extreme poverty. In almost all cities where tanker truck water is available, if households relied solely on this to meet their needs they would spend considerably more than the recommended 3% to 5% of their household income on water and sanitation.[124]

In 12 out of 15 cities analyzed, households connected to the public piped system received water intermittently, which compromises quality. In the 15 informal settlements studied, seven receive water less than 17 hours a week. Households without reliable access to piped water service obtain water from other sources, such as tanker trucks which can cost up to 52 times as much as for the same quantity of water if it were provided through the local piped water system. In informal settlements in Kampala, Lagos, and Mumbai, no households had access to piped water. In informal settlements in three cities, Cochabamba, Kampala, and Mzuzu, basic supplies of water appear unaffordable to households with average income.

The lack of attention to these factors appears to be the result of water being conceived of as a commodity. This may explain why researchers, policy analysts, and urban change agents have failed to recognize that significant numbers of low-income urban residents do not have regular supplies of affordable water. Failures of privatization combined with the continuing need to identify effective structures for water provisioning have led to the rise of corporatized water agencies. Advocates of corporatization contend it can make public services more efficient. However, it is not clear that this approach

Table 5.1 Household access to water services in 15 cities and informal settlements in the global South

City name	City-wide: percentage of households that use listed sources for all uses					Informal settlement name	Selected informal settlement: percentage of households that use listed sources for all uses				
	Piped to dwelling/yard[a]	Taps, standpipes, kiosks	Surface, ground, rain	Tanker trucks	Other, bottled		Piped to dwelling/yard	Taps, standpipes, kiosks	Surface, ground, rain	Tanker trucks	Other, bottled
Caracas	97.0	0.5	1.0	1.0	0.5	Terrazas del Alba	100.0	0.0	0.0	0.0	0.0
Cochabamba	80.0	0.0	0.0	20.0	0.0	San Miguel Km4	85.0	0.0	5.0	10.0	0.0
Rio de Janeiro	98.0	0.0	1.0	0.0	1.0	Rocinha	98.5[b]	0.0	1.0	0.0	0.5
São Paulo	96.0	4.0	0.0	0.0	0.0	Jardim São Remo	100.0[c]	0.0	0.0	0.0	0.0
Santiago de Cali	99.0	0.0	0.0	0.0	1.0	Comuna 20	98.0[d]	0.0	0.0	0.0	2.0
Bengaluru	71.0	9.0	17.0	3.0	0.0	Koramangala Slum Cluster	60.0	20.0	20.0	0.0	0.0
Mumbai	82.0	0.0	8.0	4.0	6.0	Siddarth Nagar	0.0	0.0	22.5	67.5	10.0
Colombo	86.0	12.0	1.5	0.0	0.5	Borella South GND	82.0	15.5	2.0	0.0	0.5
Karachi	28.0	3.0	10.0	25.0	34.0	Ghaziabad Sector 11½, Orangi Town	15.0	0.0	6.5	71.0	7.5
Dhaka	95.0[e]	4.0	1.0	0.0	0.0	Kallyanpur Pora Basti	7.0	92.5	0.5	0.0	0.0

(continued)

Table 5.1 (continued)

City name	City-wide: percentage of households that use listed sources for all uses					Informal settlement name	Selected informal settlement: percentage of households that use listed sources for all uses				
	Piped to dwelling/yard[a]	Taps, standpipes, kiosks	Surface, ground, rain	Tanker trucks	Other, bottled		Piped to dwelling/yard	Taps, standpipes, kiosks	Surface, ground, rain	Tanker trucks	Other, bottled
Kampala	15.0	70.0	15.0	0.0	0.0	Kalimali	0.0	90.0	10.0	0.0	0.0
Lagos	15.0	4.0	69.0	2.0	10.0	Makoko	0.0	0.0	70.0	0.0	30.0
Maputo	58.0	0.0	30.0	10.0	2.0	Nhlamankulu D	72.0	1.5	0.5	0.0	26.0
Mzuzu	67.0	28.0	0.0	0.0	5.0	Zolozolo West Ward	25.0	22.0	53.0	0.0	0.0
Nairobi	49.5	26.0	8.0	16.5	0.0	Kosovo Village in Mathare Valley	85.0[f]	15.0	0.0	0.0	0.0

Source: Beard and Mitlin, "Water Access in Global South Cities", *World Development*, 2021

[a] Figures for "piped to dwelling/yard" draw from formal sources, which are likely to underestimate the number of underserved households

[b] Most of this figure is from illegal piped water connections

[c] A portion of this figure is from illegal piped water connections

[d] 45% of this figure is from illegal piped water connections

[e] 78% of this figure is from groundwater and 22% is from the utility's water treatment plants. In Dhaka legally provided piped water combines groundwater and utility water because Dhaka has a high water table

[f] Most of this figure is from illegal piped water connections

can adequately improve access for low-income households in the global South. The focus on market-based provisioning principles has prevented public agencies from assuming responsibility for low-income households. Our analysis points to the importance of policy makers, cities, and water providers changing their collective ethos and values about water access. Then city authorities and water utilities can work together to extend the public piped networks, address intermittent services, and ensure adequate supplies of water are affordable. Most cities in the global South will require a subsidy from the national government or investment on the part of international donors, to extend and maintain piped water service to all urban residents. In turn this demands collective acceptance that universal water access is a basic human need and a public good, in the broadest social sense. While not easy to manufacture, this will require a sustained political commitment on the part of leaders, coalitions of urban change agents, and stakeholders, so investments, subsides, and other financial tools can be deployed to build and maintain piped water infrastructure systems.[125]

Public Utility Regulation and Targeted Subsidies

The recent spike in inflation has thrust popular concerns about the cost of living and consumer purchasing power into the political spotlight. In the European Union, for example, governments have responded with an estimated €300 billion of regulatory initiatives and consumption subsidies.[126] Table 5.2 provides an overview of the wide range of temporary actions taken to maintain the affordability of necessities, particularly for households of modest means.[127]

In addition to such crisis-related measures, most governments routinely regulate the tariffs that electricity, water and transport utilities charge consumers, in the interest of maintaining affordable access for their citizens. The resulting subsidies are often very substantial relative to the tariffs that would have been required to cover all operating and most capital expenses. Globally, a clear majority of water and electricity utilities do not achieve this coverage; more of them do so in advanced economies, but still far from all.[128]

In addition, many developing countries maintain a variety of direct consumption subsidies. For example, reflecting the fact that Indian households spend about 45% of their income on food, the country's Public Distribution System provides nearly 800 million people with subsidized grain through a network of a half a million "fair price" shops.[129] The programme is both a production and consumption subsidy in that it sets prices for farmers at levels that assure their standard of living, and somewhat lower prices for

Table 5.2 European Union energy cost-of-living relief measures 2021–22

Country/policy	Reduced energy tax/VAT	Retail price regulation	Wholesale price regulation	Transfers to vulnerable groups	Mandate to state-owned firms	Windfall profits tax/regulation	Business support	Other
Austria	✓							✓
Belgium	✓	✓		✓		✓	✓	✓
Bulgaria	✓	✓		✓		✓	✓	
Croatia	✓			✓			✓	✓
Cyprus	✓				✓			
Czechia	✓	✓		✓	✓	✓		✓
Denmark	✓	✓					✓	✓
Estonia	✓			✓				
Finland	✓			✓	✓		✓	✓
France	✓	✓	✓	✓		✓	✓	
Germany	✓	✓		✓	✓	✓	✓	✓
Greece	✓					✓	✓	✓
Hungary	✓	✓		✓			✓	
Ireland	✓			✓		✓	✓	
Italy	✓						✓	
Latvia	✓			✓				

Lithuania		▶					◎
Luxembourg	◎	◎				◎	
Malta	◎						
Netherlands	◎		◎	▶		◎	
Norway	◎			▶		◎	
Poland	◎			◎		◎	◎
Portugal	◎		◎	▶		◎	◎
Romania	◎			◎		◎	◎
Slovakia				□	◎	◎	
Slovenia	◎			□			
Spain	◎	◎					
Sweden	◎						◎
United Kingdom	◎			◎		◎	

Notes: We define a measure to be 'discussed' (◎) when important actors in civil society, such as political parties, have publicly discussed the measure but no formal action to implement it has been taken. By the term 'proposed' (CHECK SQUARE) we refer to measures that have been publicly announced by high government officials such as ministers. Finally, 'enacted' (☒) are all those measures already implemented
Source: Sgaravatti et al., "National Fiscal Policy Responses to the Energy Crisis", Bruegel, 2022

consumers to ensure universal affordable access to key grains. It covers two-thirds of the population and, as the Indian government's fifth-largest expenditure, costs about 5% of GDP.[130]

Subsidy schemes of this nature in developing countries are often politically sensitive owing to their central role in the lived experience and well-being of large segments of the population. Taking fuel subsidies as an example, a study found that fuel riots occurred in 41 of 217 countries between 2005 and 2018. Some countries experienced several in that period: India had seven; Indonesia had five; and China and Yemen both had three. Of the 157 countries for which monthly domestic price data were available, 73 had regimes in which prices changed every month. Over three-quarters adjusted prices at least every two months, while only around a fifth adjusted prices infrequently. The researchers found that riots were more frequent and severe in the last-mentioned group of countries—those which tended to allow larger subsidy levels to build up and make less frequent, more abrupt price adjustments.[131]

More recently, in 2022, countries as diverse as Ecuador, France, Haiti, Iran and Kazakhstan experienced social unrest triggered by consumer fuel price increases. The consumer subsidies and protections often employed by developing countries have tended to limit the impact of the recent war- and pandemic-related rise in food and fuel prices on their populations, considerably more so than in wealthier countries that tend to have fewer consumption subsidies and regulations. However, this likely portends additional pressure on the developing countries' public finances.

A 2022 IMF survey of 134 countries found that most had introduced at least one measure since the beginning of that year to shield their citizens from rising inflation (26 out of 31 advanced economies and 45 out of 103 emerging and developing economies); the lower amount of measures announced by developing countries can be probably be attributed to their higher ongoing reliance on energy and food subsidies and more limited fiscal space. More specifically:

> In advanced economies, cash and semi-cash transfers (including vouchers and utility bill discounts) were announced by the greatest number of countries (in about half of all countries), while most other measures aimed at lowering prices including reductions in value-added tax (VAT) (for example, in Belgium and Italy) and excise taxes (for example, France, Korea, and New Zealand). A cap on fuel prices was announced in Slovenia, and France provided subsidies to distributors to reduce gasoline prices. Estonia, Luxembourg, and the Slovak Republic announced measures to reduce electricity prices. In

emerging and developing economies, the most announced measures were reductions in VAT and excises (24 percent of all emerging and developing economies). This includes Poland and Turkey, which each announced a reduction in VAT rates on food and/or energy, and Côte d'Ivoire, Serbia, and Thailand, which each announced a temporary reduction or exemption of excise taxes. Some emerging and developing economies resorted to a temporary reduction or suspension of import duties (for example, Brazil, Iraq, Turkey). Finally, about 55 percent of all announced measures [were] intended to mitigate the impact of higher energy prices, 30 percent intended to mitigate the impact of higher food prices, and intention for the remaining measures is not narrowly defined.[132]

The IMF, which has traditionally encouraged the rationalization of consumer subsidies in developing countries, has nevertheless been advising during the current cost-of-living crisis that "fiscal policy [should] prioritize the protection of vulnerable groups from the burden of rising cost of living through *temporary and targeted* support while ensuring fiscal sustainability" (emphasis added).[133] It has attempted to provide more specific guidance in this regard as follows:

Countries with strong social safety nets (SSNs)

- Allow a full pass-through of higher international fuel prices to domestic users.
- Provide targeted and temporary cash transfers to vulnerable households.
  - If existing SSN programs do not adequately cover affected middle-class households, consider oneoff cash payments, smoothing energy consumption bills over time, or energy bill discounts.

Countries with weak SSNs and without existing energy and food subsidies

- Expand existing SSN programs, such as targeted transfers or child benefits, leverage measures introduced during COVID-19, and harness the power of digital tools to identify eligible households and to deliver assistance.
- Consider reducing education, health, or public transportation fees.
- If food security is a concern and all other options have been exhausted, consider temporarily lowering taxes or providing price subsidies with clear sunset clauses for basic food staples.
- Use the momentum to invest in strengthening the SSN system.

Countries with weak SSNs and with existing energy and food subsidies

- Gradually pass through higher international prices to retail prices while committing to the elimination of subsidies over the medium term.

- Carefully calibrate price increases considering the gap between retail and international prices, the available fiscal space, and the ability to put mitigating measures in place.

  – Fuel: Consider differentiating adjustment paths of domestic prices by type of fuel based on their relative weights in the consumption of different income groups.
  – Utilities: Adjust prices gradually in line with changes in costs while providing uniform lumpsum bill discounts and smoothing energy consumption bills over time.
  – Food: If a food subsidy program exists, increase rationed food prices gradually. Consider improving targeting and reducing leakages to higher income groups.[134]

This framework recognizes the importance of public policy measures to maintain affordable access to material necessities—during crises. This distinction reflects a certain long-standing intellectual tension and programmatic incoherence within the IMF and the liberal economics policy establishment more generally regarding the fundamental legitimacy of such measures. The Bretton Woods institutions are more comfortable regarding them as temporary and targeted—that is to say, ad hoc—rather than as a natural design feature of economies with endemic poverty and precarity. This is evident in the reference to "safety nets" as opposed to "social protection systems", a topic taken up in the following section. Particularly in countries plagued by large deficits of human dignity, security and capability—an inability to provide for people's basic enabling rights—the priority on the ground must be the latter, as this discussion has demonstrated and for which the original principles of liberal political economy provide clear justification.[135]

Economic Security (EcS)

There are three primary ways public policy supports the basic economic security of households and families. First is social protection, including health insurance, old-age pension benefits, disability insurance, unemployment insurance and anti-poverty programmes providing income maintenance and other benefits for the poorest. Second is worker protection based on international labour standards, including protection relating to occupational safety and health (OSH), which was recently elevated to the status of a Fundamental Principle and Right at Work (core labour standard), and arbitrary dismissal. Third is support for the asset-building of households—in particular, policy incentives regarding homeownership, private pension saving, and protection of savings of individuals (e.g., deposit insurance and regulation of investment managers).

Social Protection

As discussed above, fiscal transfers account for a significant share of household disposable income on average. This is because it is not uncommon for breadwinners to experience setbacks during their working lives which lead to disruptions in their household's labour income. Also, some households have no or proportionately few breadwinners because of their demographic profile, for example those consisting only of retirees or those with many children. Moreover, joblessness and poverty can be endemic in countries and communities, and people in them often require extra support to transcend these circumstances—to exit from cultures or geographies where poverty is deeply entrenched. For these reasons and others, a country's social protection system is a key component of its policy and institutional ecosystem for broad-based progress in living standards. It is a principal source of resilience, a shock absorber for the vagaries of economic life.

Social protection systems are not solely a luxury of rich countries. The Universal Declaration of Human Rights Article 22 states, "everyone, as a member of society, has the right to social security". In addition, SDG 1 on ending poverty includes a Target 1.3 that reads, "implement nationally appropriate social protection systems and measures for all, including floors, and by 2030 achieve substantial coverage of the poor and the vulnerable". In addition, SDG Target 3.8 calls for universal health coverage, which is one of the components of the social protection floor.

In practice, however, three-quarters of humanity lacks adequate social protection and a majority, 53%, are not covered by any form of social protection.[136] Accordingly, the current emphasis in the multilateral system is to expand the implementation of social protection floors, including particularly by extending coverage to the two billion people in the informal economy, who are typically least covered. Social protection floors are nationally defined sets of basic social security guarantees that should ensure at a minimum that over the life cycle all in need have access to essential health care and to basic income security which together secure effective access to goods and services defined as necessary at the national level.

The ILO, which is the lead multilateral organization on social protection, has a two-dimensional strategy for the promotion of national social protection floors. The strategy encompasses both basic social security guarantees ensuring universal access to essential health care and income security at least at a nationally defined minimum level (horizontal dimension), in line with its Social Protection Floors Recommendation, 2012 (No. 202), and the progressive achievement of higher levels of protection (vertical dimension) within comprehensive social security systems according to the Social Security (Minimum Standards) Convention, 1952 (No. 102).

National social protection floors should comprise at least the following four social security guarantees, as defined at the national level:

- Access to essential health care, including maternity care;
- Basic income security for children, providing access to nutrition, education, care and any other necessary goods and services;
- Basic income security for persons of active age who are unable to earn sufficient income, in particular in cases of sickness, unemployment, maternity and disability;
- Basic income security for older persons

Such guarantees should be provided to all residents and all children, as defined in national laws and regulations, and subject to existing international obligations.

Figure 5.19 illustrates that a large majority of countries have enacted legislation in most of these areas. This implies that the core challenge is one of expanding the implementation of domestic programmes, in particular extending their coverage and improving the adequacy of benefits. Figure 5.20 provides a somewhat contrasting picture of actual social protection coverage by specific population groups globally and within individual regions.

There is a clear correlation between effective coverage and income, including for vulnerable groups.[137] But while higher levels of social protection

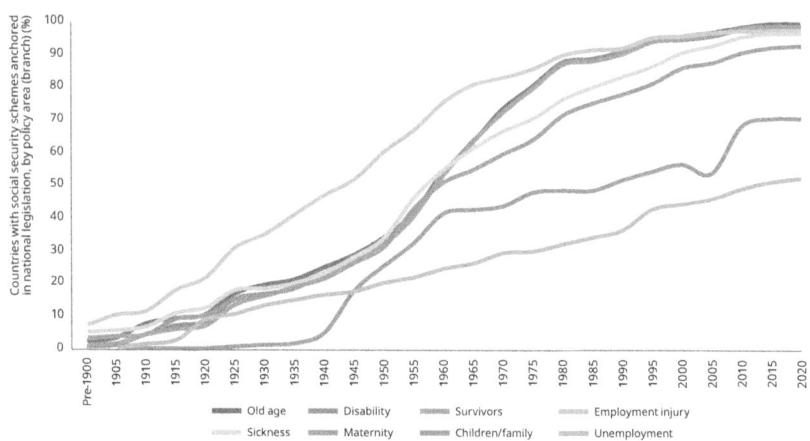

Fig. 5.19 Development of social protection programmes anchored in national legislation by policy area, pre-1900 to 2020

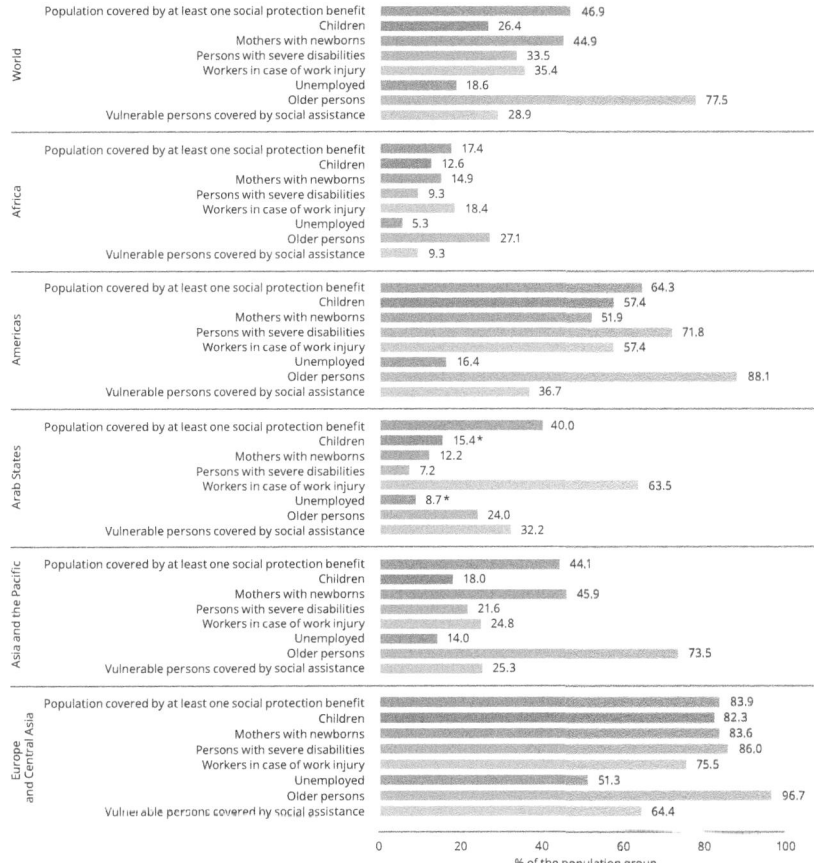

Fig. 5.20 SDG indicator 1.3.1: effective social protection coverage, global and regional estimates, by population group, 2020 or latest available year

coverage are usually associated with countries that have high levels of economic development, some poorer countries, such as Botswana, Cabo Verde, China and Timor-Leste, have demonstrated that sustained efforts to extend coverage can be effective at any level of development. The evidence suggests that all countries can pursue a high-road social protection strategy, starting from whatever their current situation may be and working progressively towards achieving universal social protection that is, accordingly to ILO guidance, comprehensive, adequate, resilient and sustainable.[138]

Even among high-income countries, there is considerable variation in social protection system coverage and benefit levels, suggesting that many countries have considerable scope to accelerate progress on inclusion and resilience through greater activation of their social security programmes, irrespective of their level of economic development. For example, as illustrated in Fig. 5.21, public pension benefit levels vary among high-income countries from roughly 30% to 40% of income replacement in the cases of Japan, Australia, Canada and the United States, to 60% to 70% in the cases of France, the Netherlands, Spain and Austria.

Similarly, public spending on family benefits is quite disparate. Among advanced economies, it ranges from a low of 0.6% of GDP in the United States, which is a clear outlier, to around 1.6% in Japan, Canada and the Netherlands and about 3% in France and the United Kingdom. The OECD average is 2.1%, three-and-a-half times higher than the US rate of public expenditure on children.[139] This is surely part of the explanation for the unusually high level of child poverty in the US (20%) mentioned above. Figure 5.22 illustrates the range of such support among 90 developing countries.

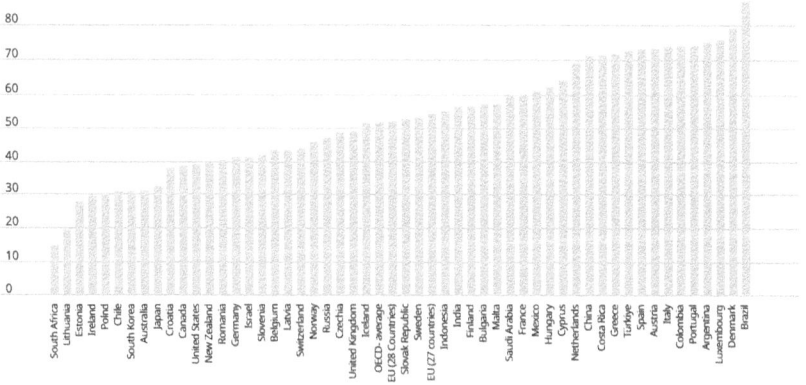

Source: OECD R&D Tax Incentives Database, April 2022.

Fig. 5.21 Gross pension replacement rates, men, percentage of pre-retirement earnings, 2020 or latest available

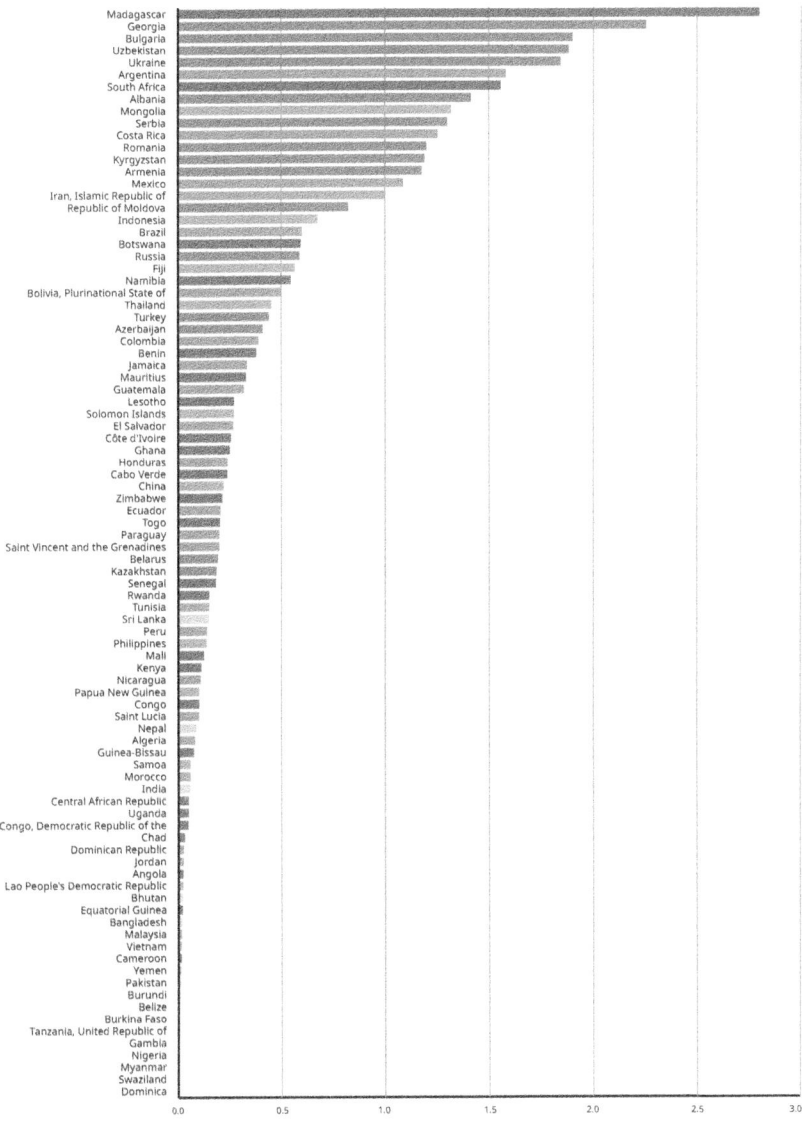

Fig. 5.22 Spending on child benefit packages in 90 low- and middle-income countries, by country (percentage of GDP)

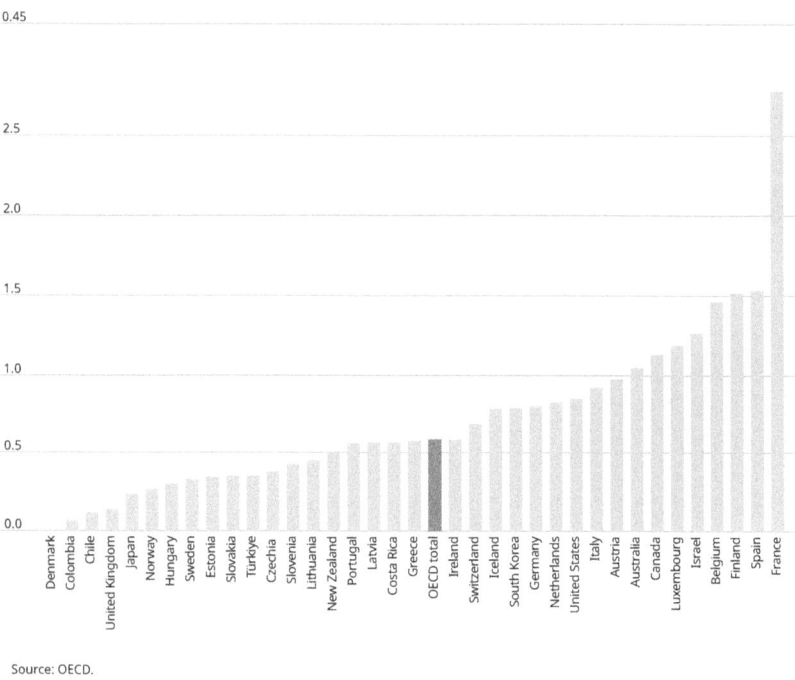

Fig. 5.23 Public unemployment spending (Percentage of GDP, 2021 or latest available)

Unemployment insurance is another dimension of social protection in which policy design and effort vary widely among countries at similar levels of economic development. Figure 5.23 summarizes this variability among OECD member countries by displaying the extent of public expenditure. This particular metric does not account for the prevailing level of unemployment and thus may somewhat exaggerate differences in the degree of policy support among countries. But Fig. 5.24 provides more specific comparison of coverage and benefit levels for select OECD and middle-income countries. While workforce coverage shows a reasonably strong correlation with national income (perhaps reflecting the higher share of informal workers in developing countries), income replacement rates vary considerably within and across both groups of countries, suggesting that many have considerable agency to further ease the transition of workers who lose their jobs.[140]

Percentage of the unemployed population

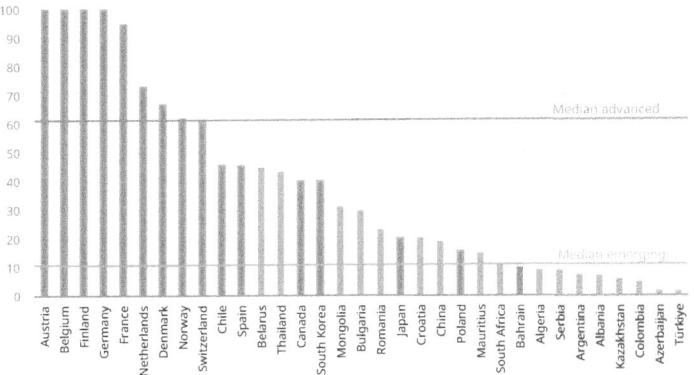

Note: The figure reports the share of unemployed individuals receiving unemployment insurance in selected countries. Blue columns refer to selected advanced economies and green columns refer to emerging economies. Data refer to 2015 (or closest available year). Data for Bahrain and Algeria refer to 2010 and 2003, respectively.
Source: ILO (2017) and authors' calculations for Mauritius.

Average replacement rates
Share of previous income

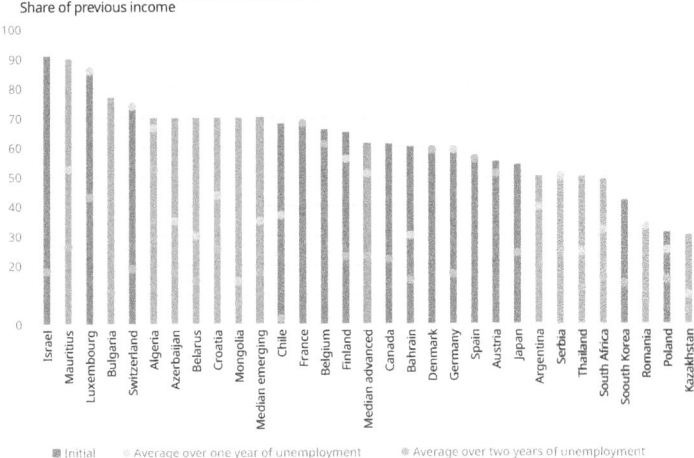

Note: Data refer to 2015 for OECD countries and most recent information for other countries. Blue columns refer to selected advanced economies and green columns refer to emerging economies. Replacement rates for OECD countries consider also cash incomes as well as income taxes and mandatory social security contributions paid by employees; while values for non-OECD countries do not take them into account. For this reason, replacement rates are not directly comparable across countries.
Source: Asenjo and Pignatti, "Unemployment Insurance Schemes around the World", ILO, 2019.

Fig. 5.24 Coverage of unemployment benefits and average replacement rates

Worker Protection

Workplace injury and exposure to hazards causing disease can have a devastating impact on the economic security of households. For this reason, OSH concerns were the subject of many of the first international labour standards established in the 1920s and 1930s. Only recently, however, during the COVID-19 pandemic, was OSH elevated to the status of a Fundamental Principle and Right at Work. As a result, governments are now obligated to respect, realize and promote two key OSH legal conventions regardless of whether they have formally adopted them in domestic legislation. Thus, the key policy and institutional variable on this important aspect of social protection is less the "what" than the "how", namely how to mobilize the necessary rigour of regulatory implementation and enforcement as well as firm responsibility and worker education.

As for the crucial role of regulatory oversight in advancing compliance, labour inspectorates are woefully under-resourced in many jurisdictions. As the table in Fig. 5.25 illustrates, the level of economic development tends to matter; rich countries tend to have more inspectors per working population than middle-income countries, and low-income countries generally have the fewest. However, the rigour of labour regulation enforcement is not foreordained by level of economic development; it remains a policy choice, as illustrated by the accompanying scatter plot graphic. This graphic shows that the relationship between the strictness of *de jure* labour law and the rigour of its de facto enforcement is highly heterogeneous, including among countries at similar levels of economic development.[141]

Europe is a case in point. According to the European Trade Union Council, safety inspections declined by a fifth between 2010 and 2018, falling from 2.2 million annual visits to 1.7 million. There were 232,000 fewer visits in Germany and a 50% reduction in Portugal, for example. In all, the number of labour inspectors declined by 1000 across the European Union, and more than a third of European countries no longer meet the ILO's standard of having one labour inspector per 10,000 workers.

Labour inspection is particularly challenging in the informal sector, which encompasses an estimated 60% of employment in the world, or two billion people. "Informal employment" is defined as all remunerative work (i.e., both self-employment and wage employment) that is not registered, regulated or protected by existing legal or regulatory frameworks, as well as non-remunerative work undertaken in an income-producing enterprise. Informal workers, 93% of whom live in emerging and developing countries, do not have secure employment contracts, workers' benefits or

Number of labour inspectors and inspections per worker by income

Income	Inspectors		Inspections	
	Average	No. countries	Average	No. countries
Low income	1.25	29	1.03	11
Lower-middle income	5.38	50	37.22	34
Upper-middle income	9.84	52	62.39	41
High income	12.23	66	137.80	45
World	8.24	197	76.61	131

Notes: The classification of countries follows the World Bank definition. The table presents the simple average across countries of the number of labour inspectors per 100,000 workers, and the number of labour inspections conducted per year per 10,000 workers. Figures are for the period 2000–12.

The negative correlation across countries between enforcement and labour law

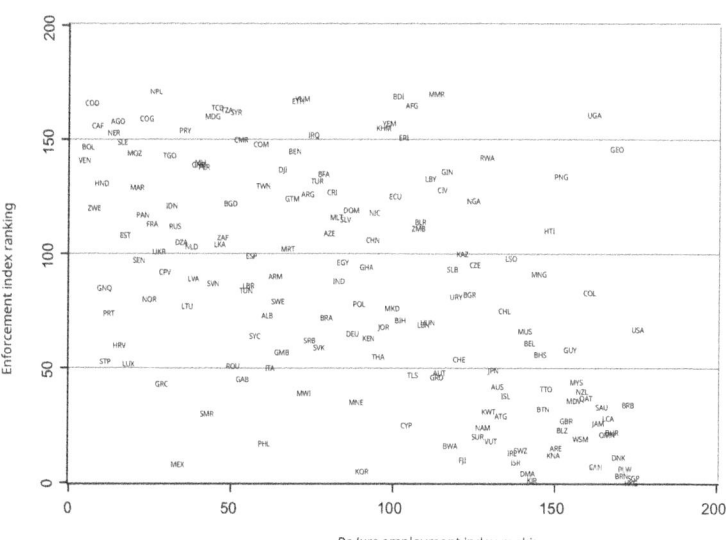

Notes: The horizontal axis is a ranking based on the *de jure* employment index wherein countries with more protective regulations have a higher ranking. The vertical axis is a ranking based on the enforcement index wherein countries with higher enforcement (labour inspectors and fines) have a higher ranking. The linear model between these variables equals Ranking Enforcement Index = 130.7 – 0.53 * Ranking Employment Law Index.
Source: Kanbur and Ronconi, "Enforcement Matters", *International Labour Review*, 2018.

Fig. 5.25 Labour inspection

workers' representation. The majority lack social protection, rights at work and decent working conditions.

Labour inspection interventions usually take place in the context of the traditional model of labour relations, with its clearly defined components (employer, employee and work contract) and workplaces that are easily accessible. This approach in the informal economy can only have a minimal impact, since, by definition, it falls outside the typical more formal pattern of labour relations in advanced economies. The ILO has prepared a guide that seeks to narrow this gap by proposing an intervention methodology adapted to the informal economy. It frames a participatory approach to: making concrete and gradual improvements with respect to working conditions in specific sectors or activities, OSH, and the organization of work (and production units); supporting the promotion of Fundamental Principles and Rights at Work; encouraging the formalization of the informal economy; and broadening social security coverage.[142]

Asset-Building

A disproportionate share of household wealth tends to be owned by households with the highest incomes. Indeed, wealth inequality tends to be even more pronounced than income inequality. But private household wealth is for many people a critical source of resilience against unforeseen shocks. Some countries seek to encourage and protect asset-building among lower- and middle-income households through incentives for homeownership and employee stock or business ownership and protection for the savings of retail investors through bank deposit insurance and asset management consumer protections.

Homeownership

The breadth of homeownership in a country is shaped by a complex mix of financial system, taxation, and zoning policies, among other things. Housing is the principal asset of the middle class; the share of housing in total assets of the middle three quintiles of the income or wealth distribution is larger than 60% in the majority of OECD countries.[143] And countries with higher rates of ownership tend to be less unequal, as illustrated in Fig. 5.26.

Countries employ mortgage lending, income and property tax, and residential zoning rules in complex ways to influence the nature and extent of homeownership. If the mix of such policies is not carefully considered, it can have the unintended result of reinforcing rather than mitigating inequality.[144] A study of 44 developed and developing countries found a mean homeownership rate of 73.9% in 2015.[145] Table 5.3 displays these rates for a subset of this group. In reflecting upon the factors contributing to these different outcomes, the authors of the study observed that

> government tax policy and regulations appear to play an important role in countries with below-average homeownership rates. For example, consider

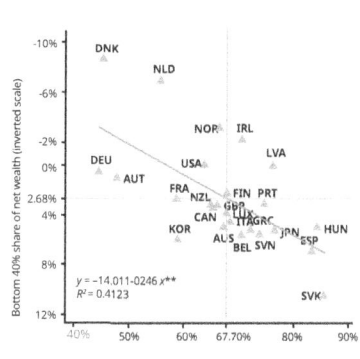

Fig. 5.26 High-homeownership countries tend to exhibit low wealth inequality

Table 5.3 Global Home ownership rates by country

	Homeownership rate %			Change in homeownership rate		
	1990	2005	2015	1990–2005	2005–2015	1990–2015
Bulgaria	89.8	85.4	82.3	−4.4	−3.1	−7.5
Canada	62.6	67.1	67.0	4.5	−0.1	4.4
Czechia	38.4	73.5	78.0	35.1	4.5	39.6
Denmark	54.5	66.6	62.7	12.1	−3.9	8.2
Finland	67.0	71.8	72.7	4.8	0.9	5.7
France	54.4	61.8	64.1	7.4	2.3	9.7
Germany	37.3	53.3	51.9	16.0	−1.4	14.6
Ireland	80.0	78.2	70.0	−1.8	−8.2	−10.0
Italy	64.2	72.8	72.9	8.6	0.1	8.7
Japan	63.2	63.1	64.9	−0.1	1.8	1.6
Mexico	78.4	71.3	71.7	−7.1	0.4	−6.7
Singapore	87.5	91.1	90.8	3.6	−0.3	3.3
Slovenia	68.0	83.2	76.2	15.2	−7.0	8.2
Spain	77.8	86.3	78.2	8.5	−8.1	0.4
Sweden	41.0	68.1	70.6	27.1	2.5	29.6
Switzerland	31.3	38.4	51.3	7.1	12.9	20.0
United Kingdom	65.8	69.2	63.5	3.4	−5.7	−2.3
United States	63.9	68.9	63.7	4.9	−5.2	−0.3
Average	62.5	70.6	69.6	8.1	−1.0	7.1

Notes: Owing to differing census and survey years, many figures in the table are from a year or two before or after the listed year, or the average between two nearby values
Source: Goodman and Mayer, "Homeownership and the American Dream", *Journal of Economic Perspectives*, 2018

the evolution of homeownership in (the former) West Germany and the United Kingdom ... Both countries pursued a similar policy of subsidizing post-war rental construction to rebuild their countries. However, in intervening years, German policies allowed landlords to raise rents to some extent and thus finance property maintenance while also providing "protections" for renters. In the United Kingdom, regulation strongly discouraged private rentals, whereas the quality of public (rental) housing declined with undermaintenance and obtained a negative stigma. As well, German banks remained quite conservative in mortgage lending. The result was that between 1950 and 1990, West German homeownership rates barely increased from 39 to 42 percent, whereas United Kingdom homeownership rates rose from 30 to 66 percent. Interestingly, anecdotes suggest that many German households rent their primary residence, but purchase a nearby home to rent for income (which requires a large down payment but receives generous depreciation benefits). This allows residents to hedge themselves against the potential of rent increases in a system that provides few tax subsidies to owning a home. Switzerland also has a low homeownership rate, and once again, tax regulations favor renting over owning ... [Researchers have concluded] that income tax policy, especially the tax on imputed rents, as well as the high price of owning relative to renting are key determinants of why many more Swiss households are renters than in other countries. On the other side of the equation, the Netherlands, Switzerland, and the United States all have relatively generous mortgage interest deductions.[146]

Housing taxation is one of the most important policy tools in promoting homeownership and, in some cases, creating an incentive for owner-occupied versus rental housing investment. For example:

- First, the vast majority of OECD countries tax rental income, but most do not tax imputed rents for homeowners (Denmark, Greece, the Netherlands and Switzerland are the exceptions, although this is generally at low rates). To some extent, property taxes replace taxes on imputed income in many countries, but revenue from property taxes tends to be low and they are commonly based on outdated property values. Property taxes are also to some extent de facto fees for local services as opposed to taxes on the imputed rental income from housing. In addition, if flat rates apply, property taxes may have less scope than income taxes to be progressive, and less scope to redistribute, particularly if levied at the local level.
- Second, tax relief for mortgage interest provides a significant advantage to debt-financing homeowners in many OECD countries, allowing homeowners to deduct mortgage interest payments from their personal income tax. The benefit provided by mortgage interest relief tends to outweigh the combined effect of all other taxes levied on a debt-financed housing investment.

- Third, owner-occupied dwellings are often exempted from taxes on capital gains, while this is typically not the case for capital gains on rental housing.
- As a result, countries effectively subsidise home ownership through their tax system—meaning that the tax credits and deductions available to homeowners are higher than the taxes that are levied on the dwelling over its lifetime. Because high-income and high-wealth households tend to own a larger share of housing assets relative to lower-income households (in terms of more expensive primary residences as well as investments in secondary residences), they accrue even greater benefits from housing taxation policies that provide disproportionate advantages to homeowners. In addition, policy such as tax relief for mortgage interest often provides larger benefits to taxpayers at higher income brackets who own larger homes and are taxed at higher marginal rates.[147]

The bottom line is that countries need to contextualize their strategies for expanding homeownership within a broader set of objectives for housing policy—improving the quality and affordability of housing for all and not just those most likely to be interested in buying a home of their own.

Employee Stock and Business Ownership
Employee stock ownership is significant in many countries. Equity ownership of the firms in which they work provides employees with an additional opportunity to share the gains from their increased productivity. However, there can be downside risks as well, which regulation needs to guard against. In particular, the use of stock distributions to employees to fund pension plans creates the potential for diversification risks—that is, the prospect that workers could lose not only their income but also a big share of their wealth if their firm goes out of business.

As of 2017, Europe had about nine million employee shareholders compared with over 30 million in the United States. European employee shareholders held €388 billion in shares of their companies (almost entirely large listed firms) versus US$3.8 trillion held by their counterparts in US companies (a third of them small and medium-sized enterprises). Differences in fiscal incentives are part of the reason for this difference, as is the lack of a coherent EU-wide policy scheme.[148]

Cooperatives are another important form of worker equity ownership. There is a strong tradition of worker cooperatives in a number of European and other countries. An estimated 800 million people around the world are members of cooperatives.[149] The economic activity of the largest 300 cooperatives (the "Global 300") as of 2014 was equivalent to the ninth-largest national economy,[150] with France generating the largest share of revenue (28%), followed by the United States (16%), Germany (14%), Japan (8%), the Netherlands (7%), the United Kingdom (4%), Switzerland (3.5%), Italy (2.5%), Finland (2.5%), South Korea (2%) and Canada (1.75%).[151] Fiscal and other government incentives matter for this form of worker ownership as well.[152]

Environmental Security (EnS)

Serious degradation of the environmental setting of a household—the surrounding air, water, soil or natural habitat—can severely impair its standard of living. This impairment can take the form of illness and disease, diminished income and employment or lost access to some of life's basic necessities. It can occur suddenly and severely or gradually and insidiously. In short, this "factor of distribution" has the potential to disrupt—or strengthen—any and all of the other four.

Neoclassical economics, with its central focus on allocative efficiency and production, is not designed to respond to major environmental challenges, certainly not of the severity and pervasiveness of those humanity faces in the twenty-first century. As argued in Chap. 4, its mental model of growth and development, as symbolized in the aggregate production function, provides no explicit entry point for the internalization of positive or negative environmental externalities. This is an increasingly problematic flaw in a world facing economically destabilizing environmental threats.

For example, national economic policies have yet to fully assimilate the implications of the Paris climate agreement. According to Climate Action Tracker, as of March 2022, 33 countries and the European Union had set a net-zero target, and more than 100 countries had proposed—or were considering—such a target. Some 7500 companies, 1100 cities, and institutional investors managing over US$130 trillion in assets had also committed to set net-zero targets. However, none of the 38 countries Climate Action Tracker has evaluated has future targets and current policies that are consistent with the Paris climate agreement goal of limiting global warming to 1.5 °C—or, at most, well below 2 °C—above pre-industrial levels. Only nine have targets and policies that would be consistent with that outcome if they made moderate improvements; the targets and policies of the rest either require substantial modification or are outright counterproductive.[153] Moreover, much of the action promised by those countries and companies setting net-zero targets is backloaded despite the fact that the feasibility of these targets depends crucially on emissions falling rapidly, by about 45%, over the next decade. Scientists advise that current national climate commitments, even when fully implemented, would lead to an estimated 2.4 °C to 2.8 °C—i.e., catastrophic—level of global warming.[154]

As discussed in Chap. 2, the environmental performance of a country is only partially related to its level of economic development. Yes, richer countries have a greater capacity to expend resources and pay higher prices if required in order to grow sustainably. But many aspects of environmental sustainability do not incur incremental costs. Quite a few save money and support growth, including those related to improving resource efficiency. Indeed, failure to arrest severe environmental degradation can severely retard development and risk catastrophic losses—the loss of shelter, community or even life itself. Examples include water shortages from unsustainable use of groundwater, collapse of fisheries because of overfishing, endemic asthma and pulmonary disease from chronic air pollution, devastating floods because riverbeds have been altered by uncontrolled soil erosion, and highly destructive forest fires and coastal storm surges intensified by global warming.

Over the past decade, there has been an explosion of policy analysis, guidance and measurement regarding these challenges. There is no shortage of frameworks, best practices, and metrics available to policymakers under the rubrics of green economy, blue economy, green growth, sustainable development, etc. These tools all fundamentally seek to capture the synergies and minimize the adverse trade-offs of the parallel pursuit of strong, socially inclusive and environmentally sustainable development. They all involve the administration of both carrot and stick—policies and institutional characteristics that appropriately incentivize investments and purchasing and production decisions in the public and private sectors.

As for policy frameworks, the UNEP was a pioneer with its Green Economy report, which made "a compelling economic and social case for investing two per cent of global GDP in greening ten central sectors of the economy in order to shift development and unleash public and private capital flows onto a low-carbon, resource-efficient path".[155] The OECD has also produced comprehensive policy guidance in its Green Growth Strategy[156] and related set of country performance indicators.[157] These two institutions, along with the Asian Development Bank, UNDP and World Bank, subsequently collaborated on a green growth policy "toolkit" for G20 countries.[158] All of these frameworks remain relevant resources for national policymakers, as does the Green Growth Knowledge Platform, a research partnership created by the Global Green Growth Institute, OECD, UNEP and World Bank.[159]

With respect to performance metrics, in addition to the OECD Green Growth Indicators the Sustainable Development Solutions Network (SDSN) has compiled an extensive set of indicators that track country progress in achieving the SDGs. Many of the goals relate to environmental sustainability: SDG 6 on clean water and sanitation; SDG 7 on affordable and clean energy; SDG 11 on sustainable cities and communities; SDG 12 on responsible consumption and production; SDG 13 on climate action; SDG 14 on life underwater; and SDG 15 on life on land. The SDSN's SDG Index and country-specific dashboards present myriad parameters by which to assess and plan improvements in a country's environmental security.[160] Its analysis finds that most countries are well off track in making progress towards the 2030 SDG targets at all levels of economic development. Indeed, a third set of metrics, the Global Green Growth Institute's Green Growth Index shows considerable variation in scores among countries in the same region, as illustrated in Fig. 5.27.[161]

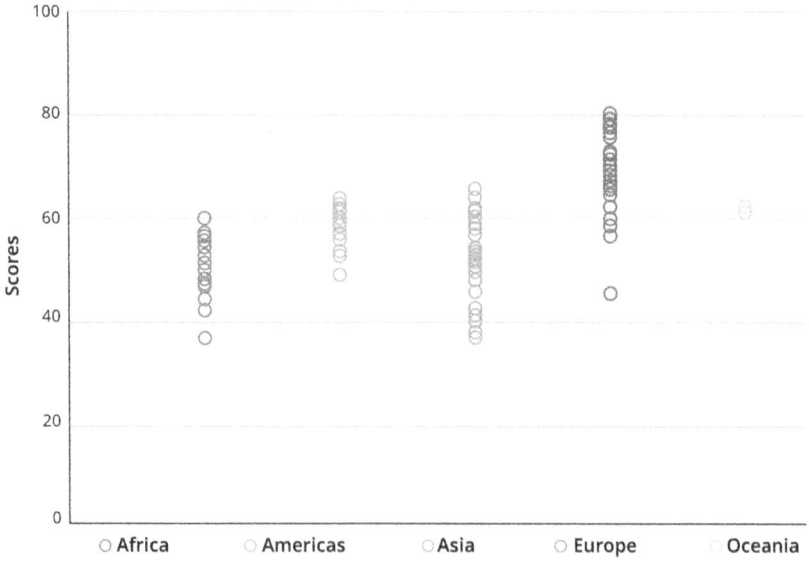

Source: Global Green Growth Institute.

Fig. 5.27 Distribution pattern of country scores for the Green Growth Index by region, 2020

Sectoral policy frameworks and performance metrics have been developed more recently. Particularly notable in this respect are SDSN's transformation pathways,[162] the Mission Possible Partnership focused on hard-to-abate industries,[163] and the World Business Council for Sustainable Development's Pathways projects and reports.[164] In addition, a coalition of think tanks has produced an evaluation of progress in 40 sectors and enabling factors relative to the IPCC's 2030 interim targets for a 1.5 °C scenario. If found that

> change is heading in the right direction at a promising but insufficient speed for 6 indicators, and in the right direction but well below the required pace for 21. Change in another 5 indicators is heading in the wrong direction entirely, and data are insufficient to evaluate the remaining 8. Getting on track to achieve 2030 targets will require an enormous acceleration in effort. Unabated coal in electricity generation, for example, must be phased out six times faster than recent global rates. Improvements in cement production's carbon intensity must increase much more quickly—by a factor of more than 10. And reductions in the annual deforestation rate must accelerate 2.5 times faster.[165]

Such sector-specific strategies are increasingly complemented by targets and disclosure frameworks. In particular, the Science-Based Targets Initiative is the leading framework for the setting of corporate net-zero greenhouse gas emission targets, and the ISSB is building a global baseline framework for the disclosure by companies of material sustainability-related aspects of their strategy and performance. It is backed by the International Financial Reporting Standards Foundation, which oversees the world's financial accounting standards, as well as the world's securities markets regulators (International Organization of Securities Commissions [IOSCO]) and is being built upon the foundation of voluntary frameworks pioneered years ago by the Climate Disclosure Standards Board,[166] Sustainability Accounting Standards Board and Value Reporting Foundation,[167] Task Force on Climate-Related Financial Disclosures[168] and Global Reporting Initiative.[169] An analogous voluntary framework with respect to nature-based (biodiversity) reporting, the Task Force on Nature-Related Financial Disclosures, is at an earlier stage of development.[170] And the UN High-Level Expert Group on the Net-Zero Commitments of Non-State Entities has issued important guidelines for ensuring the environmental additionality and credibility of—that is, avoiding greenwashing in—corporate net-zero targets and disclosures.[171]

These targeting, measurement and reporting protocols with respect to the private sector's impact on environmental security are important to the growing efforts within the financial system to internalize sustainability considerations in capital allocation decisions. National policy has a critical role to play in scaling the application of them through regulation. As mentioned previously, a large and growing number of financial regulators are beginning to implement policy changes in this regard, particularly the more than 100 members of the NGFS. Indeed, some of the Network's pioneering members are financial regulatory agencies of developing countries that are deploying a combination of restrictions, incentives and outright directives—that is, carrots and sticks. Complementing these regulatory initiatives is a market-led effort on the part of institutional investors to set and disclose investment portfolio decarbonization targets, the Glasgow Financial Alliance for Net-Zero.[172]

Some countries are also applying a range of policy carrots and sticks to commerce and procurement. For example, six countries are negotiating to eliminate tariffs on a list of "environmental and environmentally friendly" goods and services, an arrangement they hope will attract the participation of more countries over time.[173] In addition, many governments are instituting procurement preferences for environmentally friendly products and services domestically, including the European Union, which has an extensive framework in this regard that can serve as a positive example for other jurisdictions.[174] The Japanese government maintains a pioneering regulatory scheme to incentivize continuous improvement in the production and procurement of resource-efficient goods and services. Under its Top Runner programme,[175] manufacturers are effectively obliged to surpass a weighted average value for all their products per category for each predetermined target year.

Another increasingly important aspect of strengthening an economy's aggregate distribution function with respect to both environmental and social sustainability relates to a "just transition"—that is, approaches by which stronger policy measures to internalize environmental externalities can be designed and implemented without jeopardizing economic and social progress. In 2015, the ILO issued an extensive set of high-level policy guidelines in this respect, and more recently the United Nations Framework Convention on Climate Change (UNFCCC) has issued related policy guidance for countries (summarized in Fig. 5.28).[176]

Biodiversity and natural ecosystems are another aspect of environmental security requiring priority attention. As summarized in Chap. 2, the world

5 HUMAN-CENTRED NATIONAL ECONOMIC POLICY: INSTITUTIONALIZING... 213

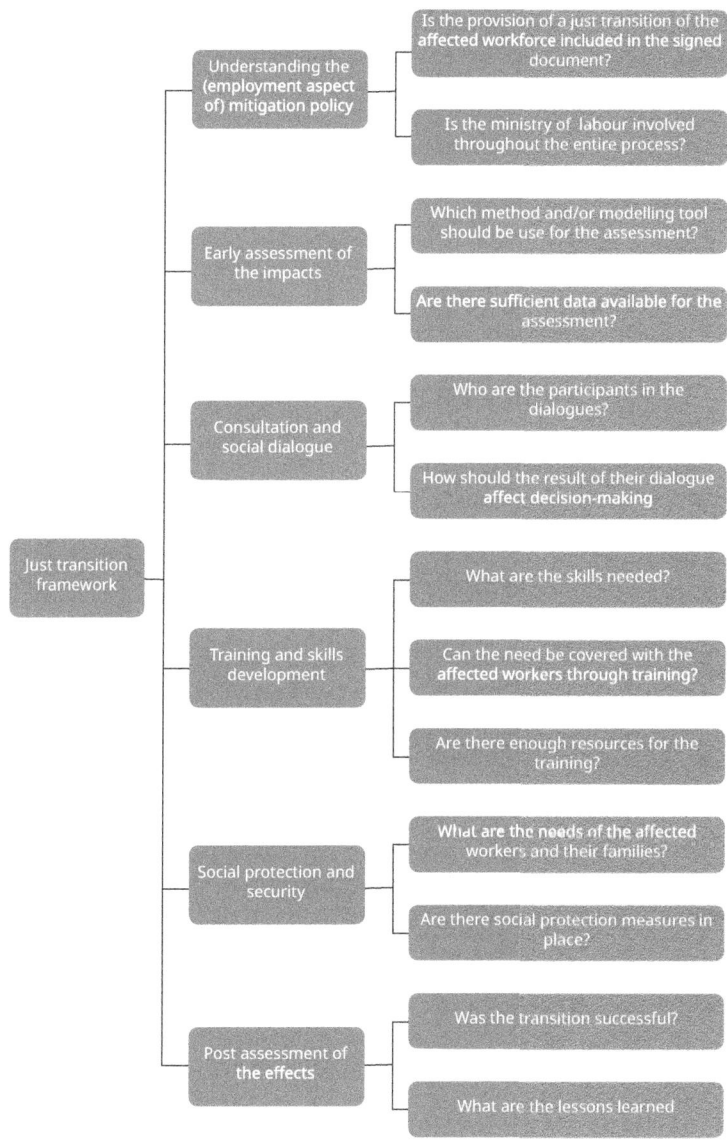

Source: ILO and UNFCC.

Fig. 5.28 Elements of a just transition

is experiencing an accelerating rate of species extinction. The recent Kunming-Montreal Global Biodiversity Framework sets out an ambitious international action plan to bring about a transformation in society's relationship with biodiversity, with the objective of ensuring that by 2050 a shared vision of "living in harmony with nature" is fulfilled. The Framework comprises 21 targets and 10 "milestones" for 2030, including:

- Restore 30% of degraded ecosystems globally (on land and sea) by 2030.
- Conserve and manage 30% of areas (terrestrial, inland water, and coastal and marine) by 2030.
- Stop the extinction of known species, and by 2050 reduce tenfold the extinction risk and rate of all species (including unknown ones).
- Reduce risk from pesticides by at least 50% by 2030.
- Reduce nutrients lost to the environment by at least 50% by 2030.
- Reduce global footprint of consumption by 2030, including through significantly reducing overconsumption and waste generation and halving food waste.
- Reduce the rate of introduction and establishment of invasive alien species by at least 50% by 2030.
- Mobilize finance for biodiversity from all sources, domestic and international—both public and private—of at least US$200 billion per year by 2030.
- Identify by 2025 and eliminate by 2030 a total of at least US$500 billion per year in subsidies harmful to biodiversity.[177]

Countries are increasingly promoting greater application and improved valuation of ecosystem services through policy.[178] The UN Millennium Ecosystem Assessment defined four categories of such services:

1. **Provisioning Services.** A provisioning service is any type of benefit to people that can be extracted from nature. Along with food, other types of provisioning services include drinking water, timber, wood fuel, natural gas, oils, plants that can be made into clothes and other materials, and medicinal benefits.
2. **Regulating Services.** A regulating service is the benefit provided by ecosystem processes that moderate natural phenomena. Regulating services include pollination, decomposition, water purification, erosion and flood control, and carbon storage and climate regulation.

3. **Cultural Services.** A cultural service is a non-material benefit that contributes to the development and cultural advancement of people, including how ecosystems play a role in local, national, and global cultures; the building of knowledge and the spreading of ideas; creativity born from interactions with nature (music, art, architecture); and recreation.
4. **Supporting Services.** Ecosystems themselves couldn't be sustained without the consistency of underlying natural processes, such as photosynthesis, nutrient cycling, the creation of soils, and the water cycle. These processes allow the Earth to sustain basic life forms, let alone whole ecosystems and people. Without supporting services, provisional, regulating, and cultural services wouldn't exist.[179]

Work is ongoing to develop approaches to measuring the benefits of such services in specific community or project settings in order to strengthen the design and implementation of policy incentives, which remain at a formative stage.[180] There is also rising interest in the practice of so-called "regenerative agriculture":

> an alternative means of producing food that, its advocates claim, may have lower—or even net positive—environmental and/or social impacts ... [through] processes (e.g., use of cover crops, the integration of livestock, and reducing or eliminating tillage), outcomes (e.g., to improve soil health, to sequester carbon, and to increase biodiversity), or combinations of the two.[181]

As part of its Green New Deal, the European Union's Farm to Fork and Biodiversity Strategies aim to make European food production the global standard with respect to sustainability. These strategies include a range of ambitious targets intended to put the EU food system on a transformative path towards greater sustainability. Those with the greatest relevance to agricultural production include the following:

- agriculture to contribute to a reduction of at least 55% in net GHG emissions by 2030;
- reduction by 50% of the use and risk of chemical pesticides, and reduction in use of more hazardous pesticides by 50% by 2030;
- reduction of nutrient losses by at least 50% while ensuring that there is no deterioration in soil fertility. This will reduce the use of fertilisers by at least 20% by 2030;
- reduction by 50% of sales of antimicrobials for farmed animals and in aquaculture by 2030;
- reaching 25% of agricultural land under organic farming by 2030;
- a minimum of 10% area under high-diversity landscape features.[182]

A recent landmark study of regenerative agriculture practices by European science academies concluded,

> Our results demonstrate that many of the analysed practices show synergies between carbon capture and storage and enhancing biodiversity (although sometimes with modest effect sizes), while not having clear large negative effects on food production, especially in the long term. Practices that show synergies include the following: *increased diversification within and among crops, introduction of permanent and perennial crops, expanded agroforestry and intercropping, keeping green plant cover on all farm fields during all seasons, and reduced tillage.* We also found some examples of clear trade-offs (e.g. conversion of arable land to grasslands increase carbon storage and biodiversity but food production decrease [*sic*]). Practices that show clear synergistic effects should be given considerable attention in plans by member states for implementation of the new Common Agricultural Policy (CAP). Recent studies also suggest that the capacity of grasslands to capture and store carbon may have been underestimated, and that permanent grasslands be considered more strongly when developing policies on carbon farming in Europe.[183]

The study ends by framing an extensive policy agenda. Other countries may wish to observe and learn from Europe's evolving experience in this important new field, which aims to strike a better balance between agricultural livelihoods and environmental sustainability and security.

CONCLUSION

This chapter has sought to elaborate on some of the domestic policies and institutional features that are most relevant to the task of strengthening an economy's aggregate distribution function in order to grow and develop in a more inclusive, sustainable and resilient manner. As the data presented here have demonstrated, countries at all levels of economic development have ample policy space to make major improvements in one or more dimensions of median household living standards. They can do so by following the golden rule of human-centred economics, which is to devote at least as much policy attention and effort to strengthening their economy's distribution function as to its production function, specifically by investing in policies and institutional capacity relating to household employment and entrepreneurial opportunity, disposable income, availability and affordability of material necessities, and economic and environmental security on a systematic and sustained basis. This is a *structural* way of improving the social quality as well as quantity of growth—that is, median household living standards as well as productive output or GDP.

Inequality, environmental degradation, and precarity and fragility are not inherent or immutable features of market economies. A better balance can be struck between economic growth and social welfare if policymakers deliberately conceive, pursue and measure national economic performance through both of these lenses simultaneously. They must abandon the reflex of standard liberal economics to assume, whether explicitly or implicitly, that broad progress in these core dimensions of living standards trickles down inevitably from higher national income. A certain intentionality is required to optimize both—a sustained process of institutional deepening and investment to foster movement closer to the frontier of good policy and institutional practice in the aggregate distribution function's five domains.

This ongoing process of institutional improvement should be assigned the same level of priority as policies traditionally relied upon to promote the quantity of growth (GDP): macroeconomic, trade and financial stability policies. Such a recalibration and rebalancing of economic policy is the way that countries can realize more of the living standards potential of their economies, narrowing their "welfare gap" irrespective of their level of national income.

In sum, this analysis has shown that all countries have considerable agency or policy space to strengthen inclusion, sustainability and resilience—to run their economies in a more human-centred fashion, rejecting the traditional trickle-down, capital-centric logic of standard liberal economics. But this will require them to rebalance their priorities, processes and personnel to reflect a more intentional approach to strengthening household living standards through ongoing structural–institutional reform as part and parcel of their growth and development strategy.

That said, no country is an island in today's globally integrated economy in which finance, trade and technology cross borders in rapid and complex ways. Many economies face difficult constraints on public finances and domestic policy space more broadly, particularly lower-middle-income and low-income ones. For this reason, the two-lens, production function plus distribution function approach of human-centred economics has important implications for the priorities and conduct of international economic governance and cooperation as well, and that is the topic of the next chapter.

Notes

1. World Economic Forum, "Inclusive Development Index 2018: Summary and Data Highlights", https://www3.weforum.org/docs/WEF_Forum_IncGrwth_2018.pdf
2. Pooja Balasubramanian, Francesco Burchi and Daniele Malerba, "Does Economic Growth Reduce Multidimensional Poverty? Evidence from Low and Middle-Income Countries", Discussion Paper No. 288, Georg-August-Universität Göttingen, Courant Research Centre—Poverty, Equity and Growth (CRC-PEG), 2021, pp. 13–14, https://www.econstor.eu/bitstream/10419/249449/1/1787158713.pdf
3. M.J. Wolf et al., *2022 Environmental Performance Index*, New Haven, Yale Center for Environmental Law & Policy, 2022, https://epi.yale.edu/downloads/epi2022report06062022.pdf
4. Matej Bajgar, Giuseppe Berlingieri, Sara Calligaris, Chiara Criscuolo and Jonathan Timmis, "Industry Concentration in Europe and North America", OECD Productivity Working Paper No. 18, 21 January 2019, https://doi.org/10.1787/2ff98246-en
5. Flavio Calvino, Chiara Criscuolo and Rudy Verlhac, 2020. "Declining Business Dynamism: Structural and Policy Determinants", OECD Science, Technology and Industry Policy Paper 94, 2020, p. 6, https://ideas.repec.org/p/oec/stiaac/94-en.html
6. Ibid., p. 9.
7. Ibid., pp. 7–8.
8. G. Gutierrez and T. Philippon, "How EU Markets Became Free: A Study of Institutional Drift", NBER Working Paper 24,700, June 2018, p. 1, https://www.nber.org/papers/w24700
9. See G. Gutiérrez and T. Philippon, "The Failure of Free Entry", NBER Working Paper 26001, June 2019, https://www.nber.org/papers/w26001
10. Thomas Philippon, "The Economics and Politics of Market Concentration", *The Reporter*, No. 4, 2019, https://www.nber.org/reporter/2019number4/economics-and-politics-market-concentration
11. Ibid.
12. Robert Anderton, Benedetta Di Lupidio and Barbara Jarmulska, "Product Market Regulation, Business Churning and Productivity: Evidence from the European Union Countries", European Central Bank Working Paper 2332, November 2019. https://www.ecb.europa.eu/pub/pdf/scpwps/ecb.wp2332~53142f69bc.en.pdf
13. Anu Bradford, Adam S. Chilton, Chris Megaw and Nathaniel Sokol, "Competition Law Gone Global: Introducing the Comparative Competition Law and Enforcement Datasets", *Journal of Empirical Legal*

Studies, Vol. 16 (2019), p. 411, https://scholarship.law.columbia.edu/faculty_scholarship/2514

14. https://info.worldbank.org/governance/wgi/
15. For an overview of research on the detrimental economic effects of corruption, see Transparency International, "The Impact of Corruption on Growth and Inequality", *Anti-Corruption Helpdesk*, 15 March 2014, https://www.transparency.org/files/content/corruptionqas/Impact_of_corruption_on_growth_and_inequality_2014.pdf
16. Transparency International, "People and Corruption: Citizens' Voices from around the World", *Global Corruption Barometer*, 2017, https://images.transparencycdn.org/images/GCB_Citizens_voices_FINAL.pdf
17. See Cecilie Wathne and Matthew C. Stephenson, "The Credibility of Corruption Statistics: A Critical Review of Ten Global Estimates", U4 Anti-corruption Resource Center, 2021, https://www.u4.no/publications/the-credibility-of-corruption-statistics.pdf
18. See, for example, Klaus Gründler and Niklas Potrafke, "Corruption and Economic Growth: New Empirical Evidence", Ifo Working Paper No. 309, August 2019, https://www.ifo.de/DocDL/wp-2019-309-gruendler-potrafke-corruption-growth.pdf; Arusha Cooray and Ratbek Dzhumashev, "The Effects of Corruption on Labour Market Outcomes", *Economic Modelling*, Vol. 74 (2018), pp. 207–18, https://www.sciencedirect.com/science/article/abs/pii/S0264999318300051; Arlette Beltran, "Does Corruption Increase or Decrease Employment in Firms", *Applied Economics Letters*, Vol. 23, No. 5 (2015), pp. 361–4, https://www.tandfonline.com/doi/abs/10.1080/13504851.2015.1076137?journalCode=rael20&
19. See, for example, Brendan O'Boyle, Emilie Sweigart and Benjamin Russell, "Fighting Corruption: What Works/What Doesn't", *Americas Quarterly*, 11 July 2019, https://www.americasquarterly.org/article/fighting-corruption-what-works-what-doesnt/; Kaunain Rahman, "Select Anti-corruption Success Stories", CMI U4 Anti-corruption Resource Center and Transparency International, 28 March 2022, https://www.u4.no/publications/select-anti-corruption-success-stories.pdf
20. https://www.transparency.org/en/cpi/2021
21. Americas Society and the Council of the Americas and Control Risks, "The Capacity to Combat Corruption Index: Assessing Latin America's Ability to Detect, Punish and Prevent Corruption", June 2022, https://www.as-coa.org/sites/default/files/inline-files/CCC_Report_2022_0.pdf
22. Commonwealth Secretariat, "Commonwealth Anti-Corruption Benchmarks", April 2021, https://production-new-commonwealth-files.s3.eu-west-2.amazonaws.com/s3fs-public/documents/Anti-Corruption%20Benchmarks_UPDF.pdf?VersionId=03OFUohyOBCaaTiuxzUowudOUc.tq7pX

23. https://oecd-public-integrity-indicators.org/
24. https://www.land-links.org/document/infographic-why-land-rights-matter/
25. Hossein Azadi and Eric Vanhaute, "Mutual Effects of Land Distribution and Economic Development: Evidence from Asia, Africa, and Latin America", *Land*, Vol. 8, No. 96 (2019), p. 8.
26. See, for example, https://cdn.landesa.org/wp-content/uploads/FactSheet_AFR_GrowEconomy.pdf and https://cdn.landesa.org/wp-content/uploads/FactSheet_IND_GrowEconomy.pdf
27. Ricardo Fort, "Land, Inequality and Economic Growth", *Agricultural Economics*, Vol. 37, Nos 2–3 (2007), pp. 159–65, https://onlinelibrary.wiley.com/doi/abs/10.1111/j.1574-0862.2007.00262.x
28. P. Keefer and S. Knack, "Polarization, Politics and Property Rights: Links between Inequality and Growth", *Public Choice*, Vol. 111 (2002), pp. 127–54, https://www.socialcapitalgateway.org/content/paper/keefer-p-knack-s-2002-polarization-politics-and-property-rights-links-between-inequali
29. Jakob Svensson, "Investment, Property Rights and Political Stability: Theory and Evidence", *European Economic Review*, Vol. 42, No. 7 (1998), pp. 1317–41, https://www.sciencedirect.com/science/article/abs/pii/S0014292197000810
30. Chris Jochnick, "How Land Rights Can Grow the Economy", *Thomson Reuters Foundation News*, 14 June 2016, https://news.trust.org/item/20160614132200-91jwi/
31. Laura Tuck and Wael Zakout, "Seven Reasons for Land and Property Rights to Be at the Top of the Global Agenda", *Land Portal*, 25 March 2019, https://landportal.org/blog-post/2019/03/seven-reasons-land-and-property-rights-be-top-global-agenda
32. https://www.landexglobal.org/en/methodology/
33. Mariana Mazzucato and William Lazonick, "The Risk–Reward Nexus in the Innovation–Inequality Relationship: Who Takes the Risks? Who Gets the Rewards?" *Industrial and Corporate Change*, Vol. 22, No. 4 (2013), p. 1123, https://ec.europa.eu/futurium/en/system/files/ged/ind_corp_change-2013-lazonick-1093-128_0.pdf
34. See, for example, Milton Friedman, "A Friedman Doctrine: The Social Responsibility of Business Is to Increase Its Profits", *New York Times*, 13 September 1970, https://www.nytimes.com/1970/09/13/archives/a-friedman-doctrine-the-social-responsibility-of-business-is-to.html
35. The International Accounting Standards Board defines "materiality" thus: "Information is material if omitting, misstating or obscuring it could reasonably be expected to influence the decisions that the primary users of general purpose financial statements make on the basis of those financial

statements, which provide financial information about a specific reporting entity." https://www.ifrs.org/news-and-events/news/2018/10/iasb-clarifies-its-definition-of-material/

36. For a fuller discussion of this topic, see Richard Samans and Jane Nelson, *Sustainable Enterprise Value Creation: Implementing Stakeholder Capitalism through Full ESG Integration*, Cham, Palgrave Macmillan, 2022, pp. 22–8, https://link.springer.com/book/10.1007/978-3-030-93560-3
37. See, for example, CFA Institute and CFA Society Germany, "Stakeholder Capitalism in Action: Spotlight on Germany's Works Councils", December 2021, https://www.cfainstitute.org/-/media/documents/article/position-paper/cfa-germany-stakeholder-web.pdf
38. Anne-Lise Bance, "The European Model of Shareholder Foundations: A Source of Inspiration for Entrepreneurs", Prophil, 2017, http://www.step-lausanne.org/wp-content/uploads/2015/08/STEP-05092017-Presentation-Lausanne-ALB-5septembre.pdf
39. See, for example, Donald Kalff, "An EU Boost to Sustainable Corporate Governance", CEPS Policy Insights No. 2022–25, July 2022, https://www.ceps.eu/ceps-publications/an-eu-boost-to-sustainable-corporate-governance/
40. See, for example, Akanksha Jumde, "Legislated Corporate Social Responsibility (CSR) in India: The Law and Practicalities of Its Compliance", *Statute Law Review*, Vol. 43, No. 2 (2022), pp. 170–97, https://academic.oup.com/slr/article-abstract/43/2/170/5841990?redirectedFrom=fulltext
41. See B Lab, "The Legal Requirement for Certified B Corporations," https://www.bcorporation.net/en-us/about-b-corps/legal-requirements
42. Samans and Nelson, *Sustainable Enterprise Value Creation*, p. 28.
43. State-owned enterprises are common in a wide range of economies. See, for example, Przemyslaw Kowalski, Max Büge, Monika Sztajerowska and Matias Egeland, "State-Owned Enterprises: Trade Effects and Policy Implications", OECD Trade Policy Paper No. 147, 24 April 2013, pp. 21–3, https://www.oecd-ilibrary.org/trade/state-owned-enterprises_5k4869ckqk7l-en;jsessionid=jIy1ksPmZLhQGJ0Agl3tOhrsqj728TXIhYiLMbnK.ip-10-240-5-142
44. For further information about this innovative approach, see the Fourth Sector Group, an advisory and advocacy organization established to promote the concept and practice: https://www.fourthsector.org/
45. See, for example, ILO, "Advancing the 2030 Agenda through the Social and Solidarity Economy", ILO Position Paper, 26 September 2022, https://www.ilo.org/global/topics/cooperatives/sse/publications/WCMS_856876/lang%2D%2Den/index.htm

46. See, for example, OECD, *OECD Corporate Governance Factbook 2021*, Paris, 2021, https://www.oecd.org/corporate/OECD-Corporate-Governance-Factbook.pdf
47. https://data.imf.org/?sk=F8032E80-B36C-43B1-AC26-493C5B1CD33B
48. For a good overview of the post-crisis reforms, see IMF, *Global Financial Stability Report. A Decade after the Global Financial Crisis: Are We Safer?*, Washington, DC, 2018, pp. 55–87, https://www.imf.org/en/Publications/GFSR/Issues/2018/09/25/Global-Financial-Stability-Report-October-2018
49. See BIS, "Basel III Monitoring Report", February2022, https://www.bis.org/bcbs/publ/d531.htm#:~:text=The%20final%20Basel%20III%20minimum,increase%20at%20end%2DDecember%202020
50. See, for example, FSB, "Enhancing the Resilience of Non-bank Financial Intermediation", Progress Report, 1 November 2021, https://www.fsb.org/wp-content/uploads/P011121.pdf
51. J. Benes and M. Kumhof, "The Chicago Plan Revisited", IMF Working Paper WP/12/202, 2012, pp. 9–11, https://www.imf.org/external/pubs/ft/wp/2012/wp12202.pdf
52. See, for example, Swiss Finance Institute, "Global Financial Regulation, Transparency, and Compliance Index (GFRTCI)", SFI Public Discussion Note, 2021, https://www.sfi.ch/resources/public/dtc/media/gfrtci2021_en_web_20210308.pdf; Deniz Anginer, Ata Can Bertay, Robert Cull, Asli Demirgüç-Kunt and Davide S. Mare, "Bank Regulation and Supervision Ten Years after the Global Financial Crisis", World Bank Policy Research Working Paper No. 9044, October 2019, https://documents1.worldbank.org/curated/en/685851571160819618/pdf/Bank-Regulation-and-Supervision-Ten-Years-after-the-Global-Financial-Crisis.pdf
53. A capital adequacy ratio of 20% of total assets would be more in line with the requirements of financial stability as well as historical practice. See, for example, John Vickers, "Safer but Not Safe Enough", keynote address at 20th International Conference of Banking Supervisors, Abu Dhabi, 29 November 2018, https://www.bis.org/bcbs/events/icbs20/vickers.pdf and Anat Admati et al., "Healthy Banking System is the Goal, Not Profitable Banks," *Financial Times*, November 9, 2010 https://www.ft.com/content/63fa6b9e-eb8e-11df-bbb5-00144feab49a
54. See, for example, Kurt von Mettenheim and Oliver Butzbach, eds., *Alternative Banking and Financial Crisis*, London, Routledge, 2015 https://www.routledge.com/Alternative-Banking-and-Financial-Crisis/Mettenheim-Butzbach/p/book/9781138663084; Roland Benedikter, *Social Banking and Social Finance: Answers to the Economic Crisis*,

New York, Springer, 2011, https://link.springer.com/content/pdf/10.1007/978-1-4419-7774-8.pdf; Cyrus R. Vance Center for International Justice, "Public Banking around the World: A Comparative Survey of Seven Models", 2021, https://www.vancecenter.org/wp-content/uploads/2021/10/Public-Banking-Around-the-World-A-Comparative-Survey-of-Seven-Models.pdf

55. NGFS, "Annual Report 2021", March 2022, especially pp. 6–7, https://www.ngfs.net/en/annual-report-2021; see also https://unepinquiry.org/
56. See https://www.ifrs.org/groups/international-sustainability-standards-board/
57. See FSB, "Assessment of Shadow Banking Activities, Risks and the Adequacy of Post-crisis Policy Tools to Address Financial Stability Concerns", 3 July 2017, https://www.fsb.org/wp-content/uploads/P300617-1.pdf
58. See, for example, Gregg Gelzinis, "Strengthening the Regulation and Oversight of Shadow Banks: Revitalizing the Financial Stability Oversight Council", Center for American Progress Report, 18 July 2019, https://www.americanprogress.org/article/strengthening-regulation-oversight-shadow-banks/
59. See George Pennacchi, "Narrow Banking", *Annual Review of Financial Economics*, Vol. 4 (2012), pp. 3–8, https://gpennacc.web.illinois.edu/GPNarrowBankARFE.pdf; B. Summers, "Loan Commitments to Business in U.S. Banking History", *Federal Reserve Bank of Richmond Economic Review*, September 1975, pp. 15–23.
60. Adair Turner, "Credit, Money and Leverage: What Wicksell, Hayek and Fisher Knew and Modern Macroeconomics Forgot", speech at Stockholm School of Economics Conference on "Towards a Sustainable Financial System", 12 September 2013, pp. 11–12, https://cdn.evbuc.com/eventlogos/67785745/turner.pdf
61. Julius Krein, "The Value of Nothing: Capital versus Growth", *American Affairs*, Vol. 5 No. 3 (2021), https://americanaffairsjournal.org/2021/08/the-value-of-nothing-capital-versus-growth/
62. Benes and Kumhof, "The Chicago Plan Revisited", p. 4.
63. I. Fisher, "100% Money and the Public Debt", *Economic Forum*, April–June 1936, pp. 406–20 as summarized in Benes and Kumhof, "The Chicago Plan Revisited", p. 4.
64. See, for example, Brett Fiebiger, "'The Chicago Plan Revisited': A Friendly Critique", *European Journal of Economics and Economic Policies: Intervention*, Vol. 11 No. 3 (2014), pp. 227–49, https://www.elgaronline.com/view/journals/ejeep/11-3/ejeep.2014.03.02.xml
65. Public–Private Infrastructure Advisory Facility (PPIAF) and World Bank, "Who Sponsors Infrastructure Projects? Disentangling Public and Private

Contributions", 2017 m https://ppi.worldbank.org/content/dam/PPI/documents/SPIReport_2017_small_interactive.pdf
66. See, for example, B. Sanchez-Robles, "Infrastructure Investment and Growth: Some Empirical Evidence", *Contemporary Economic Policy*, Vol. 16, No. 1 (1998), pp. 98–108; Dave Donaldson, "Railroads of the Raj: Estimating the Impact of Transportation Infrastructure", *American Economic Review*, Vol. 108, Nos 4–5 (2018), pp. 899–934; Matias Herrera Dappe and Mathilde Lebrand, "Infrastructure and Structural Change in the Horn of Africa", World Bank Policy Research Working Paper No. 9870, 2021, https://openknowledge.worldbank.org/handle/10986/36646; Mathilde Lebrand, "Infrastructure and Structural Change in the Lake Chad Region", World Bank Policy Research Working Paper No. 9899, 2022 https://openknowledge.worldbank.org/handle/10986/36845
67. Mariano Moszoro, "The Direct Employment Impact of Public Investment", IMF Working Paper 121/31, 6 May 2021 https://www.imf.org/en/Publications/WP/Issues/2021/05/06/The-Direct-Employment-Impact-of-Public-Investment-50251
68. https://bpp.worldbank.org/
69. https://www.gihub.org/explore-our-work/
70. Gerben Bakker, Nicholas Crafts and Pieter Woltjer, "The Sources of Growth in a Technologically Progressive Economy: the United States, 1899–1941", LSE Economic History Working Paper No. 269, October 2017, pp. 11, 14, 35, http://eprints.lse.ac.uk/85081/1/WP269.pdf
71. See OECD, "Compendium of Information on R&D Tax Incentives, 2021", March 2021, https://www.oecd.org/sti/rd-tax-stats-compendium.pdf
72. This summary of the relevant OECD data is drawn from Daniel Bunn, "Tax Subsidies for R&D Spending and Patent Boxes in OECD Countries", Tax Foundation Fiscal Fact No. 754, March 2021, https://files.taxfoundation.org/20210315164148/Tax-Subsidies-for-RD-Spending-and-Patent-Boxes-in-OECD-Countries.pdf?_gl=1*13cfjtn*_ga*MTcwMjE5MzcONC4xNjY2NDM0NDU4*_ga_FP7KWDV08V*MTY2NjQzNDQ1OC4xLjEuMTY2NjQzNTM1MS42MC4wLjA
73. Moszoro, "The Direct Employment Impact of Public Investment", p. 1.
74. See, for example, Ricardo Haussman, "Economic Development and the Accumulation of Know-How", *Welsh Economic Review*, Vol. 24 (Spring 2016), pp. 13–16, https://growthlab.cid.harvard.edu/files/growthlab/files/2016-5-hausmann-welsh-economic-review.pdf; Ricardo Hausmann, César A. Hidalgo, Sebastián Bustos, Michele Coscia, Alexander Simoes and Muhammed A. Yıldırım, *The Atlas of Economic Complexity: Mapping Paths to Prosperity*, Cambridge, MA, MIT Press, 2013 https://growthlab.cid.harvard.edu/files/growthlab/files/atlas_2013_part1.pdf

75. https://rcc.harvard.edu/knowledge-technology-and-complexity-economic-growth
76. See, for example, Cesar A. Hidalgo, "The Policy Implications of Economic Complexity", May 2022, https://arxiv.org/ftp/arxiv/papers/2205/2205.02164.pdf; Jose Manuel Salazar Xirinachs, Irmgard Nubler and Richard Kozul-Wright, *Transforming Economies: Making Industrial Policies Work for Growth, Jobs and Development*, Geneva, ILO, 2014, https://labordoc.ilo.org/discovery/fulldisplay/alma994851413402676/41ILO_INST:41ILO_V2
77. See, for example, Karl Aiginger and Dani Rodrik, "Rebirth of Industrial Policy and an Agenda for the 21st Century", *Journal of Industry, Competition and Trade*, Vol. 20, No. 2 (2020), pp. 189–207, https://link.springer.com/article/10.1007/s10842-019-00322-3
78. Justin Yifu Lin and Yong Wang, "Structural Change, Industrial Upgrading, and Middle-Income Trap", *Journal of Industry, Competition and Trade*, Vol. 20 (2020), p. 360.
79. See, for example, Ma Huimin, Xiang Wu, Li Yan and Han Huang, "Strategic Plan of 'Made in China 2025' and Its Implementation", in Richard Brunet-Thornton and Felipe Martinez, eds, *Analysing the Impacts of Industry 4.0 in Modern Business Environments*, Hershey, PA, IGI Global, 2018, pp. 1–23, https://www.researchgate.net/publication/326392969_Strategic_Plan_of_Made_in_China_2025_and_Its_Implementation; Institute for Security and Development Policy, "Made in China 2025: Backgrounder", June 2018, https://isdp.eu/content/uploads/2018/06/Made-in-China-Backgrounder.pdf; State Council of the People's Republic of China, "Made in China 2025", trans. Center for Security and Emerging Technology, 8 March 2022, https://cset.georgetown.edu/wp-content/uploads/t0432_made_in_china_2025_EN.pdf
80. https://www.wipo.int/global_innovation_index/en/2022/?utm_source=google&utm_medium=cpc&utm_campaign=Global+Innovation+Index+2022+%28EN%29%3A+Search+Campaign&utm_content=search+ads&gclid=Cj0KCQjwqc6aBhC4ARIsAN06NmPhAHH3aKB9HPtEwb-oLvxGapfjDYFuLRb6TcNt4IinbwCwF0kDCPMaAgE1EALw_wcB
81. https://atlas.cid.harvard.edu/rankings
82. https://oec.world/en/rankings/eci/hs6/hs96
83. See these and related data at United Nations Educational, Scientific and Cultural Organization (UNESCO), *Global Education Monitoring Report 2021/22. Non-State Actors in Education: Who Chooses? Who Loses?*, Paris, https://unesdoc.unesco.org/ark:/48223/pf0000379875/PDF/379875eng.pdf.multi
84. See https://data.worldbank.org/indicator/SE.PRM.CMPT.ZS?locations=XM

85. Rebecca Winthrop and Eileen McGivney, "Why Wait 100 Years: Bridging the Gap in Global Education", Brookings Institution Center for Universal Education, 2015, pp. 10–14, https://www.brookings.edu/wp-content/uploads/2015/06/global_20161128_100-year-gap.pdf
86. UNESCO, *Global Education Monitoring Report 2021/22*, p. 377.
87. UNESCO and World Bank, "Education Finance Watch 2022", 2022, p. 21, https://unesdoc.unesco.org/ark:/48223/pf0000381644/PDF/381644eng.pdf.multi
88. UNESCO, *Global Education Monitoring Report 2021/22*, p. 381.
89. Ibid., p. 400.
90. OECD, *Education at a Glance 2021: OECD Indicators*, Paris, 2021, p. 233, https://www.oecd-ilibrary.org/docserver/b35a14e5-en.pdf?expires=1666534127&id=id&accname=guest&checksum=992818DCCB2AD005D91BE3DD6AE0F208
91. Ibid., p. 359.
92. Ibid., p. 52.
93. https://data.oecd.org/socialexp/public-spending-on-labour-markets.htm
94. OECD, *Education at a Glance 2021*, p. 245.
95. See, for example, OECD, *Engaging Young Children: Lessons from Research about Quality in Early Childhood Education and Care*, Paris, 2018, https://doi.org/10.1787/9789264085145-en; OECD, "How Does Access to Early Childhood Education Services Affect the Participation of Women in the Labour Market?" Education Indicators in Focus No. 59, 2018, https://doi.org/10.1787/232211ca-en
96. See OECD, *Education at a Glance 2021*, pp. 161–5, for the data and analysis presented here on early childhood education.
97. ILO Declaration on Fundamental Principles and Rights at Work, 1998, https://www.ilo.org/declaration/lang%2D%2Den/index.htm
98. This information is drawn from ILO, Walk Free and International Organization for Migration (IOM), *Global Estimates of Modern Slavery: Forced Labour and Forced Marriage*, Geneva, 2022, https://www.ilo.org/wcmsp5/groups/public/%2D%2D-ed_norm/%2D%2D-ipec/documents/publication/wcms_854733.pdf
99. This information is drawn from ILO and UNICEF, *Child Labour Global Estimates 2020: Trends and the Road Forward*, New York, 2021, https://www.ilo.org/wcmsp5/groups/public/%2D%2D-ed_norm/%2D%2D-ipec/documents/publication/wcms_797515.pdf
100. See https://www.ilo.org/integration/themes/mdw/lang%2D%2Den/index.htm
101. See https://www.imf.org/external/about/econsurv.htm#country
102. See, for example, Federal Statistical Office, Swiss Confederation, "Household Income and Expenditure", https://www.bfs.admin.ch/bfs/

en/home/statistics/economic-social-situation-population/income-consumption-wealth/household-budget.html; National Bureau of Statistics of China, "Households' Income and Consumption Expenditure in the First Quarter of 2022", 20 April, 2022, http://www.stats.gov.cn/english/PressRelease/202204/t20220420_1829910.html; German Statistical Office, "Income, Receipts, Expenditure", 2 December 2022, https://www.destatis.de/EN/Themes/Society-Environment/Income-Consumption-Living-Conditions/Income-Receipts-Expenditure/Tables/income-expenditure-d-lwr.html;jsessionid=B47383B7A7FA476C0A5FE19B792C7377.live712

103. These figures are based on the calculations of the Wage Indicator Foundation: https://wageindicator.org/salary/wages-in-context/minimum-wages-living-wages

104. The calculations presented here for the United States are derived from a different source from that of those presented for other countries. See Stephanie Moser, "A Calculation of the Living Wage", *Living Wage Calculator*, 19 May 2022, https://livingwage.mit.edu/articles/99-a-calculation-of-the-living-wage

105. See ILO, *Social Dialogue Report 2022: Collective Bargaining for an Inclusive, Sustainable and Resilient Recovery*, Geneva, 2022, p. 15, https://www.ilo.org/wcmsp5/groups/public/%2D%2D-dgreports/%2D%2D-dcomm/%2D%2D-publ/documents/publication/wcms_842807.pdf

106. Ibid., p. 69.

107. "Trade union density" refers to the share of employees within an economy who are union members. See https://ilostat.ilo.org/topics/union-membership/

108. https://www.ilo.org/dyn/normlex/en/f?p=NORMLEXPUB:20060:0::NO:::

109. https://www.ilo.org/shinyapps/bulkexplorer48/?lang=en&segment=indicator&id=SDG_0882_NOC_RT_A

110. https://www.oecd-ilibrary.org/sites/8483c82f-en/index.html?itemId=/content/component/8483c82f-en#:~:text=The%20poverty%20rate%20is%20a,median%20prevailing%20in%20each%20country.

111. Pierre Bachas, Matthew Fisher-Post, Anders Jensen and Gabriel Zucman, "Globalization and Factor Income Taxation", World Bank Policy Research Working Paper 9973, March 2022, https://openknowledge.worldbank.org/bitstream/handle/10986/37160/Globalization-and-Factor-Income-Taxation.pdf?sequence=1&isAllowed=y

112. OECD, "Understanding Differences in Health Expenditure between the United States and OECD Countries", September 2022, https://www.oecd.org/health/Health-expenditure-differences-USA-OECD-countries-Brief-July-2022.pdf

113. For an overview of government policies on the payment of child allowances or family benefits, see Overseas Development Institute and UNICEF, *Universal Child Benefits: Policy Issues and Options*, London and New York, 2020, https://www.unicef.org/media/72916/file/UCB-ODI-UNICEF-Report-2020.pdf
114. The ICECSR was adopted by the UN General Assembly on 16 December 1966 and entered into force on 3 January 1976: https://www.ohchr.org/en/instruments-mechanisms/instruments/international-covenant-economic-social-and-cultural-rights
115. See https://tbinternet.ohchr.org/_layouts/15/treatybodyexternal/TBSearch.aspx?Lang=en&TreatyID=9&DocTypeID=11; Icelandic Human Rights Centre, "The Right to an Adequate Standard of Living", https://www.humanrights.is/en/human-rights-education-project/human-rights-concepts-ideas-and-fora/substantive-human-rights/the-right-to-an-adequate-standard-of-living
116. See https://sdgs.un.org/goals/goal6
117. See https://sdgs.un.org/goals/goal2
118. See https://sdgs.un.org/goals/goal7
119. See https://sdgs.un.org/goals/goal11
120. These data are drawn from various UN agencies' statistical reports, many related to their respective responsibilities for reporting on progress towards the SDGs. See, for example, https://unstats.un.org/sdgs/dataportal
121. See https://outlook.gihub.org/
122. Marianne Fay, Sungmin Han, Hyoung Il Lee, Massimo Mastruzzi and Moonkyoung Cho, "Hitting the Trillion Mark: A Look at How Much Countries Are Spending on Infrastructure", World Bank Policy Research Working Paper 8730, February 2019, pp. 36–47, https://papers.ssrn.com/sol3/papers.cfm?abstract_id=3327648
123. Jonathan Woetzel, Nicklas Garemo, Jan Mischke, Priyanka Kamra and Robert Palter, "Bridging Infrastructure Gaps: Has the World Made Progress?" McKinsey, 13 October 2017, https://www.mckinsey.com/capabilities/operations/our-insights/bridging-infrastructure-gaps-has-the-world-made-progress
124. Victoria A. Beard and Diana Mitlin, "Water Access in Global South Cities: The Challenges of Intermittency and Affordability", *World Development*, Vol. 147 (2021), p. 7, https://reader.elsevier.com/reader/sd/pii/S0305750X21002400?token=75ABA20AA9FC548A77FC4C8C79875337356FD6BC7231CA56A0861B5D4B39D225ADE12BE3BF1528CA00AC82328DBD27B7&originRegion=eu-west-1&originCreation=20221101131226
125. Ibid., p. 12.

126. *Reuters*, "Eurozone Bill for Cost-of-Living Crisis Nears 300 Billion Euros", 7 September 2022, https://www.reuters.com/markets/europe/euro-zone-bill-cost-living-crisis-nears-300-bln-euros-2022-09-07/
127. Giovanni Sgaravatti, Simone Tagliapietra, Cecilia Trasi and Georg Zachmann, "National Fiscal Policy Responses to the Energy Crisis", Bruegel, 21 October 2022, https://www.bruegel.org/dataset/national-policies-shield-consumers-rising-energy-prices
128. For a good overview of the nature and extent of explicit and implicit subsidies typically employed with respect to water and electricity utility services, see Kristin Komives, Vivien Foster, Jonathan Halpern and Quentin Wodon, *Water, Electricity and the Poor: Who Benefits from Utility Subsidies?*, Washington, DC, World Bank, 2005, pp. 21, 26, http://web.worldbank.org/archive/website01214/WEB/IMAGES/WATER_-2.PDF
129. World Bank, "Schemes to Systems. The Public Distribution System: Anatomy of India's Food Subsidy Reforms", 21 February 2019, https://www.worldbank.org/en/news/feature/2019/02/21/schemes-to-systems-public-distribution-system
130. *Business Standard*, "India's Food Subsidies Plan Needs to Improve Coverage, Plug Leakages", 13 March 2022, https://www.business-standard.com/article/current-affairs/india-s-food-subsidies-plan-needs-to-improve-coverage-plug-leakages-122030600092_1.html#:~:text=The%20Centre%20has%20allocated%20about,public%20distribution%20system%20(PDS).
131. Neil McCulloch, Davide Natalini, Naomi Hossain and Patricia Justino, "An Exploration of the Association between Fuel Subsidies and Fuel Riots", *World Development*, Vol. 157 (2022), https://reader.elsevier.com/reader/sd/pii/S0305750X22001255?token=B50987B9CC6D0D24837C552C12DAA5C2B9E5B9DB42B272DEC516A6F5A5FBC53B2C2DA4B58040A15A0711FF2B8B1BD70E&originRegion=eu-west-1&originCreation=20221101163356
132. David Amaglobeli, Emine Hanedar, Gee Hee Hong and Céline Thévenot, "Fiscal Policy for Mitigating the Social Impact of High Energy and Food Prices", IMF Note No. 2022/001, 7 June 2022, pp. 4–5, https://www.imf.org/en/Publications/IMF-Notes/Issues/2022/06/07/Fiscal-Policy-for-Mitigating-the-Social-Impact-of-High-Energy-and-Food-Prices-519013
133. Nadia Calviño, "Chair's Statement for the Forty-Sixth Meeting of the IMFC", IMF Press Release No. 22/357, 14 October 2022, https://www.imf.org/en/News/Articles/2022/10/14/pr22357-imfc-chair-statement-forty-sixth-meeting-of-the-imfc
134. Ibid., p. 1.

135. See related discussion in Chapter 3.
136. ILO, *World Social Protection Report 2020–22: Social Protection at the Crossroads—in Pursuit of a Better Future*, Geneva, 2021, p. 45. https://www.ilo.org/wcmsp5/groups/public/@ed_protect/@soc_sec/documents/publication/wcms_817572.pdf
137. Ibid., p. 48.
138. Ibid., p. 49.
139. https://www.oecd-ilibrary.org/social-issues-migration-health/family-benefits-public-spending/indicator/english_8e8b3273-en?parentId=http%3A%2F%2Finstance.metastore.ingenta.com%2Fcontent%2Fthematicgrouping%2F3ddf51bf-en
140. Antonio Asenjo and Clemente Pignatti, "Unemployment Insurance Schemes around the World: Evidence and Policy Options", ILO Research Department Working Paper No. 49, October 2019, https://www.ilo.org/wcmsp5/groups/public/%2D%2D-dgreports/%2D%2D-inst/documents/publication/wcms_723778.pdf
141. Ravi Kanbur and Lucas Ronconi, "Enforcement Matters: The Effective Regulation of Labour", *International Labour Review*, Vol. 157, No. 3 (2018), pp. 334, 340, https://onlinelibrary.wiley.com/doi/10.1111/ilr.12112
142. ILO, *A Guide on Labour Inspection Intervention in the Informal Economy: A Participatory Method*, Geneva, 2018, p. 4, https://labordoc.ilo.org/discovery/delivery/41ILO_INST:41ILO_V1/1252219420002676
143. Orsetta Causa, Nicolas Woloszko and David Leite, "Housing, Wealth Accumulation and Wealth Distribution: Evidence and Stylized Facts", OECD Economics Department Working Paper No. 1588, 16 December 2019, p. 22, https://www.oecd.org/officialdocuments/publicdisplaydocumentpdf/?cote=ECO/WKP(2019)58&docLanguage=En
144. See, for example, *The Economist*, "Home Ownership Is the West's Biggest Economic-Policy Mistake", 16 January 2020, https://www.economist.com/leaders/2020/01/16/home-ownership-is-the-wests-biggest-economic-policy-mistake
145. Laurie S. Goodman and Christopher Mayer, "Homeownership and the American Dream", *Journal of Economic Perspectives*, Vol. 32, No. 1 (2018), pp. 31–58, https://www.jstor.org/stable/pdf/26297968.pdf?refreqid=excelsior%3Afa1440899dd3b6533e8398357284d6f5&ab_segments=&origin=&acceptTC=1 (and Online Appendix Table A-1.1, https://www.aeaweb.org/content/file?id=6340)
146. Ibid., pp. 34–5.
147. OECD, *Housing and Inclusive Growth*, Paris, 2020, pp. 57–8, https://www.oecd-ilibrary.org/docserver/6ef36f4b-en.pdf?expires=1667575003&id=id&accname=ocid195767&checksum=9ECB429B62F

D28573359012BCCB8D414; Bethany Millar-Powell, Bert Brys, Pierce O'Reilly, Yannic Rehm and Alastair Thomas, "Measuring Effective Taxation of Housing: Building the Foundations for Policy Reform", OECD Taxation Working Paper No. 56, 12 January 2022, https://www.oecd-ilibrary.org/docserver/0a7e36f2-en.pdf?expires=1667575324&id=id&accname=guest&checksum=C7176EA1AAB5546AF53E044728657CD1

148. European Federation of Employee Share Ownership, "Employee Share Ownership: The European Policy", May 2019, http://www.efesonline.org/LIBRARY/2018/Employee%20Share%20Ownership%20%2D%2D%20The%20European%20Policy.pdf; and for a good global overview of employee ownership structures and policy incentives, see Corey Rosen, "Laws to Encourage Broad-Based Employee Ownership Outside the US", National Center for Employee Ownership, 14 October 2013, https://www.nceo.org/articles/employee-ownership-laws-outside-us

149. Stirling Smith, *Promoting Cooperatives: A Guide to ILO Recommendation 193*, Manchester, Cooperative College, 2004, p. 19, https://www.ilo.org/wcmsp5/groups/public/%2D%2D-ed_emp/%2D%2D-emp_ent/%2D%2D-coop/documents/instructionalmaterial/wcms_160221.pdf

150. Anthony Murray, "Global 300 Cooperatives Generate $1.6 Trillion Revenue", *Co-operative News*, 31 October 2011, https://www.thenews.coop/36622/sector/global-300-co-operatives-generate-16-trillion-revenue/

151. Hilary Abell, *Worker Cooperatives: Pathways to Scale*, Takoma Park, MD, Democracy Collaborative, 2014, p. 4, https://project-equity.org/wp-content/uploads/2017/02/Worker-Cooperatives-Pathways-to-Scale.pdf

152. See, for example, Monica C. Adeler, "Enabling Policy Environments for Co-operative Development: A Comparative Experience", *Canadian Public Policy / Analyse de Politiques*, Vol. 40, Supplement I (2014), pp. S50–9, https://www.jstor.org/stable/24365089

153. https://climateactiontracker.org/methodology/cat-rating-methodology/

154. S. Boehm et al., *State of Climate Action 2022*, Berlin, Systems Change Lab, 2022, p. 2, https://doi.org/10.46830/wrirpt.22.00028

155. See, for example, UNEP, "Towards a Green Economy: Pathways to Sustainable Development and Poverty Eradication—a Synthesis for Policymakers", 2011, https://sustainabledevelopment.un.org/content/documents/126GER_synthesis_en.pdf; UNEP, "Advancing the Transition to an Inclusive Green Economy: A Policy Review Manual", 2020, https://wedocs.unep.org/bitstream/handle/20.500.11822/34422/GEPM.pdf?sequence=1&isAllowed=y

156. OECD, *Towards Green Growth*, Paris, 2011, https://www.oecd-ilibrary.org/docserver/9789264111318-en.pdf?expires=1667734246&id=id&accname=ocid195767&checksum=DF0E9F868F07539EF7590CD970ECF30B
157. OECD, *Green Growth Indicators 2017*, Paris, 2017, https://www.oecd-ilibrary.org/docserver/9789264268586-en.pdf?expires=1667734355&id=id&accname=ocid195767&checksum=46DB896BDAB1674661D1D4E344817A8B
158. Asian Development Bank, United Nations, OECD and World Bank, "A Toolkit of Policy Options to Support Inclusive Green Growth: Submission to the G20 Development Working Group", 2012 https://www.afdb.org/fileadmin/uploads/afdb/Documents/Generic-Documents/A%20Toolkit%20of%20Policy%20Options%20to%20Support%20Inclusive%20Green%20Growth.pdf
159. See https://www.greengrowthknowledge.org/
160. Jeffrey D. Sachs, Guillaume Lafortune, Christian Kroll, Grayson Fuller and Finn Woelm, *Sustainable Development Report 2022. From Crisis to Sustainable Development: The SDGs as Roadmap to 2030 and Beyond*, Cambridge, UK, Cambridge University Press, 2022, https://irp.cdn-website.com/be6d1d56/files/uploaded/UNSDSN%20SDR22%20WEB%20V6%20290522.pdf
161. Global Green Growth Institute, "Green Growth Index 2021: Measuring Performance in Achieving SDG Targets", GGGI Technical Report No. 22, December 2021, pp. 24, 38, https://greengrowthindex.gggi.org/wp-content/uploads/2022/10/2021-Green-Growth-Index.pdf
162. Jeffrey D. Sachs, Guido Schmidt-Traub, Mariana Mazzucato, Dirk Messner, Nebojsa Nakicenovic and Johan Rockström, "Six Transformations to Achieve the Sustainable Development Goals", *Nature Sustainability*, Vol.2(2019),pp.805–14,https://resources.unsdsn.org/six-transformations-to-achieve-the-sustainable-development-goals-sdgs?_ga=2.26179453.1752853351.1667746049-812053377.1667652826
163. The Mission Possible Partnership is a collaboration of the Energy Transitions Commission, Rocky Mountain Institute, We Mean Business Coalition and World Economic Forum: https://missionpossiblepartnership.org/about/
164. https://www.wbcsd.org/
165. Boehm et al., *State of Climate Action 2022*.
166. https://www.cdsb.net/
167. https://www.valuereportingfoundation.org/
168. https://www.fsb-tcfd.org/
169. https://www.globalreporting.org/
170. See https://tnfd.global/

171. United Nations, "Integrity Matters: Net-Zero Commitments by Businesses, Financial Institutions, Cities and Regions", Report from the UN High-Level Panel on the Net-Zero Emissions Commitments of Non-State Entities, 8 November 2022, https://www.un.org/sites/un2.un.org/files/high-level_expert_group_n7b.pdf
172. https://www.gfanzero.com/
173. See Agreement on Climate Change, Trade and Sustainability involving New Zealand, Costa Rica, Finland, Iceland, Norway and Switzerland: https://www.beehive.govt.nz/release/joint-statement-agreement-climate-change-trade-and-sustainability-accts-mc12; and for further background see G. Hufbauer, R. Melendez-Ortiz and R. Samans, eds, *The Law and Economics of a Sustainable Energy Trade Agreement*, Cambridge, UK, Cambridge University Press, 2016, https://www.cambridge.org/core/books/law-and-economics-of-a-sustainable-energy-trade-agreement/06B92421E2074E8F89C9431CC05E424B
174. European Commission, *Buying Green: A Handbook on Green Public Procurement*, Luxembourg, Publications Office of the European Union, 2016, https://ec.europa.eu/environment/gpp/pdf/Buying-Green-Handbook-3rd-Edition.pdf
175. See IEA, "Top Runner Programme", 15 August 2019, https://www.iea.org/policies/1945-top-runner-programme
176. UNFCCC, "Just Transition of the Workforce and the Creation of Decent Work and Quality Jobs", Technical Paper, 2017, https://unfccc.int/sites/default/files/resource/Just%20transition.pdf
177. https://www.cbd.int/article/cop15-cbd-press-release-final-19dec2022
178. See, for example, J.B. Rule et al., "Connecting Ecosystem Services Science and Policy in the Field", *Frontiers of Ecology and the Environment*, Vol. 19, No. 9 (2021), pp. 519 25, https://esajournals.onlinelibrary.wiley.com/doi/epdf/10.1002/fee.2390; J.B. Rule, Steven E. Kraft and Christopher L. Lant, *The Law and Policy of Ecosystem Services*, Washington, DC, Island Press, 2007.
179. https://www.nwf.org/Educational-Resources/Wildlife-Guide/Understanding-Conservation/Ecosystem-Services
180. See, for example, Lydia P. Olander et al., "Benefit Relevant Indicators: Ecosystem Services Measures that Link Ecological and Social Outcomes", *Ecological Indicators*, Vol. 85 (2018), pp. 1262–72, https://www.sciencedirect.com/science/article/pii/S1470160X17307811;

Pamela McElwee, "The Metrics of Making Ecosystem Services", *Environment and Society: Advances in Research*, Vol. 8 (2017), pp. 96–124, https://www.envirosociety.org/wp-content/uploads/2016/05/ares080105.pdf

181. Peter Newton, Nicole Civita, Lee Frankel-Goldwater, Katharine Bartel and Colleen Johns, "What Is Regenerative Agriculture? A Review of Scholar and Practitioner Definitions Based on Processes and Outcomes", *Frontiers in Sustainable Food Systems*, Vol. 4 (2020), https://www.frontiersin.org/articles/10.3389/fsufs.2020.577723/full
182. European Academies Scientific Advisory Council, *Regenerative Agriculture in Europe: A Critical Analysis of Contributions to European Union Farm to Fork and Biodiversity Strategies*, Halle, 2022, p. v, https://www.interacademies.org/sites/default/files/2022-04/EASAC%20Report%20RegenerativeAgriculture_April_2022_WEB.pdf
183. Ibid., p. 1.

Open Access This chapter is licensed under the terms of the Creative Commons Attribution 4.0 International License (http://creativecommons.org/licenses/by/4.0/), which permits use, sharing, adaptation, distribution and reproduction in any medium or format, as long as you give appropriate credit to the original author(s) and the source, provide a link to the Creative Commons licence and indicate if changes were made.

The images or other third party material in this chapter are included in the chapter's Creative Commons licence, unless indicated otherwise in a credit line to the material. If material is not included in the chapter's Creative Commons licence and your intended use is not permitted by statutory regulation or exceeds the permitted use, you will need to obtain permission directly from the copyright holder.

CHAPTER 6

Human-Centred International Economic Policy: Institutionalizing Inclusion, Sustainability and Resilience in International Economic Governance and Cooperation

This book has argued that the living standards of nations should no longer be treated in economic theory and policy as essentially a residual consideration, an inevitable, trickle-down by-product of the wealth of nations. To this end, Chap. 4 proposed a series of reforms of the standard liberal economic growth and development model. These concepts would explicitly integrate into the heart of the model an extensive ecosystem of policies and institutional features that have a more direct and tangible bearing on the lived experience of people than do the traditional preoccupation of top economists and economic policymakers—macroeconomic, trade and financial supervision policies.

In an important sense, this rebalanced model would return economics to its classical political economy roots by more explicitly contextualizing the pursuit of allocative efficiency and productive output as means to the more fundamental social purpose of broad-based progress in household living standards. This is the bottom-line way most people and their societies evaluate national economic performance. It also reflects the broader concept of economic progress that three of the field's most important original theorists and codifiers—Adam Smith, John Stuart Mill and Alfred Marshall—had in mind, as discussed in Chap. 3.

The original version of the chapter has been revised. A correction to this chapter can be found at https://doi.org/10.1007/978-3-031-37435-7_8

© The Author(s) 2024, corrected publication 2024
R. Samans, *Human-Centred Economics*,
https://doi.org/10.1007/978-3-031-37435-7_6

In order to instrumentalize this conceptual reformulation, I have argued that both theory and policy need to adopt an explicit, co-equal focus on increasing allocative efficiency and productive output through markets and a stable macroeconomy, on the one hand, and diffusing gains in living standards through a spectrum of relevant institutions, on the other. I break down this spectrum into five policy domains, representing them as a system—an aggregate distribution function. I further posit that it is the combination and interaction of this function with the aggregate production function of an economy that determines its median standard of living or aggregate social welfare. Economic scholarship and policy practice should be centrally concerned with optimizing an economy's aggregate social welfare function, that is to say, its aggregate production *and* distribution functions. This includes capturing positive synergies between the two, since the feedback loops between them can be either virtuous or vicious, depending upon policy and circumstance.

In other words, countries should devote at least as much policy attention and investment to the aggregate distribution as to the aggregate production function of their economy. This is the golden rule of a more human-centred approach to economic growth and development, the key to making them more socially inclusive, environmentally sustainable, and resilient. In practical terms, this means progressively increasing investment in the policy incentives and institutions, described in greater depth in Chap. 5, that reinforce household employment and entrepreneurial opportunity, disposable income, availability and affordability of material necessities, and economic and environmental security. Such an ongoing process of institutional upgrading to strengthen what is in effect an economy's social contract, narrowing its welfare gap relative to the feasible frontier, needs to be a central pillar of every country's development strategy and translated into both policy and budgeting. This is all the more important during disruptive transformations that produce more churn—winners and losers—in the world of work, which can widen inequality and insecurity, other things being equal.

The mid twenty-first century is shaping up to be such a period of accelerated socioeconomic stratification, driven by the digital, environmental, demographic, geopolitical and other transformations underway. In such circumstances, it behoves countries to take a more deliberate and systematic approach to protecting and promoting median living standards, as demonstrated by the growing political call for a "just transition" with respect to climate change. The aggregate distribution function and welfare gap notions presented in Chaps. 4 and 5 represent a way for countries to operationalize a just transition at a systemic, as opposed to merely project-by-project, level. As such, these tools should become an integral part of national strategies to intensify climate action.

Just as this reformulated approach to growth and development requires a reorganization of policy priorities and resource allocation at the national level, so it has profound implications for international economic governance and cooperation. Multilateral organizations and other important economic governance arrangements will need to substantially adjust their priorities and policy advice and increase their level of material assistance in support of this agenda of institutional deepening within countries—that is, this ongoing upgrading of national social contracts in the areas represented by the aggregate distribution function. In particular, international macroeconomic, financial, and trade and technology governance and cooperation will need to be restructured to reflect this rebalanced model of economic progress, which considers inclusion, sustainability and resilience to be endogenous to growth and development rather than a trickle-down residual.

This chapter presents such a human-centred reform agenda for international economic policy, placing the *living standards* of nations at the heart of three key dimensions of global economic governance and cooperation: international macroeconomic policy cooperation; the international financial architecture; and international trade and technology governance. The following sections outline some of the most important corresponding changes required in these three areas of international economic policy. Taken as a whole, this agenda would be transformational, enabling the major acceleration of social inclusion, climate action and other aspects of economic, societal and environmental ecosystem resilience that the world's political leadership has promised to deliver by agreeing to the SDGs, Paris climate and Kunming-Montreal biodiversity agreements and ILO Centenary Declaration and Global call to action for a human-centred recovery from the COVID-19 crisis that is inclusive, sustainable and resilient. At the same time, these deep reforms are financially feasible, insofar as they are not dependent upon big increases in bilateral aid budgets. And they are politically feasible, in that they would simply activate much more fully the existing capital and capabilities, and in many cases stated intentions and current initiatives, of the principal international economic organizations.

INTERNATIONAL MACROECONOMIC POLICY ANALYSIS AND ADVICE

The Bretton Woods institutions—the IMF and World Bank—are the most important institutional sources of macroeconomic policy analysis and advice in the world economy, particularly vis-à-vis developing countries. They are the primary custodians and agents of the prevailing growth and development model insofar as the external borrowing of developing countries is often linked to fiscal choices and policy reforms negotiated with their teams. The IMF has two additional important modes of influence in this regard: the global pronouncements of its managing director and chief economist; and its annual country consultations under Article IV of its charter.

The IMF's recent leadership has been increasingly supportive of placing greater weight on inclusion, sustainability and resilience. However, this directional signalling has yet to be fully defined in operational terms, and country advisory and lending activities remain largely in line with the standard liberal development model—the so-called Washington Consensus. Yes, the Fund has been calling for the protection of social spending, including targeted and temporary fiscal support for the most vulnerable, and it has taken important initiatives to increase the financing available to member countries through an extraordinary distribution of Special Drawing Rights (SDRs) and related establishment of a facility, the Resilience and Sustainability Trust (RST), to channel some of these from developed to developing countries. However, the translation of these messages and initiatives into country policy advice and lending remains a work in progress, more procedural and incremental than structural and impactful, including in the case of this new Trust and the G20's recent debt relief initiative, the Common Framework for Debt Treatments (Common Framework).

The UN Secretary-General challenged this incremental pace of change in letters to G20 finance ministers, central bank governors, and leaders in the autumn of 2022.[1] He called for markedly increased financial support for the poorest and most vulnerable of humanity in the face of a global cost-of-living crisis and lagging progress on the SDGs and climate change. However, such a transformation in international cooperation is unlikely to be realized absent a fundamental shift in thinking about the nature of economic development and the corresponding purpose of international economic governance and cooperation.

In the standard liberal growth and development model encapsulated by the Washington Consensus, social spending and sustainable development initiatives like the SDGs are socially desirable adjuncts of economic growth and the structural transformation of economies. They are implicitly viewed as worthy but subordinate objectives that are largely downstream from (made possible by) the success of a country's growth and transformation strategy. In IMF language, they are not "macro-critical" factors. The Fund considers an issue macro-critical if "it affects, or has the potential, to affect domestic or external stability, or global stability. Exchange rate, monetary, fiscal, and financial sector policies are macro policies and always considered important for stability. Other domestic policies can also be macro-critical when they affect stability."[2]

Thus, the IMF administers policy advice through the lens of macroeconomic stability, which is the institution's formal mandate. But macroeconomic stability can be construed narrowly (e.g., sustainable fiscal balances and low inflation in the near to medium term) or more broadly (e.g., progress in median living standards and labour force participation and productivity sufficient to sustain social and political order in addition to sound public finances and monetary conditions, given the interdependence of these considerations). The Fund has been moving in the direction of the latter, particularly in the messaging of its prior and current managing directors on such issues as jobs, social protection and climate change. However, it has made slow progress in translating these signals into specific protocols to guide the policy advice it dispenses to countries. This leaves the impression that, for the time being, the organization has a more expansive definition of macro-criticality at the global than at the country level. It recognizes the potentially critical nature of these issues conceptually but appears not yet to have a practical model to guide implementation in programmes and consultations on the ground in a systematic fashion.

The key to resolving this seeming disconnect between global messaging and country operations at the IMF as well as the World Bank is for these organizations to acknowledge, first, that GDP growth and production-based measures of development are an incomplete, top-line measure of development, whereas broad progress in living standards is the bottom-line result that societies seek. Second, given that their de facto policy influence extends well beyond macroeconomic stability in the case of the Fund and development project financing in that of the Bank, they have both an implicit mandate and critical responsibility to adapt their operational frameworks so that they properly weight institutional factors that drive the diffusion of progress in living standards. This means recognizing the *macro-development* criticality (macro-criticality in a larger economic policy sense than macroeconomic stability alone) of the institutional features of a country's social contract that support inclusion, sustainability and resilience, and hard-wiring them into their policy advice and programmatic support to developing countries.

This is the crux of the transformation required in these institutions for them to move beyond their Washington Consensus default operating mode on the ground—that is, beyond an unduly narrow conception of their role and responsibility with respect to global economic progress and stability in an era that is markedly different than the one in which their original mission and working methods were framed. Other conceptual replacements for the Washington Consensus have been proposed in recent years. Some cover a portion of this substantive terrain but remain more directional than practical. Others are far-reaching but essentially seek to compensate *ex post* for the skewed and unsustainable outcomes of markets through fiscal measures rather than re-engineer the growth model itself to improve these outcomes. Still others reject the very premise of economics as it has been practised for 250 years by prescribing low or no economic growth, but this is an unattractive, politically unrealistic option for the world's many poor countries, as discussed in Chap. 2.

To use a modern metaphor, rather than patch or work around the flaws in the operating system of liberal economics with respect to inclusion, sustainability and resilience, the proposals made in this book seek to re-engineer its source code. Liberal economics requires a systems upgrade in order to bring its performance into alignment with the original specifications set by Adam Smith, John Stuart Mill and Alfred Marshall in the eighteenth and nineteenth centuries, as discussed in Chap. 3. Those original design principles (e.g., the economy serves a larger social purpose: improving general welfare and the human condition) remain valid; however, bugs have accumulated in the operating system's software (see Chaps. 3 and 4) such that it is struggling to keep pace with changing circumstances and user requirements. As a result, the neoclassical synthesis—neoliberal operating system software—is not fully fit for purpose in this new era in which inclusion, sustainability and resilience matter as much as growth for many societies and their political leaders. Indeed, these qualities are a valuable *source* of growth at a time of diminishing returns from and prospects for macroeconomic stimulus and trade liberalization.

I have characterized this elsewhere as a "Roosevelt Consensus" model of growth and development.[3] In response to the inequality, insecurity and financial instability of the late nineteenth and early twentieth century, the two Presidents Roosevelt spearheaded an extensive process of institutional deepening in the United States that effectively rebalanced the country's growth and development model, rendering it more inclusive, sustainable and resilient. This period of institution-building and reform across corporate and financial governance, labour and anti-trust regulation, social and environmental protection, skills and infrastructure development, etc. lasted eight decades across both Democratic and Republican presidential administrations. The Square Deal, New Deal, New Frontier and Great Society programmes, among others, built out the aggregate distribution function of the US economy in a way that created a positive feedback loop with the economy's production function, a virtuous circle between increased equity (rising median living standards and an expanded middle class) and robust growth that propelled US labour productivity and living standards to remarkable heights.

This growth and development model could just as well be called the "Bismarck", "Beveridge" or "Nordic Consensus". The German Chancellor pioneered elements of it in the late nineteenth century, and during the first half of the twentieth century multiple European societies enacted institutional reforms similar to those in the United States. The liberal economics establishment, including the IMF and World Bank, which are its institutional embodiment on the world stage, need to rebalance their working methods by renewing this appreciation of the macro-development criticality of an economy's living standards diffusion mechanism—the institutional ecosystem that plays a crucial role in driving inclusion, sustainability and resilience as well as growth. This is a formula for *structurally* and thus durably correcting the overshooting of neoliberalism—its systemic underappreciation of and underinvestment in this institutional dimension of economic policy.

What would this Roosevelt Consensus and macro-development criticality approach look like in action—in the country advisory work of international economic organizations including the IMF and World Bank? Two major, interrelated changes are required: one concerns data and analysis and the other relates to the way that country consultations are organized and conducted.

First, a more structured and rigorous assessment of the relative strength of country policies and institutions in the five domains of the aggregate distribution function is needed. These data should be assembled, appropriately contextualized and then integrated into a combined macroeconomic and structural–institutional analysis of the country's policy choices and pathways vis-à-vis both macro-criticality in the traditional macroeconomic stability sense and macro-development criticality in the larger aggregate social welfare function sense described in Chap. 4. As with the wearing of glasses, employing these two lenses at the same time will improve the depth perception and peripheral vision of the policy analysis and advice provided to governments.

These wider and more connected data and analyses are required to produce a sharper stereoscopic image of a country's output and welfare gaps—and its policy options for narrowing these in a manner consistent with macroeconomic stability. Fiscal policy—the level of public investment in the aggregate distribution function's key institutional domains—is the sensible place to start.

The IMF emphasized the importance of social spending in its 2019 "Strategy for Engagement on Social Spending".[4] The organization and particularly its managing director at the time, Christine Lagarde, deserve credit for seeking to clarify the extent to which social spending can be emphasized within the boundaries of the IMF's macroeconomic stability-oriented, mandate. The Fund requires there to be a clear nexus with "the principles set forth in the Integrated Surveillance Decision, which establish that policies other than exchange rate, monetary, fiscal, and financial sector policies are also examined in the context of surveillance only to the extent that they significantly influence present or prospective balance of payments or domestic stability,"[5] which is to say, fiscal stability, price stability, or growth.

But even as it cites this restrictive interpretation of macro-criticality the strategy seems to open the door to going beyond it by referring to spending adequacy as one of the three channels by which social spending can be macro-critical and posing the question: "is social spending adequate for inclusive growth and protecting the vulnerable?" It also refers to "distributional objectives" in several places, endorses the setting of quantitative "social spending floors" and cites a survey of views of its mission chiefs in which

> social spending was [considered] macro-critical in nearly 80 percent of countries, with 70 percent reporting that policy advice was provided in this area … The reasons given for macro-criticality of social spending were

diverse, going beyond traditional fiscal sustainability considerations, and varied by countries' income level: for advanced economies, expected social spending pressures (especially from population ageing) and achieving authorities' distributional objectives; for emerging market economies, achieving the authorities' distributional objectives, risks to social or political stability posed by insufficient spending levels, and large social protection gaps; and for low-income developing countries, large coverage gaps in education and health as well as risks to social or political stability.[6]

Thus, there is a certain tension, or cognitive dissonance, in the IMF's guidance to itself on this important subject. The organization appears to be caught between a laudable desire to recognize the critical importance *for growth and development* of inclusion, sustainability and resilience (the social contract), on the one hand, and its long-standing institutional *raison d'être* as the international system's guardian of balance-of-payments stability and emergency lender in the event of crisis, on the other. In short, it is struggling within the constraints of its official mandate to remain fully fit for purpose in today's circumstances—to reconcile its long-standing official concept of macroeconomic criticality with the increasingly important and even more complex demands of macro-development criticality.

The IMF has come a long way in its thinking during the past decade and deserves credit for trying to find a way out of this organizational box. But a box it is, which brings us to the second fundamental shift required to adapt the macroeconomic dimension of international economic governance to human-centred economics and the pre-eminent importance of living standards: governance architecture. Instead of continuing to try to shoehorn a macro-development approach to criticality into the Fund's macroeconomic stability mandate, the time has come to solve this problem through organizational innovation.

In strategic reorganizations, form is supposed to follow function. The world needs the IMF to fulfil its unique and vital function as the leading provider of policy advice and lending with respect to fiscal and monetary stability, as well as the ultimate guardian of the international monetary system and global financial stability. It was never intended to be a development institution; other multilateral organizations, both general and specialized, were created for this purpose. Despite its good intentions, the Fund's efforts to justify social spending on macroeconomic stability grounds and its recent foray into development lending through the establishment of the RST are unsatisfactory halfway measures, for the reason that they do not play to the Fund's core competencies or mandate, forcing it to engage in certain intellectual and operational contortions. These initiatives have arisen essentially because of inadequacies in the development cooperation architecture, including a certain narrowness of the country policy analysis and advice of multilateral development banks (MDBs) and a lack of coherence between these and the analysis and advice of the Fund.

MDBs underinvest in analysis and lending with respect to many of the key institutional drivers of broad progress in household living standards, such as labour ministry capacity to enforce worker rights, support training and facilitate workforce transitions; social protection system benefit coverage and adequacy (versus narrower safety net programmes); competition and anti-corruption rules and enforcement capacity; corporate and financial system regulation; subsidization to ensure the affordability of material necessities, etc. Such economic institution-building tends to take a back seat in these organizations to basic health, education and infrastructure systems and trade and industrial policy, particularly as it relates to export production. This may have a certain logic in very poor countries where it is of paramount importance to increase productive output. But most of the world's poor people live in middle-income countries where marginalization and exclusion are the primary problem, rather than basic human needs and overall national income. In these countries, strengthening the institutional ecosystem underpinning the economy's aggregate distribution function is a paramount development imperative.

In principle it is the MDBs and, in the case of labour markets and social protection, the ILO that should be assembling the data and analysis in these domains and participating with the IMF in a *collective* analysis of a country's welfare gap and the policy options available to overcome it. These institutions as well as the OECD, which has unparalleled data and analysis of its member countries in many of the aggregate distribution function's structural policy domains, are best positioned to identify the policy and spending targets that are macro-development critical. As development institutions, this is *their* function, not the IMF's.

Their analysis and advice need to be better connected with the IMF's macroeconomic stability analysis and advice. Human-centred economics views national economic performance stereoscopically, through the twin prisms of the aggregate production and distribution functions. These cover distinct policy terrains and require different competencies, but the analysis of them needs to be joined up rather than conducted in silos. Countries don't consider macroeconomic and development policy in isolation from each other. They have a right to expect the responsible multilateral agencies to improve the substantive coherence and reduce the operational transaction costs (the number of meetings) of their analysis and advice in these respects. Moreover, an understanding of the interdependencies and synergies between the two functions—between opportunities to reduce country output and welfare gaps—is absolutely crucial; indeed, it is where these external advisers with their global experience can add particular value.

Thus, a *structural* interface is required between the IMF and multilateral development institutions in their policy advisory functions, in contrast to current ad hoc arrangements. While the data-gathering and technical assistance of the IMF, World Bank, ILO and OECD (for its more limited number of member countries) should remain specialized and distinct, their data and analysis need to be connected and placed into an integrated picture of macroeconomic *and* development criticality, with a corresponding set of policy recommendations for realizing both the growth *and* living standards potential of the country in question.

From an organizational behaviour standpoint, this is a tall order. Established bureaucracies don't easily cooperate like this. They usually require a forcing mechanism of some sort. Outright integration, a merger of the policy surveillance and consultation functions of the organizations, is the most drastic option. But that would go too far; the world needs these institutions to maintain, indeed strengthen, their specialized competencies and analytical tools. More appropriate would be a joint country surveillance and consultation service—joint task forces that would prepare integrated analysis and policy recommendations for the benefit of these organizations' mutual client countries. This should be a standing function, a Joint Office of Multilateral Country Analysis and Consultation, for example, which would coordinate the cross-organizational task forces that would conduct the country-specific analyses and consultations. Their work would coincide in timing with the IMF's Article IV preparations and in-country consultations in order to ensure substantive coherence and minimize country transaction costs.

The Joint Office should also be assigned one global responsibility. It should prepare a joint report of the four organizations plus the World Trade Organization (WTO) and United Nations Conference on Trade and Development (UNCTAD) every other year on the progress of global development and their combined contribution thereto. This Global Economic Progress Report by the principal multilateral economic organizations should be jointly signed by their heads and delivered to G20 leaders and the UN secretary-general as well as made public. It, too, would serve as a useful forcing mechanism for policy coherence and operational synergy.

Let us return to the question of how to build out the data required for a more granular and actionable picture of the strength of economies' aggregate distribution functions. First, with respect to social spending, a set of recommended reference ranges should be estimated for relevant dimensions of such spending for different typologies of countries (e.g., low-income; lower-middle-income; upper-middle-income and high-income). At a minimum, these ranges should be constructed for: health and non-health social protection systems; labour market institutions and programmes; infrastructure in areas corresponding to material necessities; and education. They should be accompanied by reference ranges for fiscal revenues, including with respect to total revenues and the shares generated from taxation of labour, capital, consumption, imports, etc. These fiscal spending and resource mobilization reference ranges should be broad enough (overlapping the categories of countries) to account for the significant diversity of country contexts and choices but narrow enough to provide a meaningful sense of what constitutes good policy practice and minimum thresholds (social spending floors). They could be expressed as a share of GDP or the national budget or both (or indeed by other metrics).

Considerable work would need to go into the development and refinement of these indicative fiscal reference ranges by the Joint Office. In some cases, existing country data may be insufficient to derive a confident picture of good or minimum acceptable practice, particularly for low-income countries. At the other end of the spectrum, the analysis is likely to be more granular and disaggregated for high-income countries, covering many more aspects of spending in light of the OECD's vast collection of relevant data, as highlighted in Chap. 5. Indeed, one of the priorities of this effort should be to improve the availability of such data in developing countries, supported by increased development cooperation funding for their national statistical agencies.

Table 6.1 presents an indicative set of fiscal expenditure and revenue reference ranges derived from existing, publicly available data for four income groups of countries: high income; upper-middle income; lower-middle income; and low income. The table is intended to be more illustrative and suggestive than definitive and prescriptive, particularly in view of the limited availability of data in developing countries for certain

Table 6.1 Fiscal expenditure and revenue reference ranges

Expenditure indicator	Income group	Lowest performance	"Good practice" Median	80th percentile	"Leading practice" Highest performance
Total social benefits (% GDP)[a]	High–income	3.07	12.97	21.12	25.40
	Upper–middle	1.77	8.40	12.16	17.35
	Lower–middle	0.40	1.15	4.14	14.81
	Low–income	0.04	0.14	1.29	2.05
Domestic general government health expenditure (% GDP)[b]	High–income	1.9	5.75	7.82	9.3
	Upper–middle	0.6	3.7	4.58	15.2
	Lower–middle	0.2	2.0	3.58	9.3
	Low–income	0.5	1.05	1.86	2.7
Total expenditure on social protection, excluding health (% GDP)[c]	High–income	0.9	12.75	18.92	24.4
	Upper–middle	0.7	6	9.32	16.1
	Lower–middle	0.1	2	6.7	16.2
	Low–income	0	0.7	1.8	2.8
Secondary education (% GDP)[d]	High–income	0	1.60	2.01	2.38
	Upper–middle	0.33	1.45	1.87	2.47
	Lower–middle	0	3.68	3.68	3.76
	Low–income	n.a.	n.a.	n.a.	n.a.
Spending on social protection for unemployment (% GDP)[d]	High–income	0	0.54	1.17	2.04
	Upper–middle	0	0.03	0.19	0.45
	Lower–middle	0	0.01	0.08	0.31
	Low–income	n.a.	n.a.	n.a.	n.a.
Public spending on active labour market policies in OECD countries (% GDP)	OECD countries	0.10	0.36	0.72	1.89
Investment on infrastructure, both private and public (% GDP)[e]	High–income	0.85	2.39	2.75	3.58
	Upper–middle	1.46	2.99	4.69	6.37
	Lower–middle	3.37	5.1	7.11	10.55
	Low–income	4.5	n.a.	n.a.	15.96
Spending on R&D both private and public (% GDP)[f]	High–income	0.08	1.47	2.88	4.8
	Upper–middle	0.03	0.36	0.94	2.14
	Lower–middle	0.06	0.2	0.47	0.72
	Low–income	n.a.	n.a.	n.a.	n.a.

(*continued*)

Table 6.1 (continued)

Revenue indicator	Income group	Lowest value	Median	80th percentile	Highest value
Total tax revenues (% GDP)[f]	High–income	1.1	22.04	28.83	44.13
	Upper–middle	1.81	19.22	23.35	29.15
	Lower–middle	5.29	16.5	22.5	40.67
	Low–income	1.93	11.04	13	19.76
Taxes on income, profits and capital gains, levied on corporates[f]	High–income	0.05	2.85	4.60	8.35
	Upper–middle	0.78	2.91	4.00	5.98
	Lower–middle	1.13	3.19	4.28	21.02
	Low–income	1.31	1.71	2.32	6.36
Taxes on capital (% NDP)[g]	High–income	0	0.08	0.11	0.18
	Upper–middle	0.03	0.06	0.09	0.12
	Developing countries	0	0.04	0.06	0.11
Taxes on labour (% NDP)[g]	High–income	0	0.22	0.29	0.41
	Upper–middle	0.01	0.07	0.15	0.21
	Developing countries	0.01	0.03	0.06	0.24

[a]Source: IMF, Government Finance Statistics
[b]Source: GGHE-D, WHO
[c]Source: ILO
[d]Source: IMF, COFOG
[e]Source: Global Infrastructure Hub
[f]Source: IMF
[g]Source: Globalization and Factor Income Taxation Dataset, Bachas et al.

indicators; however, reference ranges such as these would provide the basis for clearer and more coherent policy guidance and accountability on the part of the multilateral economic organizations and the governments they serve. The table characterizes "good practice" as the level of spending between the 50th and 80th percentiles of the distribution of existing country practice, and "leading practice" from the 80th percentile threshold and above. By enabling countries to benchmark themselves against their peers, such an approach would give them a specific yet objective sense of the realm of the possible, that is, the extent of available policy space for countries at their level of GDP per capita.

Table 6.2 presents similar reference ranges for a number of other salient aspects of the aggregate distribution function's underlying policy and

Table 6.2 Decent work indicator reference ranges

Indicator	Income group	"Good practice" Lowest performance	Median	"Leading practice" 80th percentile	Highest performance
Informal employment rate	High-income	53.5	15.1	6.1	3.5
	Upper-middle	80.1	51.8	31.9	5.7
	Lower-middle	91.7	80.6	61	44.1
	Low-income[a]	96.9	94.8	83.8	79.5
Youth NEET 15–24 years	High-income	27.9	12.6	8.6	5.8
	Upper-middle	46.4	24.4	17.6	9.2
	Lower-middle	52	27.4	17.5	10.2
	Low-income[a]	41	31.3	26.3	24.3
Child labour rate 5–11 years	High-income	n.a.	n.a.	n.a.	n.a.
	Upper-middle	44.2	5.9	3.1	1.1
	Lower-middle	35	9.9	4.4	0.1
	Low-income	39.2	23.7	15.6	13.4
Employees with low pay rate	High-income	23.4	17.0	8.0	2.7
	Upper-middle	28.7	20.3	17.1	0.3
	Lower-middle	33.7	33.7	33.7	33.7
	Low-income	n.a.	n.a.	n.a.	n.a.
Gender wage gap	High-income	30.0	12.4	9.2	2.2
	Upper-middle	24.6	-0.1	-7.2	-35.8
	Lower-middle	26.9	8.2	3.0	-24.9
	Low-income[b]	43.8	28.6	5.3	-5.5
Employment in excessive working time (more than 48 hours/week)	High-income	46.5	10.2	7.4	2.1
	Upper-middle	39.4	19.6	12.8	1.1
	Lower-middle	55.8	32.4	17.5	4.3
	Low-income[a]	46.4	22.9	18.9	18.9
Occupational injury frequency rate, fatal[b]	High-income	4.9	1.7	1.2	0.7
	Upper-middle	5.9	3.7	2.9	0
	Lower-middle	10.0	5.0	3.2	1.0
	Low-income	n.a.	n.a.	n.a.	n.a.
Labour inspection (inspectors per 10,000 employed persons)	High-income	0.1	0.9	1.2	3.2
	Upper-middle	0.2	0.3	0.9	1.4
	Lower-middle	0	0.5	0.9	31.6
	Low-income	n.a.	n.a.	n.a.	n.a.
Collective bargaining rate	High-income	7.4	27.3	90.0	99
	Upper-middle	2.4	24	37.0	57.7
	Lower-middle	1.6	16.8	41.1	62.9
	Low-income	1.0	14.8	30.2	30.2

(*continued*)

Table 6.2 (continued)

Indicator	Income group	Lowest performance	Median	"Good practice" 80th percentile	"Leading practice" Highest performance
Trade union density	High-income	6.0	23.4	49.1	91.4
	Upper-middle	3.2	12.7	20.5	29.4
	Lower-middle	4.8	14.4	30.8	38.1
	Low-income	5.9	11.8	20.3	23.8
Income inequality (90:10 ratio)	High-income	105	20.0	10.8	4.8
	Upper-middle	349	32.7	18.2	4.3
	Lower-middle	1370	90.6	24.9	5.7
	Low-income	4977	269	91.9	52.7
Labour share of gross value added	High-income	25.7	55.8	58.9	68.8
	Upper-middle	10.2	46.8	51.9	61.4
	Lower-middle	29.6	42.3	47.7	69.4
	Low-income	21.2	40.9	42.2	58.3

Source: ILOSTAT 2019 data unless otherwise indicated. See ILOSTAT for additional information
[a] Data for 2018
[b] Data for 2017

institutional ecosystem, particularly those relating to the ILO's Decent Work Agenda. The data are drawn from the ILO's statistical database and cover a range of output or performance indicators. Some of these correspond to areas of social expenditure included in Table 6.1 and can inform a judgement as to whether such spending is adequate. For example, when spending is near the top of the performance range of a peer group of countries but performance on the corresponding decent work indicators lags, then the *efficiency* of administrative or fiscal effort may be the primary problem. Conversely, when both indicators lag on a given issue, *greater investment*—i.e., increased fiscal effort—is presumptively warranted and should be supported and at a minimum protected during a crisis by the IMF, the World Bank and other international organizations and bilateral donors.

In sum, multilaterally promulgated reference ranges like these for peer groups of countries could improve governments' priority-setting and resource allocation with respect to the promotion of broad living standards. They could also improve the accountability of national governments to their citizens and of international organizations to their member governments. Benchmarking can be a powerful tool if it is applied constructively and with due regard for differing country circumstances, and if it is combined with strategic engagement and relevant financial and technical support from international institutions. These tables demonstrate the huge range of country performance and investment that exists among countries at a similar level of economic development on nearly every fiscal and decent work indicator. The difference between the median and 80th-percentile performance is typically on the order of 50% to 300%, and the median is often three to six times higher than the lowest value. In other words, most countries have large amounts of unutilized policy space to strengthen their social contracts, even allowing for inevitable differences in national social, historical and political circumstances. Objective, comparable data such as these can help countries to move more forthrightly to instrumentalize the golden rule of human-centred economics— the rebalancing of emphasis on growth and median living standards, and the more serious search for synergies between the two called for in these pages.

Basic agreement by the IMF, World Bank, ILO and OECD on empirical reference ranges like these for the key institutional domains of the aggregate distribution function would enable the operationalization of the reformed notion of macro-criticality presented above. This in turn could transform not only the macroeconomic policy advice but also the lending and debt relief conditionality for developing countries, helping to ensure that national policymakers and international financial institutions (IFIs) do not throw the baby out with the bathwater when devising debt-restructuring and emergency lending packages and related policy reforms during balance-of-payments crises.

INTERNATIONAL FINANCIAL ARCHITECTURE: DEVELOPMENT AND CLIMATE FINANCE[7]

Over the past several years, the international community has adopted a consensus of goals for rendering global development more inclusive, sustainable and resilient. In 2015, the governments of the world agreed to the 2030 Agenda, including the 17 SDGs, as well as the Paris climate agreement. In 2019, governments and business and labour organizations of the ILO's 187 member states agreed to its Centenary Declaration for the Future of Work, followed in 2021 by a roadmap for the Centenary

Declaration's accelerated implementation in a Global call to action. In 2020, WHO and other stakeholders created the Access to COVID-19 Tools Accelerator (ACT-A) initiative, followed in 2022 by the G20's creation of the Pandemic Prevention Financial Intermediary Fund to help countries strengthen their resilience to health crises. And, in 2022, a Global Biodiversity Framework was agreed in Montreal setting a number of long-term targets in this area of environmental protection, as outlined in Chap. 5.

Together, these international instruments outline a far-reaching vision for the reform of the world economy to meet the pressing demands expressed by societies everywhere: greater economic well-being and equality as well as health and environmental security. But this agenda remains essentially a statement of shared aspiration. Implementation is lagging badly across the board, frustrating citizens and undermining the credibility of both national leaders and multilateral institutions—that is to say, those who made these very public promises and the system that produced them.

The primary obstacle to implementation is a lack of financial resources, especially in developing countries where most of humanity resides. If one takes this agenda at face value—as a genuine expression of humanity's will articulated by its duly designated leaders—then it is hard to escape the conclusion that the world economy is suffering from a systemic misallocation of private capital and underinvestment of public capital. The top priority for international governance and cooperation in the decade to come, beyond addressing wars and other military threats to peace and security, must be to raise and redirect the finance necessary to satisfy these priorities.

To be certain, donor governments are unlikely to provide a large and sustained increase in bilateral foreign assistance after having run extremely high fiscal deficits to support their domestic economies during the pandemic. In any event, the trillions required for this agenda, in particular the investments required to implement the SDGs and the nationally determined contributions (NDCs) under the Paris climate agreement, far exceed the current level of global official development assistance of about US$170 billion per year.[8]

However, these are extraordinary times. When the pandemic struck, many governments suspended existing rules and assumptions and used monetary and fiscal policy in creative ways to leverage the balance sheets of their central banks and treasuries to meet pressing domestic needs.[9]

They re-evaluated the limits and cost–benefit trade-offs of public borrowing and found a way to mobilize unprecedented levels of financial resources.

How might the same necessity-is-the-mother-of-invention combination of imagination and determination be applied to the international finance institutions in order to drive the implementation of these multilateral commitments at speed and scale? This is the most consequential question facing the international financial architecture in general and development cooperation in particular.

Three types of additional financing are required. Each is feasible using the existing capital and capabilities of IFIs in a more catalytic and networked manner. They are:

- One-off or relatively time-limited acute needs in developing countries which can be financed only through public grants or highly concessional loans (for example, sovereign debt restructuring; COVID-19 vaccines, tests and treatment; catalytic investments to establish or extend social protection systems; and accelerated replacement and avoidance of coal-fired power generation plants).
- Large, multi-year requirements that generate cash flows and can therefore be financed through a blend of public and private investment; they are so big that they can only be adequately financed by engaging private investment (for example, investment in SDG-related sustainable infrastructure and industry).
- Smaller, multi-year technical assistance and institutional capacity-building requirements typically financed with grants and concessional assistance (for example, the design and administration of labour, social protection, anti-corruption, tax, environmental, competition and financial system policies and frameworks).

The IMF and MDBs have unexploited potential to mobilize a step change in the resources available to developing countries in each of these three respects. Leaders face growing pressure to respond decisively to the large and urgent financing needs of developing countries with respect to the SDGs, digital and climate transitions, and pandemic recovery and the related cost-of-living crisis. The most feasible way they could do so would be to harness the existing international financial architecture more effectively, leveraging the public capital their countries have already invested in the IMF and MDBs more efficiently and expansively in three corresponding respects: (1) better deploying IMF's unique capacity to issue and channel SDRs; (2) improving the utilization of capital and updating the business model of MDBs to catalyse public–private financing of sustainable infrastructure and industry at much higher volumes; and (3) strengthening bilateral and multilateral support of the institutional deepening of their client countries' aggregate distribution functions.

If government representatives of developed and developing country governments on the boards of these institutions were to rally around the three corresponding sets of initiatives outlined below, the combined effect would be to generate between 2024 and 2030 in excess of US$2 trillion of additional resources for these critical financing needs in poor countries. This sum is nearly twice the projected level of global official development assistance over this period. It would represent an average increase in external flows each year for the next seven years of about 4% of GDP for the 82 economies classified by the World Bank as low income or lower-middle income, or more than 3% of annual GDP for an expanded group of 110 economies having a GDP per capita below US$7500. This US$2 trillion estimate does not include the substantial additional domestic resources that developing countries would have an incentive to mobilize in response, which could yield a further US$1 trillion or more.

Such a large increase in international financing for development represents the difference between continued incremental and truly transformational progress on the poverty and inequality challenges as well as environmental and health risks that humanity faces. It matches the additional external financing requirements for emerging and developing economies other than China that were estimated in four related areas by an international team under the guidance of Lord Nicholas Stern. This work was based on the global estimates he prepared for the G7 under the UK presidency during 2021.[10] Specifically, the London School of Economics/Brookings Institution team determined that an increase in annual investment of between 5% and 6% of GDP would ultimately be needed in these countries to address key SDG objectives, with half coming from external (international) public and private financing.[11] This is the same amount—an additional 3% of GDP per year from 2023 until the end of the decade—that would be generated by the three reforms outlined below of the existing international financial architecture.

IMF Special Drawing Rights

IMF SDRs are the closest thing the world economy has to the quantitative easing measures many governments applied domestically during the 2008–09 financial and 2020–21 COVID-19 crises (and Japan has applied for decades). They are an international form of liquidity injection by fiat, in this case by a decision of the IMF's board.

For only the fourth time in its history, in August 2021, the organization's Executive Directors approved a general allocation of SDRs, equivalent to US$650 billion, as well as plans for the voluntary channelling of some of them from developed countries to developing countries.[12] This extraordinary issuance of SDRs would never have happened had it not been for the dire financial position in which the pandemic had placed many poor countries; however, they received less than a third of the allocation, according to the IMF's quota system. While these funds have been very useful to these countries, their financing requirements are larger still, with rising inflation and interest rates increasing their external debt service obligations and shifting their terms of trade unfavourably as food and fuel import bills mount.

Developed countries and China have little need for their US$441 billion majority share of these new SDRs.[13] And while several have pledged a total of more than US$80 billion of them to the Fund's new mechanism for rechannelling such resources from rich to poor countries, the RST, this facility took a year to launch, and uptake of its assistance remains slow. The prospects for developing country participation is uncertain given the policy conditions and market stigma attached to borrowing from the IMF.

It is increasingly apparent that this well-intended and much-anticipated initiative is not configured to make more than a modest contribution to the large financing needs of these countries, even though it was these requirements that motivated the issuance in the first place. This is principally because of the reserve asset character of SDRs framed by the Fund's Articles of Agreement, which reflects the organization's original purpose as a provider of temporary emergency liquidity to countries facing a balance-of-payments crisis. The onlending or swapping of foreign exchange reserves between countries is a common device to insure against a liquidity crisis—a cascading contraction of credit driven by a loss of confidence in a country's currency or public finances. Once a country devalues and/or restores market confidence by restructuring its public finances, its current account typically returns to surplus, allowing it to reaccumulate foreign exchange reserves and reverse the swap.

By contrast, the stated purpose of the RST is to finance fiscal expenditures—essentially development projects—in the areas of pandemic prevention, climate mitigation and adaptation, and other unspecified "resilience and sustainability" expenditure priorities of countries. Unlike foreign exchange swap lines, these have no self-equilibrating or self-financing mechanism. They are outright exercises in support of fiscal, not monetary, policy. And yet the guidance of the IMF and the expectation and often the domestic legal requirements of lending countries is that they maintain an on-demand, in-full claim on the SDRs they transfer to other countries as if they were engaging in a monetary swap rather than a long-term concessional development loan. This is the practical significance of the "reserve asset character" of SDRs upon which the Fund and donor countries are insisting.

This internal contradiction is preventing the initiative from fully achieving its stated purpose. In addition, the IMF is neither mandated nor staffed to make development project loans—this being the role of the MDBs—and developing countries tend to be wary of subjecting themselves to Fund macroeconomic (e.g., budget policy) conditionality. As a result, the RST has not been set up for success and therefore is bound to disappoint.

When advanced economy governments opened the financial spigots at home during the Great Financial Crisis and COVID-19 pandemic, many of them dispensed with any such self-limiting or self-liquidating constraint. Some have maintained their quantitative easing—extraordinary liquidity provision—for years and have done so while massively expanding their fiscal deficit, effectively monetizing the latter with the former. If the international community is serious about tackling climate change at the scale and pace agreed in the Paris climate agreement, as well as preventing and responding adequately to pandemics, then it will need to do something analogous with the international financial architecture. It must find a way to inject liquidity into the world economy for these extraordinary, emergency purposes in a similarly straightforward and scaled—not contorted and incremental—manner. This can be achieved either by relaxing the "reserve asset character" constraint of SDR rechannelling in this particular instance (for example, through a special, time-limited amendment to this aspect of the Articles of Agreement) or by working creatively around it, for example by steering rechannelled SDR allocations to MDBs in the form of hybrid capital contributions that they then use to increase their financing to developing countries for the RST's intended purposes.[14]

The requirement that SDRs retain their reserve asset character is fundamentally a political, not technical, constraint. Governments on the IMF's board could simply decide to issue a different kind of extraordinary liquidity governed by different rules than in the past. And in this case they would be entirely justified in doing so. Climate action and pandemic prevention and response are not just global public goods; they are global public imperatives. Delayed or otherwise insufficient action on them anywhere ultimately threatens the security of people everywhere, regardless of geographic location, social status or personal wealth. The sheer scale and time sensitivity of the climate action required to keep global warming within the Paris climate agreement's well-below-2 °C outer limit, and the political necessity for this economic transformation to be accompanied by an orderly and just transition in the world of work, provide sufficient justification for such a temporary departure from the Fund's rules in order to place the international financial architecture in a position to better serve humanity in its hour of need. Indeed, given the absence of viable financing alternatives for the rapid acceleration of emissions reductions urgently recommended by the scientific community, it would be imprudent of governments *not* to do so. There is little to no chance of this order of magnitude of additional liquidity having any material effect on inflation in a world economy whose estimated broad money supply and outstanding stock of debt exceed US$80 trillion and US$300 trillion, respectively.

The prospect of catastrophic climate change later this century in the absence of decisive action during the next decade is too important a matter to be left to technocrats struggling to fit a square peg into a round hole. Freeing the international system from the binding constraints of a financial architecture designed three-quarters of a century ago in a very different economic and political context is the essential challenge facing international monetary and development cooperation today. How the boards of these institutions and their political masters in capitals answer this challenge will determine whether the international community fulfils the promises made to humanity with respect to inclusion, sustainability and resilience in the 2030 Agenda, Paris climate agreement, ILO Centenary Declaration and recent WHO pandemic initiatives.

To be specific, a framework that enabled the outright donation by developed countries and China of 60% of their share of the recent SDR issuance, or a similarly sized new issuance, would generate about US$265 billion in supplemental funding for low- and lower-middle-income countries. This large amount would make a transformational difference in the ambition and pace of debt restructuring that many of them will require as a result of the triple whammy of pandemic, inflation and interest rate increases. It would also make possible a scaling of multilateral financing for four critical dimensions of climate and pandemic action if coupled with certain structural changes in the RST. The three climate action elements are areas in which early, massive financing—well above business as usual in development cooperation and climate finance—is essential if humanity is to retain a realistic prospect of not breaching the agreed 1.5 °C and well-below-2 °C limits (as opposed to continuing on the world's current 2.7 °C trajectory). They are areas in which a strategic, top-down intervention is particularly required to compensate for the inadequate pace of the prevailing bottom-up architecture of Paris climate agreement NDCs and related development and climate finance cooperation.

To this end, two classes of SDRs should be established, whether through a modification of the terms of the August 2021 issuance or through a new, similarly sized, issuance. One class, perhaps called "Series A", would function according to existing rules, essentially financing the purposes for which SDRs were originally intended: domestic uses, repayments of debt owed to the IMF, or supplemental hard currency reserves held for a rainy day. This is essentially the bilateral tranche in the sense that its use is determined and executed by the governments of individual recipient countries. Low-income and most middle-income countries would receive 100% of their standard quota-based allocation in the form of these Series A SDRs.

By contrast, high-income countries and China would receive 60% of their quota-based allocation in the form of a second class of SDRs. These "Series B" SDRs would be available to them exclusively for deposit (rechannelling) into a restructured RST or the Poverty Reduction and Growth Trust (PRGT), up to a sublimit of one-sixth of their allocation in the case of contributions to the PRGT to support developing country debt relief. Series B SDRs can be thought of as the multilateral tranche of SDRs in the sense that their use would be mediated exclusively through multilaterally administered funding windows, particularly the four RST ones detailed below dedicated to the global public good imperatives of accelerated climate action and pandemic resilience. Moreover, they would differ from Series A SDRs (and all previous issuances of SDRs) in that they would be exempted from the IMF's reserve asset accounting and interest accrual treatment and activated only upon a request by the country in question to deposit them in the RST or PRGT. If an individual high-income country or China decided not to activate its Series B allocation and deposit it in these facilities, then this part of its SDR allocation would be credited to an IMF suspense account (not the country's own account) for the duration of the RST's existence, or until the country did decide to activate it and deposit it in the RST or PRGT.

In addition, the RST's terms of reference would be revised. Rather than making loans itself to countries, the RST would be restructured into these four wholesale funding windows, each of which would enter into operating agreements with accredited facilities (principally MDBs) that would do the actual lending on the basis of the highly concessional terms prescribed by the IMF's board (e.g., 20-year maturity and a 10½-year grace period, with borrowers paying an interest rate with a modest margin over the three-month SDR rate).[15] The four windows would target four acute, non-recurring financing gaps faced by developing countries which threaten the security of every citizen on the planet by preventing humanity from asserting control over global climate change and pandemics, and would do so in part by addressing the highly unequal and potentially destabilizing secondary economic and social effects of these challenges.

Specifically, the RST windows would be dedicated to financing: (a) accelerated retirement and replacement of coal-fired power plants and abatement of industrial methane emissions within the time frame advised by the UNFCCC (Global Energy Transition Mechanism); (b) creation and expansion of social protection floors, which are the most effective and comprehensive way that societies insure their people against deprivation and dislocation and are thus crucial for a just climate transition (Global Accelerator on Jobs and Social Protection for Just Transitions); (c) acceleration of basic research into renewable energy and low-carbon land use technologies on a collaborative, open-access basis (Green Revolution 2.0); and (d) two WHO-coordinated pandemic response and prevention initiatives (ACT-A/COVAX and Pandemic Prevention Financial Intermediary Facility). Series B SDR-based loans by accredited facilities would not be subject to IMF macroeconomic policy conditionality; they would be subject only to the project-based terms and conditions of the administering MDBs. To the extent practicable, accredited facilities would be encouraged to standardize such terms and conditions, coordinate their technical advisory and project development activities and collaborate in diversifying the risk of their loan portfolios relating to the four RST windows.

RST Window 1: Coal Power Plant Retirement and Replacement and Industrial Methane Abatement (Global Energy Transition Mechanism) As important as comprehensive action is on all of the key drivers of greenhouse gas emissions, nothing is more vital in the race to stabilize atmospheric concentrations of these gases by the mid-twenty-first century than halting the burning of coal and preventing the installation of new coal-fired power generation capacity. Even if no new coal plants were built, the existing global fleet would consume most of the world's remaining carbon budget of roughly 440 gigatons of carbon dioxide under a moderate-probability scenario of 1.5 °C in global warming, including a third of the budget in just the next ten years.[16] For this reason, unabated coal-fired power generation must decline rapidly—much faster than use of oil and natural gas—if the world is to have a realistic chance of achieving either of the Paris climate agreement's 1.5 °C or well-below-2 °C goals: an 80% reduction by 2030 to achieve the 1.5 °C goal or the same reduction by 2038 to remain under the 2 °C limit, as well as virtual elimination (a 97% decline) within the following 10 years in both cases (Fig. 6.1).[17]

Although plans for many new plants have been cancelled in recent years, some 1000 coal boilers are still under construction or are being planned and permitted around the world, equating to around a quarter of

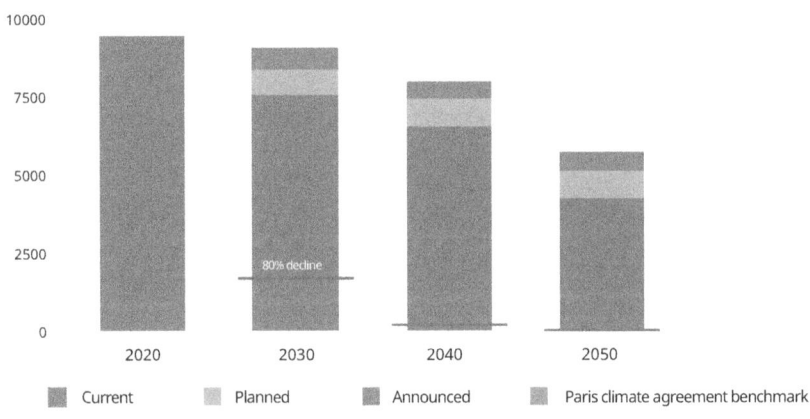

Source: Climate Analytics, "Global and regional coal phase-out requirements of the Paris Agreement: Insights from the IPCC Special Report on 1.5°C", September 2019.

Fig. 6.1 Paris 1.5°C goal requires 80% drop in coal-fired power by 2030

existing capacity.[18] Coal is thus a central factor driving the current trajectory of nearly 3 °C in global warming,[19] which the bottom-up NDC process of the Paris climate agreement has yet to substantially alter on the ground. A strategic, top-down initiative is required to intervene directly in power markets around the world with the financial inducements necessary to replace and avoid coal at the pace required over the next decade to avoid a lock-in of atmospheric greenhouse gases at concentrations incompatible with the mid-century targets set out in the Paris climate agreement.

Over the next several years, developed and upper-middle-income countries would donate US$80 billion of their Series B SDRs into this RST window, which would have a mandate to enter into operating agreements with MDBs that would structure arrangements, similar to the Asian Development Bank's Energy Transition Mechanism (ETM),[20] to: (a) buy out existing coal-fired power plants in low- and middle-income countries for the purpose of accelerating their retirement from service within a maximum of 15 years and work with their owners to redeploy the proceeds into new clean power construction projects; (b) offer financial inducements to sponsors of planned coal-fired plants which are sufficient to convince them to switch to the construction of clean power alternatives; and (c) finance a just transition for affected workers and their communities.

This RST financing would enable the international financial architecture to scale the Asian Development Bank's ETM approach around the globe. They could syndicate tranches of mature projects among themselves and other investors to diversify risk and multiply the impact of the SDRs they receive from this window. MDBs could leverage this US$80 billion in SDR donations three to four times over using additional donor and private sector funding in order to generate the estimated US$300 billion to US$350 billion needed to replace and avoid the majority of coal power generation in low- and middle-income countries by 2035.[21] Such an initiative would likely also have the effect of raising the ambition level of wealthier coal-burning countries that have the resources—but not yet the political will—to phase out coal-fired generation within this timeframe, such as China (which accounts for half of all such capacity), the United States, European nations and the Russian Federation. Indeed, these countries could be encouraged to make use of their SDRs for this purpose. Between the share of resources allocated for this purpose from the first SDR issuance, the matching funds borrowed on the market, and a comparable, or perhaps even larger, share of resources allocated from a possible second SDR issuance in 2027 or 2028—as well as the incentive effects that this bold effort would have on other countries—the world would have a viable strategy for confronting what is arguably the single biggest obstacle to the fulfilment of the Paris climate agreement.

RST Window 2: Social Protection Floors (Global Accelerator on Jobs and Social Protection for Just Transitions)
Less than half of the global population is eligible for basic social protection, a baseline level of support for the poorest and most vulnerable members of society. Most countries that lack full social protection floors, as defined by the ILO Social Protection Floors Recommendation, 2012 (No. 202),[22] have the potential to provide such services through better public financial management and realistic increases in tax revenues over time.[23]

However, in low-income countries, the required amount of domestic resources amounts to an estimated 15.9% of GDP, the equivalent of 45% of current tax revenues. Any aspiration to narrow substantially the social protection floor financing gap in such countries—estimated to be US$77.9 billion per year[24]—through domestic resource mobilization alone is not realistic. The IMF estimates that they have the capacity to finance up to a third of their combined US$500 billion in SDG implementation needs, including in the area of social protection, through an increase of 5% of GDP in tax revenues (up from very low levels) over a decade.[25] A catalytic matching international financial contribution for social protection would cost in the neighbourhood of an average of US$15 billion per year over the next seven years, an amount that could be covered in large part by wealthier countries in the form of SDR donations as part of a global effort to facilitate a just transition to climate change, including the replacement of coal power plants and reduction of energy poverty, while accelerating progress towards SDG 1 regarding the elimination of extreme poverty (Table 6.3).

In fact, most low-income and lower-middle-income countries have relatively young populations, meaning that they have the potential, from an actuarial perspective, to establish or expand basic social protection through the right combination of contributory and general financing arrangements supported by a catalytic round of financing from international cooperation. The UN Secretary-General has launched an initiative, the Global Accelerator on Jobs and Social Protection for Just Transitions, with this purpose.[26] A collaborative effort of relevant UN agencies and MDBs, it plans in its initial four years to support 30 developing countries in the

Table 6.3 Financing gap for achieving universal social protection coverage in 2020 in billions US$ and as a percentage of GDP (low- and middle-income countries only)

	Gap in billion US$ 4 SP areas[a]	Gap as % of GDP 4 SP areas	Gap in billion US$ health care	Gap as % of GDP health care	Total gap in billion US$	Total gap as % of GDP
Subregional groups						
Arab States	15.1	4.5	10.2	3.0	25.2	7.5
Central and Western Asia	86.6	7.9	15.2	1.4	101.8	9.3
East Asia	58.1	0.4	132.9	0.9	190.9	1.3
Eastern Europe	32.8	1.6	21.8	1.1	54.6	2.7
Latin America and the Caribbean	272.1	6.1	61.1	1.4	333.2	7.5
North Africa	31.5	4.7	24.1	3.6	55.6	8.3
Northern, Southern and western Europe	5.0	5.7	1.9	2.1	6.9	7.8
Oceania	1.5	4.5	0.9	2.7	2.4	7.2
South-east Asia	48.2	1.8	46.3	1.7	94.5	3.5
South Asia	94.8	2.3	94.8	2.3	189.6	4.6
Sub-Saharan Africa	61.8	3.7	75.1	4.5	136.9	8.2
Income groups						
Low-income countries	36.2	7.4	41.8	8.5	77.9	15.9
Lower-middle-income countries	173.8	2.4	189.1	2.6	362.9	5.1
Upper-middle-income countries	497.4	2.1	253.4	1.1	750.8	3.1
All low- and middle-income countries	**707.4**	**2.2**	**484.2**	**1.5**	**1191.6**	**3.8**

Source: ILO World Social Protection Report 2020–22, estimates based on World Social Protection Database 2020 and Stenberg et al. (2017), using WHO methodologies and databases (2017)
[a] The four policy areas of social protection (excluding health care): children, maternity, disability and old age

design of labour market adjustment and social protection system expansion programmes and domestic resource mobilization strategies, combined with an increase in complementary international financing. Its ultimate goal is to help countries create 400 million decent jobs, including in the green, digital and care economies, and to extend social protection coverage to the four billion people currently excluded.

In the spirit of earlier proposals for a global social protection fund,[27] this SDR window's concessional financing would help the ILO, which coordinates the initiative's Technical Support Facility, and accredited SDR implementing partners such as MDBs to organize matching commitments to countries that have sound plans to expand the coverage and/or benefit levels of their social protection systems (or to make permanent the temporary benefits provided during the pandemic) on the basis of solid domestic resource mobilization strategies. In addition to addressing the most acute crisis-related social welfare needs of those countries, such an international social protection financing initiative, perhaps on the order of the SDR equivalent of US$80 billion over the next seven years, would give practical effect to the commitment of the international community to achieve universal social protection, including social protection floors, as reflected in SDG Target 1.3.

RST Window 3: Basic Research on Renewable Energy and Low-Carbon Land Use Technologies, Including Their Development and Diffusion in Developing Countries (Green Revolution 2.0)
Given the slow pace of actual greenhouse gas emissions reduction,[28] and incremental progress in policy implementation (as opposed to long-term goal-setting),[29] the world is clearly going to require a series of technological breakthroughs if it is to have any realistic prospect of meeting the Paris climate agreement goals and averting catastrophic atmospheric warming later in this century. Public and private investment and scientific engagement in this challenge have increased significantly in recent years, but both remain well short of what is required. In its *Net Zero by 2050* report, the International Energy Agency (IEA) estimated that unlocking the next generation of low-carbon technologies would require huge increases in global public RD&D (research, development and demonstration) investment, including as much as US$90 billion in demonstrations alone by 2030.[30] A strategic "top-down" injection of substantial additional financing over the next decade is needed to multiply the impact of the growing bottom-up engagement of individual investors and scientists. An RST

SDR window to blend international "global public good" financing with that of government and academic research programmes would be a smart investment—indeed a prudent insurance policy—for humanity given the enormity of the challenge and slowness of progress to date.

Global public sector "clean" energy research expenditures totalled about US$12 billion in 2018, having risen considerably in the years leading up to the 2008–09 global financial crisis and plateaued thereafter.[31] Renewable energy research comprises about US$5 billion of this amount, along with about US$2 billion in power and storage technologies, US$600 million in hydrogen and fuel cells and US$4 billion in other cross-cutting technologies. According to the IEA, government spending on energy R&D worldwide, including with respect to demonstration projects, has fallen as a share of GDP from a peak of almost 0.1% in 1980 to just 0.03% in 2019. It has concluded that,

> without a major acceleration in clean energy innovation, reaching net-zero emissions by 2050 will not be achievable. Technologies that are available on the market today [can] provide nearly all of the emissions reductions required to 2030 ... to put the world on track for net-zero emissions by 2050. However, reaching net-zero emissions will require the widespread use after 2030 of technologies that are still under development today. In 2050, almost 50% of CO2 emissions reduction [will have to] come from technologies currently at demonstration or prototype stage. This share is even higher in sectors such as heavy industry and long-distance transport. Major innovation efforts are vital in this decade so that the technologies necessary for net-zero emissions reach markets as soon as possible.[32]

Mission Innovation is a global clean energy research cooperation of 22 governments, including the European Commission representing the European Union's 27 member states. In 2021, it launched "a decade of action and investment in research, development and demonstration to make clean energy affordable, attractive and accessible for all".[33] Its members reportedly have boosted their clean energy investments by a total of US$18 billion since the initiative's launch during the Paris climate agreement negotiations in 2015, including over US$5 billion in 2020. Mission Innovation would be a suitable recipient of matching or otherwise complementary investment from the RST window and could be accredited by it subject to appropriate rules regarding the licensing and broad diffusion of the breakthrough technologies the cooperation co-finances. An SDR allocation of the equivalent of US$50 billion over seven years would effectively double the world's public investment in renewable and related energy RD&D during the coming pivotal decade.

Ten per cent of this window's allocation (the SDR equivalent of US$5 billion) should be allocated to governmental and academic RD&D in climate-resilient agricultural technologies and techniques, particularly for application in developing economies. A doubling of such research is possible with these funds over the next seven years and could be delivered through accreditation of existing multilateral and philanthropic partners such as the Consultative Group for International Agricultural Research[34] and the Rockefeller Foundation, which catalysed the first Green Revolution in the mid twentieth century.

RST Window 4: Pandemic Response and Prevention (ACT-A/COVAX Initiative and Pandemic Prevention, Preparedness and Response Fund)
The COVID-19 pandemic appears as of this writing to be transitioning from an immediate and acute public health crisis to an ongoing but lower-intensity challenge to national health care systems. As the WHO has observed:

> The pandemic may soon be over, but COVID-19 is here to stay. As the world adapts and learns to live with this virus, countries (and the partners that support them), have started the transition to long-term COVID-19 control. A key part of this transition will see the mainstreaming of current COVID-19 emergency work into routine public health and disease control programmes, some of which may need to be adapted to take on these additional functions. Given that the SARS-CoV-2 virus continues to circulate and evolve, countries will need to maintain capacity to surge in response to future COVID-19 waves while this transition is underway.[35]

From April 2020 to September 2022, donors pledged a total of US$23.7 billion to the COVID-19 ACT-Accelerator initiative coordinated by the WHO, including US$16.1 billion for vaccines, US$1.7 billion for therapeutics, US$1.4 billion for diagnostics, US$2.3 billion for the Health Systems Response Connector and US$ 2.2 billion allocated across the Accelerator's pillars. The initiative currently expects funding requirements to fall off significantly as the disease becomes more of a mainstream challenge for national health systems; however, it has observed that "if a new, significant and more deadly variant emerges, which evades current countermeasures, tens of billions of dollars could be rapidly required to mount an effective emergency response on a global scale".[36]

A new Pandemic Prevention Financial Intermediary Fund was established and launched on the margins of the 2022 G20 Leaders' Summit under Indonesia's presidency.[37] Its mission is to "provide a dedicated stream of additional, long-term financing to strengthen pandemic prevention, preparedness and response (PPR) capabilities in low- and middle-income countries and address critical gaps through investments and technical support at the national, regional, and global levels".[38] Approximately US$1.6 billion had been pledged to the Fund as of early 2023, a level that pales in comparison with these gaps, particularly since the Fund also has a mandate in such important related areas of health system capacity-building as anti-microbial drug resistance and the intersection of human health, animal health and the environment.

The history of such initiatives is that funding tends to fall behind need with respect to both level and timing. Establishment of this RST SDR window at a base level of US$10 billion, with the possibility to expand its resources in the event of a new pandemic or lethal COVID-19 variant, would reverse this legacy and significantly enhance the resilience of societies and economies around the globe.

SDRs and Developing Country Debt Relief and Reduction
Finally, high-income countries and China would have the option of transferring up to one-sixth of their Series B SDR allocation to the IMF's PRGT to support accelerated developing country debt restructuring. Even before the pandemic struck, 25 countries were already spending more on debt service than on social spending for education, health and social protection combined, according to UNICEF.[39] Since then, elevated food and fuel import costs, rising US dollar interest rates, depreciating exchange rates as well as ongoing pandemic-related domestic expenditure have made it more difficult for many developing countries to service their external debts.

The World Bank reports that nearly 60% of low-income countries are experiencing or at high risk of debt distress and that 69 low- and middle-income countries saw their public debt service payments rise by an estimated 35% in 2022.[40] The deteriorating financial position of many low- and middle-income countries led the Bank's president to warn,

The debt crisis facing developing countries has intensified. A comprehensive approach is needed to reduce debt, increase transparency, and facilitate swifter restructuring—so countries can focus on spending that supports growth and reduces poverty. Without it, many countries and their governments face a fiscal crisis and political instability, with millions of people falling into poverty.[41]

The United Nations reported that, in 2022, 25 developing countries paid more than 20% of total government revenue in external debt service—a number of countries not seen since the year 2000 at the beginning of the Heavily-Indebted Poor Country (HIPC) Initiative. Moreover, as of early 2023, measured on the basis of a combination of credit-ratings, debt sustainability ratings, and bond spreads, more than 50 developing countries, including many middle-income countries, were suffering from severe debt problems; 26 of 91 developing countries with credit ratings were currently rated at "substantial risk, extremely speculative or default", up from 10 countries at the beginning of 2020.[42] The UNDP estimates that 54 countries are experiencing severe debt problems:

> [F]irst [are those] with a credit rating of either *"substantial risk, extremely speculative or default"* (26 countries). Added to these are [those] that do not have a credit rating but have a Debt Sustainability Assessment (DSA) risk rating of either *"in distress"* or at *"high risk of distress"* based on the latest country DSAs (23 countries). Finally, added are countries that do not meet the two ratings criteria above, but where sovereign bond spreads are more than 10 pp over US Treasury bonds (5 countries). In total this comes to (at least) 54 ... with severe debt problems, which is 40 percent of all low- and middle-income countries ... Not providing the debt relief needed will come at great human cost, as these 54 countries account for close to 18 percent of the global population and more than 50 percent of all people living in extreme poverty.[43]

Thus far, the international community's response to this debt overhang has been to move in the right direction by organizing a temporary suspension of debt service payments for many countries during 2020 and 2021 and proposing a framework for the permanent restructuring of the stock or terms of such debt thereafter. However, this G20 Common Framework on Debt Treatments is proceeding very slowly and likely to be overtaken by both the economics and politics of the problem.

Twice in the past forty years, the international financial architecture faced a similarly widespread deterioration in the external debt position of developing countries. In both cases, it responded hesitantly and incrementally for several years before belatedly recognizing reality and implementing a comprehensive process of debt restructuring as the economic pain and social unrest mounted.

The international community should abbreviate this familiar cycle by rapidly building upon the Common Framework to increase its ambition while applying lessons learned from these earlier episodes. The Baker Plan in response to the Latin American debt crisis of the 1980s, as well as the HIPC Initiative of the late 1990s, were forced to change course after a number of years of remaining well behind the curve of country and market conditions. Three years after its inception, the HIPC Initiative was relaunched as the Enhanced HIPC Initiative at the G8 Cologne Summit in 1999 and supplemented by the Multilateral Debt Relief Initiative in 2005. It ultimately yielded about US$125 billion of debt reduction and restructuring for 36 countries.[44] Bilateral (governmental) and multilateral (mainly MDBs and the IMF) creditors accounted for 37% and 48%, respectively, of this relief, which was delivered in stages. In general terms, countries would receive up to 67% relief of their bilateral debts on a net present value basis while they implemented an economic strategy agreed with the IMF and World Bank. After a few years of progress in implementation, they received a wider and deeper package of relief from bilateral, private and multilateral creditors, often reaching 100% in the case of their official creditors.

The Common Framework is a useful debt workout architecture to build upon in that it includes both traditional "Paris Club" and important newer bilateral creditors, such as China, the United Arab Emirates (UAE) and Turkey, and aims to achieve debt relief from private creditors on comparable terms. However, unlike the Common Framework, the Enhanced HIPC Initiative signalled its intention to include the credit of multilateral institutions, creating the prospect of truly comprehensive debt relief. Moreover, as developing countries went into their negotiations with bilateral creditors they were given a sense of the level of ambition of the exercise—the potential magnitude of relief they could obtain, if necessary, once they reached their "completion point", when they would become eligible for full debt relief (which was originally set as 80%, then reset as 90% in 1999 and as 100% in the mid-2000s). By contrast, the Common Framework is ambiguous in this regard, some of its documentation suggesting that debt write-offs would be restricted to "the most difficult cases".[45] Through knowing that the Enhanced HIPC process aimed to be comprehensive and truly substantial, developing countries were more motivated to participate than they currently are in the Common Framework, where this larger context and level of ambition are lacking.

That said, the Enhanced HIPC Initiative had several weak points. First, the process was long and slow. By 2009, only 15 countries had reached the completion point. Second, its coverage was somewhat arbitrarily limited, excluding countries that were not eligible for the World Bank's International Development Association (IDA) programme. Third, the crucial debt sustainability analysis methodology on which the depth of debt reduction was based focused mainly on financial ratios (e.g., debt stock/GDP and debt service/exports) and too little on economic development criteria, that is to say, the level of external debt service consistent with measures of economic and social sustainability rather than fiscal sustainability alone. Finally, private creditor participation was suboptimal, and multilateral debt reduction was constrained by the reliance of these institutions in part on individual member governments to fund their participation in debt reduction packages.

Similarly to the way the HIPC Initiative evolved, the G20 should reformulate and relaunch its Common Framework, assimilating certain lessons of the Latin American Brady Plan and Enhanced HIPC debt relief experiences. First, it should state a clear policy goal of offering a full set of low- and middle-income countries in debt distress—such as the 51 on the UNDP list referenced above (excluding the special and large cases of Ukraine, Venezuela and Argentina)—a framework for the negotiation of comprehensive debt reduction sufficient to restore a level of debt sustainability that is consistent with progress on sustainable development in general and the protection and progress of the most vulnerable and marginalized citizens in particular. To this end, it should signal its readiness to work on a country-by-country basis to achieve debt relief of as much as 67% to 80%, on a net present value basis, if that is what is required to achieve such debt sustainability. It should further commit to developing this new sustainability methodology by applying the more human-centred, two-lens economic growth and development model described in these pages, including by explicitly incorporating quantitative reference ranges for key policy drivers of broad living standards, such as those outlined in the preceding section of this chapter which pertain to social spending and decent work.

Second, with respect to the comprehensiveness of debt relief, the Common Framework should state an ambition to include private and non-Paris-Club official debt on a similar basis as Paris Club debt and to require full transparency in this regard. It should indicate that multilateral debt will be included as well, albeit possibly in a staged manner following bilateral and private sector agreements and perhaps at a lower rate reflecting these institutions' preferred creditor status. The PRGT-related SDR allocation should be applied for this purpose, helping to fund the participation of multilateral institutions without them having to resort to bilateral contributions, on the one hand, and, on the other, financing the buyback of private debt that has been deeply discounted in the market (or the collateralization of debt restructured via negotiation) as with the Brady Plan in the 1990s.

The multilateral debt reduction delivered under the Enhanced HIPC Initiative cost about US$42 billion,[46] roughly the same amount in nominal terms that would be mobilized if all advanced economies and China allocated 10% of their SDR allocation to the PRGT as suggested above. Thus far, there has been disagreement about the role of multilateral debt reduction in the Common Framework, potentially because of its resource implications for these institutions and their government shareholders. The application of this tranche of SDRs to this purpose could help to resolve these differences and enable the Common Framework to fulfil its stated mission of providing significant financial relief to developing countries whose financial position has been substantially and adversely affected by today's multiple crises.

Such a relaunch of the Common Framework to address the immediate developing country debt crisis should be coupled with a set of longer-term reforms intended to prevent the next one. The world economy has repeated many times the cycle of unsustainable lending followed by a crisis and workout. Several proposals for a standing sovereign debt restructuring framework have been made over the years, including by the IMF, but they have never gained political traction. In any event, they, too, are a form of *ex post*—that is, second-best—solution, since they are focused on making the restructuring of unsustainable debts more orderly and timely rather than on preventing them in the first place.

External shocks happen from time to time, and economic growth and development is not a linear, predictable process. What may look like a sustainable debt burden one year could turn into a serious headache for a country soon thereafter, depending on the evolution of domestic and external economic conditions sometimes beyond its control. Sovereign borrowers currently bear most of this risk; the terms of their debt service generally do not adjust unless there is a default or renegotiation. In recent years, however, countries and IFIs have begun experimenting with debt issues whose coupons vary with the economy's performance, that is, the country's underlying capacity to pay. Examples include the United States' and United Kingdom's inflation-linked bonds, the natural-disaster-linked debt issues of a few Caribbean countries and a number of initiatives to create sustainability-linked bond structures.[47]

The development- and sustainability-linked bond markets are in their infancy; however, interest and deal flow in them is growing. Stakeholders recently agreed on a set of principles to guide the development and application of these instruments and the key performance indicators (KPIs) to which they are linked.[48] The IFIs ought to invest in the development of this market, including by building the necessary market infrastructure, underwriting and syndicating early large-scale deals, including in debt buyback as well as new loan arrangements that they sponsor, and distilling and promoting best practices.[49] This contribution, combined with a continued effort to establish the inclusion of collective action clauses in sovereign bond contracts as customary practice,[50] could substantially rebalance the relative burden of risk assumed by sovereign creditors and borrowers and in so doing *structurally* reduce the frequency and severity of developing debt crises.

MDB-Led Public–Private Financing of Sustainable Infrastructure and Industry

The single biggest obstacle to the attainment of the SDGs is the large financing gap for low-carbon and job-rich sustainable energy, water, sanitation, digital, transport and other infrastructure. In developed countries, this gap exists primarily because of a lack of political imagination and will, rather than a lack of private savings or of public capacity to borrow and tax. However, in developing countries, where the largest gaps in sustainable infrastructure exist, it is a different story.

The IMF estimates that an increase in annual investment of 4% of GDP will be required by 2030 in middle-income developing countries in order for them to achieve the Paris climate agreement goals and the SDGs.[51] Sustainable infrastructure accounts for half to two-thirds of this gap, depending on the country. This incremental financing requirement is comparable to the scale of funding mobilized for Western European countries by the Marshall Plan. The financing gap in 49 lower-income countries is much higher relative to the size of their economies, at 15% of GDP. However, given the small size of these economies, this amounts to around only 0.5% of world GDP, or US$500 billion.

These estimates imply an annual incremental investment gap for sustainable infrastructure in developing countries of around US$1 trillion between now and 2030. This is around five times the level of annual official development assistance and private philanthropy delivered to developing countries. However, it is not beyond the reach of two other, more scalable, sources of development finance: domestic resource mobilization (tax base broadening and more efficient tax administration) and private portfolio and direct investment from both domestic (developing country) and international investors. Thus, the second major proposed reform of the international financial architecture aims to accelerate the implementation of SDG-related sustainable infrastructure and industry in developing countries by expanding these two sources of investment. It uses major increases in the latter to incentivize the reforms necessary to mobilize more of the former, not unlike the way in which the Marshall Plan leveraged aid from the United States to secure commitments of locally matched financing and supportive policies in European countries after the Second World War.

MDBs should play a critical catalytic role in this process. Private investment firms around the world manage assets in excess of US$120 trillion, of which only 5% are allocated to infrastructure and just 1% to developing country infrastructure. Approximately 10%, or US$12 trillion, of these assets were actually earning a *negative* yield until recently, and an additional large share were earning less than 1%. By contrast, infrastructure funds have historically generated a return of 10% to 15%.[52] This skewing of global capital away from investment in sustainable infrastructure that is employment intensive and that reduces greenhouse gas emissions is not even justified by the level of risk; average default rates on infrastructure assets are below those on non-financial corporates, and African infrastructure credits have lower default rates than European and US infrastructure assets.[53]

A two- to three-percentage-point shift in portfolio allocation by institutional investors to developing country sustainable infrastructure would cover this biggest of SDG and climate financing gaps and, in so doing, open an enormous opportunity for decent work creation in developing countries by virtue of the relative employment intensity of infrastructure projects. This shift could be catalysed through a concerted effort of MDBs to share and diversify the risks perceived by international institutional investors, blending in their own capital and partial guarantees, attracting local currency financing provided by developing country governments and investors, and aggregating infrastructure projects into syndicated packages large enough to be of interest to major institutional investors. The MDBs could offer such financial structuring and risk mitigation support to countries that meet certain minimum levels of domestic resource mobilization (such as tax collection as a share of GDP) and local currency project co-financing. MDB participation would be conditioned on safeguards to ensure financial additionality and integrity and proper public governance and oversight, including those reflected in the Blended Finance Guidance[54] produced by the OECD and in the Equator Principles,[55] as well as adherence to international labour, human rights and environmental standards, including those enshrined in ILO core labour standards and other conventions.

Most MDBs have considerable underutilized capital headroom[56]—an estimated US$750 billion of additional space in their collective capital structures without putting into jeopardy their AAA credit ratings—to expand such co-financing and risk-sharing as well as more traditional direct lending and grant provision.[57] They could comfortably utilize two-thirds of this available room on their balance sheets over the next several years, applying 40% of this amount to additional lending and grants and leveraging the other 60% three to four times over in private flows by scaling their co-financing, partial guarantee and portfolio-recycling activities. This would generate over US$1 trillion in additional external financing for SDG-related sustainable infrastructure and industry, which could be structured in such a way as to stimulate significant additional domestic resource mobilization and local currency financing.

The public–private, domestic–international and cross-multilateral institution cooperation necessary to solve this global market failure will not occur on its own, even if it would yield a two-for-one payoff of the highest political importance: big increases in employment and reductions in greenhouse gas emissions. Although the MDBs and some of their bilateral development agency partners have the necessary balance sheet room and risk mitigation and asset packaging and syndication tools, they lack the political mandate from their boards and the alignment of their senior staff to move rapidly in this direction on an individual basis, let alone a coordinated one. Breaking this logjam will require the kind of cross-cutting political leadership that world leaders under the auspices of the G20 or the UN financing-for-development initiative could provide, building on the strong network of developed and developing country governments already engaged in these processes.

Multilateral and Bilateral Financing of Domestic Economic Institution Building

The two financing initiatives described above would have the added benefit of freeing MDBs to shift more of their traditional activities and resources towards helping countries strengthen the distribution functions of their economies. Development cooperation has chronically underinvested in the design and proper staffing and implementation of the public administrative functions that are crucial to the level of inclusion, sustainability and resilience—and thus dynamism and resilience—of an economy. It has traditionally placed relatively little emphasis on helping countries build effective public institutions in such areas as:

- labour ministries and social protection system agencies that oversee critical social standards and benefits, including vis-à-vis the informal economy and other insecure forms of work that are so prevalent in developing countries;
- environmental ministries that set and enforce compliance with key standards;
- tax agencies that enable adequate and equitable domestic resource mobilization;
- independent anti-corruption, competition and financial regulatory authorities that ensure fair treatment of working families and small businesses;
- institutions of social dialogue—such as worker and employer organizations—that facilitate social participation in the setting of government and enterprise strategies and practices, giving these a solid foundation of citizen confidence and support.

Most of the world's poor people now live in middle-income countries where the primary challenge is not fulfilling basic human needs but, rather, including more of their population in the development process. The robustness of the kinds of economic institutions listed above is what chiefly determines whether countries succeed in doing so at scale over time. Technical and budget support for the design and administrative capacity of these critical public institutions and their rulebooks should be made a top priority for MDBs (and bilateral donor agencies), especially—but not exclusively—in middle-income countries. Properly resourced programmes of this sort—including Decent Work Country Programmes,[58] which help countries translate ILO labour and social protection standards into rights and protections of workers and their families on the ground—should routinely accompany trade liberalization agreements and country lending programmes in such countries.

As MDBs shift a larger proportion of their financial activities to efforts to catalyse far larger amounts of private investment through a more efficient use of their capital in co-financing and risk mitigation activities, they should be able to devote more of their energy and expertise to providing a service the private sector cannot supply: helping to build the public institutional infrastructure on which competitive and socially just markets rest. This change, on top of the greatly increased direct lending and co-financing enabled by a more expansive use of their capital, as well as the crash effort to incentivize a rapid decline in coal-related greenhouse gas emissions around the world, represents the refinement in the "business model" of MDBs necessary to apply them more fully to the priorities of the multilateral system in the twenty-first century.

A Financing Strategy to Match the Ambition and Urgency of Multilaterally Agreed Agendas

These three financing initiatives would provide the international community with the bold resource mobilization strategy it needs to have a much better chance of achieving its agreed objectives with respect to inclusion, sustainability and resilience. By generating an additional US$2 trillion in international financing for sustainable development over the next several years, these initiatives would enable the establishment of a new doctrine of development cooperation corresponding to the deeper level of interdependence that humanity is experiencing in this century and reflecting the universal threats posed especially by climate change and pandemics. To be specific, any low-income or lower-middle-income country that formulated a well-considered national strategy for the use of additional financing for these critical aspects of sustainable development would be assured access to a large boost in external flows to leverage the resources they mobilized domestically for these purposes.

This is the nature of the stronger partnership between developed and developing countries, the public and private sectors, and the Bretton Woods institutions and UN system that is necessary to make the decade of action for sustainable development a reality and to manage the risk of climate change and pandemics. In the absence of such an initiative, it is difficult to imagine how the large financing needs of developing countries with respect to the SDGs, decent work, climate change and pandemic PPR can be met.

As illustrated in Fig. 6.2, the US$2 trillion estimate assumes that: (a) developing countries not including China have received around 32% of the 2021 SDR allocation (US$209 billion); (b) developed countries and China (which has the largest foreign exchange reserve holdings in the world) would donate 60% of their share to the RST and PRGT for these four common purposes (US$265 billion); (c) MDBs would utilize roughly two-thirds of their US$750 billion in additional capital headroom, of which 40% would be devoted to increased lending and concessional

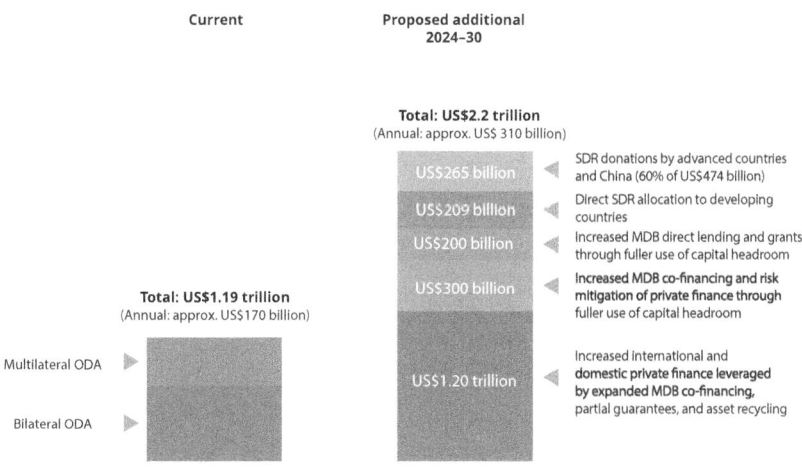

Source: Author's calculations.

Fig. 6.2 Tripling annual official development assistance (ODA) related external flows to low- and lower-middle-income countries from 2024 to 2030

assistance (US$200 billion); and (d) MDBs would deploy the remaining 60%, or US$300 billion, to catalyse private investment in SDG-related sustainable infrastructure and industry through co-financing, partial guarantees and portfolio recycling, leveraging US$4 of private capital for every US$1 in MDB capital (US$1.2 trillion).

Per the discussion above, financing mobilized through the SDR donation part of this proposal would be allocated through the four IMF RST windows as well as a restructured G20 Common Framework supported by its PRGT facility as outlined above (see Table 6.4).

These amounts do not include the additional domestic resources that developing countries would likely mobilize in order to attract such complementary international financing, including in the form of local-currency-denominated investments in sustainable infrastructure and increased tax revenues to support the expansion of social protection systems. This could add a further US$750 billion to US$1 trillion to the total resources mobilized by this package. Finally, a second SDR issuance could be considered for the latter part of the 2020s, in particular to maintain the momentum on climate action and the implementation of the broader 2030 Agenda.

The tangible human impact of this more effective use of the public capital already invested in the international financial architecture would be

Table 6.4 Resilience and Sustainability Trust (RST) allocation of rechannelled SDRs

	(US dollar equivalent, billions)
RST Window 1: Coal retirement and replacement and industrial methane abatement (Global Energy Transition Mechanism)	80
RST Window 2: Social protection floors (Global Accelerator on Jobs and Social Protection for Just Transitions)	80
RST Window 3: Basic research on renewable energy and low-carbon land use technologies (Green Revolution 2.0)	50
RST Window 4: Pandemic response and prevention (ACT-A/ COVAX Initiative and Pandemic Prevention, Preparedness and Response Fund)	10
PRGT: Developing country debt relief and reduction (Revised G20 Common Framework on Debt Treatment)	45
Total	265

Source: Author's calculations

profound, including for each of the dimensions of household living standards represented in the aggregate distribution function of countries. For example:

- **Jobs:** The employment effects of this additional US$2 trillion in external financing of SDG investment needs in developing countries would be transformational—especially from the major share that would go to finance employment-intensive sustainable infrastructure and industry projects in the energy, water, transport, sanitation, housing, digital, land use, health and education sectors. This additional external financing would enable the creation of tens of millions of jobs, helping to fill a gap that still exists from the pandemic in much of the developing world. The gross employment creation potential of investing adequately in the SDGs has been estimated at over 300 million jobs by 2030, representing more than 10% of the workforce.[59] Global unemployment stands at around 220 million individuals, with young people accounting for approximately a third of this number and experiencing an unemployment rate of around 13% and a labour underutilization rate three times higher than that of adults in the prime of their working life. The energy system aspect of this investment agenda is, by itself, projected to generate 18 million net additional jobs globally by 2030.[60] Coal power replacement and avoidance are projected to generate three to four times as many jobs as will be displaced—an estimated four million more in construction alone over the next decade.[61] Moreover, shifting to a net-zero-carbon economy through healthier and more sustainable diets, which reduce meat and dairy consumption while increasing plant-based foods, could create even more jobs. For example, the Inter-American Development Bank and the ILO estimate that 15 million net new jobs could be created in Latin and America and the Caribbean by 2030 as a result of the transition to net-zero emissions in agriculture and plant-based food production, renewable energy, forestry, construction and manufacturing. In sum, this bold financing agenda would go a long way towards filling the large hole in the labour market that existed before—and was widened much further by—the COVID-19 pandemic.
- **Entrepreneurial opportunity:** This international resource mobilization agenda would also create enormous opportunity for sustainable enterprise, including small businesses. The Business and

Sustainable Development Commission estimates that achieving the SDGs would create up to US$12 trillion in market opportunities across four economic systems representing 60% of the real economy: food and agriculture, cities, energy and materials, and health and well-being.[62] Progress towards the SDGs is well behind schedule, and these increased financial flows would go a long way towards fully funding national sustainable development plans in poor countries and placing the 2030 Agenda on track more generally. Such additional investment in the real economy is sorely needed to compensate for the effects of the COVID-19 pandemic.

- **Disposable income, economic security and poverty reduction:** This large and sustained increase in investment in employment-intensive infrastructure, industry and health systems would boost household income, expand the availability of material necessities and reduce poverty substantially. Better water, energy, sanitation, transport, housing and digital systems would also boost economic growth, as would the increased domestic funding of health and education which would likely result from the additional fiscal space opened by comprehensive packages of permanent debt relief. In addition, the large sums this financing initiative would make available for social protection floor expansion would place the multilaterally agreed goal of universal social protection within reach, with all that this implies for eliminating the worst forms of poverty that disproportionately afflict the most vulnerable groups in society. Similarly, adequate funding of pandemic PPR would enhance the resilience of entire societies and indeed the world economy.

- **Environmental security:** This ambitious mobilization of the international financial architecture would also open a viable path towards the stabilization of global warming by the middle of the twenty-first century. First, it would make possible the steep reduction in coal-fired emissions over the next ten years that is a *sine qua non* for achieving the 1.5 °C and well-below-2 °C scenarios by ensuring that such action also takes place in developing countries with sizable emissions, thereby removing any "free-rider" pretext for richer coal-burning nations to delay their own decisive action. Second, it would massively boost investment in climate-related sustainable infrastructure and industry in other sectors, further accelerating the low-carbon economic transition of economies and delivering on the unfulfilled US$100 billion per year promise of climate financing that developed countries made to developing countries as part of the Paris climate agreement. The stakes for humanity in rapidly getting on to the 1.5 °C or well-below-2 °C curve, and making much faster progress on other key aspects of environmental security such as water stress, biodiversity loss and soil degradation, are extremely high. The current trajectory of nearly 3 °C in global warming is projected to render large parts of the tropics essentially uninhabitable and to turn severe droughts and related fires that are currently once-in-a-century events into relatively common experiences that will occur every two to five years in most of Africa, Australia, Southern Europe, southern and central United States, Central America, the Caribbean and parts of South America.[63] Below 2 °C of warming, global average sea levels will likely rise by 30 to 60 centimetres by 2100. However, warming of over 2 °C will likely cause sea levels to rise by 61 to 110 centimetres in the same period. Under these circumstances, high-tide flooding that is currently expected only once a century would inundate many large cities and communities as often as every year, and some small island nations would likely become uninhabitable.[64]

In sum, mobilizing this additional US$2 trillion would make a huge difference to median living standards and human welfare more generally. These positive potential impacts demonstrate what taking multilaterally agreed economic, social and environmental goals more seriously would mean for people on the ground—for the human condition in the twenty-first century. They also demonstrate the enormous opportunity cost for humanity of the current incremental pace of change in development and climate finance.

This strategy to make more effective use of the existing international financial architecture is certainly ambitious, but it is not pie in the sky. The IMF and MDBs have previously used each of the approaches suggested here, just not at scale or as a central organizing principle of their activities. To be certain, strong collective leadership on the boards of these institutions will be necessary to bring about these changes, building on the options and recommendations of two related independent expert groups organized as part of the Italian and Indian G20 presidencies in 2019 and 2023, respectively.[65] This could be a useful focus of the G20 and UN financing-for-development initiative: leveraging their high-level political character to build the coalition of developed and developing countries within these boards that is necessary to effect such changes. Many shareholder governments and top MDB executives are committed to galvanizing and modernizing these organizations to enable them to serve the international community much more effectively in its unprecedented hour of need. The strategy outlined in this chapter would help them to harness the balance sheets and expertise of these institutions to much greater effect for this purpose.

Such a global resource mobilization partnership would greatly accelerate implementation of the objectives set out in the Paris climate agreement, 2030 Agenda (SDGs), ILO Centenary Declaration for the Future of Work and Global call to action, WHO-coordinated ACT-A/COVAX and Pandemic Fund initiatives and the 2022 Kunming-Montreal Global Biodiversity Framework. Its efficient leveraging of the resources of developed and developing countries and the public and private sectors would have certain parallels to the great international resource mobilization effort of the twentieth century: the Marshall Plan, designed to help Europe recover from the devastation of the Second World War.

The Marshall Plan, or the "European Recovery Program" as it was formally known, provided around 3% of recipient country GDP in aid per year over four years (1948 to 1951), comparable in magnitude to the additional international flows that the proposals presented here would generate for the world's lower-income and lower-middle-income countries over the next seven years. The aid provided through the Marshall Plan built on a similar level of assistance provided by the United States in 1946–47; however, it differed in several important respects. First, it was a multi-year programme, providing greater certainty and continuity. Second, it financed far more than basic needs; it was a multifaceted *recovery* programme that supported the reconstruction of infrastructure, the expansion and modernization of industry, and improvements in labour productivity through training and technical cooperation. Third, it required a matching commitment of local currency funds from recipient countries. These were deployed in support of policy reforms intended to sustain the economic momentum and social support of the recovery. Such reforms prioritized capital investment, technical and managerial capacity, and market competition, thereby strengthening European industry's competitiveness and capacity to generate employment, as well as reducing public debt, which created fiscal space for the important expansion of social protection systems that took place during this period. About half of the war debts of Germany were eventually forgiven, and repayment of the rest was deferred and linked to the country's capacity to pay (its levels of economic growth and exports). Fourth, the Marshall Plan had a distinctly public–private character. Multi-stakeholder councils were formed in recipient countries to advise on the best use of the grants and loans available through the programme, and the overall leader of the programme was a prominent business executive recruited from American industry.

As such, the Marshall Plan was far more than an aid—or crisis response—initiative; it was a crisis *recovery-and-reform* initiative that helped post-war Europe literally build back faster and better, avoiding major social unrest and political instability in the process. It not only supported a return of economic output to pre-war levels within a few years, but also corrected a number of structural and institutional weaknesses that had hampered the performance of European economies during the interwar period.[66] In other words, the Marshall Plan played a crucial catalytic role in the post-war rebalancing of Europe's economic growth model and social contract, which in turn enabled decades of strong, socially inclusive economic progress.

An analogous effort is needed today on a global scale to help economies and societies build forward faster and better from recent crises. A Marshall-Plan-like recovery-and-reform strategy is required to supplement and, ultimately, supplant the individual, largely crisis response, measures of nations, as important as these have been. As was the case in Europe after the Second World War, the speed and sustainability of recovery depend on reinforcing the key building blocks of broad-based economic and social progress: widely available employment and training; stronger worker and social protection; the deepening of other public institutional frameworks that enable more inclusive and dynamic growth; increased investment in the real economy; and, in today's context, accelerated and more equitable progress on the pandemic and climate change. Such increased social investment is also the key to achieving a just transition from our fossil-fuel-based energy system.

The architects of the Marshall Plan—as well as the UN system and the Bretton Woods institutions—deliberately sought to learn from the mistakes of the interwar period. There are analogous lessons to be learned today about the nature of the growth and development model of recent decades, in particular its socially and environmentally unbalanced nature and the deep-rooted perceptions of unfairness that this has engendered in parts of the world. These frustrations are reflected on the street and in government councils in a wide range of countries. They are manifest most visibly at international level in the long-standing stalemate at the WTO and the increasingly contentious debate within the UNFCCC about the unfulfilled commitment made by developed countries to provide US$100 billion per year in climate finance to poorer countries.

Industrialized countries, which hold the majority of votes in IFIs and have the world's largest capital markets, bear certain historical responsibilities with respect to global inequality[67] and climate change.[68] The pandemic and global warming are further entrenching inequalities and perceptions of injustice around the world. This would be an appropriate moment for these countries, in the interests of the long-term cohesion of the international system as well as their own national security, to provide a fresh round of leadership to and support for these institutions, inspired by the admonition enshrined in the foundation stones of the ILO's original headquarters which paraphrases its 1919 Constitution: "Si vis pacem, cole justitiam"—"If you desire peace, cultivate justice."

There has been much discussion in recent years about placing greater emphasis on global public goods in the operations of the Bretton Woods institutions and regional MDBs. The foregoing analysis demonstrates that the resources exist within them to drive a Marshall-Plan-like effort to greatly increase investment in the people of low- and middle-income developing countries other than China (which has ample international reserves)—in their health, productivity and economic opportunity, as well as in their social and environmental security. This would enable the international community to emerge from the current set of crises faster, stronger and more politically cohesive, while laying the foundation for the more inclusive, sustainable and resilient growth and development model to which world leaders have been aspiring since the Great Financial Crisis.[69]

This optimization of the international financial architecture's existing capital and capabilities would enable countries containing nearly two-thirds of humanity, accounting for almost half of global GDP,[70] to benefit from a US$2 trillion step change in external investment in the employment, basic necessities and social protections of their people between 2023 and 2030. It would also bring the international financing of global climate change to multiples of the US$100 billion per year target that has never been met, while fully funding the new Pandemic Fund, increasing its current committed funding sixfold. The resulting sustained increase in median household income, labour productivity and consumer confidence would raise aggregate demand and economic growth within developing economies and far beyond them, creating a virtuous circle of more rapid and resilient *global* growth and development.

In other words, the multilateral system already has the means at its disposal to become a truly transformational force for the reversal of global disease, inequality and greenhouse gas emissions, strengthening social cohesion and political stability along the way. These are the most important IFI reforms that are necessary to unlock that potential. The United Nations has called for a "decade of action"[71] on the SDGs and the Secretary-General has presented a supporting "SDG Stimulus" proposal[72]; this agenda would go a long way towards bringing about the more networked and effective form of multilateralism required to make such action and financing a reality.[73]

International Trade and Technology Governance

Trade and technology present special challenges for the practice of human-centred economics. Per the original insights of Adam Smith and David Ricardo, international trade and investment liberalization promotes resource allocation efficiency by facilitating specialization of production in areas of current or nascent comparative advantage. It also often embodies—introduces into the receiving economy—productivity-enhancing technologies and processes. In short, these two areas of international economic policy and cooperation are key drivers of GDP—the *quantity* of economic growth. The extent to which they also contribute to broad-based progress in living standards—the social *quality* of growth—depends importantly on the institutional context into which they are introduced, the robustness of the host country's aggregate distribution function.

Much has been made in recent years about the tendency of trade liberalization and technology adoption to widen inequality. But increased inequality and insecurity are not preordained outcomes of international economic integration and technical progress. They are potential risks, but not inherent or immutable ones. Governments can mitigate them by in parallel increasing investment at home in worker protections, skills and transitions, social protection systems and the enabling environment for entrepreneurship and innovation—what the ILO calls the "institutions of decent work". This is the international economic policy corollary of the golden rule of human-centred domestic economic policy described in Chap. 5—namely, that governments at all levels of economic development should place at least as much emphasis on strengthening the distribution functions as the production functions of their economies, especially during periods of economic transition and transformation.

International trade and investment agreements need to be routinely accompanied by increased domestic investment in the institutions of decent work if globalization (and regional economic integration) is to be become a more reliable force for broad progress in living standards. It is the combination of the two that helps to advance efficiency as well as inclusion as an economy integrates more deeply into the world economy. Unfortunately, this combined approach is largely missing from both economic practice and pedagogy, partly because these two policy portfolios are highly segmented—i.e., siloed—in both governments and international economic governance, and partly because of the subordinate treatment of institutions generally by the neoliberal growth and development paradigm of the past two generations.

It was not supposed to be this way. The first clause of the WTO's 1994 charter, drawn directly from the precursor 1947 General Agreement on Tariffs and Trade (GATT), states,

> Recognizing that their relations in the field of trade and economic endeavour should be conducted with a view to raising standards of living, ensuring full employment and a large and steadily growing volume of real income and effective demand, and expanding the production of and trade in goods and services, while allowing for the optimal use of the world's resources in accordance with the objective of sustainable development, seeking both to protect and preserve the environment and to enhance the means for doing so in a manner consistent with their respective needs and concerns at different levels of economic development ...[74]

Similarly, the ILO's 1944 Philadelphia Declaration, agreed only months before the Bretton Woods conference establishing the IMF and World Bank, stated,

> Believing that experience has fully demonstrated the truth of the statement in the Constitution of the International Labour Organisation that lasting peace can be established only if it is based on social justice, the Conference affirms that:
>
> (a) all human beings, irrespective of race, creed or sex, have the right to pursue both their material well-being and their spiritual development in conditions of freedom and dignity, of economic security and equal opportunity;

(b) the attainment of the conditions in which this shall be possible must constitute the central aim of national and international policy;
(c) all national and international policies and measures, in particular those of an economic and financial character, should be judged in this light and accepted only in so far as they may be held to promote and not to hinder the achievement of this fundamental objective;
(d) it is a responsibility of the International Labour Organization to examine and consider all international economic and financial policies and measures in the light of this fundamental objective;
(e) in discharging the tasks entrusted to it the International Labour Organization, having considered all relevant economic and financial factors, may include in its decisions and recommendations any provisions which it considers appropriate.

In short, modern international trade, labour and financial institutions were born with a certain logical hierarchy in their stated purpose. Trade and financial cooperation were explicitly conceived as means to improved living standards, material well-being and social justice rather than as objectives in their own right, with the expectation that they would be closely coordinated with labour and social security cooperation so as to "ensur[e] full employment and a large and steadily growing volume of real income and effective demand". The parallel reference to their intended contribution to environmental objectives was added later, in the 1990s, as the international community became more conscious of their critical importance for living standards, material well-being and social justice.

This original human-centred framing of the international economic architecture implied a certain degree of coordination, even co-creation, among these institutions. But such structural coherence in trade, labour, environmental and technology policy never developed within multilateral system. It has begun to emerge plurilaterally, particularly in preferential trading arrangements (PTAs) such as free trade agreements. Over 100 regional trade agreements, covering 140 economies, contain labour provisions,[75] and nearly 300 different environmental provisions can be found in the texts of about 630 PTAs.[76] But most of these provisions are more general and aspirational than specific and binding. And most developing countries lack sufficient institutional capacity to adequately implement and enforce them, which leads all too often to regulatory arbitrage and a race-to-the-bottom dynamic among multinational companies under constant market pressure to reduce costs. This deficit in the policy coherence and operational connectivity of international trade, technology, labour, environmental and development institutions is a signal failing of the past two generations of international economic governance. It impedes the human-centred rebalancing of the world economy that citizens and their political leaders have been appealing for since the 1999 Seattle WTO ministerial meeting by perpetuating policymakers' treatment of trade liberalization and technical progress as objectives in themselves rather than as instruments that need to be accompanied by proper investment in domestic institutions in order to produce a higher quality as well as quantity of economic growth. Following are some of the most important policy coherence and operational connectivity reforms required to bring these organizations more fully into alignment with the first principles enshrined in their charters in this regard—with a Roosevelt Consensus vision of growth and development emphasizing the co-equal importance of institutions and living standards, on the one hand, and market forces and growth, on the other.

Trade, Decent Work and Development Cooperation

The Decent Work Agenda of stronger domestic investment in people— their employment opportunities, capabilities and transitions as well as their labour and social protections—provides the most effective pathway for ensuring that the gains to living standards from international economic integration are shared as widely as possible. International trade, labour, and development cooperation institutions could do far more to work in concert to support member states in this regard, strengthening the multilateral trading system in the process.

The WTO and ILO could lead the way by jointly articulating and facilitating implementation in countries of the fundamental principle that integration in the world economy and domestic investment in the Decent Work Agenda go hand in hand. Trade liberalization and increased investment in labour and social protection institutions are necessary complements with important synergies for living standards, employment and sustainable development. For example, a WTO–ILO Trade and Decent Work programme of policy guidance and dialogue, technical and capacity-building assistance, and research and thought leadership would send the right signals to interested member states. This should be reinforced by development cooperation institutions providing additional resources to countries that choose to follow this guidance and increase their investment in these institutions as part of their engagement in regional free trade areas and other PTAs or their implementation of WTO obligations.

Such a stronger facilitative, as opposed to mainly legal, approach could go a long way towards strengthening the coherence of trade and labour policies on the ground while respecting the terms of the 1996 WTO Singapore Declaration, which excluded negotiations on labour norms in the WTO. At the same time, it would advance the objectives of the ILO's 1998 Declaration on Fundamental Principles and Rights at Work and 2008 Declaration on Social Justice for a Fair Globalization, which stated, respectively, that "labour standards should not be used for protectionist trade purposes" and that "the violation of fundamental principles and rights at work cannot be invoked or otherwise used as a legitimate comparative advantage".

More specifically:

- **Policy dialogue:** The WTO and ILO could jointly articulate this more human-centred model of trade and investment integration in a range of international fora, including their respective governing bodies. They might also co-sponsor policy dialogues involving trade and labour ministries for the purpose of encouraging the cross-fertilization of country experience and good practice. And they might offer to support national social dialogues that engage employer and worker organizations in discussion with governments about the identification of priorities and the formation of national Trade and Decent Work strategies.
- **Technical and capacity-building assistance:** The two organizations could also engage in a joint effort to mobilize additional development cooperation resources to support implementation of the Decent Work Agenda in developing country member states engaged in international trade and investment liberalization. Investment in the institutions of work, including the translation of international labour standards into national law and implementation mechanisms and the establishment or expansion of social protection systems, requires a sustained commitment of resources and technical expertise. As argued above, this aspect of institutional capacity-building has been underemphasized by development cooperation institutions, despite its central importance for the inclusiveness of trade in developing and developed countries. The ILO and WTO could work

together to address this challenge by encouraging donors to strengthen support for developing country member states that seek assistance with decent work capacity-building strategies as part of their trade and investment liberalization efforts. Additional funding mobilized for this purpose could be administered through a new "Aid for Trade and Decent Work" facility or as a new track within the existing Aid for Trade initiative, which over the years has devoted only a small fraction of its resources to this crucial aspect of the enabling environment for inclusive trade and development.[77]

The two organizations could work to connect interested countries to specific sources of relevant expertise and financial assistance. For example, with respect to skills development the ILO's Skills for Trade and Economic Diversification programme works with policymakers and industry to identify those sectors with growth potential and then identify the skills needed in those industries and build up the capacity of training providers to meet them. The programme develops a chain of economic analysis and partnerships that can turn the potential of trade into the reality of more diversified economies and the creation of more productive and decent jobs. Industry skill councils and other partnerships target training on genuine trade and employment growth opportunities and reduce the risks of skills mismatches. They also open opportunities for smaller businesses along the value chain. The ILO's Better Work programme, which it operates in partnership with the International Finance Corporation of the World Bank to promote decent work and better business practices in the garment industry, could be a model for other industrial sectors facing particular widespread decent work deficits.

Finally, at the request of member states participating in PTAs that include labour provisions, the ILO could offer its technical support in the implementation and monitoring of such provisions supported by social dialogue. Its recent role in facilitating the strengthening of Mexican labour institutions and supporting dispute resolution aspects of the US–Mexico–Canada Agreement (USMCA) is a potential model on which to build in this regard.[78]

- **Analytical tools:** The WTO and ILO could also work more closely together to develop and disseminate analytical tools countries can use to proactively assess their priority challenges and opportunities with respect to trade and decent work. For example, in recent years the ILO has developed the following resources:

i. *Trade and Decent Work: Indicator Guide.*[79] This *Guide* offers a broad set of labour market indicators for trade policy assessment which can be used in studies examining the nexus between trade and the quantitative and qualitative aspects of employment. In addition to framing the indicators most suitable for analysing the impact of trade policy on the labour market, the *Guide* facilitates the use of these indicators in macro- and micro-assessments by providing an overview of measurement approaches, relevant data sources, links to trade theory, and empirical evidence.
ii. *Trade and Decent Work: Handbook of Assessment Methodologies.*[80] This *Handbook* presents and compares methodologies for assessing the impact of trade on various areas of decent work. It traces approaches ranging from the macro- (country), through the meso- (industry/sector), to the micro-level (firms and workers), examining their strengths and weaknesses. Particular attention is paid to the micro-level, since analysis at that level, especially using linked employer–employee data sets, allows one to understand better the distributional effects of trade.
iii. *Labour Provisions in Trade Agreements Hub.*[81] The ILO's Labour Provisions in Trade Agreements database and web portal provides an extensive, structured compilation of labour provisions in trade agreements. Drawing upon the WTO's Regional Trade Agreements Information System (RTA-IS) database, it provides access to the text of labour provisions in over 100 RTAs representing 140 economies. This represents just under a third of the total of 357 RTAs in force and notified to the WTO as of early 2023. The database could be extended to include labour provisions of major international investment agreements in a further stage of research.
iv. *Sectoral and value chain analytics.* The ILO has developed a survey and mapping methodology for measuring the decent work deficits in an industry/sector as part of its work on global supply chains. The aim is to introduce transparency and data (quantitative and qualitative) in industries that are most relevant to trade. This approach could be further developed to expand understanding of the impact, both positive and negative, of international trade and supply chains on decent work. It could look at employment and skills indicators as well as forced labour indicators. The methodology offers flexibility in the type of indicators measured and could help stakeholders develop policies and action to address these deficits, building eventually into a database of

information that goes beyond and complements existing databases such as the World Input–Output Database.

- **Multilateral framework development:** The two organizations might eventually wish to consider collaborating on the development of a framework for integrating facilitative and normative aspects of the relationship between trade and decent work in the WTO's Trade Policy Review Mechanism, potentially as part of a broader process aiming to include sustainable development considerations more fully in this important function of the WTO. Broader uptake of the analytical tools and policy dialogue opportunities outlined above could ultimately enable a joint WTO–ILO global analysis of PTA labour provisions and a corresponding discussion of the lessons learned from their implementation and facilitation. Such a comparative analysis could be a useful point of departure for an eventual discussion among PTAs co-convened by the WTO and ILO on opportunities to align their provisions with good or best practice in this area and facilitating increased development assistance to fill institutional capacity gaps. Such a structured process of normative alignment and increased investment would have the virtue of reducing complexity for companies and other stakeholders and creating synergies with the growing movement for labour-related due diligence of firms within their global supply chains, such as the requirements recently enacted by the German government[82] and under development in the European Union.[83] This might even make possible one day a multilateral accord on Trade and Decent Work, perhaps modelled on the WTO Trade Facilitation Agreement in which developing countries undertake different levels of obligations as a function of their capacity to implement them, supported by the dedication of additional resources for this purpose by development cooperation institutions. The USMCA replacing the North American Free Trade Agreement represents leading practice in this respect. Signed in 2018, its labour provisions are the culmination of 35 years of iterative development of US trade policy. They represent a major step beyond the treatment of labour issues in earlier trade and investment preference programmes and free trade agreements with respect to both facilitation and enforcement.[84] Novel features in the Agreement's labour chapter include over US$200 million in institutional capacity-building assistance to support Mexican implementation; a presumption of a link between any alleged labour rights violations and trade flows unless proved otherwise by the respondant; and creation of a Rapid Response Mechanism with a cascading series of time-limited investigation, consultation and adjudication processes.

In sum, a rebalanced and more cooperative normative *and* facilitative approach to trade and labour issues, organized at the plurilateral level but enabled by a much deeper collaboration among the WTO, ILO and multilateral and bilateral development institutions, could provide a pragmatic basis for moving the international debate on trade and labour beyond where it has been stuck since the WTO Singapore Declaration a quarter of a century ago. With the right blend of policy innovation and trade–labour–development institutional coherence, substantial progress is possible on this crucial but politically sensitive aspect of a more inclusive model of globalization.

Trade, Digitally-Enabled Services and Decent Work

The availability of cloud infrastructure and computing services to store, process and communicate information has accelerated the pace of technological change.[85] The COVID-19 pandemic and the counter-measures implemented by firms and governments (e.g., remote work, digital passes, virtual meetings) have accelerated the digitalization of the economy and workplaces, including the automation of management practices and human resource (HR) policies. Algorithmic management, surveillance and tracking, and other feedback mechanisms are increasingly being used by firms in sectors such as logistics, transportation and storage services, manufacturing, and health care, among others, to organize, monitor and evaluate the performance of work.[86]

Algorithmic management is not entirely new, and many of its key features have historical precedents in Max Weber's idea of bureaucratic organization[87] and Frederick Winslow Taylor's scientific management.[88] However, digital technologies are enabling the parcelling, distribution and monitoring of tasks in real time and at scale, including in ways that span regulatory jurisdictions and national boundaries. The adoption of algorithmic management techniques can provide assistance, direction, prediction and more to management and employees, which can lead to increased productivity. However, it can also create new challenges for workers' rights and job quality. For instance, surveillance through algorithmic management, wearable devices and other sensors can have adverse effects on worker well-being and retention, and the use of algorithms in the recruitment and performance evaluation of workers can perpetuate or create new forms of discrimination, especially if the data used for predicting such algorithms are biased.[89]

While adoption of these tools and practices may be at an early stage, it is already clear that they present significant risks as well as opportunities for decent work and median living standards.[90] One open and troubling question for public policy is the extent to which they are being applied in a manner that treats labour like a commodity—a twenty-first century version of Taylorism and Fordism. Another is whether on balance they promote the replacement or augmentation of labour, sometimes also referred to as "destructive" versus "transformative digitalization".[91]

While the jury may still be out on these questions at a macro-level, we already know that the use of algorithms and other digital devices is profoundly changing workplaces—that is, the conditions under which work is carried out and employment contracts and relationships are structured. This transformation raises new questions for labour regulation—for example, regarding algorithms making decisions about worker contracts; new psychosocial and physical OSH risks[92]; or regulations in various domains which are no longer fully fit for purpose. The ILO is undertaking a stocktaking of relevant national regulation and international norms with a view to identifying gaps as well as good practices that may merit broader and more consistent application given the cross-border nature of many of the firms that use such tools.

These digital tools and practices have further exposed the limits of labour regulation bounded by physical jurisdictions and conceived for the production of tangible products. Jobs that were once considered "non-tradable" and thus protected from global competition—such as that of an administrative assistant—have now become a tradable service, readily available through a digital platform at a competitive price. The limitations of state-based regulation were already apparent in a world economy increasingly characterized by cross-border supply chains, but platform work and other forms of cross-border digital employment relationships and human resource management practices are compounding these weaknesses.[93]

Thus, digitally-enabled services present a new frontier for international trade policy and its relationship with decent work. Their importance in terms of value added is growing rapidly, as are the heterogeneity and complexity of their treatment by national regulation. Absent an agreed baseline level of international practice, a race-to-the-bottom competitive dynamic could take hold in the coming years. Thus far, PTAs have been the primary venue for policy coordination in this domain, but so far such agreements have focused mainly on market access issues, such as data localization, and placed limited emphasis on safeguards for workers and consumers.

Employee and consumer data protection and portability, on the one hand, and enterprise algorithmic management accountability are two of the most common challenges in this domain, relevant to both platform and more traditional forms of work. As such, they are good starting points for the development of common international principles and standards through a process of international dialogue involving trade, labour and other relevant policymakers. The result of such deliberations could be a model trade agreement chapter on Trade, Digitally-Enabled Services and Decent Work, which could be integrated into existing or new PTAs.

A 2022 ILO background paper prepared for a meeting of experts on decent work in the platform economy made the following observations, which are equally relevant to non-platform work in companies that utilize these services:

> the advances made by platforms and their capacity to capture data have led to growing concern about the protection of workers' personal data, and legal instruments on data protection are appearing or being reassessed in virtually every region of the planet.[94]
>
> Examples of these are the OECD Guidelines Governing the Protection of Privacy and Transborder Flows of Personal Data (revised in 2013), which have had a decisive influence on initiatives taken in many parts of the world, and the General Data Protection Regulation in Europe (2016). But it is the ILO code of practice on protection of workers' personal data (1997) which could guide the actions of platforms in this regard, especially the application of the following basic rights: (i) to be informed about personal data being held and about its processing; (ii) having access to personal data regardless of whether it undergoes automated processing; (iii) the possibility to request the deletion or correction of inaccurate or incomplete personal data; (iv) a guarantee that decisions concerning a worker should not be based solely on the automated processing of that worker's personal data; and (v) a guarantee that the processing of personal data should not lead to any discrimination.
>
> Furthermore, in platform work it is especially important to have portability of data from one platform to another, so as to provide a curriculum vitae

that can facilitate mobility between platforms and transfer a worker's ranking from one platform to another. This portability is now one of the most commonly made recommendations on platform work[95] and is already recognized as a right of individuals by the General Data Protection Regulation (Article 20) and by the Standards for Personal Data Protection for Ibero-American States (Article 30).

But if one thing characterizes platform work, it is algorithmic management. It is an algorithm that offers and grants services or tasks to workers, defines their time slots, calculates the rankings on which their activities and income depend, and decides whether they will continue to provide services for the platform or remain deselected from it. However, little or nothing is known about the algorithm by the workers who are subject to its dictates because it is opaque and at times incomprehensible to them. Also, algorithmic decisions are not always neutral. The data that feed into algorithms can contain biases which ultimately introduce discrimination into the decisions taken by them.

This is not simply a possibility, there are already examples. In Italy, a judgment has declared that the algorithm used by a delivery platform causes discrimination among delivery drivers because it does not take into account the reasons why they might not perform services in a slot previously selected by them or cancel a slot 24 hours in advance, those reasons perhaps being that they are exercising their right to strike or are ill.[96] In the Netherlands, a judgment confirmed the right of a transport platform to use an algorithm for taking decisions, but also its obligation to make transparent the data and main evaluation criteria fed into the algorithm so that workers can understand them and test their lawfulness.[97]

What many people regard as a key factor in relation to algorithmic decisions is the need to recognize their existence and their legitimacy in platforms' decision-making, and to submit the algorithms to a process of transparency and evaluation. Some national policies point in this direction. In Spain, Law No. 12/2021 of 28 September ... regulates the right of worker representatives to obtain information on "the parameters, rules and instructions at the basis of the algorithms ... which influence decision-making that can affect working conditions [and] access to and retention of employment" (one single article). *However, there is a regulatory vacuum within the ILO on this matter.*[98]

In 2019, the ILO's independent Global Commission on the Future of Work went further and called for a multilateral governance system that would require platforms and their clients to respect certain minimum rights and protections.[99] The Commission drew its inspiration from the

ILO Maritime Labour Convention, 2006 (No. 186), which sets a guiding precedent because it concerns seafarers who transcend geographical borders and involves multiple parties operating across different jurisdictions. The Commission suggested that an analogous approach could be considered for digital labour platforms, and it called for a "human-in-command" requirement in the regulation of data use and algorithmic accountability across the world of work. The tripartite ILO Centenary Declaration subsequently called in more general terms for "policies and measures that ensure appropriate privacy and personal data protection, and respond to challenges and opportunities in the world of work relating to the digital transformation of work, including platform work".[100]

A combination of hard-law and soft-law regulatory frameworks at the plurilateral and perhaps one day multilateral levels is needed to adequately address the challenges the digital economy poses to trade and decent work. The place to begin is an international regulatory dialogue and process of policy coordination to clarify and then narrow the regulatory gaps and discontinuities and to reinforce the application of universal labour standards.[101] This process could focus initially on developing a common baseline of safeguards regarding employee and consumer personal data protection and portability as well as enterprise algorithmic accountability. It could be extended over time to other decent work aspects of trade in digitally enabled services, including but not limited to digital labour platforms. These could include OSH protections and the use of algorithmic monitoring, work–life balance in remote work, transparency in platform ratings and rankings, and remote worker–management cross-border dispute resolution.

Trade and Climate Change

The most important current deficit of policy coherence between the international trade and environment regimes is in the area of climate change. This disconnect risks creating major political tension in the coming years, particularly in light of the European Union's plans to implement unilaterally a Carbon Border Adjustment Mechanism (CBAM) in 2026.[102] Under this initiative, additional import duties would be levied on certain industrial products according to their carbon intensity relative to that of competing European products. Such tariffs would very likely be challenged under and quite possibly violate the WTO's rules,[103] leading to potential retaliation against them.

For years, the multilateral trading system has sought to maintain a certain degree of openness to and interoperability with national and international environmental policy developments. Its jurisprudence has accorded a measure of deference to multilateral environmental agreements. And it has blessed plurilateral negotiations among 18 parties on an Environmental Goods Agreement aiming to eliminate tariffs on a number of environment-related products. However, the post-war trade architecture, including the WTO, has never faced an environmental challenge of the magnitude and urgency of climate change or the coming dispute over carbon border adjustments in particular.

With the scientific community warning that the window available to meet the Paris climate agreement's goals is beginning to close, it is time for the trading system to get ahead of this curve and shift from a reactive and incremental posture into a more proactive and catalytic mode. It can and should become an influential driver of climate action rather than merely seek to avoid becoming an obstacle to it. This will require a new geometry of both trade and climate cooperation, including a different cast of diplomats from that which produced the Kyoto and Paris accords.[104] Foreign and environment ministries were the key players in the creation of the UNFCCC's Kyoto Protocol in 1997 and the Paris climate agreement in 2015, with crucial input from the scientific community through assessments organized through the IPCC. This time around, economic ministries (finance, trade, energy, transport, infrastructure, development, technology) will need to be centrally engaged, with active input from the business, financial and civil society communities.

While the climate diplomacy of the past two decades has taken place at the multilateral level in the United Nations, this new economic phase will require a more purpose-built and variable configuration. Since the speed and volume of greenhouse gas emissions reductions is what matters most, a universal, multilateral approach will be unnecessary and even counterproductive. Global emissions are concentrated in a limited number of locations and industrial sectors, so there is no need to seek unanimous agreement among the United Nations' nearly 200 member states.

The best approach would be for a group of like-minded major economies to use their combined market power to speed the diffusion of low-carbon goods and services by aligning their policy incentives and standards in ways that create greater economies of scale and lower transaction costs for producers. A coalition of countries with big markets and ambitious environmental goals as well as supportive business communities could together accelerate a shift of production and consumption patterns, directly at first within their own sizable collective share of the world economy and then indirectly in other markets as these expanded economies of scale drive down production costs of low-carbon goods and services and make them more affordable globally.

Examples of climate-related economic cooperation have begun to emerge over the past several years. For example, the Major Economies Forum, WTO environmental goods negotiations, Carbon Pricing Leadership Coalition,[105] RE100,[106] the FSB Task Force on Climate-Related Financial Disclosures,[107] and other initiatives have all taken important steps forward. But, relative to the challenge the world faces, these are baby steps—fledgling and uncoordinated efforts that unfortunately are not yet making a major difference in production and consumption patterns where they would most affect global emissions.

A vanguard coalition of countries could, however, generate a significant change in the pace of low-carbon adoption in the world economy by working together in a new kind of international trade and investment alliance to shift the relative prices of the high- and low-carbon goods and services within their markets. Indeed, a growing chorus of citizens and business, civil society and international organization leaders have been calling for the introduction of "a price on carbon". This drumbeat is growing louder, but it is an appeal that suffers from being too narrowly focused, potentially to the point of making the perfect the enemy of the good.

The most effective way to shift the relative prices of low- and high-carbon alternatives would indeed be to impose a broad carbon tax or implement a national cap-and-trade scheme. But these policies have been slow to spread, and when adopted—often at considerable political cost—they have yielded modest results relative to the scale and speed of transformation that are required. While the idea of putting a price on carbon may appear to be a magic bullet, in the real world it has so far been a disappointment.

The focus of climate change strategy therefore needs to expand beyond carbon pricing on an economy-wide basis to using a much larger set of policy tools to shift relative prices with respect to specific carbon-intensive products, as well as magnifying the combined market pull of these incentives by jointly applying them across as many of the world's largest markets as possible.

There are multiple ways, beyond a broad tax or cap-and-trade scheme, to shift the relative prices of high- and low-carbon goods in an economy, whether via tariffs, procurement, financing, corporate governance, subsidies and performance-based technical standards, or targeted tax, investor disclosure, or emissions-trading rules and policies. Some of these instruments have the potential to influence prices directly, others more indirectly through a shift in purchasing behaviour that generates expanded economies of scale for low-carbon technology producers.

The actors relevant to this broad economic agenda are currently scattered across many different ministries, international organizations, and industries. Each has no shortage of challenges and priorities on its traditional turf, which is why the machinery of international economic cooperation has remained so quiet in the fight against climate change for so many years. Only presidents and prime ministers—whose authority spans finance, trade, development, infrastructure, energy and technology ministers—can galvanize the necessary domestic and intergovernmental action. And only they can compel the engagement of the key business leaders in their societies who are needed to co-design and support such a strategy.

Leaders of the European Union, Japan, South Korea, Canada, Brazil, China, the United Kingdom and the United States have all articulated support for accelerated climate action. A critical mass of them could translate these good intentions into much more decisive action by agreeing to create a new kind of international economic agreement to collectively scale market incentives for low-carbon adoption. By creating a low-carbon economic zone that aims to take full advantage of the growing price competitiveness of clean technology and industrial products, they would add fresh momentum to humanity's race against time, propelling faster adoption of clean technology in a group of the world's most important economies and driving down the relative prices of these products worldwide in the process.

This new type of "trade" agreement could take a flexible approach to the terms of membership, requiring each member country to commit to implementing at least half of the policies on its agreed action agenda within a certain number of years, while encouraging all to adopt as many as possible over time. Its policy menu could include: zero tariffs for a defined set of low-carbon goods and services[108]; common energy efficiency standards for government procurement of energy-intensive goods and services; mutual recognition of technical standards for related goods and services; minimum, time-bound targets for the reduction of fossil fuel subsidies[109]; a trade dispute peace clause and consistent rules on the use of clean energy subsidies; implementation of the forthcoming ISSB global baseline climate disclosure standards for corporations; coordination of efforts within the boards of multilateral development banks to have them make more effective use of their balance sheets to mobilize the private finance necessary for climate mitigation and adaptation in key developing countries[110]; alignment of policies in carbon-intensive sectors such as maritime, aviation, cement, steel, and oil and gas; coordination of basic and applied clean energy research to avoid wasteful duplication and to speed the rate of technical progress[111]; linkage of emissions-trading systems; and mutual recognition of the rough equivalency of domestic carbon pricing and regulatory schemes to avoid the tit-for-tat imposition of border adjustment taxes on one another's carbon-intensive products in the name of industrial competitiveness.

Such an open, expanding low-carbon zone within the world economy would help to scale up demand for low-carbon goods and services by embedding and aligning price advantages for them through linked trade, procurement, regulatory, tax and investment rules. A virtuous cycle of policy leadership, technological innovation and market forces would ensue. And the risk of border adjustment tax disputes relating to differences among national carbon emissions reduction approaches could recede as member countries use this green trade alliance as a mechanism to recognize the equivalency of effort of each other's carbon pricing and regulatory policies and eventually to negotiate a common framework at either the national level or within key industrial sectors.

An international climate action leadership club of this nature need not be restricted to national governments. City and provincial governments could be invited to accede to those elements of the menu within their jurisdiction, particularly with respect to procurement rules and energy efficiency product regulations.

Supplementing the trade and climate cooperative architecture in this manner would accelerate the implementation of the Paris climate agreement by speeding up the underlying economic transformation that is needed before nation-states can fully realize the political commitments they have made.

The world urgently needs to build on the Paris climate agreement, not rest on its laurels by hoping for the best from voluntary national plans. The best way to do so is to think beyond the current, largely siloed, trade and climate regimes—beyond the WTO and regional free trade agreements, on the one hand, and the UNFCCC and Paris climate agreement, on the other. In particular, economic institutions and policies need to be at the centre of this new effort—and that will only happen if a group of the most like-minded heads of government of major economies compels it. Only they can cut the Gordian knot of fragmentation and inattention that has plagued international economic cooperation on climate change for so many years.

A number of useful building blocks for such an approach have recently been established. Principal among them is the "Climate Club" which was agreed during the German government's presidency of the G7 in 2022. The Club will focus initially on facilitating the decarbonization of hard-to-abate industrial sectors, but it will also include a strategic dialogue on industrial "carbon leakage" and "platform for alignment, matchmaking on a voluntary basis and creating synergies between cooperation and funding instruments, thereby improving the enabling environment for industry decarbonisation in emerging economies and developing countries". The Club will have a flexible architecture in terms of both substance and membership. It has indicated that members are not required to participate in every workstream; other economic aspects of climate cooperation may be added to its agenda over time; and other "climate-ambitious" non-G7 countries are welcome to join.[112]

This is a promising example of the new enabling architecture the world will need this century to stimulate faster climate action where it is most needed in the world economy—and to avoid trade disputes in the process. If the most important industrial economies can agree on a framework to recognize the rough equivalency of each other's disparate approaches to internalizing climate-related externalities in their industrial production—whether through direct regulation or market mechanisms or the infinite possible combinations of the two—then this will obviate the need for them to impose carbon border levies, avoiding a cascade of major trade disputes that the WTO is not adequately designed to adjudicate.

Another potentially complementary building block in this regard is the recent effort by the OECD to develop an agreed methodology for estimating the carbon mitigation effectiveness of various policy instruments. Its Inclusive Forum on Carbon Mitigation Approaches aims to "develop a rigorous assessment of cross-country and country-level mitigation policies by taking stock of price-based and non-price-based climate change mitigation policies and assessing the impact of different policy approaches on greenhouse-gas emissions".[113] Such analysis could form the basis of the kind of mutual recognition regime that will be needed to avoid border adjustments and trade disputes among major industrial exporters. The Forum aims to include both OECD and non-OECD members.

Major economies should embrace and build on these initiatives to create the more comprehensive plurilateral trade and climate architecture I describe above, taking inspiration from not only the German G7 initiative but also another nascent green trade alliance of smaller and more ambitious countries, the Agreement on Climate Change, Trade and Sustainability.[114] A sizable group of countries from both of these exercises might even seek to launch and complete later in the 2020s a results-oriented Climate Change Round of plurilateral trade negotiations that incorporates several of the approaches presented here. Such a high-profile initiative would contrast with the commercially oriented, single-undertaking multilateral rounds of negotiations of prior decades, including the most recent one that failed, the Doha Round. This is the essence of the deeper policy coherence and operational connectivity between the international trade and environmental regimes which are necessary to speed the industrial decarbonization of major economies while avoiding a debilitating trade war among them triggered by the unilateral imposition of carbon border levies.

Conclusion: Making the Sum of International Economic Cooperation Greater Than Its Parts

Since the Great Financial Crisis, there has been a great deal of discussion about updating the international economic architecture to address global challenges, particularly with respect to enhancing inclusion, sustainability and resilience. But there has been relatively little progress in the past 15 crisis-ridden years, with the exception of macroprudential policy and the creation of the FSB. Part of the reason for the relative stasis in international economic governance has been the lack of a core logic—a set of guiding principles or design specifications to guide the renovation project. The absence of a new compass setting, combined with the siloed way in which the principal international organizations are governed by different sets of ministers, the reticence of the G20 despite its mission as the "premier forum for international economic cooperation", and a conspicuous lack of engagement and investment of political capital by leaders, has produced a decade of well-meaning but marginal progress.

This chapter has presented a blueprint for a major institutional renovation of international economic cooperation guided by the human-centred, living-standards-of-nations logic set out in Chap. 4. The blueprint would insert social contract institution-building into the heart of macroeconomic policy advice and analysis, including debt sustainability methodology, defining "macro-criticality" in a larger development sense more explicitly and quantitatively. It would transform international development and climate finance by tripling such investment flows for more than 80 of the poorest countries for the remainder of the 2020s, finally responding at scale to the increasingly urgent appeals of poor and vulnerable developing countries, such as those included in the Bridgetown Initiative.[115] This reform agenda would also retire and replace most of the world's coal-fired power-generating capacity over the next 15 years and double investment in renewable energy research and development—frontally attacking humanity's biggest near-term obstacle and literally doubling down on its best long-term hope for the fulfilment of the Paris climate agreement, respectively. At the same time, it would institutionalize a rebalanced, high-road model of international trade integration by coordinating trade, labour, climate change and development cooperation to a far greater extent through new types of plurilateral trade agreements, including one that could help to prevent a global trade war by creating a more workable solution than unilateral action to the thorny issue of climate leakage. Finally, it would give the WTO a new lease on life as the convenor of discussions among plurilateral trade agreements and their members about how the best normative and facilitative features of such agreements could ultimately be knit together into a reconstituted, high-road multilateral trading system that captures the potential synergies of these policy domains and sidesteps related political sensitivities of developing countries.[116]

This far more ambitious and integrated deployment of the principal international economic organizations would instrumentalize a human-centred, Roosevelt Consensus model of economic growth and development and make the multilateral system a much more potent force for sustainable development and the interests of developing countries in particular. These are the practical building blocks of a strengthened "global social contract" that would help build trust among nations and bind them more closely to the multilateral system and liberal international order for a generation or more to come. Specifically, this tripling of external financing and structural enlargement of domestic policy space would enable participating developing countries to accelerate their reduction of poverty, inequality and marginalization—that is, to significantly raise the living standards of their people. This is the top domestic political priority of virtually every developing country government, irrespective of political philosophy. With such important tangible economic and political benefits on the table, they would be much more likely to engage with advanced economies in constructing a rebalanced, high-road model of trade and globalization with respect to labour and environmental considerations in the manner outlined above, all the more so because these issues would be dealt with first and foremost as *development* issues rather than solely as legal ones.

This fundamental reorientation of international economic governance and cooperation would represent a sharp break with the past approach of developed countries, which essentially control the agenda of the primary international economic organizations and have never brought financial resources of sufficient scale to the table in either multilateral trade or environmental discussions. Nor have they, until recently, as in the USMCA, connected in a substantial way the facilitative with the normative aspects of international trade policy in plurilateral arrangements, with the notable exception of the European Union in the course of its enlargement into Southern and Eastern Europe.

US President Dwight D. Eisenhower reportedly once said that sometimes the best way to solve a difficult problem is to enlarge it. The past 25 years have shown that trade ministers do not have the political wherewithal within the confines of their portfolio to modernize the trading system in a manner that brings along the overwhelming majority of nations. The problem needs to be expanded to include other aspects of international economic cooperation. A more networked and decisive deployment of the principal international institutions is required to rescue the system from its current slide into the law of the jungle.

There is a growing risk that the world economy will splinter into a *negative-sum-game* dynamic of competing trade blocs which would be self-defeating in the long run for all concerned. The diplomatic stakes are high. The stability and very character of the trading system as a net positive or negative force for international peace are increasingly being put into question as this slide continues.

Participants in the 1944 Bretton Woods conference and the 1947 Geneva negotiations leading to the GATT and UN Conference on Trade and Employment in Havana, were very focused on understanding and applying lessons from the descent into the law of the jungle they witnessed in the 1920s and 1930s. Their original vision was for an international economic architecture spanning monetary, development and trade institutions whose guiding stars would be stability and development.[117] They viewed the architecture they were designing as creating a vital institutional underpinning for world peace through a *positive-sum-game* dynamic of mutually beneficial trade and financial cooperation between advanced and developing economies. Circumstances intervened in the ensuing years to prevent the realization of important parts of this holistic strategy; however, it is still a valid one and has become an imperative in the twenty-first century.

This is undeniably an ambitious agenda. But it is also a feasible one in the sense that it can be accomplished with the resources already invested in existing institutions and built on top of their most relevant existing initiatives. These priority reforms would bring the impact of the IMF, MDBs, ILO, WTO, UNFCCC, OECD and other international organizations into far greater alignment with humanity's consensus vision of the world we want for our children and grandchildren as expressed in a string of multilateral declarations over the past decade. They would improve the effectiveness and thus political value of the multilateral system for all countries, thereby reinforcing respect for its underlying liberal principles of universal human rights, rule of law, self-determination, territorial integrity and the peaceful diplomatic resolution of disputes.

Although it may take a global political crisis to prompt governments to take such decisive action to strengthen the multilateral system and make it more responsive to people's daily concerns, this is wholly unnecessary. There is no technical or financial barrier—just a shortfall in imagination and leadership. And yet, if history and human nature is any guide, governments may not engage sufficiently until such a grave threat to world order emerges.

As it happens, one may well be forming around the liberal tradition that gave rise to the multilateral system in the first place. This challenge, and the relevance of human-centred economics to it, is taken up in the concluding chapter.

Notes

1. https://news.un.org/pages/wp-content/uploads/2022/10/SG-letter-to-G20-Finance-Ministers-Central-Bank-Gov.pdf and https://news.un.org/pages/wp-content/uploads/2022/11/EOSG-2022-07680-ENG-Generic__SG-letter-to-G20-leaders-G20-Bali-Summit-SIGNED.pdf

2. IMF, "Guidance Note for Surveillance under Article IV Consultations", 20 March 2015, p. 36, https://www.imf.org/en/Publications/Policy-Papers/Issues/2016/12/31/Guidance-Note-for-Surveillance-Under-Article-IV-Consultations-PP4949
3. See Richard Samans and Jonathan Jacoby, "Virtuous Circle: Strengthening Broad-Based Progress in Global Living Standards", Center for American Progress, December 2007, http://cdn.americanprogress.org/wp-content/uploads/issues/2007/12/pdf/virtuous_circle.pdf?_ga=2.173664682.846694337.1673179683-2073450468.1673179683
4. IMF, "A Strategy for IMF Engagement on Social Spending", June 2019.
5. Ibid., p. 21.
6. Ibid., pp. 21–2.
7. This section is drawn from and builds upon Richard Samans, "Financing Human-Centred COVID-19 Recovery and Decisive Climate Action Worldwide: International Cooperation's Twenty-First Century Moment of Truth", ILO Working Paper 40, 7 October 2021, https://www.ilo.org/global/publications/working-papers/WCMS_821931/lang%2D%2Den/index.htm
8. https://data.oecd.org/oda/net-oda.htm
9. For example, in the 2021 Carbis Bay G7 Summit Communiqué, the leaders of the G7 noted that, "to mitigate the impact of the pandemic, we have provided unprecedented support to citizens and businesses, including to retain jobs and support incomes and keep businesses afloat, totalling over US$12 trillion including fiscal support and liquidity measures", equivalent to around 35% of their combined annual GDP.
10. Nicholas Stern, *G7 Leadership for Sustainable, Resilient and Inclusive Economic Recovery and Growth: An Independent Report Requested by the UK Prime Minister for the G7*, London, London School of Economics and Political Science, 2021, https://www.lse.ac.uk/granthaminstitute/publication/g7-leadership-for-sustainable-resilient-and-inclusive-economic-recovery-and-growth/
11. Amar Bhattacharya, Meagan Dooley, Homi Kharas and Nicholas Stern, *Financing a Big Investment Push in Emerging Markets and Developing Economies for Sustainable, Resilient and Inclusive Recovery and Growth*, London, Grantham Research Institute on Climate Change and the Environment, London School of Economics and Political Science, and Washington, DC, Brookings Institution, 2022, https://www.lse.ac.uk/granthaminstitute/publication/financing-a-big-investment-push-in-emerging-markets-and-developing-economies/
12. See IMF, "Questions and Answers on Special Drawing Rights (SDRs)", 23 August 2021, https://www.imf.org/en/About/FAQ/special-drawing-right. For further information about options and related techni-

cal considerations, see Mark Plant, "The Challenge of Reallocating SDRs: A Primer", Center for Global Development, August 2021. https://www.cgdev.org/publication/challenge-reallocating-sdrs-primer
13. Andrés Arauz, Kevin Cashman and Lara Merling, "Special Drawing Rights: The Right Tool to Use to Respond to the Pandemic and Other Challenges", Center for Economic Policy Research, April 2022, p. 16, https://cepr.net/wp-content/uploads/2022/04/SDR-Usage-PDF.pdf
14. The African Development Bank has pioneered this approach. See African Development Bank, "Leveraging the Power of Special Drawing Rights", 26 May 2022; Mark Plant, "A Valentine's Day Gift for the AfDB's Campaign for SDR Recycling—but Now We Need More than Heart", Center for Global Development, 15 February 2023, https://cgdev.org/blog/valentines-day-gift-afdbs-campaign-sdr-recycling-now-we-need-more-heart
15. IMF, "Proposal to Establish a Resilience and Sustainability Trust", IMF Policy Paper No. 2022/013, 18 April 2022, p. 2, https://www.imf.org/en/Publications/Policy-Papers/Issues/2022/04/15/Proposal-To-Establish-A-Resilience-and-Sustainability-Trust-516692
16. Kasia Tokarska and Damon Matthews, "Refining the Remaining 1.5C 'Carbon Budget'", *Carbon Brief*, 19 January 2021, https://www.carbonbrief.org/guest-post-refining-the-remaining-1-5c-carbon-budget/; IEA, "Global Energy Review 2021: Assessing the Effects of Economic Recoveries on Global Energy Demand and CO_2 Emissions", https://iea.blob.core.windows.net/assets/d0031107-401d-4a2f-a48b-9eed19457335/GlobalEnergyReview2021.pdf
17. Paola A. Yanguas Parra, Gaurav Ganti, Robert Brecha, Bill Hare, Michiel Schaeffer and Ursula Fuentes, "Global and Regional Coal Phase-out Requirements of the Paris Agreement: Insights from the IPCC Special Report on 1.5°C", *Climate Analytics*, September 2019, pp. 10–11, https://climateanalytics.org/media/report_coal_phase_out_2019.pdf
18. https://globalenergymonitor.org/projects/global-coal-plant-tracker/. See also Global Energy Monitor, Sierra Club, CREA, Climate Risk Horizons, GreenID and Ekosfe, "Boom and Bust: Tracking the Global Coal Plant Pipeline", April 2021, p. 15, https://globalenergymonitor.org/wp-content/uploads/2021/04/BoomAndBust_2021_final.pdf; Ted Nace, "A Coal Phase-out Pathway for 1.5°C", CoalSwarm and Greenpeace International, October 2018, https://www.greenpeace.org/static/planet4-international-stateless/2018/10/7df76ee5-coalpathway-final.pdf; Jason Bordoff, "Yes, We Can Get Rid of the World's Dirtiest Fuel", *Foreign Policy*, 26 August 2020, https://foreignpolicy.com/2020/08/26/coal-mining-electricity-climate-change/
19. https://climateactiontracker.org/global/temperatures/
20. See https://www.adb.org/what-we-do/energy-transition-mechanism-etm

21. For the basis of these estimates and a description of one way of structuring such an initiative, see Donald P. Kanak, "For Health and Climate: Retiring Coal-Fired Electricity and Promoting Sustainable Energy Transition in Developing Countries", Program on International Financial Systems, Harvard University, 12 August 2020, https://www.pifsinternational.org/wp-content/uploads/2022/09/Coal-retirement-mechanism-v10.1-full-length-1.pdf
22. *Adopted by 184 countries,* Recommendation No. 202 *defines "social protection floors" as nationally defined sets of basic social security guarantees that should ensure, as a minimum, that, over the life cycle, all persons in need have access to essential health care and basic income security which together secure effective access to goods and services defined at the national level as necessary.* https://www.ilo.org/dyn/normlex/en/f?p=NORMLEXPUB:12100:0::NO::P12100_INSTRUMENT_ID:3065524
23. ILO, "Financing Gaps in Social Protection: Global Estimates and Strategies for Developing Countries in Light of the COVID-19 Crisis and Beyond", *Social Protection Spotlight,* 17 September 2020, https://www.social-protection.org/gimi/RessourcePDF.action?id=56836
24. Fabio Durán-Valverde, José F. Pacheco-Jiménez, Taneem Muzaffar and Hazel Elizondo-Barboza, "Financing Gaps in Social Protection: Global Estimates and Strategies for Developing Countries in Light of the COVID-19 Crisis and Beyond", ILO Working Paper 14, October 2020, https://www.ilo.org/wcmsp5/groups/public/%2D%2D-ed_protect/%2D%2D-soc_sec/documents/publication/wcms_758705.pdf
25. *Vitor Gaspar,* David Amaglobeli, Mercedes Garcia-Escribano, Delphine Prady and Mauricio Soto, "Fiscal Policy and Development: Human, Social, and Physical Investment for the SDGs", IMF Staff Discussion Notes No. 19/03, 23 January 2019, https://www.imf.org/en/Publications/Staff-Discussion-Notes/Issues/2019/01/18/Fiscal-Policy-and-Development-Human-Social-and-Physical-Investments-for-the-SDGs-46444
26. See ILO, "Global Accelerator on Jobs and Social Protection for Just Transitions", https://www.ilo.org/global/topics/sdg-2030/WCMS_846674/lang%2D%2Den/index.htm
27. See, for example, UN General Assembly, "Global Fund for Social Protection: International Solidarity in the Service of Poverty Eradication", Report of the Special Rapporteur on Extreme Poverty and Human Rights, Olivier de Schutter, A/HRC/47/36, https://documents-dds-ny.un.org/doc/UNDOC/GEN/G21/093/37/PDF/G2109337.pdf?OpenElement
28. In 2020, the COVID-19 crisis slowed the global economy, resulting in a decrease of global carbon dioxide emissions of about 5%. In 2021, global anthropogenic fossil carbon dioxide emissions rebounded and increased

by 5.3% relative to 2020, totalling 37.9 gigatons or carbon dioxide or just 0.36% below 2019 levels. See M. Crippa et al., *CO2 Emissions of All World Countries*, Ispra, Italy, European Commission Joint Research Centre, 2022, https://edgar.jrc.ec.europa.eu/report_2022

29. See https://climateactiontracker.org/countries/
30. IEA, *Net Zero by 2050: A Roadmap for the Global Energy Sector*, Paris, 2021, p. 6, https://iea.blob.core.windows.net/assets/deebef5d-0c34-4539-9d0c-10b13d840027/NetZeroby2050-ARoadmapfortheGlobalEnergySector_CORR.pdf
31. Fang Zhang, Kelly Sims Gallagher, Zdenka Myslikova, Easwaran Narassimhan, Rishikesh Ram Bhandary and Ping Huang, "From Fossil to Low Carbon: The Evolution of Global Public Energy Innovation", WIREs Climate Change, Vol. 12, No. 6 (2021), p. 8, https://wires.onlinelibrary.wiley.com/doi/epdf/10.1002/wcc.734
32. IEA, *Net Zero by 2050*, pp. 184–6.
33. See http://mission-innovation.net/
34. See, for example, CGIAR, "CGIAR 2030: Research and Innovation Strategy", https://cgspace.cgiar.org/bitstream/handle/10568/110918/OneCGIAR-Strategy.pdf; CGIAR, "Investment Prospectus 2022–2024", https://www.cgiar.org/research/investment-prospectus/
35. WHO, "ACT-Accelerator Transition Plan (01 October 2022 to 31 March 2023)", 28 October 2022, p. iv, https://www.who.int/publications/m/item/act-accelerator-transition-plan-(1-oct-2022-to-31-mar-2023)
36. Ibid., p. 33.
37. See World Bank, "G20 Hosts Official Launch of the Pandemic Fund", press release, 30 November 2022, https://www.worldbank.org/en/news/press-release/2022/11/12/g20-hosts-official-launch-of-the-pandemic-fund
38. World Bank, "FAQs: Financial Intermediary Fund for Pandemic Prevention, Preparedness and Response", 30 June 2022, https://www.worldbank.org/en/topic/pandemics/brief/factsheet-financial-intermediary-fund-for-pandemic-prevention-preparedness-and-response
39. UNICEF, "COVID-19 and the Looming Debt Crisis", April 2021, https://www.unicef-irc.org/publications/pdf/Social-spending-series_COVID-19-and-the-looming-debt-crisis.pdf
40. World Bank, *International Debt Report 2022: Updated International Debt Statistics*, Washington, DC, 2022, https://openknowledge.worldbank.org/bitstream/handle/10986/38045/9781464819025.pdf?sequence=8
41. World Bank, "Debt-Service Payments Put Biggest Squeeze on Poor Countries since 2000", press release, 6 December 2022, https://www.worldbank.org/en/news/press-release/2022/12/06/

debt-service-payments-put-biggest-squeeze-on-poor-countries-since-2000
42. United Nations, "United Nations Secretary-General's SDG Stimulus to Deliver Agenda 2030", February 2023, p. 4, https://www.un.org/sustainabledevelopment/wp-content/uploads/2023/02/SDG-Stimulus-to-Deliver-Agenda-2030.pdf
43. Lars Jensen, "Avoiding 'Too Little Too Late' on International Debt Relief", UNDP Development Futures Series Working Paper, October 2022, p. 6, https://www.undp.org/publications/dfs-avoiding-too-little-too-late-international-debt-relief
44. IMF, "Heavily Indebted Poor Countries (HIPC) Initiative and Multilateral Debt Relief Initiative (MDRI): Statistical Update", IMF Policy Paper No. 2019/028, 2019, https://www.imf.org/en/Publications/Policy-Papers/Issues/2019/08/06/Heavily-Indebted-Poor-Countries-HIPC-Initiative-and-Multilateral-Debt-Relief-Initiative-MDRI-48566
45. Dennis Essers and Danny Cassimon, "Towards HIPC 2.0? Lessons from Past Debt Relief Initiatives for Addressing Current Debt Problems", University of Antwerp Institute of Development Studies Working Paper 2021.02, 2021, p. 13, https://www.uantwerpen.be/en/research-groups/iob/publications/working-papers/wp-2021/wp-202102/
46. IDA and IMF, "Heavily Indebted Poor Countries (HIPC) Initiative and Multilateral Debt Relief Initiative (MDRI): Statistical Update", 15 March 2016, p. v, https://documents1.worldbank.org/curated/en/123261467999692988/pdf/104810-BR-SecM2016-0137-IDA-SecM2016-0082-Box394885B-OUO-9.pdf
47. See, for example, Finance for Biodiversity Initiative, "Greening Sovereign Debt Performance: Shared Risk and Rewards in Financing the Transition", March 2022, pp. 17–19, https://www.naturefinance.net/resources tools/greening-sovereign-debt-performance/; World Bank, *Sovereign Green, Social and Sustainability Bonds: Unlocking the Potential for Emerging Markets and Developing Economies*, Washington, DC, 2022, https://thedocs.worldbank.org/en/doc/4de3839b85c57eb958dd207 fad132f8e-0340012022/original/WB-GSS-Bonds-Survey-Report.pdf
48. See International Capital Markets Association, "Sustainability-Linked Bond Principles: Voluntary Process Guidelines", June 2020, https://www.icmagroup.org/assets/documents/Regulatory/Green-Bonds/June-2020/Sustainability-Linked-Bond-Principles-June-2020-171120.pdf
49. For an example of the elements of such an agenda, see Finance for Biodiversity Initiative, "Greening Sovereign Debt Performance", pp. 20–4.

50. See, for example, Indermit Gill and Lee C. Buchheit, "Targeted Legislative Tweaks Can Help Contain the Harm of Debt Crises", *Brookings Future Development*, 27 June 2022, https://www.brookings.edu/blog/future-development/2022/06/27/targeted-legislative-tweaks-can-help-contain-the-harm-of-debt-crises/; Blanca Jimena Talera, "Potential Statutory Options to Encourage Private Sector Creditor Participation in the Common Framework", World Bank Equitable Growth, Finance and Institutions Note, 2022, https://documents1.worldbank.org/curated/en/099802006132239956/pdf/IDU0766c0f2d0f5d0040fe09c9a0bf7fb0e2d858.pdf
51. See Vitor Gaspar, David Amaglobeli, Mercedes Garcia-Escribano, Delphine Prady and Mauricio Soto, "Fiscal Policy and Development: Human, Social and Physical Investments for the SDGs", IMF Staff Discussion Note No. 2019/003, 23 January 2019, https://www.imf.org/en/Publications/Staff-Discussion-Notes/Issues/2019/01/18/Fiscal-Policy-and-Development-Human-Social-and-Physical-Investments-for-the-SDGs-46444
52. These estimates are drawn from Blended Finance Taskforce, *Better Finance, Better World*, London, 2018, pp. 47–50, https://s3.amazonaws.com/aws-bsdc/BFT_BetterFinance_final_01192018.pdf
53. Ibid.
54. OECD, *The OECD DAC Blended Finance Guidance*, Paris, 2021, https://www.oecd-ilibrary.org/development/the-oecd-dac-blended-finance-guidance_ded656b4-en
55. https://equator-principles.com/about-the-equator-principles/
56. See, for example, the independent expert report commissioned by the G20 in 2021: Bank of Italy, *Boosting MDBs' Investing Capacity: An Independent Review of Multilateral Development Banks' Capital Adequacy Frameworks*, 2022, https://www.dt.mef.gov.it/export/sites/sitodt/modules/documenti_it/rapporti_finanziari_internazionali/rapporti_finanziari_internazionali/CAF-Review-Report.pdf
57. See, for example, Chris Humphrey, "All Hands on Deck: How to Scale Up Multilateral Financing to Face the COVID-19 Crisis", Overseas Development Institute, April 2020, https://odi.org/en/publications/all-hands-on-deck-how-to-scale-up-multilateral-financing-to-face-the-covid-19-crisis/; Riccardo Settimo, "Higher Multilateral Development Bank Lending, Unchanged Capital Resources and Triple-A Rating: A Possible Trinity after All?" Bank of Italy Occasional Paper No. 488, April 2019, https://papers.ssrn.com/sol3/papers.cfm?abstract_id=3432994
58. https://www.ilo.org/global/about-the-ilo/how-the-ilo-works/organigramme/program/dwcp/lang%2D%2Den/index.htm

6 HUMAN-CENTRED INTERNATIONAL ECONOMIC POLICY... 313

59. Business and Sustainable Development Commission, *Better Business, Better World*, London, 2017, https://d306pr3pise04h.cloudfront.net/docs/news_events%2F9.3%2Fbetter-business-better-world.pdf
60. ILO, Greening with Jobs: World Employment and Social Outlook 2018, Geneva, 2018, p. 42, https://www.ilo.org/wcmsp5/groups/public/%2D%2D-dgreports/%2D%2D-dcomm/%2D%2D-publ/documents/publication/wcms_628654.pdf; SystemIQ, The Paris Effect: How the Climate Agreement *Is* Reshaping the Global Economy, London, 2020, https://www.systemiq.earth/wp-content/uploads/2020/12/The-Paris-Effect_SYSTEMIQ_Full-Report_December-2020.pdf
61. Goldman Sachs, "Carbonomics: The Green Engine of Economic Recovery", 16 June 2020, 15, https://www.goldmansachs.com/insights/pages/gs-research/carbonomics-green-engine-of-economic-recovery-f/report.pdf
62. Business and Sustainable Development Commission, *Better Business, Better World*.
63. *The Economist*, "Three Degrees of Global Warming Is Quite Plausible and Truly Disastrous", 24 July 2021, https://www.economist.com/briefing/2021/07/24/three-degrees-of-global-warming-is-quite-plausible-and-truly-disastrous
64. IPCC, Special Report on the Ocean and Cryosphere in a Changing *Climate*, Cambridge, MA, Cambridge University Press, 2019, https://www.ipcc.ch/srocc/chapter/summary-for-policymakers/
65. See G20 Indian Presidency, "G20 Roadmap for the Implementation of the Recommendations of the G20 Independent Review of Multilateral Development Banks' Capital Adequacy Frameworks," July 2023, https://www.g20.org/content/dam/gtwenty/gtwenty_new/document/G20_Roadmap_for_MDBCAF.pdf; and G20 Indian Presidency, "Strengthening Multilateral Development Banks, The Triple Agenda: Report of the Independent Expert Group," Volume 1, June 30, 2023, https://www.cgdev.org/sites/default/files/The_Triple_Agenda_G20-IEG_Report_Volume1_2023.pdf.
66. See, for example, Curt Tarnoff, "The Marshall Plan: Design, Accomplishments and Significance", Congressional Research Service, 18 January 2018, https://sgp.fas.org/crs/row/R45079.pdf; J. Bradford DeLong and Barry Eichengreen, "The Marshall Plan: History's Most Successful Structural Adjustment Program", National Bureau of Economic Research Working Paper No. 3899, November 1991, https://papers.ssrn.com/sol3/papers.cfm?abstract_id=226738
67. For an overview of research on the legacy of colonialism in this regard, see Patrick Ziltener and Daniel Kunzler, "Impacts of Colonialism: A Research Survey", *Journal of World-Systems Research*, Vol. 19, No. 2 (2013), pp. 290–311, http://jwsr.pitt.edu/ojs/jwsr/article/view/507

68. See, for example, Hannah Ritchie, "Who Has Contributed Most to Global CO2 Emissions?" *Our World in Data*, 1 October 2019, https://ourworldindata.org/contributed-most-global-co2
69. See, for example, Richard Samans, "Beyond Business As Usual: G-20 Leaders and Post-crisis Reconstitution of the International Economic Order", Center for American Progress, September 2009, https://cdn.americanprogress.org/wp-content/uploads/issues/2009/09/pdf/g20.pdf?_ga=2.33791972.457127072.1628340596-66874698.1628340596
70. According to World Bank figures, low- and middle-income countries other than China accounted for about 46% (US$36 trillion) of global GDP (US$78 trillion) in 2021 (and about 65% or 5.1 billion of the world's 7.8 billion people).
71. https://www.un.org/sustainabledevelopment/decade-of-action/
72. United Nations, "United Nations Secretary-General's SDG Stimulus to Deliver Agenda 2030," https://www.un.org/sustainabledevelopment/wp-content/uploads/2023/02/SDG-Stimulus-to-Deliver-Agenda-2030.pdf
73. See the UN Secretary-General António Guterres' vision of "networked multilateralism" and a "renewed social contract" in his landmark report to the UN General Assembly upon the United Nations' 75th anniversary: United Nations, *Our Common Agenda: Report of the Secretary-General*, New York, 2021, pp. 65–8 and 22–34, respectively, https://www.un.org/en/content/common-agenda-report/assets/pdf/Common_Agenda_Report_English.pdf
74. Agreement Establishing the World Trade Organization, 1994, https://www.wto.org/english/docs_e/legal_e/04-wto.pdf
75. See https://www.ilo.org/global/research/projects/trade-decent-work/WCMS_835479/lang%2D%2Den/index.htm
76. Axel Berger, Clara Brandi and Dominique Bruhn, "Environmental Provisions in Trade Agreements: Promises at the Trade and Environment Interface", German Development Institute Briefing Paper 16/2017, 2017, p. 1, https://www.idos-research.de/uploads/media/BP_16.2017.pdf
77. See WTO and OECD, *Aid for Trade at a Glance 2022: Empowering Connected, Sustainable Trade*, Paris, OECD, 2022, p. 16, https://www.oecd-ilibrary.org/docserver/9ce2b7ba-en.pdf?expires=1673201329&id=id&accname=guest&checksum=FFE5441158DF9F118C839A9900AD5864
78. ILO, "Conclusion of Observation Mission in Silao, Guanajuato", Briefing Note, 19 August 2021, https://www.ilo.org/americas/sala-de-prensa/WCMS_817105/lang%2D%2Den/index.htm
79. ILO, *Trade and Decent Work: Indicator Guide*, Geneva, 2021, https://www.ilo.org/global/publications/WCMS_821843/lang%2D%2Den/index.htm

80. ILO, *Trade and Decent Work: Handbook of Assessment Methodologies*, Geneva, 2021, https://www.ilo.org/global/publications/WCMS_821841/lang%2D%2Den/index.htm
81. https://www.ilo.org/LPhub/
82. See for example Lönig, "Implementing the German Supply Chain Due Diligence Act", Briefing Paper, https://loening.org/wp-content/uploads/Loening-Lieferkettengesetz-LkSG-Paper.pdf
83. See European Commission, "Just and Sustainable Economy: Commission Lays Down Rules for Companies to Respect Human Rights and Environment in Global Value Chains", press release, 23 February 2022, https://ec.europa.eu/commission/presscorner/detail/en/ip_22_1145
84. See, for example, US Department of Labor Bureau of International Labor Affairs, "Labour Provisions and the United States–Mexico–Canada Agreement", https://www.dol.gov/agencies/ilab/our-work/trade/labor-rights-usmca; Martin Myant, "Making Labour Provisions in Trade Agreements Work", European Trade Union Institute Policy Brief 2022.04, 2022, https://www.etui.org/sites/default/files/2022-03/Making%20labour%20provisions%20in%20free%20trade%20agreements%20work-2022.pdf; Maria Anna Corvaglia, "Labour Rights Protection and its Enforcement under USMCA: Insights from a Comparative Legal Analysis", *World Trade Review*, Vol. 20, No. 5 (2021), pp. 648–67, https://www.cambridge.org/core/journals/world-trade-review/article/labour-rights-protection-and-its-enforcement-under-the-usmca-insights-from-a-comparative-legal-analysis/C24881E4D72CDEAD0A78463875C5CE8C
85. ILO, *World Employment and Social Outlook 2021: The Role of Digital Labour Platforms in Transforming the World of Work*, Geneva, 2021, https://www.ilo.org/wcmsp5/groups/public/%2D%2D-dgreports/%2D%2D-dcomm/%2D%2D-publ/documents/publication/wcms_771749.pdf
86. See Alex J. Wood, "Algorithmic Management Consequences for Work Organisation and Working Conditions", JRC Working Papers Series on Labour, Education and Technology 2021/07, 2021, https://ec.europa.eu/jrc/sites/default/files/jrc124874.pdf. This paper provides, from a review of the existing literature, several examples of such practices in a number of sectors.
87. Max Weber, *Economy and Society: An Outline of Interpretive Sociology*, trans. Guenther Roth and Claus Wittich, New York, Bedminster Press, 1968.
88. See Frederick Winslow Taylor, *The Principles of Scientific Management*, New York, Harper, 1911; Harry Braverman, *Labour and Monopoly Capital: The Degradation of Work in the Twentieth Century*, New York, Monthly Review Press, 1974.

89. See A. Köchling and M.C. Wehner, "Discriminated by an Algorithm: A Systematic Review of Discrimination and Fairness by Algorithmic Decision-Making in the Context of HR Recruitment and HR Development", *Business Research*, Vol. 13, No. 13 (2020), pp. 795–848.
90. See Sara Baiocco, Enrique Fernandez-Macías, Uma Rani and Annarosa Pesole "The Algorithmic Management of Work and Its Implications in Different Contexts", ILO and European Commission Background Paper, June 2022, https://www.ilo.org/wcmsp5/groups/public/%2D%2Ded_emp/documents/publication/wcms_849220.pdf
91. F. Fossen and A. Sorgner, "Mapping the Future of Occupations: Transformative and Destructive Effects of New Digital Technologies on Jobs", *Foresight and STI Governance*, Vol. 13, No. 2 (2019), pp. 10–18.
92. See P.V. Moore, "OSH and the Future of Work: Benefits and Risks of Artificial Intelligence Tools in Workplaces", European Agency for Safety and Health at Work Discussion Paper, 2019; P.V. Moore, "The Threat of Physical and Psychosocial Violence and Harassment in Digitalized Work", ILO Working Paper, 2018, https://www.ilo.org/wcmsp5/groups/public/%2D%2D-ed_dialogue/%2D%2D-actrav/documents/publication/wcms_617062.pdf
93. J. Berg, "An International Governance System for Digital Work in the Planetary Market", in M. Graham and F. Ferrari, eds, *Digital Work in the Planetary Labour Market*, Cambridge, MA, MIT Press, 2022.
94. Frank Hendrickx, "Protection of Workers' Personal Data: General Principles", ILO Working Paper 62, 5 May 2022, https://www.ilo.org/global/publications/working-papers/WCMS_844343/lang%2D%2Den/index.htm
95. See Janine Berg, Marianne Furrer, Ellie Harmon, Uma Rani and M. Six Silberman, *Digital Labour Platforms and the Future of Work: Towards Decent Work in the Online World*, Geneva, ILO, 2018, https://www.ilo.org/global/publications/books/WCMS_645337/lang%2D%2Den/index.htm
96. Judgement of the Ordinary Court of Bologna [in Italian], https://www.algoritmolegal.com/wp-content/uploads/2021/01/Sentencia-Bologna-Italia-Deliveroo-dic-2020-Original-italiano.pdf
97. *Ekker*, "Dutch Court Rules on Data Transparency for Uber and Ola Drivers", https://ekker.legal/en/2021/03/13/dutch-court-rules-on-data-transparency-for-uber-and-ola-drivers/
98. ILO, "Decent Work in the Platform Economy", reference document for the Meeting of Experts on Decent Work in the Platform Economy, Geneva, 10–14 October 2022, pp. 33–4, https://www.ilo.org/wcmsp5/groups/public/%2D%2D-ed_norm/%2D%2D-relconf/documents/meetingdocument/wcms_855048.pdf

99. ILO, *Work for a Brighter Future: Global Commission on the Future of Work*, Geneva, 2019, https://www.ilo.org/global/publications/books/WCMS_662410/lang%2D%2Den/index.htm
100. ILO Centenary Declaration for the Future of Work, 2019, https://www.ilo.org/wcmsp5/groups/public/@ed_norm/@relconf/documents/meetingdocument/wcms_711674.pdf
101. See recommendations of ILO, *World Employment and Social Outlook 2021*.
102. See Ilaria Espa, Joseph Francois and Harro van Asselt, "The EU Proposal for a Carbon Border Adjustment Mechanism (CBAM): An Analysis under WTO and Climate Change Law", World Trade Institute Working Paper 06/2022, 2022, https://www.wti.org/media/filer_public/ee/61/ee6171fd-a68d-4829-875e-d9b0c32298b5/wti_working_paper_06_2022.pdf
103. See for example Ilaria Espa, Joseph Francois and Harro van Asselt, "The EU Proposal for a Carbon Border Adjustment Mechanism (CBAM): An Analysis under WTO and Climate Change Law," World Trade Institute Working Paper 6/2022, https://www.wti.org/media/filer_public/ee/61/ee6171fd-a68d-4829-875e-d9b0c32298b5/wti_working_paper_06_2022.pdf
104. The following discussion draws from and builds upon Richard Samans, "The Paris Accord Won't Stop Global Warming on Its Own", *Foreign Policy*, 26 September 2018, https://foreignpolicy.com/2018/09/26/the-paris-accord-wont-stop-global-warming-on-its-own/. See also Gary Hufbauer, Ricardo Melendez-Ortiz and Richard Samans, eds, *The Law and Economics of a Sustainable Energy Trade Agreement*, Cambridge, UK, Cambridge University Press, 2016; Richard Samans, Ricardo Melendez-Ortiz, Harsha Singh and Sean Doherty, *E15 Initiative Synthesis Report: Strengthening the Global Trade and Investment System in the 21st Century*, Geneva, World Economic Forum, 2016, https://www.researchgate.net/publication/321341819_Strengthening_the_Global_Trade_and_Investment_System_in_the_21st_Century_-_Synthesis_Report
105. https://www.carbonpricingleadership.org/
106. https://www.there100.org/about-us
107. https://www.fsb-tcfd.org/
108. Hufbauer et al., *The Law and Economics of a Sustainable Energy Trade Agreement*.
109. OECD, *OECD Companion to the Inventory of Support Measures for Fossil Fuels 2018*, Paris, 2018, https://www.oecd.org/environment/oecd-companion-to-the-inventory-of-support-measures-for-fossil-fuels-2018-9789264286061-en.htm
110. https://www.blendedfinance.earth/better-finance-better-world
111. http://mission-innovation.net/

112. G7 Germany 2022, "Terms of Reference for the Climate Club", 12 December 2022, https://www.g7germany.de/resource/blob/974430/2153140/a04dde2adecf0ddd38cb9829a99c322d/2022-12-12-g7-erklaerung-data.pdf?download=1
113. OECD, "OECD Secretary-General Report to G20 Finance Ministers and Central Bank Governors on the Establishment of the Inclusive Forum on Carbon Mitigation Approaches", October 2022, https://www.oecd.org/g20/topics/international-taxation/oecd-secretary-general-report-g20-finance-ministers-central-bank-governors-establishment-ifcma-indonesia-october-2022.pdf
114. New Zealand Foreign Affairs and Trade, "Agreement on Climate Change, Trade and Sustainability (ACCTS) Negotiations", https://www.mfat.govt.nz/en/trade/free-trade-agreements/trade-and-climate/agreement-on-climate-change-trade-and-sustainability-accts-negotiations/
115. See Barbados Ministry of Foreign Affairs and Foreign Trade, "The 2022 Bridgetown Initiative", 23 September 2022, https://www.foreign.gov.bb/the-2022-barbados-agenda/
116. See, for example, the discussion of "modular multilateralization" in Samans et al., *E15 Initiative Synthesis Report*.
117. See, for example, E. Helleiner, *Forgotten Foundations of Bretton Woods: International Development and the Making of the Postwar Order*, Ithaca, NY, Cornell University Press, 2014.

Open Access This chapter is licensed under the terms of the Creative Commons Attribution 4.0 International License (http://creativecommons.org/licenses/by/4.0/), which permits use, sharing, adaptation, distribution and reproduction in any medium or format, as long as you give appropriate credit to the original author(s) and the source, provide a link to the Creative Commons licence and indicate if changes were made.

The images or other third party material in this chapter are included in the chapter's Creative Commons licence, unless indicated otherwise in a credit line to the material. If material is not included in the chapter's Creative Commons licence and your intended use is not permitted by statutory regulation or exceeds the permitted use, you will need to obtain permission directly from the copyright holder.

CHAPTER 7

Conclusion: Building on Keynes's Middle Way to Renew the Liberal Tradition and Multilateral System in the 21st Century

For nearly 250 years, economists have investigated with increasing precision the functioning of markets as a driver of resource allocation efficiency, capital accumulation and national wealth creation. Enormous advances in understanding have been achieved in this regard. Political economy, by contrast, is the craft of contextualizing markets, anchoring them in the service of society's broader objectives through what the field's founders called "human institution". It has receded in importance relative to economic science as an intellectual discipline and has been particularly lacking in the recent exercise of liberal economics, which for all practical purposes has conflated economic growth with socioeconomic progress and thus grossly underinvested in the institutions that enable social inclusion, environmental sustainability and human resilience and dignity.

This neoliberal experiment has frustrated the aspiration for faster and wider improvement in living standards in many countries despite their considerable economic growth; it has left a legacy of undue inequality and insecurity, leaving far too many people to compensate by working harder, incurring more debt or doing without, in spite of the overall scale of resources available within their country's economy. John Maynard Keynes had warned Friedrich Hayek about this prospect in a letter two years before his death: "Your greatest danger ahead is the probable practical failure of the application of your philosophy in the U.S. in a fairly extreme form."[1]

The original version of the chapter has been revised. A correction to this chapter can be found at https://doi.org/10.1007/978-3-031-37435-7_8

© The Author(s) 2024, corrected publication 2024
R. Samans, *Human-Centred Economics*,
https://doi.org/10.1007/978-3-031-37435-7_7

We are living now in Keynes's proverbial "long run". He made the famous quip that "in the long run we are all dead" in 1923 as a provocative rejoinder to the confident assumption of neoclassical liberalism's more doctrinaire proponents that market economies have an innate capacity to self-correct over time in response to socially unjust disequilibria, such as high unemployment.[2] He deployed his dry wit in this way to puncture and indeed lampoon the implicit trickle-down, self-regulatory mental model at the heart of neoclassical liberal economic doctrine.

To be sure, Keynes considered himself a liberal. He was an unabashed believer in the superiority of distributed economic decision-making—in this central insight of Adam Smith.[3] But he had equal conviction as a critic of the self-regulatory ethos of ordoliberalism or what is now called "neoliberalism". He came to see the bulk of his life's work as fleshing out what his biographer Lord Robert Skidelsky and others have called a "Middle Way" between laissez-faire market economics and centrally planned socialism.[4] This evolutionary journey culminated in *The General Theory of Employment, Interest and Money*, but he never felt that he had fully completed this intellectual project.

Keynes understood that the macroeconomic strategies he advocated were blunt instruments, "coarse tuning" in modern parlance, for the regulation of the great engine of market-driven output so that it runs more smoothly in social and political terms—that is to say, in terms of social justice and cohesion and thus political stability and peace. Like Smith, Mill and Marshall, he was acutely conscious of the social context of his work, of the larger purpose of economics. He had come to prominence as a sharp critic of the Treaty of Versailles following the First World War, whose draconian, socially unjust economic terms he just as presciently argued would sow the seeds of future conflict.[5]

Towards a General Theory of Institutions, Distribution and Welfare

This book can be read as an attempt to build upon the tradition of Keynes's Middle Way, which has fallen into a state of partial neglect, misinterpretation and disrepute during the past forty years of neoliberalism's ascendancy. In effect, it tries to help raise that fallen standard and hoist it to new heights in the twenty-first century by supplementing the mainly macroeconomic strategy Keynes pioneered with the systematic institutional counterpart described in Chap. 4. It further stylizes and instrumentalizes the Middle Way by conceptualizing and providing a basis for measuring countries' social welfare gaps, their areas of underperformance on median household living standards, including but not limited to employment opportunity, relative to countries having similar GDP per capita. I argue that policymakers need to be as focused on this *welfare* gap as on the output gap of their economy, which is to say at least as much on strengthening the economy's institutionally enabled aggregate distribution function, or social contract, as on increasing its market-enabled production of goods and services. This is the golden rule of human-centred economics, which for all intents and purposes is a framework for rebalancing the discipline's focus from the top to the bottom line of national economic performance, from the total production of goods and services or wealth of nations (GDP) to the median living standards of their people.

Keynes's use of fiscal and monetary policy to support the economy's propensity to consume and incentive to invest in order to boost employment and discourage less-productive, rent-seeking use of capital is essentially a production function strategy. It seeks to narrow the output gap particularly through fiscal policy's contribution to consumption and monetary policy's contribution to low interest rates and investor hurdle rates, thereby raising real economy investment and pushing the economy closer to the frontier of its potential output. In other words, it operates top-down through the main macro-channels that influence GDP or the quantity of growth, albeit often with important secondary effects on the quality of growth (e.g., through the higher real wages that tend to accompany tighter job markets).

The human-centred, living-standards-oriented approach described in these pages is a complementary "distribution function" strategy. It seeks to narrow an economy's welfare gap by systematically applying policy and institutional strategies that together increase the diffusion of gains to living standards across the economy at the household level. It supports the material well-being, prospects and security of people more directly, through a more comprehensive and concerted application of labour, social protection, financial regulation, corporate governance, anti-trust and anti-corruption, infrastructure and other measures. In other words, it operates bottom-up to improve the social *quality* of growth, albeit often with important secondary effects on the quantity of growth (e.g., through higher labour force participation and productivity and increased aggregate demand as a result of greater human capability and agency and stronger household disposable income, purchasing power and consumption).

These principles and proposals are fundamentally an agenda to strengthen the relationship between economic growth and broad progress in living standards—to rebalance the standard liberal economic growth and development model by institutionalizing inclusion, sustainability and resilience in the way that market economies develop. They are the building blocks of what might be considered a general theory of institutions, distribution and welfare. Concerted, systematic use of them would effectively open a second lane within the Middle Way, a strategy of sustained institutional deepening to complement that of Keynes's periodic fiscal and monetary coarse tuning. In other words, they offer the possibility of running an economy relatively "hot" on a stable and sustainable basis—that is to say, closer to the level of its potential productive output *and* social welfare based on the ongoing strengthening of its fundamentals (structural and institutional foundations) rather than the transitory and often difficult-to-time application of macroeconomic stimulus.

From an academic perspective, human-centred economics can be interpreted as adding a practical macroeconomic dimension to the subdiscipline of welfare economics, which has had a rather abstract, largely microeconomic focus for nearly a century. The foundation for it is a simple model of the main channels by which rising living standards propagate in an economy at the household level: the five areas of employment and entrepreneurial opportunity; disposable income; access to and affordability of material necessities; economic security; and environmental security. This "aggregate distribution function" is then translated into a policy framework, a map of the principal domains of policy and institutional strength that influence the transmission of higher household living standards through each of these five channels. This is an actionable framework for substantially improving the lived experience and material security and prospects of people throughout society, provided that governments invest in and across it on an ongoing basis as a core element of their growth and development strategy.

Chapter 5 provided extensive data demonstrating that all countries have considerable policy space to narrow their economy's welfare gap, that is, their performance on one or more such aspects of median living standards relative to the frontier of leading policy practice of peer countries. By benchmarking their policy and institutional strengths and weaknesses, and investing in and learning from their peers with respect to the latter, they can significantly improve the lived experience of their people. I call this moving closer to the frontier of their economy's living standards potential, analogous to the concept of a country's growth potential. I define aggregate social welfare for macroeconomic purposes as a function of the combination of and interaction between the aggregate production and distribution functions and suggest that much more research is needed to better understand and improve guidance to policymakers on their relative importance and synergies as well as those of their constituent factors.

This internalization of the social contract in macroeconomic theory and policy would re-anchor modern economic science in its classical political economy foundation in a key sense. Smith, J.S. Mill, Alfred Marshall and other pioneers of the field consciously contextualized markets in the more fundamental quest for broad improvement in social welfare, for the amelioration of the human condition. Each in his own words emphasized the need for markets to be accompanied by a strong social contract of institutional arrangements for this purpose. But the link between the social contract and economics has remained ill-defined and ad hoc over the years. The approach outlined in this book is an attempt to treat it in a more structured and thus actionable manner, thereby giving liberal economics a distinctly more human-centred—that is, more inclusive, sustainable and resilient—character. This is what is required to move beyond the Washington Consensus paradigm of growth and development to what I call a "Roosevelt Consensus" in recognition of the central emphasis the two presidents Roosevelt placed on the institutional construction of the social contract through the Square Deal and New Deal, respectively, during the United States' rapid industrialization in the early to mid 1900s.

It is well past time to move beyond the big-versus-small-government and socialism-versus-capitalism polemics of the twentieth century. The entire world is now living in Keynes's Middle Way to one degree or another; essentially every country operates a mixed, market-based economy as illustrated in the Social Market–Market Socialism Corporate Governance Continuum presented in Chap. 5. In effect, that policy continuum, together with its sister Financialization–Real Economy Investment Financial Regulation Continuum and the Fiscal Expenditure and Revenue and the Decent Work Indicator Reference Ranges also presented in that chapter, provide more modern and precise flight instrumentation for countries wishing to chart their course and monitor progress along the Middle Way.

These practical tools and the theoretical construct underpinning them address what is arguably the central challenge facing economics in this century: how to strengthen growth while rendering it more inclusive, sustainable and resilient; indeed how to achieve the former *through* the latter. Human-centred economics has the potential to better capture the positive synergies between the pace and pattern of economic development and thereby to reverse the current *negative* synergy between liberal economics and politics.

The long-standing disconnect between production and distribution, markets and institutions, and growth and broad living standards in the teaching and practice of liberal economics has had a history of generating serious and at times violent social and political conflict. The ongoing failure to properly confront it is a growing strategic liability for the liberal tradition in a century characterized by rapid change and not infrequent upheaval in economic life. Business as usual in economic policy under these circumstances risks a further decoupling of growth from equity, sustainability and resilience. It risks a further corrosion of the sense of hope and shared destiny that broadly rising living standards inspire in societies and a corresponding erosion of social cohesion and popular trust in political institutions and leaders. Such a dynamic is toxic to the liberal values of rule of law, human rights, social tolerance and dialogue. The response to it therefore merits urgent and decisive action rather than the complacent and incremental current pace of reform.

This goes for international economic governance and cooperation as well. Like in Keynes's time, a rebalanced Middle Way or Roosevelt Consensus approach to economic policy at the national level requires a reinforcing international policy agenda. As a chief architect of the postwar international economic system, Keynes was very focused on monetary issues, particularly the maintenance of sufficient liquidity and avoidance of deflationary pressures in the context of a system of fixed exchange rates linked to gold. In Chap. 6, I have elaborated an ambitious but politically and financially feasible reform agenda addressing serious contemporary international liquidity constraints. These include the difficult financial position of poor countries with limited fiscal space and large unmet social needs; the enormous gap in financing needed to accelerate the climate transition in line with the scientific community's recommended timeline for emissions reductions; and a systemic misallocation of private capital that handicaps progress on both of these challenges as well as others. Grossly insufficient public investment and misaligned private investment are suppressing economic growth and employment opportunity in much of the world economy, aggravating already acute social justice deficits such as vast youth employment and informal sector underemployment and growing working poverty in many developing countries as well as some developed ones. These problems are combining with the spectre of increased precarity from the spread of automation beyond manufacturing into many services and the ongoing urbanization and saturation of cities and slums in poor countries to pose a growing danger to peace and stability within and among countries.

The international community was supposed to have learned the dangers of complacency in the face of such dangers in the last century. It enshrined the principle that social justice is the ultimate foundation of peace in the ILO Constitution in 1919 following the "war to end all wars", Spanish influenza pandemic and Bolshevik Revolution, and it constructed a vast architecture of related norms and institutions following the Second World War, notably through the United Nations system and Bretton Woods institutions that Keynes helped create. But actual and perceived deficits in social justice are once again visibly tearing the social fabric of nations at all levels of economic development. Social frustration and political cynicism are spilling over into international relations, undermining the cohesion and stability of a multilateral system that was inspired by liberal values and the better angels of human nature.

To be certain, geopolitical tensions are also roiling the waters of international relations. But deficits in social and environmental justice are likely to deepen in the coming years as environmental, technological, demographic and other changes accelerate. Absent a major change in course by the international community, they could well accumulate to the point of endangering the economic and political stability of many countries at once, posing an existential threat to the multilateral system—to the liberal norms that have more or less succeeded in regulating the behaviour of states for the past 75 years. The UN Secretary-General has warned as much in his recent report on the future of multilateral cooperation, *Our Common Agenda*.[6] If projections about the human and social implications of these transformations are anywhere near accurate, then shifting the prevailing economic growth and development model from a pushing-on-a-string, trickle-down mode to a people-centred, environmentally sustainable dynamic becomes a social, economic and political imperative—a *sine qua non* for the survival of the liberal tradition and multilateral system.

THE IMPERATIVE TRINITY OF HUMAN-CENTRED ECONOMICS

In the 1970s and 1980s, there was a big debate about the extent to which an inherent trade-off existed between efficiency and equity, that is to say, between growth and social inclusion.[7] Echoes of that debate can be heard in the more recent polemic about the extent to which pro-growth policies are inherently unpopular, i.e., that good economics sometimes requires a dose of strong, socially distasteful medicine and for this reason democracies are at a disadvantage to governments less subject to regular popular electoral scrutiny. There is a germ of truth in both of these arguments; economic policymakers do sometimes face difficult trade-offs and dilemmas, some tractable and others more deep-seated or even inherent. A famous example of the latter is the Mundell–Fleming "impossible trinity" or "trilemma" of international monetary policy, namely that a country cannot pursue an independent monetary policy, maintain a fixed exchange rate and allow the free flow of capital across its borders at the same time—only two of the three are possible.[8]

Human-centred economics is the opposite of a trilemma. It presents not a quandary of three incompatible choices but the possibility of a trifecta of synergistic social and environmental, economic and political outcomes. It represents not just a possible trinity but an indispensable or imperative one for individual societies and economies as well as the world economy and international order as a whole. It represents a "triperative", so to speak.

This triple imperative is achievable if policymakers refocus their attention from the top to the bottom line of national economic performance, from growth to aggregate social welfare, from the wealth to the living standards of nations. In practical terms, this means choosing carefully where they wish to position their economies on the Social Market–Market Socialism Corporate Governance and Financialization–Real Economy Investment Financial Regulation continua, since this determines what kind of mixed economy they wish to have and how actively they wish to incentivize financial intermediation to serve the real economy and discourage it from financing rentier behaviour. At the same time, it means increasing investment in people across the weaker dimensions of their economy's aggregate distribution function or social contract on a systematic and ongoing basis, possibly using as their guide international reference ranges such as those presented in Chap. 5 pertaining to fiscal expenditure and revenue as well as decent work. Moreover, it means voting for the combined redeployment of international economic institutions to better support this agenda through the restructuring of their priorities and activities with respect to macroeconomic analysis and advice, development and climate financing, and trade and technology rules and facilitation, as outlined in Chap. 6.

I have gone to considerable lengths in these pages to spell out the social and environmental side of this triperative—how shifting to a human-centred, living-standards orientation in economic theory and policy is the key to improving inclusion, sustainability and resilience. Human-centred economics is fundamentally a strategy to invest more in people and to do so more directly across multiple dimensions of their material quality of life. Strengthening the social contracts of countries would certainly improve the distributional fairness and environmental sustainability of their economies, including by protecting the most vulnerable. There is much that can be done to strengthen median living standards in countries at every level of GDP per capita and thereby create a more just society that better fulfils the universal rights of people enshrined in the ICESCR.

However, human-centred economics is also an economic imperative in the current circumstances. It is a strategy to increase economic growth by broadening its base and strengthening its resilience. Investing more in people through tangible improvements in their household purchasing power, financial security, social protection, skills and access to decent work strengthens aggregate demand, worker productivity and investor and consumer confidence—the fundamental determinants of growth.

Such an added bottom-up impetus to growth could scarcely come at a better time for economies around the world that are struggling to wean themselves from a decade of unsustainable top-down monetary and fiscal stimulus. While crucial to stabilizing their economies during the Great Financial Crisis and COVID-19 pandemic, that growth engine has run its course, and much less policy space remains for a new round of massive deficit spending or liquidity expansion. A new engine is required not only for this reason but also because of the real possibility that generative artificial intelligence and machine learning will hollow out employment, purchasing power and aggregate demand over the next generation as much or more than digitization and globalization did during the last one. Deep decarbonization and population ageing are likely to complicate matters further, additionally disrupting the world of work.

Domestic action to improve the living-standards diffusion mechanism of economies could help to resist any secular softening of aggregate demand from these transformations, while facilitating a more orderly and socially just transition to them. At the same time, international action to redeploy the principal multilateral economic institutions to increase support for developing countries that pursue these strategies, including by overcoming the global misallocation of capital that restricts their access to financing, would support aggregate demand and economic growth in the world economy still further. By feeding this global macroeconomic virtuous circle—structurally increasing the "propensity to consume and inducement to invest" within and across countries, to invoke Keynes's framework of analysis—the application of human-centred economics has the potential to lift the living standards of all nations. It looks to be the most viable available strategy for reinvigorating the win–win, positive-sum-game promise of liberal economics in an international community that has been demonstrably losing faith in it.

This new *structural* form of demand and supply management is particularly suited to twenty-first-century circumstances, in particular to the income- and opportunity-dispersing effects of digitalization, disruptive labour market effects of decarbonization and population ageing, and enormous pent-up social demands for greater social inclusion, environmental sustainability and human resilience and dignity. This reformulation of structural economic reform, or Roosevelt Consensus model of growth and development, boils down to devoting at least as much attention to investing in and measuring the progress of key elements of an economy's aggregate distribution function as those of its aggregate production function, and doing so as an integral part of a country's development strategy. This ongoing process of institutional deepening has the potential to narrow both the output gap and welfare gap of economies. Indeed, it makes added progress on the former by addressing the latter.

For this reason, governments should expand their macroeconomic targeting and measurement beyond the familiar targets and metrics corresponding to the quantity of economic growth (e.g., GDP growth, inflation, etc.) to those corresponding to the five "factors of distribution" in their aggregate distribution functions, which relate to the social *quality* of growth. Some countries have been doing so for many years, such as China with respect to employment.[9] Others are experimenting with metrics and targets in other aspects of the aggregate distribution function, such as New Zealand's Living Standards Framework,[10] India's Ease of Living Index[11] and the non-governmental Cost of Thriving Index developed in the United States.[12] The Wellbeing Economy Alliance is a growing coalition of jurisdictions experimenting with a wide range of such alternative economic policy approaches.[13]

The key aim should be to rebalance the focus of policy from liberal economics' traditional emphasis on financial and physical capital accumulation to investment in the institutional drivers of progress in median living standards, people's lived experience, defined by the policy framework presented in Chap. 4. This two-lens—growth-and-living-standards, production-and-distribution, markets-and-institutions—perspective on economic policy produces a sharper image of economic policy performance and policy priorities, similar to the way that people see better out of two eyes than one. It also improves the resolution of objects in motion in the sense that it offers a framework for operationalizing the still largely aspirational concept of just transition, whether with respect to climate change, automation, urbanization or other economic shifts and shocks.

Consider climate change, the most urgent just transition challenge facing policymakers and economists. The jury is still out regarding whether economic growth can be sufficiently decoupled from pollution to avert the environmental catastrophe that scientists project will occur later this century based on humanity's current greenhouse gas emissions trajectory. Judging from the evidence to date, such decoupling is highly unlikely absent a paradigmatic shift in economics and economic policy.

Over the next generation, humanity will need to chart a new Middle Way in economics, this time between environmentally destructive growth and socially destructive stagnation or degrowth. In a world that still suffers from extensive poverty and social injustice, deliberate economic contraction to lower emissions is simply not politically realistic. But changing the composition of growth—improving its social quality while reducing its environmental externalities—might be. A new neoclassical-Keynesian-ecological synthesis in economics will be needed to chart this course and arrive at the destination of the major decoupling of economic progress from environmental degradation implied by the Paris climate agreement.

Constructing this new synthesis would appear to be the paramount challenge facing economic scholarship and policymaking in the 2020s and 2030s. Navigating an economically, socially and environmentally viable course between the prevailing resource-intensive model of economic growth and development and the steady-state economics many ecological economists believe is necessary to meet this challenge (let alone the more radical degrowth prescriptions of some of their colleagues) will ultimately depend on the innovative design and deployment of institutions—legal and other norms, policy incentives and public administrative capacities. One need not subscribe to the institutional approach advocated by the foremost theorist of steady-state economics, Herman Daly, (broadly speaking, regulatory caps on and the trading of natural resources and reproductive rights) to recognize that far greater extra-market intervention will be required by governments to achieve the decoupling of economic and social progress from fossil fuel energy consumption implied by their mid-century net-zero emissions commitments, of which 70 such targets had been set as of mid-2023.

Transforming the neoclassical-Keynesian synthesis model of growth and development that has endured for the past three-quarters of a century by systematically internalizing within it the institutional drivers of a green and socially just transition to a net zero world will require a different model of economic growth and development. The aggregate social welfare and aggregate distribution functions outlined in Chap. 4 provide the foundations of such a model to guide this rebalancing of national economic policy and international economic governance and cooperation. Use of these theoretical constructs and their accompanying policy framework would help to impose a certain discipline and accountability on the process, pushing economists and policymakers to strive to "solve simultaneously" for: a) growth and poverty reduction through the more efficient resource allocation techniques taught by neoclassical economics; b) full employment in decent work and social justice through robust utilization of fiscal and monetary policy as taught by Keynes and his intellectual heirs; and c) decarbonization and other critical aspects of environmental sustainability within planetary boundaries taught by ecological economics. Of course, framing and adopting a better mental model of economic progress is just half the battle; filling in the details of its implementation will be even more important and is far from straightforward. That is why practical policy and empirical research as well as education and capacity building in support of this new synthesis policy innovation, investment and integration agenda will be so important; it must become the central calling of the economics community and a high priority of adjacent social and hard sciences in academia and international organizations going forward.

Daly considered his vision of steady-state and broader ecological economics as representing a practical challenge ultimately governed by the laws of nature rather than any particular brand of politics. He believed his precepts transcended the traditional left-right political framework of analysis, as he viewed socialism and capitalism as both being caught up in "growth-mania" and thus distracted from the more fundamental requirements—the ultimate means and ultimate ends—of natural capital and social welfare, respectively.[14] This is similar to the human-centred and living standards-oriented approach to economics elaborated in these pages, which is based on its own structural critique of the neoclassical synthesis, calling out its blind spot regarding the crucial role of institutions in addressing the wider distributional considerations of inclusion, sustainability and resilience. I have argued that the systematic institutional manifestation of the social contract is the missing link of macroeconomic theory and policy practice. It is tantamount to the dark matter of development economics—a highly consequential but barely recognized force that exerts a profound influence on both the productive transformation of and propagation of living standards within economies, every bit as important as the force neoclassical economics has succeeded in making so visible to students and policymakers: factor accumulation through market-based allocative efficiency.

For those wondering how countries will be able to afford the sustained investment in their social contracts necessary to render their development more inclusive, sustainable and resilient, recall the comparative data presented in Chap. 5 demonstrating that a large number of countries at every level of economic development have ample fiscal space to increase domestic resource mobilization (taxes and fees) quite substantially even if only to the median level of their peers. And as for countries with a high ratio of tax receipts to GDP relative to their cohort, there is often plenty of room for expanding revenues by raising or shifting taxes to pollution and wealth, reducing subsidies enjoyed by wealthier segments of the population, and accounting in a more economically rational way for investments that increase their country's growth potential over the medium to long term (e.g., measures to expand labour force participation, skilling, technical progress and diffusion, and sustainable infrastructure). These expenditures warrant some degree of amortization of costs, and thus financing over several years or more, because they contribute to an enlargement of the economy over time and are thus different in character than government expenditures financing current consumption.

Indeed, one size will not fit all in the pursuit of this new synthesis. Policy and institutional mixes will differ according to political, economic, historical, demographic and other circumstances. Some advanced economies, such as Japan, are already demonstrating important characteristics of a steady state economy, e.g., very low rates of economic growth driven in part by low or outright negative population growth. They are already focusing on the goal of improving social welfare even in the absence of meaningful GDP growth through technological and policy innovation. Many poorer countries are looking to leapfrog the traditional carbon-intensive pathways of industrial development through the same.

The concepts and tools of human-centred economics presented in Chaps. 4 and 5 provide the recalibrated macroeconomic policy compass needed to navigate this new Middle Way—this neoclassical-Keynesian-ecological synthesis—on a country-by-country, polity-by-polity basis. At the same time, the major renovation of the international economic architecture outlined in Chap. 6 would promote the global coherence and sufficiency of such national efforts relative to the performance requirements humanity has set in the Sustainable Development Goals, Paris climate and Kunming-Montreal biodiversity targets and ILO Centenary Declaration for the Future of Work objectives.

The Political Imperative: Revitalizing the Liberal Tradition and Multilateral System

Human-centred economics and the new neoclassical-Keynesian-ecological synthesis it could help create would have the effect of bringing economics full circle, back to the original two-lens vision of Smith, Mill and Marshall, who viewed better markets and stronger growth as a necessary but not sufficient means to address the social injustices of their day. They were apprehensive about growing popular dissatisfaction with the working and living conditions of the Industrial Revolution and the risks these posed to political stability. Today, too, rapid technological change and environmental and demographic trends are creating powerful headwinds for governments and political parties of all philosophical stripes by exerting powerful centrifugal forces on their societies. These threaten to exacerbate inequality and insecurity beyond levels already elevated by decades of digitalisation and globalisation as well as the financial, pandemic and cost-of-living crises of the past 15 years. This dynamic is undermining social cohesion and fuelling political polarization in countries at every level of economic development irrespective of system of government.

Social fear is palpable at the prospect of a perfect economic storm in the second quarter of the twenty-first century consisting of a climate emergency and generative artificial intelligence-driven disruption of service sector employment, exacerbated by rapid population aging and the ripple effects of geopolitical tensions on international trade and investment. Perfect storm or not, these disruptive forces are likely to exert enormous additional pressure on the social fabric and political order within countries as well as on a multilateral system that was designed to move international relations finally beyond the law of the jungle.

These socioeconomically based political headwinds are particularly evident in liberal democracies, where they have combined with controversies over immigration and identity as well as the digital disintermediation of media to create enormous challenges for the political establishments of both right and left. These are countries that tend to have a particularly strong embrace of standard liberal economics and to be situated on the lefthand, less interventionist side of the Social Market–Market Socialism Corporate Governance Continuum and its Financialization-Real Economy Investment Financial Regulation Continuum counterpart. Some critics from countries whose forms of governance place them on the righthand side have recently taken to needling their liberal democratic counterparts by suggesting that their own comparatively statist political systems are inherently better suited to mobilizing the long-term real economy investments that are necessary to drive both robust economic growth and broadly based social development.

Such criticisms strike a nerve. They imply that liberalism is innately flawed—that there is a serious bug if not outright design defect in its governance operating system. These debates have contributed to the growing body of soul-searching analysis by liberals and provocations by liberalism's critics since the Great Financial Crisis.[15]

This book has sought to demonstrate that the problem is decidedly a recent bug rather than congenital flaw. The design principles laid down by the discipline's most influential founders and codifiers were sound. But a lopsided mental model of growth and development and a corresponding set of disequilibrating policy reflexes have crept into the practice of liberal economics, particularly during the past half-century.

Rising inequality and insecurity are not an iron law of capitalism or technological progress, and the choice that countries face in confronting them is not between big and small government or between socialism and capitalism. There are multiple policy and institutional levers that governments of all philosophical traditions can pull to mobilize a combined attack on the problem. The key is to recognize the critical role this structural policy ecosystem plays in shaping the inclusive and sustainable growth performance of economies and to place at least as high a priority on strengthening it as top economists and policymakers in government (most of whom are macroeconomists and bankers) have traditionally placed on improving allocative efficiency and macro-financial stability.

In today's digitally and environmentally disruptive and globally integrated economy, more direct investment in people and the practical aspects of their standard of living is the key to not only a more equitable society but also a more rapidly growing and sustainable economy. The talent, purchasing power and fair employment and entrepreneurial opportunity of people are fundamental determinants of national economic success. Ensuring that these are widely distributed across society—instead of pumping more money at owners of capital and hoping that it trickles down through their increased investment activity—is what is most important for the strength of a nation's economy and social fabric in this day and age.

In other words, a systemic–theoretical modernization of the economic model itself is required rather than patches or palliatives that address the symptoms of its shortcomings. Big-bang, silver-bullet interventions, including macroeconomic ones, should be treated with caution and considered in this larger context. The problems of inequality and economic and environmental insecurity are most effectively addressed through a more comprehensive and sustained effort to upgrade a country's growth model and social contract, including in areas in which relatively weak or underdeveloped policy incentives and institutions are behind much of the inequality, exclusion and unsustainable natural resource depletion that markets are producing in the first place. Macroeconomic stimulus or "coarse tuning" has an important role to play, including by financing these structural–institutional improvements, but it is only one and, depending on the country's circumstances, not necessarily the most important tool.

This fundamental critique corresponds more closely than the traditional political narratives of the centre-right and centre-left to the growing unease of citizens with their country's economic performance. People instinctively sense that political and business leaders have been neglecting their economy's fundamentals, especially the most important one: *them*. Strengthening skills, consumer purchasing power and business and public investment in the real economy would lift labour productivity, disposable income and aggregate demand. Adapting power, transport, water and industrial infrastructure to the requirements of the Paris climate and Kunming-Montreal biodiversity agreements would also boost employment and median incomes. Assessed against the bottom-line metric of national economic success—broad progress in living standards—these would be far more effective uses of additional public expenditures than, for example, the cuts in individual, corporate, estate and other capital income taxes that are the mainstay of trickle-down economics. A win–win–win—higher growth with greater equity and lower risk—result for the economy becomes possible when policy choices are viewed from the bottom-up, household perspective of human-centred economics rather than the top-down, corporate-boardroom vantage point of its trickle-down counterpart.

In other words, human-centred economics is kitchen-table economics—economics that is tangibly relevant to everyone. As such, it has the potential to help turn the political tide against the threat of demagogic populism and erosion of rule of law and human rights in countries facing widespread voter disillusionment and disaffection over the stagnation of living standards and hollowing out or otherwise limited prospect of industrial employment. If framed in the language of the universal values of equal access and opportunity as well as freedom from want and discrimination, the principles and tools of human-centred economics, while progressive and universalist in a Rooseveltian and United Nations Charter sense, have the potential to appeal to a much larger political coalition than either the establishment right or left currently commands.

The political affinities of people in many countries are in motion in a way they have not been for a generation or more. Especially in the wake of recent crises, people are impatient for major change. A full-court press of domestic and foreign economic policy reforms aiming to improve more directly their lived experience—making multiple aspects of their households' standard of living rather than GDP the unit of analysis and top policy priority—might impress citizens sufficiently to overcome the distraction and cynicism that have infected the political culture of so many countries in recent years.

Former US President Trump had a point when, upon announcing his candidacy in 2016, he warned about the death of the American Dream of serial generational progress in living standards. And former UK Prime Minister Truss also had a point when in 2022 she called out her country's habitually weak economic growth performance. But the programmes of both represented another instalment of trickle-down fiscal and deregulatory stimulus that continued the error of mistaking growth as the end rather than means of economic policy. They were neither a direct nor a durable response to the weakened relationship between, and sometimes outright decoupling of, national wealth creation from median improvement in living standards. Over time, such an approach is likely to widen rather than narrow this gap, leaving in its wake a bigger public debt and even bigger missed opportunity to strengthen the economy's most valuable resource, its people. This hugely inefficient use of public resources and decreasingly effective growth and development model is an artifact of the late twentieth century and generally ill-suited to the challenges of the twenty-first century.

As argued in Chap. 1, if the planned-economy socialist experiment of the twentieth century failed because of its excessive focus on equity and control to the detriment of allocative efficiency and dynamism, the ongoing experiment in neoliberal capitalism is staring its own political failure in the face for the opposite reason—an unbalanced focus on efficiency and aggregate wealth creation over the breadth of the social payoff in terms of broad progress in living standards. This is what Keynes was warning Hayek about in his letter.

A comprehensive effort to elevate the practical aspects of the material quality of people's lives to the top priority of a country's economic strategy—reconstituting capitalism by locating and rectifying the original reason for its divergence from this course—has the potential to reorder the political landscape. An agenda to systematically strengthen the social contract in ways that relieve family budgets and bolster their employment prospects and security in the event of misfortune is highly relevant to entrepreneurs and workers, Millennials and Baby Boomers, conservatives and progressives, and foreign policy realists and activists alike. The kitchen-table focus of human-centred economics, combined with its sharp critique of the way that liberal economics has been applied in recent decades, gives it the potential to take the wind out of the sails of demagogic populism by providing a sharper contrast with the financial market trading desk logic of trickle-down economics.

However, liberals need to recognize that a more effective response to demagogic populism begins with the philosophical mea culpa in which human-centred economics is grounded—a fundamental critique of the prevailing trickle-down mental model of economic progress. This is the price of admission for political and business elites seeking to make common cause with the economic insecurity and sense of aggrievement of many of their fellow citizens. Such intellectual honesty, along with the fundamental, operating-system level of the proposed reforms, creates the potential for a different and more principled version of populism that exposes the false promises and short-term political expediency of its illiberal counterpart.

High-road liberal populism can defeat low-road illiberal populism if it genuinely constitutes a doctrinal shift in the way the economy is organized—that is, if it shows that the political and business establishments are ready to join in rewriting the rules of their country's growth model in a way that properly emphasizes the ongoing institutional deepening of its social contract, and if this is communicated in the language of universal aspirations and values, including particularly the responsibility of older generations to leave their country's economic fundamentals in sound shape for younger ones. By providing people with a clearer virtuous-circle vision of their country's and the world's economic future, human-centred economics has the potential to galvanize a big-tent, left–right, working- and-professional-class governing coalition of people more interested in getting ahead than putting other people down.

It is in this sense that this substantial reformulation of macroeconomics offers a lifeline to a proud if somewhat adrift liberal tradition in the twenty-first century. The major changes described in Chaps. 5 and 6 are what domestic and international economic policy would look like if they were guided by the bottom-line focus of human-centred economics on aggregate social welfare—on the median living standards at least as much as the aggregate wealth of nations. These are the most important reforms required to arrest the world economy's current descent into a zero-sum-game, law-of-the-jungle dynamic and the many risks that this entails for international peace and security. They would provide the economic, social and environmental policy basis for the profoundly liberal people-centric (versus state-centric) vision of international relations framed by the Commission on Human Security co-chaired by Sadako Ogata and Amartya Sen following the end of the Cold War and genocides in Cambodia, Rwanda and Bosnia.[16]

Nothing would bind developing countries more tightly to the liberal principles of the current international order than an effort led by rich countries to mobilize a massive, genuinely Marshall Plan-like US$2 trillion acceleration of investment in sustainable development—in jobs, basic necessities, social protection and environmental security—as outlined in Chap. 6, all of which is feasible within the existing resource envelopes and political mandates of the principal international economic institutions. And nothing else would generate more worldwide goodwill and diplomatic capital for the present multilateral system and its main underwriters over the course of the next generation than a crash effort to invest in the most important near-term (accelerated removal and replacement of coal-fired power plants) and long-term (doubling of renewable energy and low-carbon agriculture RD&D) elements of a global strategy to avert catastrophic climate change by mid-century. In effect, these and the other major reforms of international economic cooperation outlined in Chap. 6 would constitute a new *global* social contract[17] that reflects humanity's deeper level of interdependence in the twenty-first century and provides more sufficient support to countries seeking to strengthen their *national* social contracts through strategies such as those presented in Chaps. 4 and 5. The proposed Roosevelt Consensus model of economic growth and integration would enable countries around the world to activate the aggregate distribution function of their economies much more fully, hardwiring social solidarity into them by institutionalizing inclusion, sustainability and resilience in their rules, incentives and administrative capacities, and in the process bending the arc of global development in the direction of the foundational vision of social justice expressed in the Declaration of Philadelphia.

Thus, there are compelling social, environmental, economic and political reasons to shift liberal economic governance from a capital-centred, trickle-down to human-centred, level-up logic. The economic philosophy and policy prescriptions of human-centred economics provide the compass for a major course correction towards a more socially "embedded" form of liberalism.[18] By formally integrating into economics the critical role that institutions play in translating growth into broad progress in household living standards, these prescriptions lay the foundation for improving the political responsiveness of leaders to social demands for greater inclusion, sustainability and resilience. Such a fundamental rewiring of the liberal economic mind holds the key to moving the dismal science beyond its narrow concentration on allocative efficiency and capital accumulation to a more living standards-centred, lifting-all-boats construct that focuses at least as much on the seaworthiness and ecosystem stewardship of vessels and their crews as on the level of the tide. It is the combination of the two that ultimately determines whether the entire marina rises with and profits fully and sustainably from the sea's incoming bounty.

This doctrinal departure from trickle-down economics is actually a rediscovery of one of economics' first principles expressed throughout the writings of Adam Smith, John Stuart Mill and Alfred Marshall: the economy is a social construct that requires strong institutions in multiple domains if it is to fulfil its ultimate purpose of improving the general welfare of society. Re-embracing this old insight from the eighteenth and nineteenth centuries is what is required to revitalize the liberal tradition and multilateral system in the twenty-first century.

This journey begins by taking living standards more seriously in economic theory and policy and by contextualizing the crucial role of markets and economic growth in this wider conception of socioeconomic progress. It continues by recognizing that such progress requires an active role for political economy, not only markets, just as the original theorists and codifiers of the field envisioned.

Notes

1. J.M. Keynes, Letter to F.A. Hayek, 28 June 1944, in *The Collected Writings of John Maynard Keynes*, ed. Donald Moggridge and Elizabeth Johnson, London, Macmillan, 1978, Vol. 27, p. 387.
2. J.M. Keynes, *A Tract on Monetary Reform*, London, Macmillan, 1924, https://delong.typepad.com/keynes-1923-a-tract-on-monetary-reform-1.pdf
3. See, for example, J.M. Keynes, *The General Theory of Employment, Interest and Money*, London, Macmillan, 1936, Chapter 24, Section III.
4. See, for example, R. Skidelsky, *John Maynard Keynes 1883–1946: Economist, Philosopher, Statesman*, New York, Penguin, 2003, pp. 364–75.
5. J.M. Keynes, *The Economic Consequences of the Peace*, New York, Harcourt, Brace & Howe, 1920, https://gutenberg.org/cache/epub/15776/pg15776-images.html
6. United Nations, *Our Common Agenda*.
7. See, for example, Arthur M. Okun, *Equality and Efficiency: The Big Tradeoff*, Washington, DC, Brookings Institution, 1975.
8. See, for example, Rudiger Dornbusch, "Exchange Rate Expectations and Monetary Policy", *Journal of International Economics*, Vol. 6 (August 1976), pp. 231–44; Rudiger Dornbusch, "Expectations and Exchange Rate Dynamics", *Journal of Political Economy*, Vol. 84 (December 1976), pp. 1161–76; Rudiger Dornbusch, *Open Economy Macroeconomics*, New York, Basic Books, 1980.
9. See, for example, Yadong Wang, "Employment Policy Implementation Mechanisms in China", ILO Employment Research Brief, 2017, https://www.ilo.org/wcmsp5/groups/public/%2D%2D-ed_emp/documents/publication/wcms_613367.pdf; State Council, People's Republic of

China, "China to Take Further Steps for Job Growth and Employment Stability", 14 July 2022, https://english.www.gov.cn/premier/news/202207/14/content_WS62cef248c6d02e533532db65.html; Di Yan, "China's Employment Policies and Strategies", OECD and Chinese Academy of Labour and Social Security, 2006, https://www.oecd.org/employment/emp/37865430.pdf

10. See New Zealand Treasury, "The Living Standards Framework", 28 October 2021, https://www.treasury.govt.nz/sites/default/files/2021-10/tp-living-standards-framework-2021.pdf; New Zealand Treasury, "The Living Standards Framework Dashboard", 12 April 2022, https://www.treasury.govt.nz/system/files/2022-03/lsf-dashboard-apr22.pdf
11. https://eol2022.org/Home/AboutUs#:~:text=Ease%20of%20Living%202022&text=It%20provides%20a%20comprehensive%20understanding,and%20its%20sustainability%20and%20resilience.
12. Oren Cass, "The 2023 Cost-of-Thriving Index: Tracking the Catastrophic Erosion of Middle-Class Life in America", *American Compass*, February 2023, https://americancompass.org/wp-content/uploads/2023/02/COTI_2023_Final.pdf
13. https://weall.org/
14. See the "Daly Triangle" or hierarchical relationship between the human economy and the earth in H.E. Daly, Toward a Steady-State Economy, San Francisco: W.H. Freeman, 1973, p. 8 and as graphically represented in Rachael D. Garrett and Agnieszka E. Latawiec, "What are sustainability indicators for?" in Latawiec, A. E., Berlin (Ed.), *Sustainability Indicators*, De Gruyter, 2015, https://www.researchgate.net/figure/The-Daly-Triangle-relates-natural-capital-with-human-well-being-as-the-ultimate-human_fig1_280977342 based on Donella Meadows, "Indicators and Information Systems for Sustainable Development," The Sustainability Institute, 1998, pp. 41–42, https://donellameadows.org/wp-content/userfiles/IndicatorsInformation.pdf
15. See, for example, Patrick Deneen, *Why Liberalism Failed*, New Haven, Yale University Press, 2018; John Milbank and Adrian Pabst, *The Politics of Virtue: Post-liberalism and the Human Future*, London, Rowman & Littlefield, 2016; Robert Kagan, *The Jungle Grows Back: America and Our Imperiled World*, New York, Knopf, 2018.
16. Commission on Human Security, *Human Security Now: Protecting and Empowering People*, 2003. https://digitallibrary.un.org/record/503749?ln=en
17. See, for example, 346th Session of ILO Governing Body, "The World Needs a New Social Contract Says ILO Director-General", press release, 2 November 2022, https://www.ilo.org/global/about-the-ilo/newsroom/news/WCMS_859985/lang%2D%2Den/index.htm

18. See, in particular, K. Polanyi, *Origins of Our Time: The Great Transformation*, New York, Farrar & Rinehart, 1944; John Gerard Ruggie, "International Regimes, Transactions, and Change: Embedded Liberalism in the Postwar Economic Order", *International Organization*, Vol. 36, No. 2 (1982), pp. 379–415, https://www.jstor.org/stable/2706527

Open Access This chapter is licensed under the terms of the Creative Commons Attribution 4.0 International License (http://creativecommons.org/licenses/by/4.0/), which permits use, sharing, adaptation, distribution and reproduction in any medium or format, as long as you give appropriate credit to the original author(s) and the source, provide a link to the Creative Commons licence and indicate if changes were made.

The images or other third party material in this chapter are included in the chapter's Creative Commons licence, unless indicated otherwise in a credit line to the material. If material is not included in the chapter's Creative Commons licence and your intended use is not permitted by statutory regulation or exceeds the permitted use, you will need to obtain permission directly from the copyright holder.

Correction to: Human-Centred Economics

Correction to:
R. Samans, *Human-Centred Economics*,
https://doi.org/10.1007/978-3-031-37435-7

The following corrections have been made later to the original publication of this book:

Chapter 3

Pg 105. In the image named Pioneers of Human-Centered Economic Thought, one of the names was misspelled as Thorsten Veblen. The name has now been corrected as Thorstein Veblen.

The updated versions of the chapters can be found at
https://doi.org/10.1007/978-3-031-37435-7_3
https://doi.org/10.1007/978-3-031-37435-7_5
https://doi.org/10.1007/978-3-031-37435-7_6
https://doi.org/10.1007/978-3-031-37435-7_7

© The Author(s) 2024
R. Samans, *Human-Centred Economics*,
https://doi.org/10.1007/978-3-031-37435-7_8

C2

Chapter 5

Pg 135. In the second line of the third paragraph, the text "In conceptual terms, this is the difference between its current median household living standard relative and the level that would obtain…" has been corrected as "In conceptual terms, this is the difference between its current median household living standard relative to the level that would obtain…".

Pg 162. The following text: "(per USD 1 million investment)" has been added to the caption of figure 5.7.

Pg 163. The following text: "(percent of GDP)" has been added to the caption of figure 5.8.

Pg 171. The following text: "(% point change in gender gap in labour force participation rate 2012–21)" has been added to the caption of figure 5.9.

Pg 177. The following text: "Percentage reduction of market income inequality owing to transfers and taxes, 2007–14 (or latest year), working-age population" has been added to the caption of figure 5.13.

Pg 182. The following heading has been added to figure 5.17: "Per capita health spending, 2019, adjusted for differences in purchasing power".

Pg 183. The following text has been added to the caption of figure 5.18: "(% of average wage, 2021 or latest available)".

Pg 183. In the first paragraph under the section "Availability and Affordability of Material Necessities (N)", the cross reference to chapter 2 has been revised to cross reference chapter 3.

Pg 199. The following text has been added to the caption of figure 5.22: "(percentage of GDP)".

Pg 200. The following text has been added to the caption of figure 5.23: "(Percentage of GDP, 2021 or latest available)".

Pg 201. The following text has been inserted at the end of figure 5.24: "and average replacement rates". The heading "Percentage of the unemployed population" has been added above the figure.

Chapter 6

Pg 235, in the first sentence of the second paragraph the text "output production of goods" has been replaced with "productive output".

Pg 257, in the last sentence of the first paragraph the text "quarter of a trillion dollars" has been replaced with "order of magnitude".

Chapter 7

Pg 329, in the first sentence of the first paragraph, the sentence "The key aim should be to rebalance their focus..." has been revised as "The key aim should be to rebalance the focus...".

Open Access This chapter is licensed under the terms of the Creative Commons Attribution 4.0 International License (http://creativecommons.org/licenses/by/4.0/), which permits use, sharing, adaptation, distribution and reproduction in any medium or format, as long as you give appropriate credit to the original author(s) and the source, provide a link to the Creative Commons licence and indicate if changes were made.

The images or other third party material in this chapter are included in the chapter's Creative Commons licence, unless indicated otherwise in a credit line to the material. If material is not included in the chapter's Creative Commons licence and your intended use is not permitted by statutory regulation or exceeds the permitted use, you will need to obtain permission directly from the copyright holder.

BIBLIOGRAPHY

Atkinson A. and F. Bourguignon, *Handbook of Income Distribution*, Vol. 2, Amsterdam, North-Holland, 2015.
Bank of Italy Italia, *Boosting MDBs' Investing Capacity: An Independent Review of Multilateral Development Banks' Capital Adequacy Frameworks*, 2022.
Blanchard, O. and D. Rodrik, *Combating Inequality: Rethinking Government's Role*, Cambridge, MA, MIT Press, 2021.
Blended Finance Taskforce, *Better Finance, Better World*, London, 2018.
Boucoyannis, D., "The Equalizing Hand: Why Adam Smith Thought the Market Should Produce Wealth without Steep Inequality", *Perspectives on Politics*, Vol. 11, No. 4 (2013).
Chancel, L. and T. Piketty, "Global Inequality 1820–2020: The Persistence and Mutation of Extreme Inequality", *Journal of the European Economic Association*, Vol. 19, No. 6 (2021), pp. 3025–62.
Commission on Growth and Development, *The Growth Report: Strategies for Sustained Growth and Inclusive Development*, Washington, World Bank, 2008.
Commission on Human Security, *Human Security Now: Protecting and Empowering People*, 2003.
Commons, J.R., *Legal Foundations of Capitalism*, New York, Macmillan, 1924.
Daly, H.E., *Steady-State Economics: The Economics of Biophysical Equilibrium and Moral Growth*, 2nd ed., W.H. Freeman, 1977.
Deneen, P., *Why Liberalism Failed*, New Haven, Yale University Press, 2018.
Dixson-Decleve, S., O. Gaffney, J. Ghosh, J. Randers, J. Rockstrom and P.E. Stokne, *Earth for All: A Survival Guide for Humanity*, Gabriola Island, BC, New Society, 2022.
Georgescu-Roegen, N. *The Entropy Law and the Economic Process* (Harvard University Press, 1971)

Harvey, D., *The Limits to Capital*, London, Verso Books, 1982.
Heilbroner, R. and W. Milberg, *The Crisis of Vision in Modern Economic Thought*, Cambridge University Press, 1995.
Heilbroner, R., *The Worldly Philosophers: The Lives, Times, and Ideas of the Great Economic Thinkers*, New York: Simon & Schuster, 1953.
Helleiner, G.K., International Economic Disorder: Essays in North–South Relations, Toronto, University of Toronto Press, 1981.
Hickel, J., *Less Is More: How Degrowth Will Save the World*, London, Penguin Books, 2022.
Hodgson, G.M., *The Evolution of Institutional Economics: Agency, Structure and Darwinism in American Institutionalism*, Abingdon, Routledge, 2004.
Hufbauer, G., R. Melendez-Ortiz and R. Samans, eds, *The Law and Economics of a Sustainable Energy Trade Agreement*, Cambridge, UK, Cambridge University Press, 2016.
Humphrey, C., "All Hands on Deck: How to Scale Up Multilateral Financing to Face the COVID-19 Crisis", Overseas Development Institute, April 2020.
International Energy Association (IEA), *Net Zero by 2050: A Roadmap for the Global Energy Sector*, Paris, 2021.
International Labour Organization (ILO), *Centenary Declaration for the Future of Work*, 2019a.
International Labour Organization (ILO), *Decent Work Indicators: Guidelines for Producers and Users of Statistical and Legal Framework Indicators*, 2nd version, Geneva, 2013.
International Labour Organization (ILO), Declaration on Fundamental Principles and Rights at Work, 1998.
International Labour Organization (ILO), Declaration on Social Justice for a Fair Globalization, 2008.
International Labour Organization (ILO), Global call to action for a human-centred recovery from the COVID-19 crisis that is inclusive, sustainable and resilient, 2021a.
International Labour Organization (ILO), *Work for a Brighter Future: Global Commission on the Future of Work*, Geneva, 2019b.
International Labour Organization (ILO), *World Employment and Social Outlook 2021: The Role of Digital Labour Platforms in Transforming the World of Work*, Geneva, 2021b.
International Labour Organization (ILO), "World Employment Programme: Past, Present and Future", Background Paper for the 50th Anniversary of the Launch of the WEP, 2020.
International Trade Union Confederation, "A New Social Contract", Statement of 5th ITUC World Congress, 19 December 2022.
Keynes, J.M., *The Economic Consequences of the Peace*, London, Macmillan, 1919.

Keynes, J.M., *The General Theory of Employment, Interest and Money*, London, Macmillan, 1936.
Keynes, J.M., *A Treatise on Money*, London, Macmillan, 1930.
Kindleberger, C.P., *Manias, Panics, and Crashes: A History of Financial Crises*, 1978, 4th ed., London, Palgrave Macmillan, 2001.
Kuznets, S., "Economic Growth and Income Inequality", *American Economic Review*, Vol. 45, No. 1 (1955), pp. 1–28.
Kuttner, R., *Can Democracy Survive Global Capitalism?*, New York, W.W. Norton, 2018.
Langille, Brian and A. Treblicock, *Social Justice and the World of Work: Possible Global Futures, Essays in honour of Francis Maupain*, Hart, 2023.
Latouche, S., *Farewell to Growth*, Cambridge, UK, Polity Press, 2009.
Maddison, A., *The World Economy: Historical Statistics*, Paris, OECD, 2003.
Marshall, A., *Principles of Economics*, London, Macmillan, 1890.
Marshall, A. and M. Paley, *The Economics of Industry*, 1879.
Marx, K., *Das Kapital*, Hamburg, Otto Meisner, 1867.
Maul, D., *The International Labour Organization: 100 Years of Global Social Policy*, Berlin and Geneva, DeGruyter Oldenbourg and ILO, 2019.
Mazzucato, M., *The Value of Everything: Making and Taking in the Global Economy*, London, Penguin Books, 2019.
Mill, J.S., *On Liberty*, London, Longmans, Green, Reader & Dyer, 1859.
Mill, J.S., *Principles of Political Economy*, London, John W. Parker, 1848.
Minsky, H.P., *Can "It" Happen Again: Essays on Instability and Finance*, Armonk, NY, M.E. Sharpe, 1982.
Minsky, H.P., "Capitalist Financial Processes and the Instability of Capitalism", *Journal of Economic Issues*, Vol. 14, No. 2 (1980), pp. 505–23.
Minsky, H.P., *Ending Poverty: Jobs, Not Welfare*, Annandale-on-Hudson, NY, Levy Economics Institute, 2013.
Nishizawa, T., "Alfred Marshall on Human Capital and Future Generations", *Economic Review*, Vol. 53, No. 4 (2002), pp. 305–21.
Nishizawa, T., *Alfred Marshall's Last Challenge: His Book on Economic Progress*, Newcastle upon Tyne, Cambridge Scholars, 2020.
Pigou, A.C., *The Economics of Welfare*, London, Macmillan, 1920.
Piketty, T., *Capital in the Twenty-First Century*, trans. Arthur Goldhammer, Cambridge, MA, Belknap Press of Harvard University Press, 2014.
Polanyi, K., *The Great Transformation: The Political and Economic Origins of Our Time*, New York, Farrar & Reinhart, 1944.
Pope Pius XI, *Quadragesimo anno*, 1931.
Raworth, K., *Doughnut Economics: Seven Ways to Think Like a 21st Century Economist*, White River Junction, VT, Chelsea Green, 2017.
Rockström, J. et al., "A Safe Operating Space for Humanity", *Nature*, Vol. 461 (2009), pp. 472–5.

Rodrik, D., *Has Globalization Gone Too Far?* Washington, DC, Institute for International Economics, 1997.
Rodrik, D., *Straight Talk on Trade: Ideas for a Sane World Economy*, Princeton, NJ: Princeton University Press, 2017.
Rodrik, D., A. Subramanian and F. Trebbi, "Institutions Rule: The Primacy of Institutions over Geography and Integration in Economic Development", *Journal of Economic Growth*, Vol. 9 (2004), pp. 131–65.
Rogelj, J. et al., "Mitigation Pathways Compatible with 1.5C in the Context of Sustainable Development", in IPCC, *Global Warming of 1.5°C*, Geneva, 2018.
Samans, R., "A 21st Century Square Deal", *Washington Monthly*, September 2016.
Samans, R., "Beyond Business as Usual: G20 Leaders and Post-crisis Reconstitution of the International Economic Order", Center for American Progress Policy Brief, September 2009.
Samans, R., "Financing Human-Centred Recovery from the COVID-19 Crisis and Decisive Climate Action Worldwide: International Cooperation's 21st Century Moment of Truth", ILO Working Paper 40, October 2021.
Samans, R., "Level-Up Economics: Beyond the Wealth of Nations", Institute for New Economic Thinking (INET) Working Paper, January 2020.
Samans, R., "A New Way to Measure Growth and Development: The Inclusive Development Index", *Vox EU*, March 2018a.
Samans, R., "The Paris Accord Won't Stop Global Warming on Its Own", *Foreign Policy*, 26 September 2018b.
Samans, R., "Transitioning to a New U.S. International Economic Policy", Center for American Progress Policy Brief, December 2008.
Samans, R., "Virtuous Circle: Strengthening Broad-Based Global Progress in Living Standards", Center for American Progress Policy Brief, December 2007.
Samans, R., J. Blanke, M. Drzeniek Hanouz and G. Corrigan, *The Inclusive Growth and Development Report 2017*, Geneva, World Economic Forum, 2017.
Samans, R. and N. Davis, "Advancing Human-Centred Economic Progress in the Fourth Industrial Revolution", *G20 Policy Brief*, Think 20, May 2017.
Samans, R., R. Melendez-Ortiz, H. Singh and S. Doherty, eds, *Strengthening the Global Trade and Investment System in the 21st Century: E15 Initiative Synthesis Report*, Geneva, World Economic Forum and International Centre for Trade and Sustainable Development, 2016.
Samans, R. and J. Nelson, *Sustainable Enterprise Value Creation: Implementing Stakeholder Capitalism through Full ESG Integration*, Cham, Palgrave Macmillan, 2021.
Samans, R., M. Uzan and A. Lopez-Claros, eds, *The Group of 20, IMF and International Monetary System: A Great Transformation in the Making?*, Cham, Palgrave Macmillan, 2006a.

Samans, R. et al., "Building on the Monterrey Consensus: The Untapped Potential of Development Finance Institutions to Catalyze Private Investment", World Economic Forum Financing for Development Initiative, January 2006b

Sen, A.K., *Development as Freedom*, Oxford, Oxford University Press, 1999.

Sen, A.K., "Equality of What?", in *The Tanner Lectures on Human Values*, ed. S.M. MacMurrin, Vol. 4, 2nd ed., Cambridge, UK, Cambridge University Press, 1983.

Sen, A.K., *Poverty and Famines: An Essay on Entitlement and Deprivation*, Geneva and Oxford, ILO and Clarendon Press, 1981.

Shafik, M., *What We Owe Each Other: A New Social Contract for a Better Society*, Princeton, NJ, Princeton University Press, 2021.

Skidelsky, R., *John Maynard Keynes 1883–1946: Economist, Philosopher, Statesman*, New York, Penguin Books, 2003.

Smith, A., *An Inquiry into the Nature and Causes of the Wealth of Nations*, London, W. Strahan & T. Cadell, 1776.

Smith, A., *The Theory of Moral Sentiments*, London and Edinburgh, Andrew Millar and Alexander Kincaid & J. Bell, 1759.

Solow, R., "Review of Capital and Growth", *American Economic Review*, Vol. 56, No. 5 (1966), pp. 1257–60.

Sperling, Gene B., *Economic Dignity*, Penguin Press, 2020.

Stiglitz, J., *The Price of Inequality: How Today's Divided Society Endangers Our Future*, New York, W.W. Norton, 2012.

Stoller, M., *Goliath: The Hundred Year War between Monopoly Power and Democracy*, New York, Simon & Schuster, 2020.

Sunstein, Cass R., *The Second Bill of Rights*, Basic Books, 2006.

Supiot, Alain, *The Spirit of Philadelphia: Social Justice vs the Total Market*, (London, Verso, 2012).

Sustainable Development Solutions Network, *Sustainable Development Goals Report*, Cambridge, 2022.

Temple, J., "Aggregate Production Functions and Growth Economics", *International Review of Applied Economics*, Vol. 20, No. 3 (2006), pp. 301–17.

United Nations, *Our Common Agenda: Report of the Secretary-General*, New York, 2021.

United Nations, "United Nations Secretary-General's SDG Stimulus to Deliver Agenda 2030", February 2023.

Veblen, T., "Why Is Economics Not an Evolutionary Science?" *Cambridge Journal of Economics*, Vol. 22 (1998), pp. 403–14.

Victor, P. A., *Herman Daly's Economics for a Full World: His Life and Ideas* (Routledge, 2022).

Viner, J., "Adam Smith and Laissez-Faire", *Journal of Political Economy*, Vol. 35, No. 2 (1927), pp. 198–232.

Williamson, J., "Borrowing Strategy: The Role of GDP-Linked Bonds", Washington, DC, Peterson Institute for International Economics, 2006.
Williamson, J., *The Exchange Rate System*, Washington, DC, Institute for International Economics, 1983.
Williamson, J., "What Washington Means by Policy Reform", in J. Frieden, M. Pastor and M. Tomz, *Modern Political Economy and Latin America: Theory and Policy*, New York, Routledge, 2000.
Whitaker, J.K., ed., *The Correspondence of Alfred Marshall, Economist*, Cambridge, UK, Cambridge University Press, 1996.
Wolf, M.J. et al., *2022 Environmental Performance Index*, New Haven, Yale Center for Environmental Law & Policy, 2022.
World Bank, *The East Asian Miracle: Economic Growth and Public Policy*, Washington, 1993.
World Commission on Environment and Development, *Our Common Future* (Brundtland Report), United Nations and Oxford University Press, 1987.
World Inequality Lab, *World Inequality Report 2022*, 2022.

Index[1]

A
Acton, Lord, 79
Aggregate distribution
  function, 8, 112, 114–116,
  119–125, 131, 132, 135,
  137, 139, 146, 156, 172,
  212, 216, 217, 236, 237,
  241–242, 244, 246, 248, 251,
  254, 279, 285, 321, 322,
  326, 328
Aggregate production function, 8, 87,
  112, 114, 115, 131, 208,
  236, 328
Aggregate social welfare function, 114,
  115, 120, 124, 125, 135, 236,
  242, 323
Agreement on Climate Change,
  Trade and Sustainability, 303
Aid for Trade, 290
Algorithmic management, 293,
  295, 296
Analytical tools, 290
Anti-trust regulation, 142–145

Asian Development Bank
  Energy Transition Mechanism
    (ETM), 261
Asset-building, 194, 204–208
Austrian School, 79

B
Bank for International Settlements
  (BIS), 33
Banking crises, 29
Basel III, 157
B corporations, 155
Bentham, Jeremy, 65
Biodiversity, 25, 212, 214
Bismarck, Otto von, 80, 82
Bolshevik Revolution, 5
Bretton Woods, 5, 8, 194, 238, 277,
  283, 286, 305, 325
Brookings Institution, 254
Business and Sustainable Development
  Commission, 279–280
Business dynamism, 142, 143, 145

---

[1] Note: Page numbers followed by 'n' refer to notes.

C

Capacity-building, 253, 289, 292
Capacity to Combat Corruption Index, 147
Carbon Border Adjustment Mechanism (CBAM), 297
Carbon dioxide, 26
Chicago Plan, 161, 162
Child care, 182
Child labour, 170, 171
Chile, 34
China, 12, 165
Clean energy, 265
Climate Action Tracker, 208
Climate change, 26, 134, 137, 236, 256, 257, 284, 297–300, 302, 303, 338
Climate Club, 302
Climate leakage, 304
Coal-fired power, 26, 260, 261, 304
Collective bargaining, 175, 176
Columbia University, 145
Commission on Growth and Development, 20, 21, 45n22
Common Agricultural Policy (CAP), 216
Commons, John R., 86
Commonwealth Anti-Corruption Benchmarks, 147
Competition law, 145
Cooperatives, 207
Coral, 27
Corn Laws, 78
Corporate governance, 31, 152–166
Corruption, 146, 147
Corruption Perceptions Index, 146
COVID-19 pandemic, 31, 137, 175, 202, 256, 266, 280, 293, 327
Credit
  allocation, 159, 161
  creation, 29, 157, 161

D

Daly, Herman, 39, 41, 330
Data protection, 295–297
Debt relief, 238, 258, 267–272, 280
Decent work, 61, 113, 171, 273, 276, 285, 286, 288–297
  indicators, 125, 250, 251, 323
De-growth, 40
Development economics, 92
Digitalization, 293, 294
Disposable income, 113, 114, 116, 132, 172–183, 280
Downward mobility, 18
Draco, laws of, 61

E

Early childhood education, 169
East Asian miracle, 19, 110, 139
Economic security, 113, 114, 117, 133, 194–208, 280
Ecosystem services, 214
Eisenhower, Dwight D., 305
Elephant curve, 15
Employee stock, 207
Employment and entrepreneurial opportunity, 113, 114, 116, 121, 124, 132, 141–172, 279
Enhanced HIPC Initiative, 269–271
Entail, 60
Environmental Goods Agreement, 298
Environmental Performance Index (EPI), 137
Environmental security, 113, 114, 118, 134, 208–216, 280
European Commission, 265
European Trade Union Council, 202
European Union, 154, 189, 202, 208, 212, 297, 305
  Green New Deal, 215

INDEX 351

F
Factors of distribution, 8, 112, 114, 123, 126, 131, 139, 172, 328
Factors of production, 112
Family benefits, 183, 198
Financialization–Real Economy Investment Financial Regulation Continuum, 158
Financial regulation, 62, 156–162
Financial Stability Board (FSB), 29, 159, 303
Fiscal transfers, 40
Fisheries, 27
Floyd, George, 34
Food and Agricultural Office (FAO), 27
Food prices, 29, 78, 189, 193, 194
Forced labour, 58, 170
France, 34
Friedman, Milton, 152
Fuel prices, 30, 34, 192–194

G
Gender discrimination, 171
Gender equality, 67
General Agreement on Tariffs and Trade, 286
Germany, 154, 282, 292
  West, 206
Gilets Jaunes, 34
Gladstone, William, 79
Glasgow Financial Alliance for Net-Zero, 212
Global Accelerator on Jobs and Social Protection for Just Transitions, 259, 262–264
Global Correlation Sensitive Poverty Index (G-CSPI), 22, 23
Global Energy Transition Mechanism, 259–262
Global Green Growth Institute, 210

Global Peace Index, 34
Global warming, 26, 208, 257, 260, 261, 280
Great Britain, 60, 67, 70, 78, 80, 148
Great Depression, 5, 21, 108, 161
Great Financial Crisis, 11, 29, 39, 41, 157, 162, 256, 284, 303, 327, 333
Great Transformation, 90, 92, 109
Greenhouse gas emissions, 26, 211, 260, 276, 298
Green Revolution 2.0, 259, 264–266
Gross domestic product (GDP), 1–3, 8, 32, 34, 64, 109, 112, 125, 134, 136, 137, 217, 285, 321
G20, 252, 275, 281, 303
  Common Framework for Debt Treatment, 24, 238, 268–271, 278
  Debt Service Suspension Initiative (DSSI), 24
  Global Infrastructure Hub, 163, 185

H
Hausmann, Ricardo, 165
Hayek, Friedrich, 319, 336
Health care, 182, 196, 266
Heavily Indebted Poor Country (HIPC) Initiative, 268–270
Homeownership, 204–207
House prices, 16, 17
Human capital, 73
Human-centred economics, 119–123
Human development, 95, 96
Human trafficking, 170

I
Inclusive Development Index (IDI), 126, 136
Income inequality, 13, 16, 33

India, 154, 189
  Public Distribution System, 189
Informal economy, 171, 195, 202, 204
Infrastructure investment, 185–189
Institutional deepening, 8, 20, 21, 23, 217, 237, 241, 254, 322, 328
Institutional economics, 86, 88, 111
Institution-building, 20, 21, 241, 244, 304
Institutions, 109, 110
Inter-American Development Bank, 279
Intergovernmental Panel on Climate Change (IPCC), 26, 211, 298
International Covenant on Economic, Social and Cultural Rights (ICESCR), 89, 184, 327
International Energy Agency (IEA), 264, 265
International Financial Reporting Standards Foundation, 159, 211
International Labour Conference, 83–85
International Labour Organization (ILO), xiv, 5, 32, 38, 82, 84, 125, 126, 138, 169–171, 175, 176, 195, 204, 212, 244, 264, 279, 285, 288–291, 294, 295
  Better Work, 290
  Centenary Declaration, 237, 251, 297
  Constitution, 83, 284, 325
  Decent Work Agenda, 250, 288, 289
  Declaration on Fundamental Principles and Rights at Work, 289
  Declaration on Social Justice for a Fair Globalization, 289
  Fundamental Principles and Rights at Work, 169, 204
  Global Commission on the Future of Work, 296
  Maritime Labour Convention, 297
  Philadelphia Declaration, 5, 85, 88, 286
  Skills for Trade and Diversification, 290
  World Employment Programme (WEP), 95, 96
International Land Coalition (ILC), 149
International Monetary Fund (IMF), 24, 34, 163, 172, 192–194, 238, 239, 242–245, 254–272, 281
  Financial Development Index, 156
International Organization of Securities Commissions (IOSCO), 211
International Sustainability Standards Board (ISSB), 159, 211, 301
International Union for Conservation of Nature (IUCN), 26
"Invisible hand," 2, 56, 64

J
Japan, 212
Just transition, 212, 236, 257

K
Keynes, John Maynard, xii, xiii, 87, 88, 92–94, 108, 122, 160, 319–325, 328, 336
Kunming-Montreal Global Biodiversity Framework, 214, 252, 282
Kuznets, Simon, 87, 92
Kuznets
  curve, 92
  moment, 92

L

Labour
 division of, 56
 inspection, 202, 203
 regulation, 61, 64, 202, 294
 standards, 166, 169, 170,
  175, 176, 194, 202, 274,
  289, 297
Lagarde, Christine, 242
Land governance, 148–149
League of Nations, 83
Lee, Sangheon, 92
Living wage, 61, 62, 72, 173
London School of Economics, 254
Low-carbon, 209, 264–266,
 280, 298–301
Low pay rate, 176

M

Macro-criticality, 239, 240, 242,
 251, 304
Macro-development
 criticality, 240–243
Macroeconomic stability, 239,
 240, 242–244
Macroeconomic stimulus, 119,
 122, 334
Marginalist school, 70
Marshall, Alfred, 6, 58, 65, 70, 71,
 74–77, 83, 90
Marshall Plan, 273, 282, 283
Marx, Karl, xii, 82, 90
Material necessities, 22, 113, 114,
 117, 133, 183–194
Median standard of living, 114, 131,
 135, 139, 236
Menger, Carl, 79
Middle-income trap, 19, 22, 165
Middle Way, 320, 322–324
Mill, John Stuart, 6, 58, 65–69,
 71, 86, 90

Minimum wage, 78, 173
Mission Innovation, 265
Modern Monetary Theory
 (MMT), 40
Monopolies, 61, 63
Moral philosophy, 64
Multidimensional Poverty Index
 (MPI), 22, 23
Multilateral Debt Relief Initiative, 269
Multilateral development
 banks (MDBs), 244, 254,
 256, 259, 261, 262,
 272–277, 281
Mundell–Fleming trilemma, 326

N

Nationally determined contributions
 (NDCs), 27, 252, 258
Neoclassical economics, 58, 65,
 70, 78, 208
Neoclassical-Keynesian-ecological
 synthesis, 329, 332
Neoclassical synthesis, 88, 115, 240
Neoliberalism, xi, xiii, 2, 7, 57, 88,
 134, 152, 241, 286, 319,
 320, 336
Netherlands, the, 296
Network for Greening the Financial
 System (NGFS), 159, 212
Net-zero, 208, 211, 265, 279
New Deal, 323
Northeast Asia, 154
Not in employment, education or
 training (NEET), 168

O

Occupational safety and health (OSH),
 108, 194, 202
Oceanos, 27
Ordoliberalism, 320

Organisation for Economic
 Co-operation and Development
 (OECD), 16, 17, 125, 142–144,
 147, 179, 198, 244, 246,
 274, 302
 Green Growth Indicators, 210
 Green Growth Strategy, 209
 Inclusive Forum on Carbon
  Mitigation Approaches, 302
Our World in Data, 13
Output gap, 8, 134, 135, 321

P
Paley, Mary, 72
Pandemic Preparedness, Prevention
 and Response Fund, 31, 284
Pandemic Prevention Financial
 Intermediary Fund, 252, 267
Pandemic prevention, preparedness
 and response (PPR), 267, 280
Paris climate agreement, 3, 26, 208,
 251, 252, 256–258, 260–262,
 265, 272, 281, 298, 301, 304
Pensions, 198, 207
Pew Research Group, 17
Phelan, Edward, 82
Philippon, Thomas, 143, 144
Pigou, Arthur Cecil, 75–77
Pitt, William, 78, 79
Platform work, 294–296
Polanyi, Karl, 4, 90–92, 109, 120
Policy dialogue, 289
Poverty reduction, 12, 19, 22, 23,
 137, 280
Poverty Reduction and Growth Trust
 (PRGT), 258, 267, 271, 278
Preferential trading arrangements
 (PTAs), 287, 289, 292, 295
Primogeniture, 60
Productivity growth, 56, 64, 110,
 122, 143, 162

Public goods, 60, 62, 64, 68, 74, 284
Public Integrity Indicators, 147
Public investment, 162–166, 168, 242

R
R&D, 149, 164, 165, 265
Real economy investment, 150–151,
 157, 160, 333, 334
Regenerative agriculture, 215, 216
Renewable energy, 162, 264–266, 304
Rent-seeking, 59, 93, 321
Resilience and Sustainability Trust
 (RST), 238, 255, 256,
 258–267, 278
Ricardo, David, 285
Robbins, Lionel, 75
Roosevelt, Franklin D., 84
Roosevelt Consensus, 241, 288, 304,
 323, 324, 328, 338

S
St Simonian school, 67
Sanitation, 27, 185, 186
Schooling, 167
Science-Based Targets Initiative, 211
Sea level rise, 281
Seattle, 288
Second World War, 108
Secular stagnation, 122
Sen, Amartya, 65, 94–96
Settlement Laws, 78
Skidelsky, Lord Robert, 320
Smith, Adam, xiii, 2, 6, 11, 55, 57–60,
 62–66, 70, 78–80, 86, 89, 107,
 110, 142, 148, 151, 184, 320
Social accounting matrices, 39
Social contract, xii, xiv, 5, 7, 82, 84,
 85, 89–92, 97, 120, 135, 141,
 236, 240, 243, 304, 321, 323,
 326, 338

Social dialogue, 5
Social insurance, 80, 81, 172, 177
Socialism, 82, 93, 151, 155, 336
Social Market–Market Socialism Corporate Governance Continuum, 154, 155
Social protection floor, 24, 32, 195, 196, 259, 262–264, 280
Social protection system, 125, 194, 195, 198, 264, 278, 282
Social safety net (SSN), 193, 194
Social utility functions, 108
South Africa, 34
South Korea, 19, 165
Special Drawing Rights (SDRs), 238, 254–272, 277, 278
Spence, Michael, 20
Square Deal, 323
Stakeholder capitalism, 155
Stern, Lord Nicholas, 254
Stiglitz, Joseph, 19
Stiglitz–Sen–Fitoussi Commission, 39
Structural economic reform, 124, 134, 328
Subsidies, 189, 192, 193
Supply chains, 31
Sustainable Development Goals (SDGs), 28, 32, 33, 126, 137, 138, 176, 185, 195, 210, 251, 252, 254, 262, 264, 272, 279, 280, 285
Sustainable Development Solutions Network (SDSN), 210, 211
Sustainable infrastructure, 254, 272–275, 278–280
Switzerland, 206

T
Taxation
 housing, 206, 207
 progressive, 63, 177, 179

Taylor, Frederick Winslow, 293
Technology governance, 149–150, 237
Tertiary education, 168
Theory of change, 41–43, 64
Tocqueville, Alexis de, 70
Total factor productivity, 163
Trickle-down economics, 1, 3, 4, 9, 97, 118, 121, 217, 320, 335, 336, 338
Trump, Donald, 335
Truss, Liz, 335
Turner, Adair, 160
2030 Agenda, 251, 278

U
Unemployment insurance, 81, 200
United Kingdom, 82, 148, 160, 165, 177, 206
 Financial Services Authority, 160
United Nations, 5, 268, 285, 298, 325
 Charter, 335
 financing-for-development initiative, 275, 281
 High-Level Expert Group on the Net-Zero Commitments of Non-State Entities, 211
 Secretary-General, 238, 262, 325
United Nations Children's Fund (UNICEF), 24, 267
United Nations Conference on the Human Environment, 25, 109
United Nations Conference on Trade and Development (UNCTAD), 245
United Nations Development Programme (UNDP), 96
United Nations Environment Programme (UNEP), 25, 209

United Nations Framework
 Convention on Climate Change
 (UNFCCC), 212, 259, 284
Kyoto Protocol, 298
United States, 16, 17, 34, 82, 137,
 144, 155, 161, 163, 168, 173,
 177, 198, 241, 273, 319,
 323, 328
Universal Declaration of Human
 Rights, 38, 88, 184, 195
University of Chicago, 145
US Department of Commerce, 87
US–Mexico–Canada Agreement
 (USMCA), 290, 292, 305
Utilities, 189, 194

V
Veblen, Thorstein, 86
Versailles, Treaty of, 83, 320
Volcker, Paul, 29

W
Washington Consensus, xi, 21, 41,
 97, 238–240
Washington, DC, 84
Water, 27, 28, 185, 186, 189
Weber, Max, 293
Welfare economics, 75, 77, 85, 94,
 120, 322

Welfare gap, 8, 135–141, 217, 236,
 244, 321, 322
Wellbeing Economy Alliance, 328
Whitbread, Samuel, 78, 79
World Bank, 12, 19, 24, 32, 44n8,
 44n10, 45n20, 45n22, 49n54,
 139, 148, 149, 163, 179, 185,
 239, 267
 International Development
  Association (IDA), 270
 International Finance
  Corporation, 290
World Economic Forum, 126
World Employment Conference, 96
World Governance Indicators, 145
World Health Organization (WHO),
 30, 252, 259, 266
World Meteorological Organization
 (WMO), 27
World Trade Organization (WTO),
 245, 283, 286, 288–291, 297,
 302, 304
 Singapore Declaration, 289, 293
 Trade Facilitation Agreement, 292
 Trade Policy Review
  Mechanism, 292

Z
Zero growth, 40
Zuma, Jacob, 34

SPRINGER NATURE

GPSR Compliance

The European Union's (EU) General Product Safety Regulation (GPSR) is a set of rules that requires consumer products to be safe and our obligations to ensure this.

If you have any concerns about our products, you can contact us on ProductSafety@springernature.com

In case Publisher is established outside the EU, the EU authorized representative is:

Springer Nature Customer Service Center GmbH
Europaplatz 3
69115 Heidelberg, Germany

The manufacturer's authorised representative in the EU is Springer Nature Customer Service Centre GmbH, Europaplatz 3, 69115 Heidelberg, Germany. If you have any concerns regarding our products, please contact ProductSafety@springernature.com

Printed and bound by CPI Group (UK) Ltd, Croydon, CR0 4YY

25/03/2026

02078179-0006